Smart City Citizenship

Smart City Citizenship

Dr Igor Calzada
COMPAS, Urban Transformations ESRC & Future of Cities Programmes
University of Oxford,
Oxford, United Kingdom

Digital Economy Unit and Centre for Advanced Studies,
European Commission,
DG Joint Research Centre,
European Union

ELSEVIER

Elsevier
Radarweg 29, PO Box 211, 1000 AE Amsterdam, Netherlands
The Boulevard, Langford Lane, Kidlington, Oxford OX5 1GB, United Kingdom
50 Hampshire Street, 5th Floor, Cambridge, MA 02139, United States

Library of Congress Cataloging-in-Publication Data
A catalog record for this book is available from the Library of Congress

British Library Cataloguing-in-Publication Data
A catalogue record for this book is available from the British Library

ISBN: 978-0-12-815300-0

Publisher: Joe Hayton
Acquisitions Editor: Brian Romer
Editorial Project Manager: Aleksandra Packowska
Production Project Manager: Niranjan Bhaskaran
Cover Designer: Miles Hitchen

Typeset by SPi Global, India

Contents

About the author

Dr Igor Calzada is working as a senior techno-political and social scientist in the Centre for Advanced Studies (CAS) (A5) and the Digital Economy Unit (B6) in the DG Joint Research Centre (JRC) of the European Commission (EC). His research and policy work revolves around three main projects: (i) digital transformations and the governance of human society (DigiTranScope), (ii) data ecosystems/spaces, and (iii) artificial intelligence (AI Watch). In addition, since 2012, he is a senior researcher/lecturer at the University of Oxford (UK), Urban Transformations ESRC, and Future of Cities Programmes at COMPAS, InSIS, and Oxford Martin School, where he has been conducting research and working as PI and policy adviser in smart cities and city-regions supported by several research grants and regularly funded by the (i) EU-H2020-Smart Cities and Communities-SCC-01-2015-691735-Replicate (2016–2021); (ii) ESRC-Urban Transformations (2016–2019); (iii) EU-Marie Curie-CoFund Regional Programmes (2015–2016); (iv) City-Regions project funded by Ikerbasque (2012–2014); and (v) the RSA (Regional Studies Association) (2014–2015).

His main research interest draws on how digital transformation processes driven by AI disruption in the post-GDPR current context are altering techno-political and democratic conditions of data governance for the emergence of new algorithmic citizenship regimes in European (smart) cities and regions by paying special attention to the interplay of multi-stakeholders and the creation of data co-operatives and platform co-operatives schemes from the Social Innovation perspective.

Previously, he has worked as lecturer, research fellow, associate researcher, and visiting lecturer at the (i) Universitat Oberta de Catalunya, UOC (2020); (ii) University of Strathclyde in Glasgow in the MSc in Global Sustainable Cities (UK) (2015–2019); (iii) Vrije Universiteit Brussel (Belgium) (2016–2018); (iv) Aston University in Birmingham (UK) (2014–2015); (v) University of Iceland (2014); (vi) University of Malmö (Sweden) (2013); (vii) University of Deusto-Orkestra (2014); (viii) University of Nevada, Reno (USA) (2008–2009); (ix) University of Helsinki (Finland) (2004); and (x) University of Mondragon (Spain) (2002–2012).

Alongside these academic positions, he has been awarded the following research fellowships: (i) Visiting Fellowship at Vrije Universiteit Brussel (Belgium) (2016–2017); (ii) European Commission's Cofund Regional Programmes' Marie Curie Fellowship (2015–2016); (iii) RSA's Early Career

(2014–2015) and Research Network Grants (2014–2018); (iv) Ikerbasque's Postdoctoral Fellowship (2012–2014); and (v) Caja Madrid Foundation's Doctoral Fellowship at the University of Nevada (USA) (2008–2009).

Over the last 23 years, he has been gaining an intense international profile being invited as keynote speaker worldwide (in more than 40 countries), participating in remarkable scientific conferences and events, and directly giving policy advice to governments, firms, universities, technological centres, civic groups, and NGOs.

Outside the academia, he has been director of research, technology, and innovation in the Basque regional government (Spain) (2009–2010); project director at the Mondragon Co-operative Corporation research centre in innovation for a decade (Spain) (2002–2012); and deputy director at the automotive SMEs in Spain (1999–2001). In addition, while his postdoctoral period (2012–2014), he set up an academic entrepreneurial spin-off called Translokal SL and was the director and the co-founder for the period 2014–2019.

He was awarded PhD in territorial and Social Innovation by the University of Mondragon and the University of Nevada, Reno on 11 February 2011. In addition, he obtained the MBA (Master in Business Administration) in 1999 and the Certificate of the Diploma in Advanced Studies from the University of Helsinki (Finland) and Deusto (Spain) in 2006. In addition, he was awarded with a TQM (total quality management) diploma by the EFQM, Brussels (Belgium). He graduated with first class honours in BSc (sociology) from the University of Deusto (Spain) in 1997.

He possesses an emerging track record of publications: 35 high-quality, peer-reviewed academic journal articles (published in *Transforming Government: People, Process, and Policy, Journal of Urban Technology, Sustainability, Space and Polity, Regional Studies Regional Sciences, Regional Science Policy & Practice, Data & Policy, RSA Journal,* and *Systems,* among others), 10 books, 19 book chapters, 25 policy reports, and more than 123 invited international keynotes and talks related to digital policy, smart cities, and political regionalism. In addition to this present monograph, 'Smart Cities Citizenship' through Elsevier, he will be soon releasing this monograph on city-regions throurgh Routeldge: 'Benchmarking City-Regions'.

He is a member of the editorial advisory board of the following journals:

- Transforming Government: People, Process and Policy (Emerald)
- JRC Editorial Review Board: Digital Social Sciences field editor (European Commission)
- Applied Sciences (Nature Springer)
- Smart Cities (MDPI)
- Territories: A Transcultural Journal of Regional Studies (eScholarship).

He is a British citizen and Spanish/EU national and speaks English, Basque, and Spanish.

Acknowledgements

The University of Oxford is a place with aura. This book kicked off unwittingly, its initial elaboration happened in a very unconscious manner since 2012. That year, my father passed away, the man who gave me the strength to follow my route in life (he always said *Aurrera!,* meaning 'go-ahead' in Basque, with his clumpsy but highly committed Castillian accent). This book is fundamentally dedicated to him and the strength he gave me. *Eskerrik asko, gracias, Aita.* I owe the deepest gratitude to my father. His struggles in life inspired me in my explorations and constant fieldwork research in the cities and regions worldwide that culminated in this book.

Furthermore, this book would not have existed without the wise academic and personal support and mentorship of Professor Michael Keith from the University of Oxford at COMPAS since 2012. My time as a research member at the Future of Cities and later at the Urban Transformations ESRC Programmes, under his leadership, cannot be dissociated from this book's achievement. Professor Keith knew how to push ideas ahead, and has encouraged my action research on smart cities with a comparative, international, critically constructive, and experimental predisposition and flavour. He pushed me to make applied social science that intersects urban, digital, and political transformations a constant, innovative, intellectual challenge, driving me to tackle real societal issues. Additionally, I thank everybody at COMPAS, InSIS, Oxford Martin School, and Politics and International Relations for supporting my academic work so far.

In 2012, the smart city discourse had plenty of advocates and a few of them openly focused on the b-side of the rhetoric. This book would not have been what it is today without my conversations and interactions with other academics, policymakers, practitioners, and students who provided me (sometimes even contradictory) points of view, opinions, and practices. Most importantly, these alternative conversations led me to research and look into in-depth citizenship-related issues in the so-called smart cities. I also acknowledge the contributions of all my coauthors and editors including Professor Andy Jonas, Dr. Esteve Almirall, Professor Frank Moulaert, Professor Martin Jones, Dr. John Harrison, Professor Ronan Paddison, Dr. Anna Visvizi, Dr. Tassilo Herrschel, Dr. Paul Cowie, Dr. Cristobal Cobo, Mr. Amitabh Satyam, Dr. Benjamin Hennig, Ms. Ana Arranz, Professor Henk Scholten, Dr. Max Craglia, Dr. Marina Micheli, Dr. Margeritha Di Leo, Ms. Karmele Barandiaran,

Mr. Gavin McAdam, Dr. Antonio Casado, Mr. Jokin Bildarratz, Mr. Fredrik Björk, Mr. Domenico Di Siena, Mr. Alfonso Chautón, etc.).

Similarly, I acknowledge the stakeholders for participating directly in the academic, scientific, and fieldwork action research activities that contributed to this book: H2020-Replicate-EU project's 36 partners and six city representatives, including Essen in Germany, Nilüfer in Turkey, Lausanne in Switzerland, San Sebastian in Spain, Florence in Italy, and Bristol in the UK; particularly, I thank Euken Sesé and Eli Jorge from Fomento San Sebastian.

Additionally, I thank my former colleagues and collaborators at the universities of Strathclyde in Glasgow, Aston in Birmingham (UK), Vrije Universiteit Brussels (Belgium), Iceland, Malmö (Sweden), Ikerbasque and Deusto (Spain), Nevada (USA), and Mondragon in the Basque Country (Spain).

As the Regional Studies Association (RSA) Fellow, FeRSA, my gratitude to Sally Hardy and the RSA team for supporting me in events and with publications by disseminating my research and policy contributions to reach a broader audience beyond academia. Furthermore, special thanks to the Early Career Grant received in 2014. I must also mention the assistance provided by the RSA Research Network led by the late Tassilo Herrschel and the rest of the members of the Smart City-Regional Governance for Sustainability, including Dr. Gerd Lintz, Professor Bas van Heur, Dr. Yonn Dierwechter, Dr. Stefano Di Vita, Professor Iwona Sagan, and Professor Ethan Seltzer.

I owe special thanks to the funding institutions and related people for regularly aiding my research projects with grants and fellowships, including: (i) European Commission's (EC's) JRC; (ii) EC-H2020; (iii) EC-Marie Curie Fellowship-CoFund (Alfonso Martinez-Cearra and Ana Sancho from Bilbao Metropoli-30 and Ivan Jimenez from Bizkaia Talent); (iv) Economic and Social Research Council (ESRC); (v) Visiting Fellowship at the Brussels Centre for Urban Studies at the Vrije Universiteit in Brussels (Bas van Heur, Stefan de Corte, and Elena Solonina) to convene the 'Bridging European Urban Transformations' Workshop Series 2016–2018; (vi) Basque Government and Ikerbasque (Basque Foundation for Science; Fernando Cossio, Iñigo Atxutegi, and Javier Echeverría); and (vii) Ministry of Innovation and Science of the Spanish Government.

This book was highly and directly inspired by the fieldwork action research conducted worldwide. Thus, I am grateful to those who invited me as guest keynote speaker for international conferences related to smart cities and digital innovation and those who assisted me during the fieldwork action research in the following global geolocalisations: Barcelona, Madrid, Valencia, Valladolid, Pamplona-Iruñea, Vitoria-Gasteiz, Donostia-San Sebastian, and Bilbao (Spain); Astana (Kazakhstan); Moscow (Russia); Pemba (Mozambique); Bolívar (Colombia); Boston, Washington and New Orleans (USA); Liege and Brussels (Belgium); Dublin (Ireland); Copenhagen and Kolding (Denmark); Rennes (France); Stavanger (Norway); Yinchuan (China); Brasília (Brazil); Montevideo (Uruguay); Bragança (Portugal); Vienna (Austria); Gdansk (Poland); Essen,

Hamburg, and Dresden (Germany); Lausanne (Switzerland); Nilüfer and Izmir (Turkey); Florence, Ispra, and Torino (Italy); Reykjavik (Iceland); London, Oxford, Bournemouth, Sheffield, Kent, Liverpool, Cardiff, Bristol, Edinburgh, and Glasgow (UK); and so on.

And especially I express my warmest appreciation to Ms. Lourdes Mugica Aizpuru (my mother), Ms. Arantza Kalzada (my sister), and Ana.

By the end of the road, this book could have not even existed without all these steps, particularities, details, locations, and more importantly, without the aura.

Whoever goes forward creating something new, like this book (amidst the magic Oxford aura), does it like a rower, advancing forward but paddling on his back, looking back, towards the past, towards what exists, in order to reinvent his keys.

Rephrased, inspired by Jorge Oteiza (Basque avant-garde, forward-looking, and disruptive artist).

Prologue. DECONSTRUCTING smart city citizenship: Data ecosystems and democracy

1 We are already becoming tiny chips...

'We are already becoming tiny chips inside a giant system that nobody really understands' (Harari, 2016, p. 1). So wrote Israeli historian Noah Yuval Harari about our current experience of urban living, which, increasingly, is mediated by artificial intelligence (AI) (Pak-Hang, 2020; Valle-Cruz et al., 2020). AI is now an important component of sectors such as health care, agriculture, public administration, and transportation, and is helping to address major challenges such as ageing and climate change. However, there is currently a lack of transparency in algorithmic governance systems, and this is worsened when these algorithms are integrated into already opaque governance structures in our cities (Coletta & Kitchin, 2017; Danaher et al., 2017). Moreover, over the past decade, the propagation of sensors and data collection machines in the so-called 'smart cities' by both the public and the private sector has created democratic challenges around AI, surveillance capitalism, and protecting citizens' digital rights to privacy and ownership (Cities Coalition for Digital Rights, 2019; Finn, 2017; Durán, 2019; Dyer-Witherford et al., 2019).

In 2018, the General Data Protection Regulation (GDPR) came into force in the EU (Buttarelli, 2018; European Commission, 2019b). This regulation harmonised data privacy laws across Europe and is aimed at protecting citizens' data and giving people control over their own data. Against this backdrop, a debate has emerged in European cities and regions about the role of citizens in their cities and how they control and understand their own data (Ferronato & Stan, 2018; Green, 2019; Shelton & Lodato, 2019).

Data ecosystems are the infrastructure, institutions, analytics, and data capture systems that are used to take data and relay it to the system owners, who can then alter their provision of goods and services and marketing accordingly. Little is known about the long-term sociopolitical effects of these systems, which we are increasingly reliant on. The present momentum around privacy concerns could be seen as a call to action to create democratic digital infrastructures and institutions in Europe. The public sector needs to innovate and involve a plurality of stakeholders (Mazzucato, 2015). More radically, the ownership of platforms—currently predominantly in the hands of private companies—as well

Smart City Citizenship. https://doi.org/10.1016/B978-0-12-815300-0.09986-X

as data itself could be *co-operativised* (Bauwens, Kostakis, & Pazaitis, 2019; Hardjono & Pentland, 2019; Scholz, 2014). Such an approach in Europe would trailblaze citizens' digital rights protection and avoid algorithmic extractivism and surveillance (Morozov, 2012; Zuboff, 2019).

2 AI and data ecosystems

If we allow data ecosystems and AI to develop with insufficient oversight, algorithmic disruption will have consequences in a wide range of areas, including employment, income and gender equality, privacy, bias, access, machine ethics, weaponisation, social capital, and service provision. According to Cisco ISBG, by 2020 facial recognition and individual profiling will be driven through 50 billion connected devices, all feeding data to AI platforms (Ratti & Claudel, 2016). In theory, this could make our experiences of cities far more tailored and effective as our data are used to provide the most needed services and pinpoint areas where cities are underperforming. The idea is that AI could make better decisions than humans. AI gets smarter the more data it is fed, but it also learns human and societal biases, thereby creating the conditions where the most vulnerable social groups are marginalised further. For example, the Microsoft chatbot was taught racist phrases by Twitter users. The American political scientist Virginia Eubanks' work shows how the poorest and most in need sections of society are those who are under the most surveillance by automated systems, which can often make mistakes (Eubanks, 2017; Brayne, 2020).

If it is to address some of these risks and increase public benefit, governments and the public sector need to embrace AI; unless they take more responsibility for the handling of citizens' data, for-profit companies will dominate the techno-deterministic smart cities agenda. Local and regional authorities need to show citizens that they will protect their data and rights, and that data will be used in responsible ways. Once this trust is established, people may be in turn more willing to agree to the use of AI in various government services.

The European Commission is leading the way in this field. It is developing an expanded network of digital innovation hubs, which could be central to the development of local and regional 'data ecosystems', bringing AI training, data, computing, and local partnerships together to develop AI solutions that are adapted to local and regional issues (European Commission, 2019a).

3 Digital rights in smart cities

Over the past 20 years, working collaboratively on smart cities and the technopolitics of data with local and regional authorities, firms, academics, nongovernmental organisations, and (social) entrepreneurs and activists, under several policy and research schemes, I have concluded that the smart city has been built on hubris and the false assumption that just being digitally connected or plugged in means being *smart* (Campbell, 2012; Hajer & Dassen, 2014; Marvin, Luque-Ayala, & McFarlane, 2015; Willis and Aurigi, 2018, 2020). The advocates of smart cities wrongly still think that real-time data flows can be used to optimise cities' central nervous systems through 'digital twins' (virtual models of real-world processes, products, or services) without any democratic cost (Richey & Taylor, 2018). They promise big improvements in energy savings, mobility and transport efficiency, replication capacity, and sustainable land use. Yet many smart city experiments have demonstrated the shortcomings of this point of view (Noveck, 2015).

Valuable lessons about how not to build smart cities from scratch can be drawn from Songdo in South Korea (Shwayri, 2013), Masdar in Abu Dhabi (Cugurullo, 2013) (both of which were designed to be smart, eco-friendly cities, but which remain ghost towns) and even Toronto in Canada. The Google/Alphabet Sidewalk Labs flagship project in Toronto has triggered a fierce backlash, with Google accused of infringing citizens' digital rights and thus subverting democracy. Critics are concerned that questions about who owns the data collected by Sidewalk Labs 'digital layer' are not being adequately addressed (Goodman & Powles, 2019).

In contrast, since 2015, Barcelona has been pursuing the explicit protection of digital rights through technological sovereignty by emphasising grassroots-led urban experimentation, data commons (platforms where data is considered part of the public infrastructure, or a common asset, and is stored and shared under set principles) and public return (Bakıcı, Almirall, & Wareham, 2013). How the Toronto and Barcelona experimental approaches fare in the coming years will inform policymakers around the world (Coletta, Evans, Heaphy, & Kitchin, 2018; Evans, Karvonen, & Raven, 2016; Karvonen, Cugurullo, & Caprotti, 2018; URB@Exp, 2017).

The demise of democracy is clearly already one of the biggest policy challenges of our time, and the undermining of citizens' digital rights is part of this issue (Castells, 2009; Economist, 2019; Susskind, 2018). These include a wide range of complex rights that need to be addressed alongside legal and human rights in a digital world. They include the right to be forgotten on the internet, the right to be unplugged or disconnected, the right to your own digital legacy, the right for your personal integrity to be protected from technology, freedom of speech online, the right to your own digital identity, the right to the transparent and responsible use of algorithms, the right to have a last human instance in expert-based decision-making processes, the right to equal opportunities in the digital economy, consumer rights in e-commerce, the right to hold intellectual property on the internet, universal access to the internet, the right to digital literacy, the right to impartiality on the internet, and the right to a secure internet.

So how will AI affect cities and, more directly, citizens' digital rights? How can cities control their technologies, infrastructure, and provision of services while utilising data in a democratic, citizen-led fashion?

4 Post-GDPR AI

GDPR is perhaps the first time that the EU has taken the initiative in digital matters and spoken with its own voice, blending data and smart city research and policy formulations. From here onwards, new data ecosystems are needed to consolidate a strategy for the protection of citizens' digital rights across Europe. This should entail a call to action, a need to critically map out the techno-political debate on *dataism* and, ultimately, it should identify the potential requirements to establish regulatory frameworks to protect digital rights (Holmes, 2017). It is crucial to understand how the concepts of autonomy and identity of individuals, as well as security, safety, privacy, and ownership might change under the influence of AI (Mayer-Schönberger, 2013; Sugimoto, Ekbia, & Mattioli, 2016). To build and retain trust in AI and the use of citizens' data requires critical engagement of civil society (Mayer-Schönberger & Ramge, 2018).

One direct outcome of GDPR is the Cities Coalition for Digital Rights (CCDR) movement. This broad movement already encompasses 41 international cities and has the support of the UN-HABITAT programme. Under the leadership of Barcelona and the joint strategic view of Amsterdam and New York, the network is being extended further.

Two main policy challenges are identified in this book to better react to the consequences of AI for citizens. We are referring to the emergence of platform and data co-operatives.

The first policy challenge is to gradually replace the centralised and extractive 'platform-knows-best' capitalist model of the smart city that has taken over many cities. This should be done by enacting sectoral policies in conjunction with experiment-driven 'platform co-operatives'. A platform co-operative is a co-operatively owned, democratically governed business model that establishes a computing platform and uses a website and/or mobile app to facilitate the sale of goods and delivery of services. For example, Fairbnb, a vacation rental platform, gives 50% of its revenue to local community projects; Denver's Green Taxi Cooperative is owned by its workers; and Resonate, a streaming music service, shares profits with various stakeholders.

In Barcelona, three projects on participatory democracy have set the scene for a transition towards platform co-operativism: DECODE, which provides the tools for individuals to be in control of their personal data; Decidim, which helps people, organisations, and governments to self-organise in a democratic way; and Metadecidim, the democratic community that manages Decidim projects. Platform co-operatives require a strong alliance between institutional capacity, active civic society, and entrepreneurial business ecosystems. They are social and ethical alternatives to existing commercial extractivist platforms.

The second policy challenge is how to consolidate a pan-European post-GDPR AI through 'data co-operatives'. They enable the creation of open data and personal data stores for mutual benefit. The unbridled extractivism of personal data by big tech private 'data-opolies' needs to be stopped. Local and regional authorities should establish data co-operatives in order to empower citizens to have more control over their data and give them more of a say in the services that are built on and informed by this data. This may help to rebalance the relationship between those who create data (citizens) and those who seek to exploit that data, while also creating the environment for fair and democratic exchange. Data co-operatives with fiduciary obligations to members demonstrate a promising direction for the democratic empowerment of citizens through their personal data. Without data co-operatives and their related data ecosystem, the EU might lose its opportunity to establish a pan-European post-GDPR AI strategy. Unlike in China or the United States—the data governance paradigms of which are driven by either the state or big tech corporations—the debate around data in the EU is currently open, and actually the EU has the opportunity to lead or at least internationally influence towards further humanistic and democratic approach in digital transformations, data ecosystems, and AI strategies. City and regional authorities must collaborate further on the ethical and social benefits of data capture and AI for their citizens.

5 Deconstructing the smart city citizenship: Book's structure

Could an ecosystem of data co-operatives in Europe protect citizens' digital rights and better tailor the design, implementation, and assessment of further citizen-centric AI? (Montreal AI Ethics Institute, 2020; Common Wealth, 2020; Nichols & LeBlanc, 2020). To ensure that European cities and regions employ data democratically, the public sector should take the lead alongside various stakeholders. Debating on the techno-politics of data for citizens cannot be seen as an operation of ethic washing; it should be about ownership and how to rescue democracy. Failing to do so could risk exposing European democracies to the stealthy algorithmic manipulation of collective behaviours through social media, resulting in a dystopian populism.

Beginning with the Prologue, this book therefore attempts to unfold the following topics in each chapter:

(i) Unplugging, the first chapter, presents a corrective to the smart city definition through the development of 10 dimensions from the Social Innovation (SI) perspective by avoiding the techno-determinism of the hyperconnected society.

(ii) Deciphering, the second chapter, examines the hegemonic smart city approach in the European H2020 institutional framework by pointing out that it is slowly evolving into a new citizen-centric paradigm called experimental city.

(iii) Democratising, the third chapter, unfolds and operationalises multi-stakeholders policy frameworks from the SI perspective by suggesting the ex novo Penta-helix framework—including public, private, academia, civic society, and social entrepreneurs/activists—to extend the Triple- and Quadruple-helix frameworks.

(iv) Replicating, the fourth chapter, analyses the city-to-city learning programme to reformulate the policy issue of replication among smart cities by revealing that replication might be enabled as a multidirectional, radial, dynamic, iterative, and democratic learning process, overcoming the currently unidirectional, hierarchical, mechanistic, solutionist, and technocratic approach.

(v) Devolving, the fifth chapter, elucidates the notion of data devolution as a key governance component that is enabling some cities to formulate their own smart city-regional governance policies and implement them by considering the role of the smart citizens as decision-makers rather than mere data providers.

(vi) Commoning, the sixth chapter, examines how the city of Barcelona is marking a transition from the conventional, hegemonic smart city approach to a new paradigm, the experimental city, by elaborating a strategy based on 'data commons'.

(vii) Protecting, the seventh chapter, elucidates on the need to establish pan-European data infrastructures and institutions—collectively data ecosystems—to protect citizens' digital rights in European cities and regions.

(viii) Finally, Resetting, the Epilogue of the book thus, concludes by updating the smart city citizenship amidst the current post-COVID-19 society by converging a pandemic and a data crisis.

References

Bakıcı, T., Almirall, E., & Wareham, J. (2013). A smart city initiative: The case of Barcelona. *Journal of the Knowledge Economy*, *4*(2), 135–148. https://doi.org/10.1007/s13132-012-0084-9.

Bauwens, M., Kostakis, V., & Pazaitis, A. (2019). *Peer to peer: The commons manifesto*. Westminster: University of Westminster Press.

Brayne, S. (2020). *Predict and surveil: Data, discretion, and the future of policing*. Oxford: Oxford University Press.

Buttarelli, G. (2018). *Big tech is still violating your privacy*. Retrieved from: https://www.washingtonpost.com/news/theworldpost/wp/2018/08/14/gdpr/?utm_term=.9e9ddd6cf937.

Campbell, T. (2012). *Beyond smart cities: How cities network, learn and innovate*. Oxon: Earthscan.

Castells, M. (2009). *Democracy in the age of the internet*. Retrieved from: https://llull.cat/IMAGES_175/transfer06-not01.pdf.

Cities Coalition for Digital Rights. (2019). *Declaration of cities coalition for digital rights*. Retrieved from: https://citiesfordigitalrights.org/.

Coletta, C., Evans, L., Heaphy, L., & Kitchin, R. (2018). *Creating smart cities*. Oxon: Routledge.

Coletta, C., & Kitchin, R. (2017). Algorhythmic governance: Regulating the 'heartbeat' of a city using the internet of things. *Big Data & Society*, *4*(2). https://doi.org/10.1177/2053951717742418.

Common Wealth. (2020). *Democratic Digital Infrastructure*. London: DPW.

Cugurullo, F. (2013). How to build a sandcastle: An analysis of the genesis and development of Masdar city. *Journal of Urban Technology.*, *20*(1), 23–37. https://doi.org/10.1080/10630732.2012.735105.

Danaher, J., Hogan, M. J., Noone, C., Kennedy, R., Behan, A., Paor, A. D., et al. (2017). Algorithmic governance: Developing a research agenda through the power of collective intelligence. *Big Data & Society*, *4*(2). https://doi.org/10.1177/2053951717726554.

Duran, X. (2019). *El imperio de los datos*. Valencia: Universitat de Valencia.

Dyer-Witherford, N., Kjosen, M., & Steinhoff, J. (2020). *Inhuman power: Artificial Intelligence and the future of capitalism*. London: Pluto Press.

Economist, T. (2019). *Can technology plan economies and destroy democracy?*. Retrieved from: https://amp.economist.com/christmas-specials/2019/12/18/can-technology-plan-economies-and-destroy-democracy.

Eubanks, V. (2017). *Automating inequality: How high-tech tools profile, police, and punish the poor*. NYC: St. Martin's Press.

European Commission. (2019a). *Digital innovation hubs (DIHs)*. Brussels: EC.

European Commission. (2019b). *Eurobarometer GDPR*. Retrieved from: https://ec.europa.eu/commfrontoffice/publicopinion/index.cfm/Survey/getSurveyDetail/instruments/special/search/General%20Data%20Protection%20Regulation/surveyKy/2222.

Evans, J., Karvonen, A., & Raven, R. (2016). *The experimental city*. London and New York: Routledge.

Ferronato, P., & Stan, R. (2018). *Smart citizenship: Designing the interaction between citizens and smart cities*. Limerick: University of Limerick.

Finn, E. (2017). *What algorithms want: Imagination in the age of computing*. Cambridge, Massachusetts and London, England: The MIT Press.

Goodman, E. P., & Powles, J. (2019). Urbanism under Google: Lessons from sidewalk Toronto. *Fordham Law Review* (Preprint/Draft).

Green, B. (2019). *The smart enough city: Putting technology in its place to reclaim our urban future*. Boston: MIT Press.

Hajer, M. A., & Dassen, T. (2014). *Smart about cities: Visualising the challenge for 21st century urbanism*. Amsterdam: Nai010 Publishers.

Harari, Y. N. (2016). Yuval Noah Harari on big data. In *Google and the end of free will*. Retrieved from: https://www.ft.com/content/50bb4830-6a4c-11e6-ae5b-a7cc5dd5a28c.

Hardjono, T., & Pentland, A. (2019). Data cooperatives: Towards a foundation for decentralized personal data management. *arXiv*. e-prints. Retrieved from: https://ui.adsabs.harvard.edu/abs/2019arXiv190508819H.

Holmes, D. E. (2017). *Big data: A very short introduction*. Oxford: Oxford University Press.

Karvonen, A., Cugurullo, F., & Caprotti, F. (2018). *Inside smart cities: Place, politics and urban innovation*. London: Routledge.

Marvin, S., Luque-Ayala, A., & McFarlane, C. (2015). *Smart urbanism: Utopian vision or false dawn?*. New York: Routledge.

Mayer-Schönberger, V. (2013). *Big data: A revolution that will transform how we live, work and think*. London: John Murray.

Mayer-Schönberger, V., & Ramge, T. (2018). *Reinventing capitalism in the age of big data*. London: Basic Books.

Mazzucato, M. (2015). *The entrepreneurial state: Debunking public vs. private sector myths*. London: Anthen Press.

Montreal AI Ethics Institute. (2020). *The State of AI Ethics*. Montreal: MAEI.

Morozov, E. (2012). *In the net delusion: How not to liberate the world*. London and New York: Penguin.

Nichols, T. P., & LeBlanc, R. J. (2020). Beyond apps: Digital literacies in a platform society. *The Reading Teacher.*, *74*(1), 103–109. https://doi.org/10.1002/trtr.1926.

Noveck, B. S. (2015). *Smart citizens, smarter state: The technologies of expertise and future of governing*. Cambridge, MA: Harvard University Press.

Pak-Hang. (2020). Cultural Differences as Excuses? *Human Rights and Cultural Values in Global Ethics and Governance of AI. Philosophy & Technology.*, 1–11. https://doi.org/10.1007/s13347-020-00413-8.

Ratti, C., & Claudel, M. (2016). *The City of tomorrow: Sensors, networks, hackers, and the future of urban life*. Boston: Yale University Press.

Richey, S., & Taylor, J. B. (2018). *Google and democracy: Politics and the power of the internet*. London and New York: Routledge.

Scholz, T. (2014). *Platform cooperativism vs. the sharing economcy*. Retrieved from: https://medium.com/@trebors/platform-cooperativism-vs-the-sharing-economy-2ea737f1b5ad.

Shelton, T., & Lodato, T. (2019). Actually existing smart citizens. *City*, 1–18. https://doi.org/10.1080/13604813.2019.1575115.

Shwayri, S. T. (2013). A model Korean ubiquitous eco-city? The politics of making Songdo. *Journal of Urban Technology, 20*(1), 39–55. https://doi.org/10.1080/10630732.2012.735409.

Sugimoto, C. R., Ekbia, H. R., & Mattioli, M. (2016). *Big data is not a monolith*. Cambridge, Massachusetts and London, England: The MIT Press.

Susskind, J. (2018). *Future politics: Living together in a world transformed by tech*. Oxford: Oxford University Press.

URB@Exp. (2017). *Guidelines for urban labs*. London: URB@Exp.

Valle-Cruz, D., Criado, J. I., Sandoval-Almazán, R., & Ruvalcaba-Gomez, E. A. (2020). Assessing the public policy-cycle framework in the age of artificial intelligence: From agenda-setting to policy evaluation. *Government Information Quarterly.*, *37*(4). https://doi.org/10.1016/j.giq.2020.101509.

Willis, K. S., & Aurigi, A. (2018). *Digital and smart cities*. Oxon: Routledge.

Willis, K. S., & Aurigi, A. (2020). *The Routledge companion to smart cities*. Oxon: Routledge.

Zuboff, S. (2019). *The age of surveillance capitalism: The fight for a human future at the new frontier of power*. London: Profile.

Chapter 1

UNPLUGGING smart city citizenship: Beyond the hyperconnected societies

Chapter outline

Smart City Citizenship. https://doi.org/10.1016/B978-0-12-815300-0.00001-0

1.1 Unplugging is a privilege in digitally divided and hyperconnected societies...

The term digital divide implies that the worldwide, explosive growth of the Internet, Big Data, and artificial intelligence (AI) is an uneven and multidimensional phenomenon (Ernst, 2020; Floridi, Cowls, King, & Taddeo, 2020; Kitchin, 2014). A significant body of literature in this field highlights differences between the haves and have-nots of Internet access. This distinction focuses on the binary classification of technology use considering only whether individuals use the Internet. However, a closer examination of digital technology utilisation suggests the need for a comprehensive understanding that includes effective access to the Internet, which cannot be explained exclusively by focusing on access to connectivity but must address the deep-rooted patterns of social inequality (caused by differences in income, employment, education, age, culture, and other forms of social capital) (Norris, 2001; Selwyn, 2004; Van Dijk & Hacker, 2003; Warschauer, 2004). This distinction between accessing the Internet (Rifkin, 2000) and remaining connected with friends and family reflects the need to establish a second-level digital divide that is not limited to technological infrastructure but is grounded in the social capital barriers that affect the effective access of digital technologies (Eastin & LaRose, 2000; Hargittai, 2002).

The expansion of technological development and the algorithmic disruption, which includes not only reductions in the cost of connectivity but also a pervasive pattern of surveillance capitalism (Zuboff, 2019), has increased the deployment of information-centric schemes (Ahlgren, Dannewitz, Imbrenda, Kutscher, & Ohlman, 2012). Based on this definition, a smart city is as a city in which 'investments in human and social capital and traditional (transport) and modern (ICT) communication infrastructure fuel sustainable economic growth and a high quality of life, with a wise management of natural resources, through participatory governance' (Caragliu, Del Bo, & Nijkamp, 2011, p. 70). Today, these cities represent a set of hyperconnected societies that enthusiastically embrace Information and Communication Technologies (ICT) as a key component of the infrastructure of modern cities (Chourabi et al., 2012; Floridi, 2015).

However, the social adoption of technology and technological evolution occurs at highly dissimilar rates, suggesting significant sociotechnical misalignment (Rogers, 2010). Noting this tension, this chapter considers an interesting contribution to the understanding of smart cities developed by Chourabi et al. (2012, p. 2294), who suggest ‘a comprehensive framework that consists of eight factors’. This framework is relevant to this chapter, though an update is required to address the special significance of social phenomena within the analysis of these factors. As a result, this chapter aims to reframe this framework utilising the Social Innovation (SI) approach (Grimm, Fox, Baines, & Albertson, 2013; Moulaert, MacCallum, Hillier, & Vicari, 2009; Mulgan, 2007) and add 10 dimensions of unplugging. Likewise, the often-cited definition of smart city must be enhanced to include the subtle notion of unplugging and the 10 dimensions provided in this chapter (Caragliu et al., 2011; Willis & Aurigi, 2020).

The framework adopted in this chapter is grounded in the approach provided by Chourabi et al. (2012) who established the following: (1) a comprehensive set of factors that are essential to understanding smart city initiatives; (2) a set of components not to rank smart cities but to create a framework that can be used to characterise how to envision such a city; (3) an integrative framework to explain the relationships and influences among these factors and smart city initiatives; and (4) this set of factors is also presented as a tool to support the understanding of how cities envision their smart initiatives in different contexts and for different purposes.

Table 1.1 illustrates the integrated framework for unplugging in the smart city guiding this chapter. This framework complements the research conducted by Chourabi et al. (2012) from the SI perspective focusing on the relevance of human interaction as a meta-factor of the smart city, while providing a transversal understanding of some unexplored dimensions, including the who, how, and what questions and system, governance, information, space, design, sociopolitical process, and political economy issues. This chapter follows the theoretical contributions made in the field of SI by Grimm et al. (2013), Moulaert et al. (2009), Mulgan (2007), and Morgan (2013) and builds an interdisciplinary, systemic, and multidimensional integrated framework to address the transitions that are currently occurring in smart city initiatives. This updated framework indicates possible transitions in the understanding and adoption of smart cities; while some cases indicate that technologies are accelerators of smart city 'in the box' initiatives, other experiences of smart cities in transition (such as smart citizens, Hacking the City, or FabLabs) envision new possibilities for building more democratic citizenship (Smith, 2019; Zandbergen & Uitermark, 2019).

Unplugging is a subtle notion that is emerging as a contestation to the dominant technocratic mode of urban governance (Kitchin, 2014, p. 9), that is, the so-called smart city model that demands a transition to overcome the social tensions and misalignments caused by hyperconnected societies (Floridi, 2015). Thus, unplugging is a novel trend that offers a corrective from the corporate, top-down direction of the smart city mainstream in favour of a transition towards the critical use of digital technologies enabling the construction of a more democratic citizenship. Consequently, this chapter and thus the whole book develop the following two hypotheses:

TABLE 1.1 Ten dimensions from the critical Social Innovation.

Unplugging the Smart City	1 Who	2 How	3 Systems	4 Governance	5 Information	6 What	7 Space	8 Design	9 Socio-political processes	10 Political economy
	Social and Digital Divide	Individualism vs collectivism	Socio vs technical Systems	Master planning vs emergent plan and top-down vs bottom-up—techno-politics	Overload vs scarcity—big data	Social net-working vs social capital—trust, ethics, and trans-parency	Context Collapse—Geolo-calisation—Real-time data—Profiling—Data leakage—Dat-aveillance	Ambient Commons—Data commons—Communal nature of connectivity and space	Control & Normative vs Free & Emergent—Sur-veillance Capitalism	Profitable vs unprofitable Multi-stake-holder
From	High	Individualism vs collectivism	Artificial	Top-down and master planning	Controlled	Inter-action	Fragmented	Infra-structure-centred	Control and normative	Private and financially
To	Low	Networked Individualism or neo-communi-tarianism	Integrated	Bottom-up and emergent plan	Open data	Trust	Contex-tualised	People-centred	Free and Emergent	Commu-nitarian and Socio-eco-nomically

The first hypothesis argues that according to the implementation of smart city 'in the box' cases, the relevance of face-to-face interactions (Marwick & Boyd, 2011) is increasingly dismissed (even more now in the post COVID-19 hyperconnected societies—Datta, 2020; Kitchin, 2020).

The second hypothesis suggests the existence of smart city initiatives in transition (as smart citizens, Hacking the City, or FabLabs; Calzada, 2018) along 10 interrelated dimensions that enable the construction of a more democratic citizenship.

Hence, the analysis of this chapter focuses on the following two research questions:

1. To what extent can face-to-face interactions remain at the centre of human experience (Allenby & Sarewitz, 2013) given that digitally mediated communications have replaced a large number of physical encounters?
2. To what extent can the 10 critical dimensions be identified to provide an integrated framework that illustrates a transition in the understanding of smart city?

Moderating the consumption of information could be perceived as unusual, particularly when the modern understanding of our societies (i.e. smart cities, open government, smart crowds, etc.) and technological development (i.e. telecommunication, computer, and smartphone sectors) continuously increase the value of being online continuously (24×7). This apparently paradoxical willingness to moderate access to data can be understood as a side effect of the non-stop stream of data. In hyperconnected societies, being offline is a nearly unaffordable privilege (or loss, in some cases) that very few dare to attempt. Currently, the opportunity to be offline is rarely considered to be valuable.

An increasing number of voices note benefits to not being online constantly, thus challenging the widely spread techno-enthusiasm of the knowledge society. Scholars including Turkle (2011), Morozov (2012), Gladwell (2013), and Rendueles (2013) argue that there are exaggerated expectations about how digital connectivity provides the dynamism required by ordinary cities (Robinson, 2006). Concepts such as disorder (Rosen, Whaling, Rab, Carrier, & Cheever, 2013), cyberfetishism, and sociophobics confirm increasing concern among scholars in the knowledge fields. These critics echo concerns over increasing amounts of loose social capital in our hyperconnected communities (Tayebi, 2013), neighbourhoods, cities, and societies highlighted by authors such as Bauman and Lyon (2012), Castells (2012), and Putnam (2001). As Lanier (2011, p. xiii) stated, 'You have to be somebody before you can share yourself'.

1.2 Digital natives in the smart city

Who are these digital natives (Castells, 2020; International Telecommunication Union ITU, 2013)? A puzzling collection of designations is attached to the generations that grow up in Internet-dominated, information-rich societies. These names include the net generation (Tapscott, 2009), digital natives (Prensky, 2001), millennials (Oblinger & Oblinger, 2005), Google generation (Rowlands et al., 2008), and many others (Jones, Ramanau, Cross, & Healing, 2010). Pfanner (2013) underlines the nondeterministic digital nature of young people.

Authors such as Tapscott (2009) and Prensky (2001) suggest that contemporary youth are qualitatively different from previous generations. Although the capabilities of the younger generations are open to debate, there is an emerging consensus that younger generations are exposed to an increasing amount of (digital) information (Castells, 2009; Hilbert & López, 2011; Rainie, Rainie, & Wellman, 2012). Hence, it is necessary to define who these digital natives are and how they are expected to unravel the subtle notion of unplugging as discussed in the framework (see the information in Table 1.1).

Telefónica and the Financial Times (Telefónica, 2013) conducted over 12,000 online interviews of respondents between 18 and 30 years of age in 27 countries (in North America, Latin America, Western Europe, Central and Eastern Europe, Asia, the Middle East, and Africa). That study revealed that respondents are constantly connected, spending an average of 6 hours online every day (equivalent to 2016 hours or 2.8 months per year).

According to the Oxford Internet Survey (Dutton & Blank, 2011), in a multistage sampling of 2000 people in the UK, one major change over the past decade has been the growing use of the Internet as a source of information. Compared to first-generation Internet users, the so-called next-generation users (NGUs) are shaped by the emergence of two separate but related trends: portability and access through multiple devices. NGUs are not evenly distributed, but they have higher incomes and are 'more likely than first-generation users to go to the Internet first for all kinds of information' (Dutton & Blank, 2011, p. 6). Compared to previous generations, NGUs have a more advantageous relationship with the Internet and the access to information, people, services, and other technologies it can provide, including quicker devices such as webcams, Internet connected televisions, and games consoles.

The World Internet Project (Internet Project, 2012) administered surveys to people aged 18 and older in 37 countries. That study revealed that a high percentage of users believe that going online has (somewhat or greatly) increased their contact with people who share their hobbies. Compared with other forms of social media, Internet users in many countries are more attracted to social networking and video-sharing websites (Lieberman, 2013).

The Pew Internet Project (Brenner & Smith, 2013) determined that nearly three quarters (72%) of online US adults (over 2000 respondents aged 18 years and older) use social networking sites, an increase from the 67% reported in late 2012. This increase is notable given that in 2005, only 8% of online adults reporting using social networking sites.

These data are not representative of the universe of Internet users but they illustrate clear trends in current Internet use. Rather than aiming for a generalisation, these trends signal the key role that the Internet plays in contemporary societies as a social platform that extends (amplifies) face-to-face (analogue) relationships (see the SPACE dimension). These data are relevant to the first research question regarding the dichotomy of face-to-face interaction and digitally mediated communication. Bearing in mind the ongoing transition in the smart city discourse, unplugging is a subtle notion in favour of face-to-face (analogue) social interactions. That is, unplugging emerges as a reaction to the techno-centred enthusiasm that supports smart cities (Morozov, 2012).

Rainie et al. (2012, p.7) coined the term 'networked individualism' to describe the ways in which people connect, communicate, and exchange information. This concept will be discussed as part of the how dimension of the integrated framework and highlights the opportunities and constraints of a hyperconnected and extensively networked society, that is, people who continuously and ubiquitously play and work on computers and mobile devices. These authors suggest that the shift to networked individualism has been accompanied by changes in how people behave socially and how they define the boundaries between private and public (see the discussion of the SPACE dimension) both on and offline, as well as the limits between individual and collective actions. This transformation can be observed in a growing community that is shifting from the Internet-as-novelty to the Internet-as-utility in everyday life.

According to Zygmunt Bauman (CCCB, 2013), 'Our society is addicted to information'. Dr Larry Rosen, a professor at California State University, adds, 'In our studies, the typical teen and young adult checks his or her smartphone every 15 minutes or less and if they can't check as often as they like they get anxious. This anxiety then drives the need to check in to reduce the anxiety which then begins to build again' (Richmond, 2013). In the Richmond article, Rosen explains that the more ubiquitous digital technologies become (mobile and wearable devices), the worse this problem becomes (see the INFORMATION dimension). To illustrate the magnitude of this information growth, Eric Schmidt explained, 'There were five exabytes of information created between the dawn of civilisation through 2003, but that much information is now created every 2 days'. An exabyte is equivalent to one billion gigabytes (Rooney, 2013).

In 1985, Hiltz and Turoff anticipated that 'users will be overloaded with information' (Hiltz & Turoff, 1985, p. 680). In their work, these authors emphasised the need for novel strategies to help users filter information and reduce overload. Edmunds and Morris (2000) added that rapid advances in information and communication technology have exacerbated the effects of information overload, and they highlighted the need to adopt sociotechnical strategies to overcome this situation (see the SYSTEMS dimension), such as implementing personal information management strategies and software solutions such as push technology and intelligent agents (Lanier, 2011, 2018).

Eppler and Mengis (2004) analysed a number of overlapping terms and relevant perspectives in this field, such as information overload, cognitive overload, sensory overload, communication overload, and knowledge overload or information fatigue syndrome. The authors explain information overload by comparing the amount of information supplied (e.g. the number of available communication platforms available) with the information processing capacity of an individual (i.e. the quantity of information one can integrate into a decision-making process within a specific period). In this case, information overload occurs when the supply exceeds the processing capacity (p. 326). After a comprehensive review of experiences, Eppler and Mengis observe that reducing information overload requires a combination of personal factors, information characteristics, task and process parameters, organisational design, and information technology applications.

Paradoxically, in an information society, the choice to go offline or unplug from this endless flow of data becomes a nearly unreasonable option that very few individuals make (see the WHO dimension). Factors such as identity (Buckingham, 2008), socialisation (Rheingold, 2012), and the extension of human capabilities (Richardson, 2007) make the voluntary decision to not have a digital device or not be online rather rare. In cities, as Hollands (2008) and Kitchin (2014) noted, it has been atypical to remain uninfluenced by discussions of smart cities when one of the main principles is a technology-driven understanding of modern societies. Although citizens have not necessarily chosen to become a hyper-artificial model for cities, it is increasingly challenging to embrace spontaneous, emergent, unplugged social spaces (see discussions of the GOVERNANCE and SOCIOPOLITICAL PROCESSES dimensions; Kingsley, 2013).

The idea of shaping boundaries to arbitrarily pre-establish the extent to which being online is appropriate is a solution more typical of a totalitarian system (Lupton & Mike, 2017; Van Dijck, 2014) than a society that self-regulates the adoption of appropriate 'digital dieting' (Brabazon, 2013, p. 10–60) to address the 'tsunami of data' without losing its processing capacity. In an extension of the strategies that reduce information overload suggested by Eppler and Mengis (2004), we explore the usefulness of the unplugged smart city not only to address information overload but also to explore the urban governance model of a city universally considered to be smart. The integrated framework, stemming from the SI perspective (Moulaert & MacCallum, 2019; Moulaert & Mehmood, 2020), illustrates the transition from a mainstream approach towards a more democratic understanding of smart cities. This specific aspect will be elaborated in depth in Chapter 3 (DEMOCRATISING). The updated framework (Chourabi et al., 2012) attributes a critical factor to SI in power relationships between stakeholders (an aspect that will be clearly addressed in Chapter 3). In that respect, 10 thought-provoking dimensions that can contribute to deconstructing the concept of a smart city using the so-called unplugging decalogue are proposed. Furthermore, a system of key principles aimed at creating a conceptual and analytical framework is suggested.

1.3 Unplugging: 10 dimensions from the Social Innovation perspective

How and why should we critically (Hollands, 2008; Kitchin, 2014) deconstruct the term *smart city* to suggest an integrated framework that provides an improved understanding of the ongoing transition from the mainstream definition? This chapter proposes an answer to this question as well as a decalogue of 10 dimensions.

Derridá suggested that deconstruction is one way to approach distinctions. 'Unless a distinction can be made rigorous and precise it isn't really a distinction' (Derridá, 1977, p. 126). This chapter deconstructs our understanding of a smart city and suggests a framework that is complementary to previous classic taxonomics (Chourabi et al., 2012) of the systemic and multidimensional SI perspective (Van de Broeck, Mehmood, Paidakaki, & Parra, 2019).

A deconstruction (Wolfram, 2012) of the smart city (Caragliu et al., 2011, p. 70; Cohen, 2012) is provided and articulated using 10 dimensions of unplugging, which are grounded in critical SI (Calzada, 2013a). Critical SI drives transdisciplinary research and provides a guide for collective action, which are interrelated concepts that indicate significant changes, social evolution, structures modification, and consideration of ethical norms (Moulaert, MacCallum, Mehmood, & Hamdouch, 2013, pp. 9–13). This definition suggests the importance of an analytical discussion to explore a transition that is occurring in the discourse of smart cities (Keith & Calzada, 2018).

Which dimensions should be considered to deconstruct the smart city model (Hollands, 2008)? To what extent is it possible to address sociotechnical ideological dimensions (Peck, 2013) to understand the economic and social changes occurring in modern cities (Moulaert et al., 2013, p. 18)? As Kitchin argues, '...technologies need to be complemented with a range of other instruments, policies and practices that are sensitive to the diverse ways in which cities are structured' (Kitchin, 2014, p. 10). This chapter presents 10 dimensions of a multidimensional, interrelated, and systemic combination that is explained by an epistemological focus on critical SI.

Most likely, because of the claim that the smart city paradigm has been shaped primarily by providers of large-scale technology (Microsoft-CityNext; IBM-TheSmarterCity; Kitchin, 2014), the remaining stakeholders in the urban sphere tend to explore thought-provoking alternative interpretations, such as smart citizens (Calzada, 2018; Hemment & Townsend, 2013), Hacking the City (Sterling, 2014), and FabLabs (Gershenfeld, 2005). The dominant smart city approach failed because it was not attuned to bottom-up innovation or to the complex, disruptive ways that people use technology. Furthermore, the principle 'to be smart, citizens must be connected' (Hemment & Townsend, 2013, p. 59) denotes part of the major premises in contrast with Harvey's (Harvey, 2008, p. 23) statement that refers to the notion of social transformation rather than simply digital connectivity. 'It is a right to change ourselves by changing the city'.

Hence, the smart city is perceived by critical thinkers (Hemment & Townsend, 2013; Hollands, 2008) as a top-down, master-planned vision shaped around the needs of suppliers rather than the needs of citizens (see the GOVERNANCE dimension).

While large corporate technology companies have been selling a 'Smart city in a Box' to cities (Hemment & Townsend, 2013, p. 1), this chapter opens this box to determine which dimensions can be summarised using a non-technological deterministic notion, unplugging. This perspective suggests that citizens can and should play a leading role in conceiving, designing, building, and maintaining their cities, as argued by Jacobs (1970) and Geddes (Welter, 2003) (see the SOCIOPOLITICAL PROCESSES dimension).

Montgomery (2013) raised many questions in his book 'Happy City'. For example, how much of this commonly accepted environment is based on the idea of unplugging? Why do we need to rescue unplugging in the design of our cities? Can we combine off- and online environments to create a smarter balance? He argues, 'It is not too late to rebuild the balance of life in our neighbourhoods and cities and, in so doing, to build a more resilient future' (Montgomery, 2013, p. 323). Addressing the first hypothesis, Turkle (2011) severely critiqued social networking when she referred to the overexposure of social networks while expecting more from technology than from one another. Is Sennett (2012) right when he argues that humankind has forgotten how to co-operate such that we must learn rituals, pleasure, and the politics of co-operation? What if instead we focused on the ambient commons (McCullough, 2013), the whole, subtle, and sometimes invisible notion of information that is overlooked when modern life is oversimplified as connectivity (see the DESIGN dimension)?

It is necessary for the smart city to be deconstructed to avoid techno-deterministic conditions and to observe how relevant unplugging dimensions can be to SI in a more realistic, grounded, and socially equal urban sphere. The dimensions of the unplugging decalogue are summarised in Table 1.1.

1.3.1 1st Dimension (WHO): Social and digital divide—Plugging in vs unplugging

After the increasing enthusiasm for using data to improve the life of citizens in modern societies (i.e. open data, the Internet, cloud computing; Hashem et al., 2016), the publication of a considerable amount of confidential information of (smart) citizens (see the SPACE dimension) and heads of states via espionage, surveillance, dataveillance, and theft has somewhat altered the data enthusiasm of some communities (Benkler, 2011; Brown & Marsden, 2013; Frey, 2019; Hindman, 2018; Morozov, 2012). In fact, there are hazards in certain digital applications of the smart city (IBM, 2013). While some simply collect data, others use that data to control and design citizen interactive artificial services (Lupton, 2019). First, it is relevant to determine who is plugged in and why.

Who controls citizen data and why? When big technology providers mention multiple stakeholders, they are not necessarily addressing the Penta helix model of SI (Calzada, 2013a) in which civil society, academia, activists, or entrepreneurs become central agents in the design of private and public policies. Finally, are smart city solutions currently based more on vendor push than on city government pull? What are the politics of big data in various smart cities (Bigo, Isin, & Ruppert, 2019)?

Apparently, in a smart city, everyone should be plugged as passive mass users, while the data control centre decides what to do with the information (Danaher, 2019). As Greenfield argues, 'The praxis of everyday survival goes almost entirely unrecognised in the contemporary smart city literature' (Hemment & Townsend, 2013, p. 10). The current smart city achieves nearly complete connectivity, but the concept does not attach enough importance to the tacit influence of an information-driven smart city. To what extent is it possible for smart citizens to stimulate public spaces where unplugged people are not constrained either by or because of their digital technology (Calzada, 2018)? As Greenfield (2013, p. 11) contended, 'how might we inscribe a robust conception of the right of the city in all of the technological interventions proposed, including but not limited to those intended to enhance personal mobility, citizen engagement and processes of (individual and collective) self-determination'? As the author suggested, legitimacy must be given to those who decide to live unplugged or to be connected to others without the use of technology (Cardullo, Di Feliciantonio, & Kitchin, 2019; Mayer-Schönberger, 2011).

Currently, the United Nations (Cerf, 2012) has suggested that access to the Internet is a basic human digital right (Calzada & Almirall, 2020). However, attention should not be focused solely on the rate of Internet penetration but on the capability to choose whether to be connected—in other words, possessing a critical position of why, how, and when citizens are connected or unplugged (Lane, 2019). Therefore, this dimension goes beyond instrumental factors and focuses on human interaction (see the first research question) as a central element to reduce the social divide in unplugging.

1.3.2 2nd Dimension (HOW): Individualism vs collectivism—Networked individualism and neo-communitarianism

When Tim O'Reilly founded the 2.0 paradigm, he also established the way by which cities would be structured in the network society paradigm (Castells, 1999) that involved a new combination of the individual and the collective. Bauman and Beck, among others, commented on threats to individualism in contemporary society, providing significant dimensions for this analysis.

On the one hand, there is the assumption in the smart city context that relationships are merely peer-to-peer, where ideas and relationships all arise from intimate collaborations across ubiquitous, distributed networks. Ratti (Hemment & Townsend, 2013, p. 20) called this approach 'networked specifism', Rainie et al. (2012) refer to this as ‘networked individualism’, while Turkle (2011) termed it ‘alone together’. These terms favour an ideal mix between a person and the network in a new, constructive and desirable configuration.

On the other hand, Davies (2012) observes an emerging trend of ‘neo-communitarianism’, which is defined as ‘a similar counter-movement developed within and against neoliberalism (…) a new vision of the individual is emerging’. In this context, new dynamics among citizens reshape their interactions in society, adopting either the networked individualism or the neo-communitarianism approach. While networked individualism emphasises that the individual plays the predominant role in the networked-shaped collectivism, neo-communitarianism highlights how the community may be reshaped based on the actions and behaviours of individuals. Neo-communitarianism further suggests a tension between this hybrid condition that combines individual and collective activities in a ‘communihood’ (Tayebi, 2013). Therefore, rather than suggesting a one-size-fits-all concept, unplugging can be addressed from either the individual or the collective perspective.

According to the second hypothesis, this dimension addresses the need to overcome the individualistic form in which the mainstream smart city definition has been built. Therefore, the integrated framework contributes a balance to be explored between individualism and collectivism. This dimension is intertwined with the dimensions of GOVERNANCE, FOCUS, SOCIOPOLITICAL PROCESSES, and POLITICAL ECONOMY.

1.3.3 3rd Dimension (SYSTEMS): Sociotechnical systems and strategies—Urban systems

The smart city is all about systems that are connected to individuals who are plugged into digital information devices. However, as Puel and Fernandez (2012, p. 1297) note, ‘the existence of sociotechnical systems, practices, and strategies produce urban forms which intensify social fragmentation’. Thus, how a new technical local infrastructure affects communitarian life should be considered before it is implemented.

What is the sustainable design for non-plugged or not connected urban spaces? Is it possible to better integrate the social dimension of the city with sensor-driven mainstream design? In today’s society, the smart city should overcome the initial idea of separation between designers and users (Calzada in Moulaert et al., 2013). Indeed, the main criticism of the term smart city, as Hollands (2008) noted, stems from the positive and rather naïve stance towards urban development that the term reflects.

Throughout this first chapter, Unplugging, it has referred to the mainstream smart city perspective. New Songdo (Korea), Masdar (United Arab Emirates), and PlanIT (Portugal) are clear examples of this perspective. These flagship smart cities (‘in the box’) were built from scratch as a result of closed planning between governments working alongside large IT firms, such as Microsoft,

IBM, or Cisco (Ratti, 2014). For instance, one renowned mainstream smart city is described by Cugurullo (2013, p. 34) as 'with little space for the social aspects of sustainable development and for the basic social dimension of the city'.

How can we design and co-create (see the GOVERNANCE dimension) more open, transparent, democratic, self-regulated, participatory, and less artificial (technology-driven) sociotechnical urban systems, or a dynamic city metabolism (Baccini, 1997; Watcher-Boettcher, 2017)?

1.3.4 4th Dimension (GOVERNANCE): Master planning vs emergent plan and top-down vs bottom-up—Techno-politics

Here is where unplugging the smart city forces us to examine it as an entrepreneurial city (Harvey, 2000) rather than as the sum of technological social artefacts (Pinch & Bijker, 1984) and gadgets (Lanier, 2011, 2018) being controlled by large corporations (Gray & Siddharth, 2019) (see the dimensions of GOVERNANCE, INFORMATION, and SOCIOPOLITICAL PROCESSES). This approach leads to the next dimension in observing the smart city from the SI perspective (Calzada, 2013a; Grimm et al., 2013; Pel, Wittmayer, Dorland, & Sogaard Jorgensen, 2019). Indeed, this description implies that we observe the city from a complex urban governance systemic scalar framework (Herod, 2011) and that we address the contradictions (Harvey, 2000) emerging between the macro and micro where the meso is the black box that must be unwrapped (Mintzberg, Ahlstrand, & Lampel, 1998). With respect to the current debate about governance models, the meso consists of the minutiae that are embodied in the entrepreneurial projects of the city (see the GOVERNANCE dimension). For instance, Shirky (2009) considers 'organising without organisations' and questions what happens when people are given the digital tools to collaborate without traditional organisational structures.

Nevertheless, there is an emerging trend of bottom-up participatory models, i.e. smart mobs (Rheingold, 2012), FabLabs (2020), Hacking the City (Sterling, 2014), and other interventions in public and communicative spaces that openly criticise the smart city as '...economically polarised, but also socially, culturally and spatially divided' (Hollands, 2008, p. 312). We cannot determine whether evidence-based cases of informal *peer-to-peer* encounters and physical interactions that are unplugged have improved the governance model output (see the first research question). As Williams (1983, p. 128) stated, 'Technology is never neutral, it has the potential and capacity to be used socially and politically for quite different purposes'.

Therefore, this chapter has certain contextual questions wherein the unplugging notion would fit with some hypothetical governance models (see second hypothesis). How can the smart city be a centralised vs decentralised decision-making process? (Atzori, 2017) (see the SOCIOPOLITICAL PROCESSES dimension). Can bottom-up and top-down models coexist (and, if possible, how)? Which planning paradigm is more consistent with the socially innovative smart city? As evidenced, there are many unanswered questions relating to the GOVERNANCE dimension. As Innerarity (2013, p. 70) stated, 'The perspective of governance merely reaches the conclusions dictated by the fact that current social plurality, dynamism and the complexity of the tasks with which it is charged demand, not a central governmental subject, but the cooperation of governmental and non-governmental actors, at various levels and with differing methods and tools'.

1.3.5 5th Dimension (INFORMATION): Overload vs scarcity—Big Data

Smart citizens can be understood as an alternative initiative to the technocratic determinism of the smart city approach (Calzada, 2018; Shelton & Lodato, 2019). Smart citizens prioritise bottom-up, community-driven, low-cost, and local innovative strategies rather than large-scale, urban infrastructure projects (Shepard & Simeti, 2013). Today, it is increasingly recognised that smart citizens have an interest in participating in a transition from controlled data mining to open access and user-centred systems in which the smart use of information can increase transparency, accountability, participation, and collaboration (Hecker et al., 2018) (see the SYSTEMS and INFORMATION dimensions). However, as Morozov (2013, p. 153) stated, 'Poor information diets give us new forms of ignorance—ignorance that comes not from a lack of information, but from overconsumption of it'. Information overload is increasingly common in a hyperconnected society, i.e. there is still a gap to overcome to manage this abundance of information (Floridi, 2015). The challenge is how to provide relevant information for improved decision-making without overloading citizens with endless data streams that might generate interference or information anxiety (Wurman, Leifer, Sume, & Whitehouse, 2001). Can public and open spaces facilitate information-friendly environments without having to address information overload? (see the WHO and SPACE dimensions).

McCullough (2013) proposes the management of the ambient commons of a public space, which is clearly significant to rediscovering surroundings or, as this chapter suggests, unplugging from surroundings, which is similar to Jacobs' (1970) special attention to drawing on the local knowledge of citizens. As noted by Smart (2013, p. 4), 'Individuals and business are paying the price as time-scarcity, attention-poverty and information-saturation clog the 'mental machinery' we rely on. The real smart city might use IT [information technology] to enhance democratic debates about the kind of city it wants to be and what kind of city people want to live in, a type of virtual public culture'. This idea is consistent with what Kitchin (2014) referred to as a real-time city that opens up new concerns about the needs and desires of the society. The digital and social divides must be addressed accordingly within the political realm, which makes this dimension of unplugging a relevant transition towards a more 'progressive smart city' (Hollands, 2008) as encouraged by the SI critical paradigm (Moulaert et al., 2013, p. 13) (see the WHO dimension).

1.3.6 6th Dimension (WHAT): Social networking vs social capital—Trust, ethics, and transparency

Currently, the smart city has focused on the social networking approach. With the pure definition of the imperative to be connected, we could guarantee that social capital (Putnam, 2001) is not directly achievable. One of the first principles of unplugging is the value of face-to-face and offline social interaction to gain trust among diverse urban development stakeholders (Marwick & Boyd, 2011) (see hypothesis one).

When addressing the question of whether Facebook (or a similar domain) is a complement or substitute for face-to-face interactions, Pollet, Roberts, and Dunbar (2011) admitted that time spent using technology-based social media is not associated with larger offline (face-to-face) networks or feelings of emotional closeness to offline network members (McElroy, 2019). Furthermore, Pollet et al. (2011) stated those who used social media, compared to non-users, did not have larger offline networks (see the WHO dimension, first research question, and first hypothesis). As Allwinkle and Cruickshank (2011) noted, there is an unspoken assumption surrounding the self-declaratory nature of smart cities that they foster trusting interactions and contribute to increased social capital, which is an incorrect assumption (Mulgan & Straub, 2019).

Tayebi (2013, p. 89) highlighted an alternative to the dominant notion of the smart city when he spoke of a communihood as 'the context for human and social life in the 21st century that provides opportunities for active citizenship and local activists to improve the quality of life in their communihood'. The basis of the communihood is the hybrid place-based power relations and the potential of ICT and social media. As suggested by Pollet et al. (2011), online mechanisms of socialising are not necessary proxies for face-to-face relationships.

Therefore, while the construction of social capital requires a place that allows for physical contact among its members, it could benefit from plugged-in artefacts to share and create a sense of belonging (Guibernau, 2013). The simple adoption of social networking interactions (i.e. Facebook, Twitter, WhatsApp, etc.) does not imply a direct, positive correlation, nor does it increase the rate of development of a trusting social interaction (Delacroix & Lawrence, 2019). Moreover, unplugging and face-to-face interaction spaces are of the utmost importance within the hyperconnectedness described herein (see the following dimension).

1.3.7 7th Dimension (SPACE): Context collapse—Geolocalisation—Fragmented vs contextualised—Real-time data—Profiling—Data leakage—Dataveillance

Although credit for coining the term is given to Danah Boyd (2013), the direct source of inspiration was Meyrowithz (1986) in 'No Sense of Place', whose perspectives are aligned with the term 'space of flows' proposed by Castells (1999). Space of flows, according to Castells (1999, p. 294), represents 'the material arrangements that allow for simultaneity of social practices without territorial contiguity'. In the context of the smart city, social media enable the dynamics of networked publics that are implicitly juxtaposed with an analogue era of face-to-face interaction. Therefore, the smart city may be the connected spaces that, 'by default, span multiple arenas of the actor's social world; collapsing contexts that were previously segmented' (Davis, 2013).

Nevertheless, this chapter argues that high value social capital interactions based on trust require physically contextualised environments (Keymolen & Voorwinden, 2019) (see the FOCUS and DESIGN dimensions). The smart city discourse assumes that the meaning of context collapse is socially and personally contextualised by social media interactions (Kitchin & Moore-Cherrry, 2020).

'Mobile hyperconnectivity in fuzzily bounded public-private spaces changes individuals' expectations about the availability of other people and the accessibility of information' (Rainie et al., 2012, p. 104). By no means does this statement appear valid when examining trends in urban spaces and how people behave and interact in cities (Hoque, 2013). Perhaps one of the key differences is the revalorisation of analogic urban spaces for a common shared meaning and a sense of context awareness. As McCullough (2013) suggested, people are still intent on seeing, feeling, and creating from new experiences that can be fed by any type of external stimulus over the ambient online environment (rediscovery of surroundings). This chapter calls this DESIGN dimension of the smart city from the unplugging perspective of the ambient commons.

1.3.8 8th Dimension (DESIGN): Ambient commons—Data commons—Communal nature of connectivity and space

Why do we need technology in the smart city? Given the need for technology, how should the smart city be designed (Rosner, 2018) to respond to the governance of communal data sharing (Data commons; Ho & Chuangt, 2019)? The critical definition provided by Hollands (2008, p. 307) highlighted the infrastructure-centred design of smart cities when he stated that we require 'the utilisation of networked infrastructure to improve economic and political efficiency and enable social, cultural, and urban development'. Although this is changing, there remains insufficient attention to the people-centred analysis of smart cities thus far.

By applying McCullough's (2013) term ambient commons, this chapter addresses the main challenge of urban design, which is that physical positions are progressively tagged and digitally augmented. Within this flood, attention matters more than ever (Eyal, 2014) (see the WHO dimension). The fixed forms of architecture and the city play a cognitive role in the flow of ambient information, and accordingly, this work explores current obsessions with smart phones (constant social connectivity) to rethink its focus (Wismans, Friso, Rijsdijk, de Graaf, & Keij, 2018). Therefore, there is tension between information superabundance and the perspectives of AI socio-economic and cultural contexts (Eubanks, 2017; Noble, 2018; O'Neill, 2008) (see the INFORMATION and SPACE dimensions). McCullough (2013, p. x) suggests the relevance of 'rethink attention itself, especially with respect to surroundings'. This is also explained by Anderson (2012, p. 31–32) when he highlights the do-it-yourself (DIY or new makers) revolution in which 'people working together with extraordinary new tools create a manufacturing revolution [...] Rather than top-down innovation by some of the biggest companies in the world, we're seeing bottom-up innovation by countless individuals, including amateurs' (see the GOVERNANCE dimension; see also Chapter 2 'DECIPHERING', Section 2.6.3). Thus, how can the smart city transform from an infrastructure design into a people-centred design, which requires the management of all sociopolitical decision-making processes? (Vesnic-Alujevic, Stoermer, Rudkin, Scapolo, & Kimbell, 2019).

1.3.9 9th Dimension (SOCIOPOLITICAL PROCESSES): Control and normative vs free and emergent—Surveillance capitalism

The tension between self-administered freedom and the oppressive role of AI-driven technologies and meta-organisations in the lives of citizens has been widely discussed (Cheney-Lippold, 2011; Foucault, 1975; Kellogg, Valentine, & Christin, 2020; Mattelart, 2010; Noble, 2018; Sadowski & Pasquale, 2015; Zuboff, 2019). Cities are urban spaces in permanent conflicts of interest with the sociopolitical negotiation processes within (Harvey, 2000). However, according to Hollands (2008, p. 305), the smart city paradigm has only reached as far as using 'self-promotional examples by stressing their underlying pro-business and neoliberal bias, as well as raising hidden questions about social justice and sustainability'.

There is a growing group of academics (Grimm et al., 2013; Kitchin, 2014; Morgan, 2013; Moulaert et al., 2009; Mulgan, 2007) who are conducting evidence-based research addressing the challenge of involving all sociopolitical stakeholders in a more democratic and participatory process. To the extent that we are able to reach this aim, we will build cities that are consistent with the direction of the statement, 'Being (digitally) connected is no guarantee of being smart' (Evans, 2002, p. 34) (see the WHO dimension). As discussed, one of the greatest challenges for the smart city paradigm is to connect the Penta helix of stakeholders (public sector, private sector, academia, entrepreneurs/activists, and civil society) (Calzada, 2013a, 2013b; Calzada & Cowie, 2017; see Chapter 3 'DEMOCRATISING') at the local level (Moulaert & Nussbaumer, 2004) in every city to experiment with a new *ad hoc* urban governance model (GovLab, 2013; Mulgan, 2007) that is much wider than the previous self-deterministic and uncritical (Hollands, 2008; Kitchin, 2014; Zook, 2017) smart city discourse of the mainstream approach (see the SYSTEMS dimension).

It is becoming increasingly relevant for promoters of openness and inclusiveness and for contemporary public administrations to face trade-offs and place limits on transparency. It remains unclear whether the so-called AI-driven public administrations in the post COVID-19 hyperconnected societies (Kitchin, 2020; Kuziemski & Misuraca, 2020; Mikhaylov, Esteve, & Campion, 2018) will ultimately earn the mantle of transparency or reinforce public cynicism about the digital panopticon and the dystopic 'Stasi government', which has as its final goal the diversification of the mechanisms of control and suppression rather than the use of technologies to embrace freedom (Broussard, 2018; Coglianese, 2009). These processes must be anticipated and invigorated as free and emergent rather than as controlled and normative democratic standpoints (Moore, 2018) (see the GOVERNANCE dimension).

1.3.10 10th Dimension (POLITICAL ECONOMY): Profitable vs unprofitable—Multi-stakeholder

The mainstream and dominant smart city approach is accused of being neoliberal (Brenner, 2014; Grossi & Pianezzi, 2017; Hollands, 2008; Kitchin, 2014; Milanovic, 2019; Peck, 2013). Peck (2013) actually emphasises, 'In the political-economic twilight world that has been taking shape after the crisis, it appears that neoliberalism has not gone away, but neither does it remain as it was'. As suggested by Hassan (2009, p. 80), 'Neoliberalism and digital technologies combine to produce a powerful momentum'. What we can state here is that after the technological boom of the smart city, we are now questioning the property, use, and benefits of these investments in cities. Who will benefit from the smart city? As Mulgan (2013) stated, if someone wins, someone loses, which implies that we should certainly address the social justice divide (Datta, 2015; Kitchin, Cardullo, & Di Feliciantonio, 2018) (see the WHO and HOW dimensions).

If a community (or communihood) can effectively adapt to and adopt digital technologies to address specific local, context-based community interests, there are increasing possibilities for the development of new relationships (Pazaitis, Kostakis, & Bauwens, 2017), *social* objects, and engagements that can be understood as *new currencies* of the *social* economy (Calzada, 2013b). Some suggest that this can be understood as a new form of capitalism that is self-initiated and self-organised (i.e. crowdfunding, open-source projects, etc.) and which has particular relevance to social capital even to revert it (see the FOCUS dimension) (Miller, 2006). Others from a further radical techno-political standpoint, and against the backdrop of the post COVID-19 society worldwide, suggest that there is now another form ready to revert capitalism that was making the large organisations larger and the small organisations smaller (Bastani, 2019; McChesney, 2013; Milanovic, 2019; Morozov, 2012).

1.4 Conclusion

This chapter is grounded in previous fieldwork research taking place in several countries, regions, and cities worldwide, focuses on understandings of the smart city, and proposes a 10-dimensional integrated updated framework for its critical analysis. This revision aims to contribute to an enhanced understanding of the smart city by emphasising the critical SI perspective (Grimm et al., 2013; Moulaert et al., 2009; Mulgan, 2007) and providing a continuum from the mainstream to an emergent and transitional version of the smart city (see the second hypothesis).

Answers to the two main research questions and hypotheses are summarised as follows:

1. In the broad context of hyperconnected societies (Floridi, 2015), physical encounters have been impacted by the increasing adoption of digitally mediated communications not only in number but also how the encounters have qualitatively evolved, as was demonstrated by the studies conducted by Telefónica and the Financial Times (Telefónica, 2013), the Oxford Internet Institute (Dutton & Blank, 2011), and the World Internet Project (Internet Project, 2012). This chapter indicates that the evidence that digital technologies have replaced the face-to-face interactions is unclear. Nonetheless, it is noteworthy that the fuzziness of social networking cannot be understood directly as a driver of social capital, even amidst the hyperconnectivity that characterised the post COVID-19 society.
2. Grounded in the analysis provided by Chourabi et al. (2012), technology could be considered a meta-factor in smart city initiatives. In contrast, unplugging, a subtle notion and novel trend, highlights the importance of identifying human interaction (see the focus dimension) as the key meta-factor, which is transversal for the analysis of this chapter's framework (even despite the post COVID-19 social and physical distancing boundaries). In addition to the idea of 'human interaction' as a meta-factor spread in the 10 dimensions framework, it is noteworthy that each dimension illustrates the inherent tensions and contradictions within the mainstream and dominant smart city 'in a box' approach (New Songdo, Masdar, and PlanIT) and the emergent smart city initiatives in transition (such as smart citizens, hacking the city, or FabLabs; Calzada, 2018).

This chapter concludes with 10 unresolved questions that will redefine the future research framework of this book and consequently the renewed smart city policy agenda. These 10 questions serve to summarise the previously presented dimensions. The 10 aforementioned dimensions comprise a complex interdependent corpus driven by human interaction meta-factors.

1. [The WHO Dimension] Will the smart city evolve into an urban sphere in which dwellers have the right to decide whether to be connected (Brenner, 2014)? Will unplugging be a right or a privilege? To what extent is it

possible to foresee a transition of smart cities from the high to the low social and digital divides towards more democratic, participatory, and equal smart cities (Butziaff, 2020; Schneider, 2018)?

2. [The HOW Dimension] How will the transition between individual and collective entities be organised? Will we witness new hybrid configurations by experimenting with unplugging? Can the function of the smart city be understood as a proxy for community (De Wall, 2013; Greenfield, 2013; Townsend, 2013)? Is the city a social interface in which the citizens will be able to self-design their social everyday life needs?
3. [The SYSTEMS Dimension] To what extent is it possible that dwellers can be less passive in deciding the role of urban technology systems? Will these devices serve the citizens more than the citizens serve the devices? Will the transition from an artificial system to an embedded system be understood as an opportunity for adding value to citizen experiences?
4. [The GOVERNANCE Dimension] How will the smart city avoid technocratic, dominant, and top-down governance? Are there experimental governance schemes that embrace bottom-up, emergent strategic planning and are considered to be real possibilities? Is the bottom-up innovation perspective simply wishful thinking?
5. [The INFORMATION Dimension] How realistic is it to combine open access civilian deliberative systems within a confidential, espionage-obsessed paradigm? In the big data era, is it possible to transition from controlled to open data-driven models?
6. [The FOCUS Dimension] Are open, democratic communities of individuals facing a transition from a business-led and techno-deterministic approach to socially innovative community-driven cities (Bauman & Lyon, 2012; Hollands, 2008; Moulaert et al., 2009)? Do we notice the difference between simple social interactions and trusting human ties?
7. [The SPACE Dimension] Will we observe changes in which context-collapsed information will be contextualised to enhance social interactions? To what extent can context collapse enable new opportunities for social capital?
8. [The DESIGN Dimension] Will technological devices be designed based on people's needs rather than on corporate or infrastructure interests? How can design and user interactions be improved to anticipate an ambient commons for citizens?
9. [The SOCIOPOLITICAL PROCESSES Dimension] Will the sociopolitical establishment experience a shift towards free and community-driven processes? What are the boundaries to establish these processes in the urban arena?
10. [The POLITICAL ECONOMY Dimension] Finally, will the political economy of the smart city be altered as a consequence of changes in stakeholder power relationships?

The purpose of this chapter was to present a debate as well as a cross-disciplinary research agenda about unplugging. This analysis explores new research opportunities at the intersection of the future of cities, democracy, data science, AI, digital transformations, business models, digital humanities, policy, sociology, ethnography, and smart urbanism as well as other disciplines.

References

Ahlgren, B., Dannewitz, C., Imbrenda, C., Kutscher, D., & Ohlman, B. (2012). A survey of information-centric networking. *Communications Magazine, IEEE, 50*(7), 26–36.

Allenby, B., & Sarewitz, D. (2013). *The techno-human condition*. Cambridge, MA: The MIT Press.

Allwinkle, S., & Cruickshank, P. (2011). Creating smart-er cities: An overview. *Journal of Urban Technology, 18*(2), 1–16.

Anderson, C. (2012). *Makers: The new industrial revolution*. New York: Random House.

Atzori, M. (2017). Blockchain technology and decentralised governance: Is the state still necessary? *Journal of Governance and Regulation, 6*(1), 45–62. https://doi.org/10.22495/jgr_v6_i1_p5.

Baccini, P. (1997). A city's metabolism: Towards the sustainable development of urban systems. *Journal of Urban Technology, 4*(2), 27–39.

Bastani, A. (2019). *Fully automated luxury communism*. London: Verso.

Bauman, Z., & Lyon, D. (2012). *Liquid surveillance: A conversation*. Cambridge: Polity.

Benkler, Y. (2011). Free irresponsible press: Wikileaks and the battle over the soul of the networked fourth estate. *Harvard Civil Rights-Civil Liberties Law Review, 46*(311).

Bigo, D., Isin, E., & Ruppert, E. (2019). *Data politics*. London: Routledge.

Boyd, D. (2013). Retrieved from: http://www.zephoria.org/thoughts/archives/2013/12/08/coining-context-collapse.html.

Brabazon, T. (2013). *Digital dieting: From information obesity to digital fitness*. Farnham, Surrey, UK: Ashgate Publishing, Limited.

Brenner, N. (2014). *Implosions/explosions: Towards a study of planetary urbanization*. Berlin: Jovis.

Brenner, J., & Smith, A. (2013). *The Pew Research Center's Internet & American Life Project*. Retrieved from: http://www.pewinternet.org/Reports/2013/social-networking-sites.aspx.

Broussard, M. (2018). *Artificial unintelligence: How computers misunderstand the world*. Cambridge: MIT Press.

Brown, I., & Marsden, C. T. (2013). *Regulating code: Good governance and better regulation in the information age*. Cambridge, MA: MIT Press.

Buckingham, D. (2008). *Youth, identity, and digital media* (p. 2008). Cambridge, MA: MIT Press.

Butziaff, F. (2020). Between empowerment and abuse: Citizen participation beyond the post-democratic turn. *Democratization, 27*(3), 477–493. https://doi.org/10.1080/13510347.2019.1707809.

Calzada, I. (2013a). Critical social innovation in the smart city era for a city-regional european horizon 2020. *Journal of Public Policies & Territory P3T, 2*(6), 1–20.

Calzada, I. (2013b). Knowledge building & organizational behaviour: Mondragon case. In F. Moulaert, D. MacCallum, A. Mehmood, & A. Hamdouch (Eds.), *International handbook of social innovation. Social innovation: Collective action, social learning and transdisciplinary research* (pp. 219–229). Cheltenham: Edward Elgar (UK) Publishing. https://doi.org/10.13140/RG.2.2.30748.69766.

Calzada, I. (2018). (Smart) Citizens from data providers to decision-makers? The case study of barcelona. *Sustainability, 10*(9), 3252. https://doi.org/10.3390/su10093252.

Calzada, I., & Almirall, E. (2020). Data ecosystems for protecting European citizens' digital rights. *Transforming Government: People, Process and Policy*, *14*(2). https://doi.org/10.1108/TG-03-2020-0047.

Calzada, I., & Cowie, P. (2017). Beyond smart and data-driven city-regions? Rethinking stakeholders-helixes strategies. *Regions Magazine*, *308*(4), 25–28. https://doi.org/10.1080/13673882.2017.11958675.

Caragliu, A., Del Bo, C., & Nijkamp, P. (2011). Smart cities in europe. *Journal of Urban Technology*, *18*(2), 65–82.

Cardullo, P., Di Feliciantonio, C., & Kitchin, R. (2019). *The right to the smart city*. Bingley: Emerald.

Castells, M. (1999). Grassrooting the space of flows. *Urban Geography*, *20*(4), 294–302.

Castells, M. (2009). *Communication power*. Oxford: Oxford University Press.

Castells, M. (2012). *Networks of outrage and hope: Social movements in the internet age* (p. 2012). Cambridge: Polity.

Castells, M. (2020). *Digital*. Retrieved from: https://www.lavanguardia.com/opinion/20200425/48700040274/manuel-castells-digital.html.

Centre de Cultura Contemporània deBarcelona (CCCB). (2013). *DEBATES//In Common. Education. Zygmunt Bauman (VO En Trad. Ca)*. Retrieved from: http://www.cccb.org/en/video-debates_in_common_education_zygmunt_bauman_vo_en_trad_ca-43359.

Cerf, V. (2012). Internet access is not a human right. *New York Times*, *4*, 55.

Cheney-Lippold, J. (2011). A new algorithmic identity: Soft biopolitics and the modulation of control. *Theory, Culture and Society*, *28*(6), 164–181. https://doi.org/10.1177/0263276411424420.

Chourabi, H., Nam, T., Walker, S., Gil-García, J. R., Mellouli, S., Nahon, K., et al. (2012). Understanding smart cities: An integrative framework. In *Proceedings of the 2012 45th Hawaii international conference on system sciences* (pp. 2289–2297). Washington, DC: IEEE Computer Society.

Coglianese, C. (2009). *The Transparency President? The Obama Administration and Open Government (SSRN Scholarly Paper No. ID 1433815)*. Rochester, NY: Social Science Research Network.

Cohen, B. (2012). *What exactly is a smart city?*. Retrieved from: https://www.fastcompany.com/1680538/what-exactly-is-a-smart-city.

Cugurullo, F. (2013). How to build a sandcastle: An analysis of the genesis and development of masdar city. *Journal of Urban Technology*, *20*(1), 23–37.

Danaher, J. (2019). *Automation and utopia: Human flourishing in a world without work*. London: Harvard University Press.

Datta, A. (2015). New urban utopias of postcolonial India: Entrepreneurial urbanisation in Dholera smart city, Gujarat. *Dialogues in Human Geography*, *5*(1), 3–22. https://doi.org/10.1177/2043820614565748.

Datta, A. (2020). Self(ie)-governance: Technologies of intimate surveillance in India under COVID19. *Dialogues in Human Geography*. https://doi.org/10.1177/2043820620929797.

Davies, W. (2012). The emerging neocommunitarianism. *The Political Quarterly*, *83*(4), 767–776.

Davis, J. (2013). *Context collapse: A literature review*. Retrieved from: http://www.thesocietypages.org/cyborgology/2013/01/10/context-collapse-a-literature-review.

De Wall, M. (2013). *The city as interface: How new media are changing the city*. Rotterdam: Nai Uitgevers/Publishers.

Delacroix, S., & Lawrence, N. D. (2019). Bottom-up data trusts: Disturbing the 'one size fits all' approach to data governance. *International Data Privacy Law*. https://doi.org/10.1093/idpl/ipz014.

Derridá, J. (1977). *Limited Inc*. Evanston, IL: Northwestern University Press.

Dutton, W., & Blank, G. (2011). *The internet in Britain: Oxford internet survey 2011 report*. Oxford: Oxford Internet Institute.

Eastin, M. S., & LaRose, R. (2000). Internet self-efficacy and the psychology of the digital divide. *Journal of Computer-Mediated Communication*, *6*(1).

Edmunds, A., & Morris, A. (2000). The problem of information overload in business organisations: A review of the literature. *International Journal of Information Management*, *20*(1), 17–28.

Eppler, M. J., & Mengis, J. (2004). The concept of information overload: A review of literature from organization science, accounting, marketing, MIS, and related disciplines. *The Information Society*, *20*(5), 325–344.

Ernst, D. (2020). *Competing in artificial intelligence chips: China's challenge amid technology war*. Waterloo: CIGI.

Eubanks, V. (2017). *Automating inequality: How high-tech tools profile, profile, and punish the poor*. NYC: St. Martin's Press.

Evans, S. (2002). Smart cities more than broadband networks. *Ottawa Business Journal*, 37.

Eyal, N. (2014). *Hooked: How to build habit-forming products*. London: Portfolio.

FabLabs. (2020). Retrieved from: http://fab.cba.mit.edu/about/faq/.

Floridi, L. (2015). *The onlife manifesto: Being human in a hyperconnected era*. Cham: Springer.

Floridi, L., Cowls, J., King, T. C., & Taddeo, M. (2020). How to design AI for social good: Seven essential factors. *Science and Engineering Ethics*. https://doi.org/10.1007/s11948-020-00213-5.

Foucault, M. (1975). *Surveiller et punir*. Paris: Gallimard.

Frey, C. B. (2019). *The technology trap: Capital, labor, and power in the age of automation*. Princeton: Princeton University Press.

Gershenfeld, N. (2005). *Fab: The coming revolution on your desktop—From personal computers to personal fabrication*. New York: Basic Books.

Gladwell, M. (2013). *David and goliath, underdogs, misfits, and the art of battling giants*. New York: Little, Brown and Company.

GovLab. (2013). Retrieved from: http://thegovlab.org/what-works-the-concept-of-experimental-government.

Gray, M. L., & Siddharth, S. (2019). *Ghost work: How to stop silicon valley from building a new global underclass*. Boston: HMH.

Greenfield, A. (2013). *Against the smart city (the city is here for you to use)*. New York: Do Projects. Retrieved from: http://www.youtube.com/watch?v=9keDwTBmZ3o.

Grimm, R., Fox, C., Baines, S., & Albertson, K. (2013). Social innovation, an answer to contemporary societal challenges? Locating the concept in theory and practice. *Innovation: The European Journal of Social Science Research*, *26*(4), 436–455.

Grossi, G., & Pianezzi, D. (2017). Smart cities: Utopia or neoliberal ideology? *Cities*, *69*, 79–85. https://doi.org/10.1016/j.cities.2017.07.012.

Guibernau, M. (2013). *Belonging: Solidarity and division in modern societies*. London: Polity.

Hargittai, E. (2002). The second-level digital divide: Differences in people's online skills. *First Monday: Peer-Reviewed Journal on the Internet*, *7*(4).

Harvey, D. (2000). *Spaces of hope*. Berkeley: University of California Press.

Harvey, D. (2008). The right to the city. *New Left Review*, *53*, 23–40.

Hashem, I. A. T., Chang, V., Anuar, N. B., Adewole, K., Yaqoob, I., Gani, A., et al. (2016). The role of the big data in smart city. *International Journal of Information Management*, *36*(5), 748–758. https://doi.org/10.1016/j.ijinfomgt.2016.05.002.

Hassan, R. (2009). *Empires of speed: Time and the acceleration of politics and society*. Leiden: BRILL.

Hecker, S., Haklay, M., Bowser, A., Makuch, Z., Vogel, J., & Bonn, A. (2018). *Citizen science: Innovative in open science, society and policy*. London: UCL Press.

Hemment, D., & Townsend, A. (2013). *Smart citizens*. Manchester: Future Everything Publications. Retrieved from: http://futureeverything.org/publications/smart-citizens/.

Herod, A. (2011). *Scale*. London: Routledge.

Hilbert, M., & López, P. (2011). The world's technological capacity to store, communicate, and compute information. *Science, 332*(6025), 60–65.

Hiltz, S. R., & Turoff, M. (1985). Structuring computer-mediated communication systems to avoid information overload. *Communications of the ACM, 28*(7), 680–689.

Hindman, M. (2018). *The internet trap: How the digital economy builds monopolies and undermines democracy*. New Jersey: Princeton University Press.

Ho, C., & Chuangt, T. (2019). Governance of communal data sharing. In A. Daly, K. Devitt, & M. Mann (Eds.), *Good data* (pp. 202–213). Amsterdam: Institute of Network Cultures.

Hollands, R. G. (2008). Will the real smart city please stand up? Intelligent, progressive, or entrepreneurial? *City: Analysis of Urban Trends, Culture, Theory, Policy, Action, 12*(3), 303–320.

Hoque, F. (2013). *Unplug: Not what you think it is*. Retrieved from: https://www.fastcompany.com/3013212/unplug-not-what-you-think-it-is.

IBM. (2013). *IBM smarter cities intelligent operations center*. Retrieved from: https://www.youtube.com/watch?v=onOXhk_lVNo.

Innerarity, D. (2013). *The democracy of knowledge*. London: Bloomsbury.

International Telecommunication Union ITU. (2013). *Measuring the information society 2013, executive summary*. Geneva: ITU.

Internet Project. (2012). *World internet project international report* (4th ed.). University of Southern California. Retrieved from: http://www.worldinternetproject.net/_files/_Published/_oldis/770_2012wip_report4th_ed.pdf.

Jacobs, J. (1970). *The economy of cities*. New York: Random House.

Jones, C., Ramanau, R., Cross, S., & Healing, G. (2010). Net generation or digital natives: Is there a distinct new generation entering university? *Computers & Education, 54*(3), 722–732.

Keith, M., & Calzada, I. (2018). *Back to the 'urban commons'? Social innovation thorough new co-operative forms in Europe*. Brussels: Bridging European Urban Transformations ESRC. https://doi.org/10.13140/RG.2.2.22227.27688/1.

Kellogg, K. C., Valentine, M. A., & Christin, A. (2020). Algorithms at work: The new contested terrain of control. *Academy of Management Annals, 14*(1).

Keymolen, E., & Voorwinden, A. (2019). Can we negotiate? Trust and the rule of law in the smart city paradigm. *International Review of Law, Computers & Technology*, 1–21. https://doi.org/10.1080/13600869.2019.1588844.

Kingsley, P. (2013). *Masdar: The shifting goalposts of Abu Dhabi's ambitious eco-city*. Retrieved from: http://www.wired.co.uk/magazine/archive/2013/12/features/reality-hits-masdar.

Kitchin, R. (2014). The real-time city? Big data and smart urbanism. *GeoJournal, 79*(1), 1–14.

Kitchin, R. (2020). Civil liberties *or* public health, or civil liberties *and* public health? Using surveillance technologies to tackle the spread of COVID-19. *Space and Polity*. https://doi.org/10.1080/13562576.2020.1770587.

Kitchin, R., Cardullo, P., & Di Feliciantonio, C. (2018). *Citizenship, justice, and the right to the smart City*. Maynooth: The programmable city working paper 41.

Kitchin, R., & Moore-Cherry, N. (2020). Fragmented governance, the urban data ecosystem and smart city-regions: The case of Metropolitan Boston. *Regional Studies*. https://doi.org/10.1080/00343404.2020.1735627.

Kuziemski, M., & Misuraca, G. (2020). AI governance in the public sector: Three tales from the frontiers of automated decision-making in democratic settings. *Telecommunications Policy*. https://doi.org/10.1016/j.telpol.2020.101976.

Lane, J. (2019). *The digital street*. Oxford: Oxford University Press.

Lanier, J. (2011). *You are not a gadget*. London: Penguin Book.

Lanier, J. (2018). *Ten arguments for deleting your social media accounts right now*. New York: Henry Holt & Company.

Lieberman, M. (2013). *Social: Why our brains are wired to connect*. New York: Crown Publishers.

Lupton, D. (2019). *Data selves*. Oxford: Polity Press.

Lupton, D., & Mike, M. (2017). Depends on who's got the data: Public understandings of personal digital dataveillance. *Surveillance and Society*, *15*(2), 254–268.

Marwick, A. E., & Boyd, D. (2011). I tweet honestly, I tweet passionately: Twitter users, context collapse, and the imagined audience. *New Media & Society*, *13*(1), 114–133. https://doi.org/10.1177/1461444810365313.

Mattelart, A. (2010). *The globalization of surveillance*. Cambridge: Polity.

Mayer-Schönberger, V. (2011). *Delete: The virtue of forgetting in the digital age*. Princeton: Princeton University Press.

McChesney, R. W. (2013). *Digital disconnect: How capitalism is turning the internet against democracy*. New York: The New Press.

McCullough, M. (2013). *Ambient commons: Attention in the age of embodied information*. London: The MIT Press.

McElroy, E. (2019). Data, dispossession, and Facebook: Techno-imperialism and toponymy in gentrifying San Francisco. *Urban Geography*, 1–20. https://doi.org/10.1080/02723638.2019.1591143.

Meyrowithz, J. (1986). *No sense of place: The impact of electronic media on social behaviour*. Oxford: Oxford University Press.

Mikhaylov, S. J., Esteve, M., & Campion, A. (2018). Artificial intelligence for the public sector: opportunities and challenges of cross-sector collaboration. *Mathematical, Physical and Engineering Sciences. Philosophical Transactions of the Royal Society A*, *376*(2128). https://doi.org/10.1098/rsta.2017.0357.

Milanovic, B. (2019). *Capitalism, alone: The future of the system that rules the world*. Cambridge & London: Harvard University Press.

Miller, L. M. (2006). *Competing in the new capitalism: How individuals, teams and companies are succeeding by creating the new currency of competition*. Bloomington, IN: AuthorHouse.

Mintzberg, H., Ahlstrand, B., & Lampel, J. (1998). *Strategy safari: A guided tour through the wilds of strategic management*. New York: The Free Press.

Montgomery, C. (2013). *Happy city: Transforming our lives through urban design*. London: Penguin Books.

Moore, M. (2018). *Democracy hacked: Political turmoil and information warfare in the digital age*. London: Oneworld Publications.

Morgan, K. (2013). The rise of metropolitics: Urban governance in the age of the city-region. In N. Bradford, & A. Bramwell (Eds.), *Governing urban economies: Innovation and inclusion in canadian city-regions*. Toronto: University of Toronto Press.

Morozov, E. (2012). *In the net delusion: How not to liberate the world*. NYC: PublicAffairs.

Morozov, E. (2013). *To save everything, click here: The folly of technological solutionism*. NYC: PublicAffairs.

Moulaert, F., & MacCallum, D. (2019). *Advanced introduction to social innovation*. Cheltenham: Edward Elgar (UK) Publishing.

Moulaert, F., MacCallum, D., Hillier, J., & Vicari, S. (2009). *Social innovation and territorial development*. Farnham, England: Ashgate.

Moulaert, F., MacCallum, D., Mehmood, A., & Hamdouch, A. (2013). International handbook of social innovation. In *Social innovation: Collective action, Social Learning and Transdisciplinary Research*. Cheltenham: Edward Elgar (UK) Publishing.

Moulaert, F., & Mehmood, A. (2020). Towards a social innovation (SI) based epistemology in local development analysis: Lessons from twenty years of EU research. *European Planning Studies*, *28*(3), 434–453. https://doi.org/10.1080/09654313.2019.1639401.

Moulaert, F., & Nussbaumer, J. (2004). Integrated area development and social innovation in european cities. A cultural focus. *City*, *8*(2), 249–257.

Mulgan, G. (2007). *Social innovation: What it is, why it matters and how it can be accelerated*. London: The Basingstoke Press.

Mulgan, G. (2013). *The locust and the bee*. Retrieved from: https://www.youtube.com/watch?v=8OVyX2Pg-X8#t=77.

Mulgan, G., & Straub, V. (2019). *The new ecosystem of trust*. London: NESTA.

Noble, S. U. (2018). *Algorithms of opression: How search engines reinforce racism*. NY: New York University Press.

Norris, P. (2001). *Digital divide: Civic engagement, information poverty, and the internet worldwide*. New York: Cambridge University Press.

O'Neill, C. (2008). *Weapons of math destruction: How big data inequality and threatens democracy*. London: Penguin Random House.

Oblinger, D. G., & Oblinger, J. L. (2005). *Educating the net generation*. Boulder, CO: Educause.

Pazaitis, A., Kostakis, V., & Bauwens, M. (2017). Digital economy and the rise of open cooperativism: The case of the enspiral network. *Transfer: European Review of Labour and Research*, *23*(2), 177–192. https://doi.org/10.1177/1024258916683865.

Peck, J. (2013). Explaining (with) neoliberalism. *Territory, Politics, Governance*, *1*(2), 132–157.

Pel, B., Wittmayer, J., Dorland, J., & Sogaard Jorgensen, M. (2019). Unpacking the social innovation ecosystem: An empirically grounded typology of empowering network constellations. *Innovation: The European Journal of Social Science Research*. https://doi.org/10.1080/13511610.2019.1705147.

Pfanner, E. (2013). *Young people are not as digitally natives as you think*. Retrieved from: https://bits.blogs.nytimes.com/2013/10/07/young-people-are-not-as-digitally-native-as-you-think.

Pinch, T. J., & Bijker, W. E. (1984). The social construction of facts and artefacts: Or how the sociology of science and the sociology of technology might benefit each other. *Social Studies of Science*, *14*(3), 399–441.

Pollet, T. V., Roberts, S. G. B., & Dunbar, R. I. M. (2011). Use of social network sites and instant messaging does not lead to increased offline social network size, or to emotionally closer relationships with offline network members. *Cyberpsychology, Behavior and Social Networking*, *14*(4), 253–258.

Prensky, M. (2001). Digital natives, digital immigrants part 1. *On the Horizon*, *9*(5), 1–6.

Puel, G., & Fernandez, V. (2012). Socio-technical systems, public spaces and urban fragmentation: The cases of cybercafés in China. *Urban Studies*, *49*(6), 1297–1313.

Putnam, R. (2001). *Bowling alone: The collapse and revival of American community*. New York: Simon & Schuster.

Rainie, H., Rainie, L., & Wellman, B. (2012). *Networked: The new social operating system*. Cambridge, MA: MIT Press.

Ratti, C. (2014). *Forget flying cars–smart cities just need smart citizens*. ArchDaily. Retrieved from: http://www.archdaily.com/?p=491630.

Rendueles, C. (2013). *Sociofobia, el Cambio Político en la Era de la Utopia Digital*. Madrid: Capitán Swing.

Rheingold, H. (2012). *Net smart: How to thrive online*. Cambridge, MA: MIT Press.

Richardson, I. (2007). Pocket technospaces: The bodily incorporation of mobile media. *Continuum: Journal of Media & Cultural Studies*, *21*(2), 205–215.

Richmond, S. (2013). Wearable computing is here already: How hi-tech got under our skin. In *The Independent*. Retrieved from: http://www.independent.co.uk/life-style/gadgets-and-tech/features/wearable-computing-is-here-already-how-hitech-got-under-our-skin-8721263.html.

Rifkin, J. (2000). *The age of access: The new culture of hypercapitalism, where all of life is a paid-for experience*. New York: J.P. Tarcher/Putnam.

Robinson, J. (2006). *Ordinary cities, between modernity and development*. London: Routledge.

Rogers, E. M. (2010). *Diffusion of innovations*. New York, NY: Simon and Schuster.

Rooney, B. (2013). *How do we educate in a digital world?*. Retrieved from: http://online.wsj.com/article/SB10001424127887323993804578611661116660422.html.

Rosen, L. D., Whaling, K., Rab, S., Carrier, L. M., & Cheever, N. A. (2013). Is Facebook creating "iDisorders"? the link between clinical symptons of psychiatric disorders and technology use, attitudes and anxiety. *Computers in Human Behavior*, *29*(3), 1243–1254.

Rosner, D. K. (2018). *Critical fabulations: Reworking the methods and margins of design*. Cambridge: The MIT Press.

Rowlands, I., Nicholas, D., Williams, P., Huntington, P., Fieldhouse, M., Gunter, B., et al. (2008). The google generation: The information behaviour of the researcher of the future. *ASLIB Proceedings*, *60*(4), 290–310.

Sadowski, J., & Pasquale, F. (2015). The spectrum of control: A social theory on the smart city. *First Monday*, *20*. https://doi.org/10.5210/fm.v20i7.5903.

Schneider, N. (2018). An Internet of ownership: Democratic design for the online economy. *The Sociological Review*, *66*(2), 320–340. https://doi.org/10.1177/0038026118758533.

Selwyn, N. (2004). Reconsidering political and popular understanding of the digital divide. *New Media & Society*, *6*(3), 341–362.

Sennett, R. (2012). *Together: The rituals, pleasures & politics of cooperation*. London: Penguin Books.

Shelton, T., & Lodato, T. (2019). Actually existing smart citizens. *City*, 1–18. https://doi.org/10.1080/13604813.2019.1575115.

Shepard, M., & Simeti, A. (2013). What's so smart about the smart citizen? In D. Hemment, & A. Townsend (Eds.), *Smart citizens* (pp. 12–18). Manchester: Future Everything Publications.

Shirky, C. (2009). *Here comes everybody: How change happens when people come together* (p. 2009). London: Penguin.

Smart, J. (2013). *Clarity: Clear mind, better performance, bigger results*. Chichester: Wiley.

Smith, W. (2019). Deliberative citizenship: A critical reappraisal. *Citizenship Studies*, *23*(8), 815–830. https://doi.org/10.1080/13621025.2019.1664404.

Sterling, B. (2014). *Hacking the city*. Retrieved from: http://www.wired.com/beyond_the_beyond/2011/06/hacking-the-city.

Tapscott, D. (2009). *Grown up digital: How the net generation is changing your world*. New York: McGraw-Hill Education.

Tayebi, A. (2013). Communihood: A less formal or more local form of community in the age of the internet. *Journal of Urban Technology*, *20*(2), 77–91.

Telefónica. (2013). *Telefónica global millennial survey. Today's young adults: The leaders of tomorrow*. Retrieved from: http://survey.telefonica.com/survey-findings/#sthash.CdxUFGqv.dpuf.

Townsend, T. (2013). *Smart cities: Big data, civic hackers, and the quest for a new utopia*. New York: W.W. Norton & Company.

Turkle, S. (2011). *Alone together: Why we expect more from technology and less from each other*. New York: Basic Books.

Van de Broeck, P., Mehmood, A., Paidakaki, A., & Parra, C. (2019). *Social innovation as political transformation through for a better world*. Cheltenham, UK and Northampton, MA, USA: Edward Elgar Publishing.

Van Dijck, J. (2014). Datafication, dataism and dataveillance: Big data between scientific paradigm and ideology. *Surveillance and Society*, *12*(2), 197–208. https://doi.org/10.24908/ss.v12i2.4776.

Van Dijk, J., & Hacker, K. (2003). The digital divide as a complex and dynamic phenomenon. *The Information Society*, *19*(4), 315–326. https://doi.org/10.1080/01972240309487.

Vesnic-Alujevic, L., Stoermer, E., Rudkin, J., Scapolo, F., & Kimbell, L. (2019). *The future of government 2030+: A citizen-centric perspective on new government models*. Luxembourg: Publications Office of the European Union.

Warschauer, M. (2004). *Technology and social inclusion: Rethinking the digital divide*. Cambridge, MA: MIT Press.

Watcher-Boettcher, S. (2017). *Technically wrong: Sexist apps, biased algorithms, and other threats of toxit tech*. London: W.W.Norton & Company.

Welter, V. M. (2003). *Biopolis: Patrick geddes and the city of life*. Cambridge, MA: MIT Press.

Williams, R. (1983). *Towards 2000*. London: Chatto and Windus.

Willis, K. S., & Aurigi, A. (2020). *The routledge companion to smart cities*. Oxon: Routledge.

Wismans, L. J. J., Friso, K., Rijsdijk, J., de Graaf, S. W., & Keij, J. (2018). Improving a priori demand estimates transport models using mobile phone data: A rotterdam-region case. *Journal of Urban Technology*, 1–21. https://doi.org/10.1080/10630732.2018.1442075.

Wolfram, M. (2012). Deconstructing smart cities: An intertextual reading of concepts and practices for integrated urban and ICT development. In M. Schrenk, V. V. Popovich, P. Zeile, & P. Elisei (Eds.), *Proceedings REAL CORP 2012 Tagungsband*.

Wurman, R. S., Leifer, L., Sume, D., & Whitehouse, K. (2001). *Information anxiety 2*. Indianapolis, IN: Que.

Zandbergen, D., & Uitermark, J. (2019). In search of the smart citizen: Republican and cybernetic citizenship in the smart city. *Urban Studies*. https://doi.org/10.1177/0042098019847410.

Zook, M. (2017). Crowd-sourcing the smart city: Using big geosocial media metrics in urban governance. *Big Data & Society*, *4*(1). https://doi.org/10.1177/2053951717694384.

Zuboff, S. (2019). *The age of surveillance capitalism: The fight for a human future at the new frontier of power*. London: Profile.

Further reading

Duggan, M., & Brenner, J. (2013). *The demographics of social media users* (p. 2012). Retrieved from: http://www.pewinternet.org/Reports/2013/Social-media-users.aspx.

Newton, P. W. (2012). Liveable and sustainable? Socio-technical challenges for twenty-first-century cities. *Journal of Urban Technology*, *19*(1), 81–102.

Schmidt, S. M. (2011). *Hacking the City: Interventions in urban and communicative spaces*. Gottingen: Edition Volkwang/Steidl.

Chapter 2

DECIPHERING smart city citizenship: Techno-politics of data and urban co-operative platforms

Chapter outline

2.1 Smart city citizenship at stake in the European city-regional realm

The relationship between the state and individual is at stake in the post COVID-19 societies (Calzada, 2020). According to billionaire investor and philanthropist George Soros, the giant multinational technology firms Facebook and Google have become 'obstacles to innovation, and are a menace to society' (Solon, 2018, p. 1). Amid hegemonic rhetoric about the promises of techno-centric smart cities (Angelo & Vormann, 2018), Soros recently stated at the

Smart City Citizenship. https://doi.org/10.1016/B978-0-12-815300-0.00002-2

World Economic Forum that the 'days are numbered for the two geek giants' (Solon, 2018, p 1). This idea contrasts considerably with the way these two geek giants have capitalised the side-effects of post COVID-19 societies by ensuring worldwide the pattern of surveillance capitalism (Zuboff, 2019). Moreover, the digital philosopher Evgeny Morozov has argued that the economics of these giants' data extraction is creating a world in which they build addictive services to gather citizens' data to develop artificial intelligence (AI) and machine learning solutions for the very addiction problem they created (Morozov, 2018).

Because of this timely debate, smart city citizenship is at stake in some European (smart) cities and regions, depending on how they react to the disruption to the techno-politics of data privacy, literacy, awareness, and ownership in their policies and communities caused by projects such as Google Urbanism (2018) and the *sharing economy* (exemplified by AirBnB, Uber, Cabify, and Amazon). At present, Barcelona is an archetypal case of a European city evolving towards a new citizen-centric paradigm called the *experimental city* (Calzada, 2018a, 2018b). This contrasts with Toronto, Canada, where a controversial debate about privacy, identity, and security around data has been taking place around the internationally renowned intervention called Sidewalk Labs, designed by Alphabet/Google (Sidewalk Labs, 2018). Actually Sidewalk Labs has given up on its plans to bring smart city technology to Toronto, blaming the economic uncertainty caused by the COVID-19 pandemic.

Although the relationship between technology and the city is long-standing, only since the 1990s has a clear set of terms or definitions been widely used to define certain types of approaches to cities and technologies, such as the e-city, electronic city, intelligent city, u-city, cyber city, and media city. These terms were developed as a consequence of the Internet and other computing technologies that spilled into European society and everyday city life. Information and communication networks began to significantly alter the social and structural life of the city and heralded new forms of civic governance, deliberation, and participation, as well as smart city citizenship (Willis & Aurigi, 2018). As such, the current debate about the suitability of a participatory and representative democracy is timely in the evolution of smart city citizenship and inevitably reflects on citizens' awareness of (big) data and (big) data's techno-political and psychopolitical implications (Galparsoro, 2017). These implications include transparency as 'no longer just a desirable virtue in politics but an imperative tactic if the aim is to stay clear of disrepute' (Castells, 2018, p. 101). When Han (2015) denounced transparency, he did so as a call to action against this core restrictive element of contemporary societies—people's slavery to a data-driven lifestyle (Chisnall, 2020). He advocates a fundamental imperative: the need to allow experimentation in citizens' lives as an unpredictable work of art rather than a set of scientific urban rules that fix their lives as pure hyper-plugged 'geek' slavery (Calzada & Cobo, 2015; Chisnall, 2020).

Smart cities are currently dealing with a remarkable amount of data being controlled by AI tools and devices owned by multinational corporations. This raises the question of how a smart city can ensure the privacy, identity, and security of its citizens while experimenting with an intertwined representative and deliberative democratic public expressions. In response to this question, and closely following the contours of the smart city citizenship debate, there has been a counter-reaction fuelled by the interplay of certain multi-stakeholders, highlighting the need for an ethically transparent data-driven society that reinforces the digital rights of citizens through accountable data ethics (Han, 2015; Susskind, 2018). Even more recently, a wide range of manifests, declarations, and institutional frameworks have embodied this paradigm shift (Access now, 2018; Asilomar, 2018; Barcelona City Council, 2018; IBM, 2018; Montreal Declaration Responsible AI, 2018; Telefónica, 2018; Universidad de Deusto, 2018). Therefore, this chapter aims to explain how a smart city could transition towards a more experimental urban approach, which would require rethinking data transparency, literacy, and democratic accountability based on a new deal or social contract on digital ethics and data rights (Floridi, 2018).

The growing awareness of digital rights may affect the ethics of stakeholders (citizens and institutions) particularly through their interplay (helix thinking, Calzada & Cowie, 2017). The unique role of stakeholders and their ethics may determine the balance experimental cities and regions in Europe strike between political and democratic endeavours in data-rich environments by changing the minds of unpopular critics of the technocratic smart cities. As a result of the negative side effects of big data extraction monopolies in smart cities, the so-called *data-opolies* (Stucke & Grunnes, 2017), a new set of research terms and findings are gradually surfacing, including 'algorithmic oppression' (Noble, 2018), 'platform capitalism' (Rossi, 2018; Srnicek, 2017), 'automating inequality' (Eubanks, 2017), 'technically wrong' (Watcher-Boettcher, 2017), and 'weapons of math destruction' (O'Neill, 2008).

Although the concept of the *smart city* has become popular in recent years—even a brand, at least in Europe—the initial techno-centric smart city has evolved into a socially constructed and citizen-centred smart city, which this chapter refers to as the *experimental city* (Evans, Karvonen, & Raven, 2016). The so-called techno-centric smart city uses resources cleverly and attracts money, corporate power, and private industry by offering cheap, effective solutions to social and political problems in a functional, optimised, and safe fashion. However, these smart cities are not participatory, democratic, sustainable, or fair. This smart city notion employs Han's (2015) notion of predictable and enslaving patterns forced by the 'digital and transparent society' in which the psychopolitics of data plays against individual freedom of choice, impoverishing citizens' lives through their own obsession with being controlled by big data and measured by numbers.

The smart city is a hyperconnected entity that bypasses human uniqueness, interaction capacity, and ability to self-organise transformational urban circumstances. In response to this hegemonic approach to the techno-centric smart city, the citizen-centric, or experimental, city (based on unpredictable and creative psychopolitical events, according to Han) is emerging through niche experiments that demonstrate far more nuanced democratic and co-operative service provision models for cities (Anastasiu, 2019; Clamp & Alhamis, 2010; Goldsmith & Keliman, 2017; Gupta, 2014; Hacking Inside Black Box, 2018; Keith & Calzada, 2018). This evidence reveals not only an awareness of data techno-politics and governance frameworks but also a pursuit of alternative business models characterised by urban co-operative platforms, which may open up a new post-GDPR (General Data Protection Regulation) wave of social entrepreneurial activity on the European city-regional realm (Bauwens & Pazaitis, 2018; Calzada, 2017; European Data Protection Board, 2018; Scholz, 2013, 2016; Srnicek, 2017). One such context to experiment is the EU's Horizon H2020 Smart Cities and Communities Lighthouse programme, which is the focus of the next section, which introduces the Chapter 3 'DEMOCRATISING' and Chapter 4 'REPLICATING' that examine in depth the Horizon H2020 Smart Cities and Communities Lighthouse Programme.

2.2 The European smart city policy framework: H2020 Smart Cities and Communities lighthouse projects

From the institutional and geographic standpoints, the importance of city-regions in the EU is evident (Calzada, 2015): 59% of the EU population lives in metropolitan areas, which generate 62% of all employment and 68% of the EU's GDP. Alongside this trend, the European data economy could grow 18-fold under the favourable policy and legislative conditions and could total 4% of the EU's GDP by 2020. Europe is home to many vibrant cities, each with its own unique flavour (Calzada, 2016a, 2017). Sprawling metropolises like London, Paris, and Berlin are renowned as global centres. Conversely, at least half of all EU cities are home to fewer than 100,000 people. In between, city-regional configurations of 1–3 million people are increasingly shaping daily economic and political scenarios by deeply affecting citizens' lives in terms of mobility, energy, employment, migration, democracy, and connectivity (Calzada & Keith, 2018). While cities like Lisbon and Florence radiate renaissance charm, cities like Barcelona, Amsterdam, Naples, Torino, Bologna, Vienna, Glasgow, Bristol, Helsinki, Utrecht, Dublin, and Brussels are continually experimenting with new ways to set up city-centric approaches. Several cities are already part of an experimental city-network called 'Cities Coalition for Digital Rights' (CCDR) that will be broadly analysed in Chapter 7 'PROTECTING smart city citizenship'.

The brilliant diversity of Europe's cities should be treasured. However, the continent's city-regions, though, face shared challenges. Municipalities across Europe are racing to find solutions to troubles that transcend city limits and national boundaries. For example, virtually all European cities are grappling with the challenges of urban air pollution and chronic traffic congestion. Traffic jams cost the EU around €100bn per year, while EU air quality standards are consistently breached in more than 130 European cities (European Commission, 2016).

According to the institutional rhetoric of the European Commission, smart city technologies are vital to ensure that cities (and by extension, metropolitan areas and regions) can answer the key social, political, democratic, economic, institutional, and environmental questions that current and future generations face (Caragliu, Del Bo, & Nijkamp, 2011). The European Commission has invested €280m to establish the Horizon 2020 (H2020) framework called Smart Cities and Communities, which encompasses all 12 Lighthouse projects (European Commission, 2018). The Lighthouse projects aim to deliver smart technologies to municipalities by demonstrating that technologies like electric cars and smart lampposts can be a cost-effective way of tackling some of the most profound problems facing city authorities. Since 2014, the 17 Smart Cities and Communities Lighthouse projects have focused on ensuring that people who live and work in cities can enjoy the quality-of-life benefits derived from innovative smart technologies.

In Sønderborg, innovative district heat networks are being established as part of the SmartEnCity project (2018). In Milan, under the Sharing Cities programme (2018), building retrofits are radically improving energy efficiency and reducing CO2 emissions. In Lyon, the Smarter Together programme is introducing an electric-vehicle car-sharing system and an autonomous driverless electric shuttle (SmarterTogether, 2018). San Sebastian's Replicate programme has installed smart lampposts in a bid to slash city electricity costs (Replicate, 2018).

In the Basque Autonomous Community (Spain), three relevant projects are simultaneously taking place in the three capital cities of the city-region: Replicate in Donostia-St. Sebastian, SmartEnCity in Vitoria-Gasteiz, and As-Fabrik in Bilbao (As-Fabrik, 2018). Alongside these EU-funded projects, in the broad contours of the Basque city-region, the city of Pamplona-Iruñea was recently awarded the Stardust EU-project (Stardust, 2018). At the city-regional scale of the Basque Country (Calzada, 2015), gradual efforts are attempting to provide an overarching strategic smart city-regional framework by connecting these lighthouse and strategic projects with a bottom-up network encompassing 232 'smart' municipalities in the Basque Autonomous Community. This initiative is funded by the Basque regional government through the Association of Basque Municipalities entitled EUDEL (*Asociación de Municipios Vascos*) via the strategic programme 'HerriSmartik: Smart Municipalities in the Basque Autonomous Community' (Calzada, 2016b).

The H2020 institutional framework is based on the rationale that cities achieve more when they collaborate. The lighthouse projects involve cities sharing technical learning, spreading the risk of investing in new technology, and using their scale to drive down costs via joint procurement. Technologies tested as part of the H2020 Smart Cities and Communities Lighthouse programme can then be implemented on a wider scale at a vastly reduced cost per unit. Evidence suggests that joint procurement can generate massive cost savings for cities bold enough to embrace intercity co-operation. For example, following a reorganisation of regional procurement in Austria in 2001, city authorities achieved savings of 30% and an administrative workload reduction of 60% (European Commission, 2017a).

The Lighthouse projects involve 46 lighthouse cities and 71 follower cities across Europe. They demonstrate the innovative potential of smart city technologies by allowing citizens to avert turbulent, and many times obscure, extractivist algorithmic governance practices (Lane, 2019; Lanier, 2018; Van der Zwan, Van Doorn, Duivestein, & Pepping, 2018; Wired, 2018). Consequently, local authorities are already imposing certain data governance imperatives as a result of the GDPR, which took effect in May 2018 (European Data Protection Board, 2018).

The future belongs to the European cities and regions that genuinely embrace city-to-city learning and attempt to fulfil the promise of smart cities (Calzada, 2018b; Calzada & Cobo, 2015; Coletta, Evans, Heaphy, & Kitchin, 2018). However, new social, institutional, and political transitions are required to understand how some European city-regions face new challenges while avoiding the algorithmic control of big corporations. Therefore, the point of departure of this chapter revolves around three underlying strategic underlying issues for smart cities in the EU in the years to come.

First, 'city-to-city learning' programmes will likely become the standard replication strategy in cities rather than purely predictable replicability (see Chapter 4, where H2020-Replicate project's city-to-city learning programme will be presented and analysed; in addition see Chapter 7, where the Cities Coalition for Digital Rights is presented and examined as well). Pure replicability means 'the possibility of transporting or *copying* results from a pilot case to other geographical areas' (European Commission, 2017a, p. 12; European Commission, 2018; Bable, 2018). The 'city-to-city learning programme' was experimentally implemented by the Future of Cities Programme at the University of Oxford in the Replicate Lighthouse project (City-to-City-Learning, 2018). It is also inspiring the programme HerriSmartik (Calzada, 2016b), which encompasses a network of municipalities in the Basque Autonomous Community. The 'city-to-city learning' programme aims to revise the assumption that the city is a predictable and rational machinery. This issue is entirely addressed in Chapter 4.

Second, it is similarly likely that the techno-politics of data will lead to a permanent state of monitoring (Kourtit, Elmlund, & Nijkamp, 2020). In the hegemonic and techno-centric approach of smart cities, citizens are considered pure and passive data providers (Calzada, 2018b). The current transition towards more socially constructed experimental cities suggests a new role for smart city citizenship: decision-makers co-operatively setting up platforms to avoid the monopolistic control of extractivist multinationals' algorithmic governance. These companies have increased citizens' awareness of how (big) data disruption could modify urban ecosystems by requiring further regulations to prevent companies from censoring, capturing, and monetarising data with no return to the communities in which they operate. This issue is discussed in the fourth and fifth sections of this chapter.

Third, the potential emergence of urban co-operative platforms (Scholz, 2016) as opposed to the hegemonic platform capitalistic paradigm (Parker, Van Alstyne, & Choudary, 2016; Srnicek, 2017; Stone, 2016) may start an insightful policy debate. Certain transitions are occurring from the hegemonic techno-centric smart cities' business models, represented by the H2020 official approach, to socially constructed co-operative urban platforms evolving towards experimental cities. Many European cities are increasingly advocating for the latter. Some cities are working inside the H2020 funding framework, whereas others are not. According to recent preliminary findings by the author on the analysis of H2020 fellow/follower cities (Replicate, 2018), these cities are welcome to experiment with new business models beyond the public-private partnership (PPP) framework (see Chapter 3).

Hence, the aim of the chapter is not to present a list of cities on one or the other side of this transition, but rather to describe this ongoing transition between (techno-centric) smart cities and (citizen-centric) experimental cities. However, a preliminary list of European cities currently driven by a citizen-centric approach includes Barcelona, Amsterdam, Naples, Torino, Bologna, Vienna, Glasgow, Bristol, Helsinki, Utrecht, Dublin, and Brussels. Further research is needed on this trend and to provide further evidence to support this transition.

This chapter makes two contributions to the current literature on smart cities through the techno-politics of data and urban co-operative platforms. First, it enhances the current understanding of smart cities beyond techno-deterministic and data-driven approaches by further examining what smart city citizenship would mean in European cities. Second, it contributes to understanding two main factors that make this transition possible: (i) the techno-politics of data and (ii) urban co-operative platforms. Therefore, this chapter can help policymakers, academics, private companies, NGOs, civic groups, entrepreneurs, and activists broaden the implementation of smart city projects by including citizens as decision-makers from the beginning, as citizens are essential for the democratic health of European city-regions (Urban Transformations, 2018). Ultimately, deciphering the smart city citizenship will require a distinction between the hegemonic techno-centric smart city approach and the new ongoing alternative intervention approach (the experimental city). The experimental city should blend the interdependencies between various stakeholders in response to critiques that the smart city is overly technocratic and instrumental (Cardullo & Kitchin, 2018).

Following the general introduction and the policy framework description, this chapter presents a theoretical literature review on the term 'smart city' by emphasising 10 transitions towards the 'experimental city' framework. After that, the fourth section demonstrates that citizens are considered active decision-makers rather than passive data providers in this ongoing transition.

The fifth section discusses data issues and their techno-political implications for the current understanding of the smart city. The sixth section presents the main result of this chapter, which is the notion of 'experimental cities' as a transitional citizenship framework encompassing three structural elements: (i) Urban Living Labs, (ii) Data Commons, and (iii) Urban Co-operative Platforms. Finally, the seventh section answers the three research questions formulated in the following section.

2.3 Transitions from smart cities to experimental cities

The term 'smart city' turns 28 this year. It was introduced in 1992, around the time of the historic Rio Earth Summit. Typing it into a search engine today will generate more than 15 million hits. Thus, figures for the smart city market appear similarly impressive. Persistence Market Research forecasts that global growth will balloon from its current valuation of $622 billion to $3.48 trillion by 2026, a fivefold increase in just one decade (McClelland, 2017; Racounteur, 2017).

The last 20 years of research on the smart city paradigm is fragmented and contested (Mora, Bolici, & Deakin, 2017). Although it is emerging as a fast-growing topic of scientific inquiry, much of the knowledge generated about the smart city is centred on its technologies. Therefore, this chapter investigates social and collective intelligence (smart citizenship), cultural artefacts (citizen watchdog groups), and environmental attributes (systemically sustainable), among other factors that need to be integrated into the current zeitgeist of urban innovation involving information communication technology (ICT), which is so far limited to the term 'smart city'.

The spectrum of smart city terms ranges from initial explorations of computing effects on the city (the first cybercities in 1995 envisaged what would happen when information arteries provided all kinds of information and communication services to industries and households), through to the virtual city (an online representation of a real city) and the e-city, which envisaged new forms of governance and civic participation through online forums (Willis & Aurigi, 2018). In the first years of the 21st century, these terms evolved into more city-centred terms, such as the digital city and u-city or ubiquitous city, which developed from the early internet networks and the potential of the city as a platform where people could interact and access city services in a range of ways. This notion is directly connected with the term 'experimental city', which is explained in the sixth section.

With the rise of connected technologies of smart sensors and networks, the term smart city was popularised in 2008 to capture these new forms of smart urbanism. These are a selected set of terms that emphasise key stages of development, but many more terms exist that represent more nuanced and specific aspects of technological change and the city. Looking at how terms have developed over the last 30 years shows that as technology continues to develop, new terms and labels will be created to reflect the changing nature of technology's impact on the urban space and systems.

It is noteworthy that although smart cities (Albino, Berardi, & Dangelico, 2015; Ersoy, 2017; Krivy, 2016) are already being built, they diverge considerably from the simplistic, one-size-fits-all, smart-city-in-the-box approach that has dominated mainstream institutional approaches thus far (Díaz-Díaz, Muñoz, & Pérez-González, 2017; RICS, 2017; UK Government, 2016). This raises a number of questions, such as '(i) for whom and for what purpose are smart cities being developed? (ii) Are smart cities primarily about, or should they be about, (ii.1) creating new markets and profit, (ii.2) facilitating state control and regulation, or (ii.3) improving quality of life while enhancing citizens' opportunities to participate in democracy?' (Kitchin, 2016, p. 7, 2017).

The contemporary smart city cannot be reduced to the economic value that it generates through partnerships with powerful public and private actors (Rossi, 2016, 2018). While the application of new information flows and the development of smart cities are receiving increasing attention, there is still limited understanding of the interconnections among hard and smart infrastructures and economic, political, and social systems on both metropolitan and regional scales. Furthermore, this conventional paradigm has often failed to deliver practical tools that can help people better understand and intervene in their daily realities while engaging with the various stakeholders that are important for European cities and regions. Hence, a multi-stakeholder approach is required to overcome *dataism* (Harari, 2016a), understood as the logic that oversimplifies city metabolisms, seeing them as mere assemblages or systems of data and algorithms (Morozov, 2014; Morozov & Bria, 2017, 2018; Morozov & Eno, 2017; Morozov & Harvey, 2016) rather than as ecosystems of citizens (Devish, Poplin, & Sofronie, 2016; Keith & Calzada, 2016; Kontokosta, 2016). In the sixth section, the importance of the transformational dimension of the multi-stakeholders' framework is explained by distinguishing the Triple, Quadruple, and Penta helix frameworks (see Fig. 2.1 and Table 2.3).

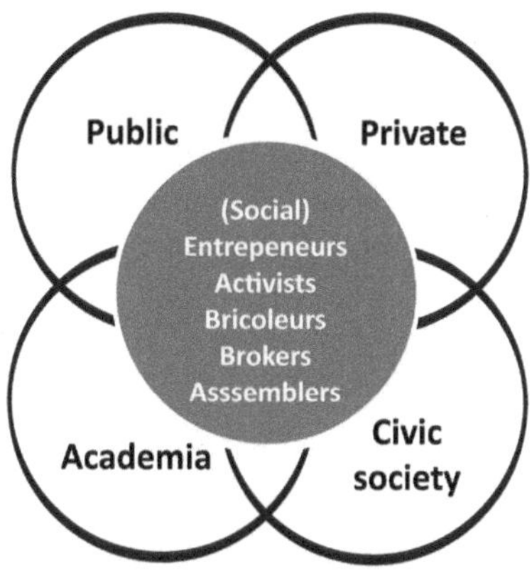

FIG. 2.1 Penta helix multi-stakeholder framework (Calzada & Cowie, 2017).

The development and use of the buzzword smart city in the planning of inner cities could be intimately connected to today's necessary urban transformations (Calzada, 2016a). There is currently a great deal of rhetoric about the importance of building smart cities, but this rhetoric does not pay attention to the elements that constitute smart city strategies and policies in diverse contexts (Kitchin, 2016). Technological solutions have often been proposed under the umbrella of the smart city buzzword without first considering citizens' needs, their ability to meet those needs and use the proposed solutions, or their socio-technical misalignment with the city itself (Campbell, 2012; Hajer & Dassen, 2014).

Thus, this chapter suggests that European city-regions should first unpack or deconstruct ('unplug') the meaning of smartness in their unique urban realities (by following consequently what it was elaborated in Chapter 1) by asking 10 underlying questions about the cities they want to create. This exercise is suggested for cities in the EU that are directly or indirectly influenced by the H2020 Smart Cities and Communities policy framework. As part of that, a wide range of stakeholders in cities and regions are debating the digital rights of citizens through accountable data ethics (see Chapter 7 'PROTECTING'). These fifteen digital rights are (i) the right to be forgotten on the Internet; (ii) the right to be unplugged; (iii) the right to a person's own digital legacy; (iv) the right of a person's integrity to be protected from technology; (v) the right to freedom of speech on the Internet; (vi) the right to a person's own digital identity; (vii) the right to the transparent and responsible usage of algorithms; (viii) the right to have a last human instance in the expertise-based decision-making processes; (ix) the right to equal opportunities in the digital economy; (x) the consumer rights in e-commerce; (xi) the right to hold intellectual property on the Internet; (xii) the right to universal access to the Internet; (xiii) the right to digital literacy; (xiv) the right to impartiality on the Internet; and (xv) the right to a secure Internet.

Safeguarding the digital rights of citizens through accountable data ethics involves 'unplugging' people's city experience, or making being digitally connected a smart experience for citizens (Ahlgren, Dannewitz, Imbrenda, Kutscher, & Ohlman, 2012; Allenby & Sarewitz, 2013). The questions below as broadly and previously presented in Chapter 1 'UNPLUGGING', are related to the framework called 'Unplugging' (Calzada & Cobo, 2015), which consists of 10 transitions. Thus, each city-region can adopt these 10 transitions from the smart cities approach and apply them to a new paradigm that this chapter explores—that of experimental cities (Evans et al., 2016). As seen in Chapter 1, the 10 transitions and questions to move the smart city from a techno-centric to a citizen-centric approach briefly were:

1. WHO: Will the smart city evolve into an urban sphere in which dwellers have the right to decide whether to be connected? (Morozov, 2017)
2. HOW: Is the city a social interface in which citizens can self-design their social and everyday needs? (Amin & Thrift, 2016)

3. SYSTEMS: Will devices serve citizens more than citizens serve devices? (Friedewald & Pohoryles, 2013)
4. GOVERNANCE: Is the bottom-up innovation perspective wishful thinking? (If You Want To, 2017; Webb & Mills, 2016)
5. INFORMATION: In the era of data, is it possible to transition from controlled to open data-driven models? (Levy, 1968)
6. FOCUS: Do citizens notice the difference between simple social interactions and human ties built on trust? (Shin & Shin, 2016)
7. SPACE: Will citizens observe changes in which context-collapsed information will be contextualised to enhance social interactions? What are the implications for the privacy and security of individuals (Carrington, 2016; Guerrini, 2016)? Context collapse is a term used by academics (Marwick & Boyd, 2010) writing about the effects of social media and the contexts they give rise to. As such, the term refers to an infinite number of contexts collapsing upon one another into a single moment of recording and having direct consequences for the public and private lives of citizens.
8. DESIGN: How can the design of places and user interactions be improved to create an 'ambient commons' for citizens? The term 'ambient commons' (McCullough, 2013) refers to the cognitive role of citizens in relation to fixed forms of architecture and the city itself when surrounded by a superabundant flow of ambient information where individual signals increasingly matter less.
9. SOCIOPOLITICAL PROCESSES: Is a shift occurring in the power dynamics between stakeholders (Blanco, Salazar, & Bianchi, 2017)?
10. POLITICAL ECONOMY: Will the political economy of the smart city, and the related techno-politics of the data governance model, be altered by any changes in stakeholder power relations? (Bumbee Labs, 2020; Eticas Consulting, 2020; Platform of Trust, 2020; Stucke & Grunnes, 2017)

Only after unpacking the techno-deterministic view of our cities ('unplugging') can citizens smartly connect ('plug') stakeholders into a wide, smart governance framework by including five types of actors, which this chapter presents in the Section 2.6.2 and Chapter 3 'DEMOCRATISING' operationalises, by introducing the Penta helix multi-stakeholder framework (Calzada, 2016a, 2017). These stakeholders are the public sector, the private sector, academia, civic society, and social entrepreneurs/activists. It is necessary to 'plug' stakeholders in by setting up a new, complex, multi-stakeholder, city-regional urbanity to transition towards real smartness in cities and regions. A dynamic power balance between stakeholders has so far been lacking in the hegemonic, technocratic, and techno-centric version of the smart city (Cowley, Joss, & Dayot, 2017). Thus, the distinction among the helixes (groups of stakeholders) is methodological. By using the Penta helix multi-stakeholders' framework, which stems from the Social Innovation (SI) perspective (Calzada, 2016a), this chapter aims to shed light on the transformational interplay created by social entrepreneurs/activists (the 'fifth helix') influencing the other stakeholders. This aspect would be empirically demonstrated in Chapter 3.

However, the position outlined in this chapter avoids a dystopian view. Instead, it embraces a constructive notion that considers the favourable conditions that exist for a potential smart city policy agenda based on urban transformations driven by SI and experimentation (Sabato, Vanhercke, & Verschraegen, 2017). Likewise, cities and regions represent powerful places in which to detect emerging processes and observe spontaneous urban transformations.

To summarise, after the negative side effects of hyperconnected societies are minimised, technology-oriented pathways towards smart cities still offer unexplored opportunities for experimentation (Calzada & Cobo, 2015; Floridi, 2018; Han, 2015). Thus, European cities and regions should embrace the transitional experiments already underway in cities such as Barcelona, Amsterdam, Naples, Torino, Bologna, Vienna, Glasgow, Bristol, Helsinki, Utrecht, Dublin, and Brussels, among many other niche experiments going on at the micro level scale (Calzada, 2017; Smarticipate, 2016; Urban Transformations, 2018).

These 10 transitions from the smart city to the experimental city paradigm lead to three open research questions regarding smart city citizenship, which constitute the core theme of this chapter:

1. What prospects exist for alternative funding and alternative business models for (smart) cities? (Kourtit & Nijkamp, 2012)
2. What practical/political interventions have been tried or are possible among businesses, local governments, academia, communities, and social entrepreneurs (Penta helix framework)? (Calzada, 2016a)
3. Is another type of (smart) city possible? That is, is there a 'third way' between the state and the market that overcomes the PPP framework? (Keith & Calzada, 2017)

2.4 (Smart) citizens are active decision-makers rather than passive data providers

Regarding smart citizenship, this chapter asks whether alternatives to the techno-deterministic approach to smart urbanism (Marvin, Luque-Ayala, & McFarlane, 2015) are flourishing. In the last few years, a new way of empowering the smart city through its smart citizens has received increased attention (Hemment & Townsend, 2013; Waag, 2016). Currently, cities such as Barcelona (Blanco et al., 2017; Eizaguirre, 2016; Eizaguirre & Parés, 2018) are embracing this new shift to an inclusive, democratic, and participative smart city by advertising accordingly: 'If you'd rather have smart citizens than smart cities... BITS, "Barcelona Initiative for Technological Sovereignty", will be in your interest' (BITS, 2016, p. 1). The Barcelona Digital Plan mostly follows Alex Pentland's (2014, p. x) principle that city-regions '[need] a "New Deal on Data" putting citizens in control of data that is about them and also creating a "Data Commons" to improve both government and private industry'. This is essentially the source of the evolution from the smart city to the experimental city paradigm, which produces clear consequences in the political economy of data governance frameworks and the entrepreneurial urban ecosystem of cities through the methodological representation of the helixes (Triple, Quadruple, and Penta).

In a recent manifesto, advocates for smart citizens (Waag, 2016) suggested that smart citizens should take responsibility for the places they live and work and the places they love, value access over ownership, and contribution over power, ask for forgiveness, not permission, appropriate technology rather than accept it as-is, and provide assistance to those who are less 'tech-savvy'. This set of principles shows that there is still a limited understanding of the interconnections between hard and smart infrastructures, as well as among economic, political, and social systems on metropolitan and regional scales. Furthermore, this new paradigm highlights the importance of overcoming the often-failed smart-city-in-a-box approach by engaging with the various stakeholders in European cities and regions.

In this direction, a study conducted in London called 'If You Want To', which developed 'an *urban co-operative platform* to map, organise, and make easily accessible green services or a sustainable lifestyle' (If You Want To, 2017, p. 1), has formulated an evidence-based view of (smart) citizens who are highly aware of their role in the world and the impact that even small individual choices may have globally. According to the preliminary conclusions of this study (Broadbent, 2017), (smart) citizens are contextually aware of the decisions they make in their daily lives—and the consequences of these decisions—when interacting with the urban realm. This awareness of both the environmental and social impacts of personal practices does not, however, translate into a sense of renunciation. On the contrary, it translates into a sense of empowerment and commitment to do things better in a smarter way that can combine personal fulfilment with collective good.

Hence, this chapter aims to rethink the dominant technocratic and technology-centric smart city discourse by presenting this new perspective on so-called smart citizens related to the emerging 'experimental city' paradigm. This new approach focuses not on imagining cities beyond or before technologies, but on accepting that city-regions are already fundamentally shaped by networked and mobile ICTs. This approach also focuses on thinking through the consequences for governance that the promises and realities of smart cities pose (Calzada, 2013a). For example, many argue that smart city-regions will inevitably revolve around generating large amounts of data and that this in itself will lead to new insights and governance strategies (Gray & Lammerhirt, 2017). However, as Acuto pointed out (Acuto, 2018, p. 165), 'data availability does not immediately translate into better-informed urban management, nor fairer, greener, and more prosperous cities'. City-regions are complex and are shaped by a wide variety of actors and organisations, which often have conflicting positions (Calzada, 2015).

Likewise, data generated about individuals in cities and regions are variable, including personally identifiable information, data exhaust, personal data trails, and participatory personal data (Leao & Izadpahani, 2016). Data about people is big data in both the cognitive sense and in the social movement sense (Shilton, 2016). Actually, not all big data are data about people, but data about people inspire much of the hope and anxiety about their material, emotional, and relational human conditions in an individual and collective way. As such, smart cities rely on data to provide and refine services that enhance the quality of citizens' lives although this may impact personal privacy (Racounteur, 2017). Thus, the aim of this chapter is to unpack how citizens are usually framed within smart city initiatives and to examine the extent to which so-called citizen-centric initiatives offer an alternative to, or simply reproduce the actually existing neoliberal smart city.

According to Cardullo and Kitchin (2018), citizens in smart cities are consistent with neoliberal citizenship and its emphasis on personal autonomy and consumer choice, with individuals performing certain roles and taking responsibility for their circumstances (entrepreneurial self) and with the marketisation and privatisation of services and infrastructures (retreat of the state and austerity policy). While citizen participation is potentially widespread, it is most often framed in a post-political way that provides feedback, negotiation, participation, and creation, but in an instrumental rather than normative or political framework. In other words, citizens are encouraged to help provide solutions to practical issues—such as producing an app, providing feedback on a development plan, or performing certain roles/responsibilities—but not to challenge or replace the fundamental political rationalities shaping an issue or plan. Instead, most citizens are empowered in the smart city by technologies that treat them as consumers or testers, people to be steered, controlled, and nudged to act in certain ways, or sources of data that can be turned into products. That is, citizens are treated as passive data providers. Citizens in the smart city perform within the bounds of expected and acceptable behaviour, rather than transgressing or resisting social and political norms as active decision-makers.

Another strand of the smart city debate emphasises the impact of the near-universal uptake of smartphones and other handheld devices as well as the impact of the internet of things—networks of data-gathering and cloud computing (Ratti & Claudel, 2016). Particularly relevant regarding 'Contact Tracing' apps in the post COVID-19 era. Many people use these devices and networks on a daily basis, but what this means for city-regional governance and the power-laden relationships among citizens, governments, and companies remains an open question. As we have observed, the centralised or decentralised nature of the network of users is crucial to judge the effectiveness and the democratic nature of the apps. All this makes truly smart city-regional governance (Herrschel & Dierwechter, 2015) exceedingly difficult, but at the same time, such governance is a fascinating and rewarding scale at which to investigate the various meanings and usages of smartness from the citizens' perspective. However, according to Tranos and Gertner (2012) and Leon (2017), the notion of smartness lacks a global interurban perspective, and, consequently, the gradual corporate acquisition of the smart city idea has been perpetuating capital accumulation by and among global cities at the international scale (Gaffney & Robertson, 2016). In Chapter 5 'DEVOLVING', a scalar examination will be developed by including case studies regarding the critical factor of devolving data to cities and regions and ultimately to citizens. Data devolution governance schemes are crucial in the post COVID-19 societies, cities, and regions, to further configure data ecosystems as an integral part of the techno-political governance instrumentarium consisting of privacy, ownership, and digital rights (Loukissas, 2019).

Recently, however, various research projects across Europe have begun to investigate alternative pathways to overcome the smartness lock-ins or entrenched ideas related to the notion of smart citizens. Most seek to develop both critical analyses and practical suggestions to tackle urban problems, such as pollution, health, safety, and mobility, through developing and using various types of mobile and networked data. These projects examine various ways of considering the interlinked notions of smart citizens and data where the so-called smart city approach has been enacted on the ground. Specifically, the research efforts sought to unpack and question the following three issues:

1. the types of knowledge gained through the production, distribution, and use of smart data (PWC, 2016);
2. the role data play in the constitution of urban expertise and in mediating and transforming the relationships among smart citizens, governments, and companies (NESTA, 2015); and
3. the ways in which data-driven knowledge and expertise tackle or reproduce inequalities in city-regions among diverse groups of (smart) citizens by provoking social exclusion patterns driven by toxic side effects of technology (Hughes, 2016).

Answering these questions shows that certain issues—such as the techno-politics of data and how smart citizens should be integrated into this realm of governance—remain crucial (Calzada, 2017; Gray & Lammerhirt, 2017). The smart city approach is being deconstructed from many angles after having recently saturated policy agendas with very little reflection and being driven by market-based urban solutions. In response, a new smart-citizen-centric paradigm is being tested by examining the 'experimental city'. These urban experiments are intriguing, because '[they are] producing a different type of city by offering novel modes of engagement, governance, and politics that both challenge and complement conventional strategies such as ongoing smart city strategies' (Evans et al., 2016, p. 9). Even in the post COVID-19 society, how can we build social capital as Bauman (2000) warned if our lives consist of selfie, peer-to-peer interactions, videoconferencing, social and physical distancing, and entirely digital life?

This chapter, therefore, explores what is new in the experimental city approach compared to the smart city approach. Cardullo and Kitchin (2018), based on Arnstein's classic contribution (Arnstein, 1968), suggest a remarkable interpretation about the scaffold of smart citizen participation. However, more nuanced research is required for context-based applications. Therefore, in an attempt to contrast the two approaches and trace the evolution from one paradigm to the other, Table 2.1 shows 10 transitions:

The information provided in Table 2.1 suggests that smart citizens are becoming the centre of current smart city transformations (Satyam & Calzada, 2017).

TABLE 2.1 From smart cities to experimental cities.

Conceptual transitions	Smart cities	Experimental cities
(Smart) citizen (Keith & Calzada, 2016)	User/data provider	Decision-maker
Techno-politics of data (Louail, Lenormand, Arias, & Ramasco, 2016)	Big data	Technological/digital/data sovereignty
Notion of the city (Anttiroiko, Valkama, & Bailey, 2013; European Commission, 2016)	As a market	As a platform
Personal data ownership (Morozov, 2014)	Owned by firms	Publicly scrutinised
Stakeholder helixes (Calzada, 2016a)	Triple or Quadruple helix	Penta helix
Business models (Bauwens & Pazaitis, 2018; Bollier, 2016)	PPP	Urban commons and urban co-operative platforms
Scalability and replicability (European Commission, 2017a)	Based on urban *solutionism*	Unpacking urban problems
Algorithmic coding and disruption (Zanouda, Al Emadi, Abbar, & Srivastava, 2017)	IoT sensor networks	Citizen-sensing
Governance (Almirall & Wareham, 2011)	E-government systems	Living labs
Causality (Angelo & Vormann, 2018)	Linear and normative	Complex adaptive systems, emergence, and dynamic capabilities

This argument emphasises three achievements of urban laboratories as new experimental settings (Karvonen & Van Heur, 2014): situatedness, change-orientation, and contingency. As such, data science could enable—or not enable—citizens' advice regarding the anticipation or even prediction of changes regarding the issues affecting people every day, which would help cities act sooner to prevent problems from escalating (Gray & Lammerhirt, 2017; NESTA, 2015).

In short, (smart) citizens (Noveck, 2015; Schuurman, De Marez, & Ballon, 2016; Thomas, Wang, Mullagh, & Dunn, 2016) are considered decision-makers rather than simple data providers insofar as their decisions depend on a relational context and their unique circumstances (see Chapter 6). Currently, within the scope of some approaches to experimental cities being implemented under the umbrella of Urban Living Labs interventions/methodologies (Almirall & Wareham, 2011; Casual Synthesis Report, 2016; Leminen, 2015; Tõnurist, Kattel, & Lember, 2017), participants—as citizens—play more of an active role as co-producers than as mere data providers. However, the techno-politics of data (NESTA, 2015), especially its ownership and governance, is an underexplored area of research. The next section discusses this area.

2.5 Techno-politics and psychopolitics of data in smart cities

According to the research firm Gartner (2016), 8.4 billion devices worldwide were connected to the Internet by the end of 2017, and this is expected to rise to 20.4 billion by 2020. However, as previous sections in this chapter highlight, some hesitation persists at the centre of the debate around what Harari (2016b) has described as *dataism*, or the religion or dogma of big data. Thus, what are the real consequences of big data for (smart) citizens? In response to this open question, Shilton (2016, p. 21) argued that 'uncertainties about how to use increasingly large sets of personal data are at the centre of social debates about the virtues of Big Data. Not all big data are data about people, but data about people inspire much of the hope and anxiety bound up in discussions of the term'. As such, the emergence of AI on the policy radar with a strong geopolitical competition around it, and the recognition that the development of AI rests firmly on the availability of massive quantities of good quality data, has also brought to the fore the need to establish European data strategies and data ecosystems (Calzada & Almirall, 2020) involving stakeholders acting with different level of agency and being represented by the Penta helix (Calzada & Cowie, 2017). How the digital and data economy develops will present significant consequences on society at large, particularly in the context of the current initiatives on AI being implemented by several public administrations worldwide. Thus, who controls not only data collection, analysis, storage, and usage but ultimately ownership? Table 2.2, inspired by Shilton's question, shows the key parameters of the techno-politics and the psychopolitics of data related to the degree of citizen participation in today's cities. Shilton's interpretation

TABLE 2.2 Citizen participation in the techno-politics and in the psychopolitics of data collection, analysis, storage, reuse, and ownership.

Citizen participation in the techno-politics and the psychopolitics of data	Collection	Analysis	Storage	Reuse	Ownership
High participation	Citizens own or control devices; data collection can be customised	Raw data accessible; citizens can conduct their own analyses	Data stored on local devices	Citizens control reuse	Citizens own their data and customise their data policy
Low participation	Citizens aware of devices; data collection can be avoided	Citizens can see visualisations or analysis of their data	Data in cloud storage with options for deletion	Reuse is restricted to aggregated forms	Data collectors use contracts to obtain citizens' consent over their own data
Little to no participation	Citizens unaware of devices; data collection cannot be avoided	Citizens are evaluated or categorised without their knowledge	Data in cloud storage with no option for deletion	Data collectors share or sell data	Data collectors own citizens' data

assumes that users with high participation—smart citizens—can control the reuse of their own data. This assumption is a reaction to the fast development of the data extractivist practices by which (smart) citizens should not only be involved in participation processes but also gain the knowledge and the ethical quality to engage autonomously in the data collection processes. The assumption may offer a way to implement data sovereignty, ownership, and commons policy frameworks. Hence, these are the key parameters in today's cities of the citizen participation in the techno-politics and psychopolitics of data collection, analysis, storage, reuse, and ownership. It is relevant to note the aftermath of the GDPR and how this new regulatory framework might foster and incentives new data governance models based on ownership such as data co-operatives and platform co-operatives through public procurement (see Chapter 7 'PROTECTING').

Regarding new sources of data collection, analysis, storage, usage, and ownership, the major obstacles to fostering a people-centred data design are in the acquisition, shareability, and licencing restrictions of the obtained data. In this respect, closer collaboration is needed between computer scientists and social and political researchers regarding the development of stronger evidence-based research on how to tackle unexplored data issues. Thus, timely research should elaborate on the need to consider individuals not only as citizens deliberating on their material conditions but also as consumers agreeing and disagreeing to the terms of service. Basically, this research could advocate for a more human-centred approach to the smart city—one that fosters interplay and interdependencies among multiple stakeholders.

When Habermas (2015) confronted technocratic and democratic smartness, he made it possible to generalise a category called smart citizens. As such, citizen interaction, engagement, involvement, participation, and deliberation are at the centre of debates around the techno-politics of data. However, how should the distrust, apathy, and open outrage that have become increasingly evident in popular political attitudes today be addressed? The misalignments between technology and the social needs of citizens in data generation constitute a common dilemma today: will data-driven cities (PWC, 2016) and devices continue to serve citizens or vice versa? In response to this question, different forms of engagement on the part of smart citizens can be discussed in relation to the techno-politics of data.

As Morozov (2014) argued, despite the plethora of technological solutions to social problems, key questions remain unanswered: for example, who gets to implement data? And what kinds of politics of data do technological solutions smuggle through the back door? Discussions highlight how seemingly simple calls for data to openly challenge existing legal norms and have potentially profound implications for users along the value chain. For example, liability risks might be passed to the end user of open data, but what if end users cannot bear those risks? If the internet of things generates continuous monitoring and commonly individualised data, how should digital scholars theorise, regulate, and show the ethical choices (Hughes, 2016) that have emerged around the legal liability surrounding the 'ownership of data'?

For a full understanding of the techno-political and psychopolitical implications of the term smart city citizenship (Noveck, 2015) and to fully actualise citizens' capacities as the main drivers of urban transformations, this chapter underlines the need for a deeper transition towards experimental cities. Considering citizens as users or data providers assume that personal data comprises a raw material that citizens take for granted as another element of the market. This should attract the attention of policymakers, as it involves underlying issues of value as well as political decisions.

Hence, citizens' data are intrinsic parts of their urban experience and their right to the city (Morozov & Harvey, 2016). Why, then, are 'smart citizens' not considered pure decision-makers rather than passive data providers? Despite this willingness to pursue sustainable futures that are more democratic than technocratic, there is still strong inertia obstructing this alternative path. In fact, the current round of 'urban experimentation differs from previous incarnations, indicating a specific type of governance fix for a neoliberal system that is struggling to move towards more sustainable forms of urban development' (Evans et al., 2016, p. 10).

To open a new path of reflection and action based on Ostrom's influential thoughts on the commons (Ostrom, 2010; Urban Transformations, 2018), which have been analysed and adapted by Subirats (2016), this chapter suggests breaking away from the individualistic vision conceived by the capitalist tradition. Subirats and Rendueles (2016) noted that this vision has progressively transferred the idea of rights to individual people. The resulting prevailing view is that only privatisation leads to growth (Mazzucato, 2018). However, Bollier (2016) argued that historically rooted individualisation processes are increasingly shaping people's communal conditions insofar as intersubjectivity matters between them (Borch & Kornberger, 2015). This notion could be fully applied to 'smartness' to explore an emerging paradigm that has not yet been established—the experimental city.

In a serious attempt to transition from the smart city to the experimental city, a deeper analysis of the techno-politics of data is needed to interpret the role of smart citizens as decision-makers rather than data providers. This notion is likely to be influenced by new conceptual explorations and empirical analyses of the urban commons (Bollier & Helfrich, 2016) being applied to data (i.e. 'Data Commons'). Data commons will be elaborated further in Chapter 6. To describe this current transition, this chapter briefly presents three European projects on participatory smart cities that reconceptualise smart citizens as decision-makers rather than data providers: Hackair Project (Collective Awareness for Air Quality) (2016), Flamenco (Project: Flanders Mobile Enacted Citizen Observatories) (2016), and City of Things (2016). Together, these projects mark a transition from the smart city to the experimental city through their analyses of the techno-politics of data.

HackAIR is a SI project (Calzada, 2013b; Sabato et al., 2017) and open technology platform for citizen observatories of air quality. The project focuses on citizen engagement and related strategies, such as crowdsourcing (citizens as sensors), distributed intelligence (citizens as basic interpreters), participatory science (citizens as participants in data collection), and extreme collaborative science (citizens as participants in defining problems and analysing data). The call to transition from the conception of citizens as data providers to citizens as decision-makers has provoked a powerful debate on the ethical dimensions of participatory innovative technologies.

The Flamenco project has developed this theme further, exploring how citizens can be empowered to tailor their own observatories based on participatory sensing and citizen science principles. An interdisciplinary team is working on the applicability of the project from the perspectives of computer science and social science.

The City of Things project explores the experimental dimensions of data-driven living labs. These dimensions are related to multi-stakeholder co-creation processes for business, user design, prototyping, and product development. Basically, these are open innovation processes that aim to connect to the user experience during the product design process (West & Bogers, 2016).

These projects demonstrate that what was once novel has become received wisdom. It is now common sense to suggest that the nature of the metropolis demands forms of knowledge that transcend the old boundaries that once divided the humanities, natural sciences, and social sciences. It has become almost self-evident that a model of knowledge production where knowledge is produced in the academy and then exported to city hall and local governance structures is inadequate for the metropolitan challenges of the 21st century. Instead, the world has moved towards a stronger sense of co-production between research and practise. The idea that the questions arise in the real world, but the answers are found in the academy, is less plausible than ever. At its worst, the smart agenda, particularly as represented in journalistic accounts, can look like the return of technocratic determinism, through the back door, whereby all urban ills are resolved through scientific solutions. Such naïve arguments are, in reality, often the belief of second-rate technocrats and third-rate academic critics.

Interestingly, the complex and open systems of urban life are being disrupted by rapid social change and powerful economic forces (Keith & Calzada, 2017). Recognising that such change is unpredictable in its disruptive form and uneven in its social consequences, one function of academic research is to speculate, test, map, and trace how disruptive algorithmic technologies restructure the relationship between the individual, data, and the city (Han, 2015). The smart citizen at the heart of the new city needs to understand both the emancipatory potential and the divisive consequences of different moments of disruptive innovation. As described in the next section, the function of Urban Living Labs (Karvonen & Van Heur, 2014) as forms of urban governance that act entirely as proxies among stakeholders is to show the choices at stake rather than to provide singular solutions to problems. How citizens make these choices then becomes a mediation of scientific expertise and deliberative democracy.

This section has highlighted how data-driven issues present new pathways for conducting research and implementing policy (Zanouda et al., 2017). However, to unpack data ('unplug'), the underlying social, ethical, and political implications of the technical capacity to store and distribute information through the power of data science must be considered. Dystopian visions and technocratic utopias alike demand rigorous scrutiny in research and public debate to optimise the chance of shaping a better future city.

Concerning the ethical, psychological, and political dimensions of the ownership of data, urban experiments are gaining traction in cities all over the world as a way to stimulate alternatives and steer change (Caprotti & Cowley, 2016). Policymakers, designers, private companies, and third sector organisations are initiating innovations to test alternative visions of local economic development, social cohesion, environmental protection, expansion of the creative sector, the evolution of policy, service delivery, infrastructure provision, academic research, and more. The concept of experimentation feeds on the attractive notions of innovation and creativity (both individual and collective) while reframing the focus of sustainability from distant targets and government policies to concrete and achievable actions that can be undertaken by a wide variety of urban stakeholders in specific places. The ability of urban experiments to be radical in their ambitions while limited in their scope underpins a vibrant debate in both the policy and academic worlds regarding the ability of such experiments to initiate genuine change. Are these activities extensions of business, as usual, spatially limited, and captured by a familiar cast of dominant interests? Or can they generate real alternatives and stimulate profound transformation?

To explore these questions, the next section reflects on the promises and perils of experimentation as an increasingly alternative framework of urban governance that is moving beyond the structural mistakes of the so-called smart city, which has been the dominant mode thus far.

2.6 Experimental and pandemic post-COVID-19 citizenship as a transitional citizenship phase?

This section is divided into three subsections that discuss the three structural elements of the experimental city. In the first subsection, (smart) citizens are situated within the milieu of the Urban Living Labs as a way in which experimentation occurs within the city. The second subsection examines whether the Data Commons can offer any alternative to PPPs by pursuing a 'third way' of governing urban assets and enabling (smart) citizens to provide services themselves. The third subsection explores the extent to which considering (smart) citizens as decision-makers or citizen makers in the broader realm of the city could create a potential ecosystem of Urban Co-operative Platforms (i.e. platform and data co-operatives) as alternatives to capital-based forms of business.

In the backdrop of the post COVID-19 aftermath, this subsection anticipates the need to reset the smart city citizenship in light of novel needs that are surfacing from the everyday life of citizens (Allam & Jones, 2020). However, while effective protocols in regard to the sharing of health data is emphasised, urban Data Commons, on the other hand, specifically relating to urban health and safe city concepts, is still viewed from the national perspective without approaching the side effects for citizens. Thus, we may ask whether the current experimental and pandemic post COVID-19 citizenship could be understood as a transitional smart city citizenship phase. The Epilogue section of the book will revolve around this question.

2.6.1 Urban Living Labs: Strategies for experimenting within the city

In smart city and smart specialisation strategy (S^3) policy discourses (European Commission, 2016, 2018), governance interventions have been proposed in European cities and regions without appropriately considering the stakeholders, their multiple expectations, and their visions of a possible and desirable urban future. As such, smart technological solutions have not always focussed on how technologies are used by (smart) citizens, and at times, the smart city's modes of governance have been misaligned with citizens and stakeholders.

In this context, to understand the interdependent challenges and opportunities for different stakeholders, this chapter focuses on the dynamics of urban complexity, experimental research, and alternative policy approaches to cities and regions. This section is an invitation to rethink urban Europe based on the notion of an experimental laboratory that produces research and policy interventions. Urban Living Labs, exemplified by networks such as the European Network of Living Labs (ENoLL, 2017), enact projects that include active user involvement, real-life settings, multi-stakeholder participation, multi-method approaches, and co-production.

In contrast, the smartness of some European urban strategies is dominated by a technological discourse centred on data aggregation represented by early adopter H2020 Lighthouse projects, such as Triangulum, Remourban, and Growsmarter (analysed in Chapter 4), which allows the city-region to be managed by a fixed public-private partnership governance model (Moisio & Jonas, 2018). Nonetheless, in the complex multi-stakeholder urbanity that is flourishing around Europe, the shortcomings of the contemporary city must not be forgotten (Calzada, 2016a).

Paralleling the mainstream approach of smart cities, urban laboratory initiatives, generally placed under the loose banner of Urban Living Labs (Gascó, 2017; Urry, 2014), have been increasingly emerging in the newest H2020 Lighthouse projects from 2015 to 2020 as Chapter 4 will present. They are seen as an approach to speeding up socio-technological innovation that involves multi-stakeholders in co-production processes and as a form of collective urban governance and experimentation within the city that addresses the sustainability challenges and opportunities created by urbanisation. Currently, the ways that city innovation policies propose highly spatially specific and potentially transformative stakeholder-helix strategies (Triple, Quadruple, or Penta) are worth examining. These policies recognise that strategies are cross-sectoral, involving the research base, private capital, and public expenditure of civil society. In the next subsection, the suitability of expanding from Triple and Quadruple helixes to the Penta helix is described by suggesting that citizens require an active and entrepreneurial role among fixed institutional settings to ensure their full capacity as a system's transformers and as democratisers of urban life (Calzada & Cowie, 2017).

The enormous potential for experimental forms of governance in many European city-regions is expressed by ongoing Urban Living Labs initiatives, such as the Urban Living Partnership (Birmingham, Bristol, Leeds, Newcastle, and York) (Urban Transformations, 2017), JPI-Urban Europe (2017), and many international programmes, such as ENoLL (2017), Mistra Urban Futures (2017), BMW Guggenheim Urban Labs (2017), Urban Lab+ (2017), the Guangzhou International Award for Urban Innovation (2017), Rockefeller 100 Resilient Cities (2017), GUST snapshots (2017), and urb@exp (2017).

The notion of Urban Living Labs is normally attributed to Professor William Mitchell of the Massachusetts Institute of Technology (MIT). MIT Living Labs (2017) aimed to bring together interdisciplinary experts to develop, deploy, and test—in actual living environments—new technologies and strategies for a design that responds to this changing world. People from the outside world were invited into living laboratories where ethnographers and other researchers observed how they used newly invented information technology. Popularised in the USA, the notion generated traction in Europe; its diverse practices complicated what different actors believed the lab concept entailed. There have been numerous attempts to define an Urban Living Lab, but there is no firm consensus in the literature. So, in what ways are Urban Living Labs, as the new experimental initiatives of the applied social sciences, the correct—or at least a feasible—type or scale of intervention? According to Spilhaus (1964, p. 1141), 'the city is a completely interacting system and thus, the experiment must be a total system. Nobody knows the answers to city living in the future, and, when answers are unknown, experiment is essential'.

Despite the lack of consensus on the definition and building of Urban Living Labs in the emerging body of relevant policy initiatives and research (Keith & Calzada, 2017), the following questions can explore how notions of experimentation inform new ways of urban living:

1. What does the integration of interdisciplinary and place-based knowledge practices mean? How can urban studies bring together expertise in areas such as computing, mapping, politics, economics, digital anthropology, spatial analysis, and urban planning?

2. How can policymakers address multi-stakeholder helix strategies? What 'are' the roles of the private sector, public authorities, academia, civil society, and entrepreneurs/activists in these Urban Living Lab initiatives? What 'should' these roles be?
3. How can Urban Living Labs transcend the current governance constraints of the smart specialisation policy agenda in Europe?
4. What makes the Urban Living Lab approach attractive and novel?
5. How are Urban Living Lab initiatives being operationalised in contemporary urban governance initiatives for sustainability and in low carbon cities?
6. What prospects are there for alternative funding and alternative business models for cities and regions in Europe?
7. What are the practical and political interventions needed within multi-stakeholder approaches, and what are the potential concerns about data techno-politics?
8. Is another urban governance model possible—a 'third way' between state and market? (OECD/KIPF, 2016)

To operationalise the transition from the understanding of (smart) citizens as decision-makers rather than data providers, the next subsection explores the notion of the urban commons, particularly through Data Commons, as related to the strategic role of institutions, in fostering regional ecosystems of experimentation that engage the public sector, the private sector, academia, civic society, and social entrepreneurs/activists in the Penta helix framework (see Fig. 2.1). Penta helix framework, stemming from a SI perspective, will be employed as a methodological guideline in several chapters of this book (Chapters 3–7). Section 2.6.2 briefly presents the main rationale of Penta helix framework. This endeavour focuses on experimentalism rather than smartness, which can help examine how urban governance requires considering the Data Commons beyond PPP. Questions 6–8, are responded at the end of this chapter and will be operationalised in Chapters 6 and 7 by responding to them in-depth through the case study of Barcelona.

2.6.2 Experimenting with the Data Commons: The Penta helix multi-stakeholder framework

According to Karvonen and van Heur (2014), the experimental city approach champions the promise of experimental processes to promote urban innovations related to environmental protection, social cohesion, capitalist expansion, the development of the creative sector, policy improvements, infrastructure provision, academic research, and more. It is important to recognise that the notion of the experimental city is related to a wider discursive field that includes Triple helix early formations, applied innovation, engaged research, transdisciplinarity, living laboratories, and the co-production of knowledge. As such, experimental urbanism (Amin & Thrift, 2016) taps into ideas of urban change as inherently multidisciplinary, data-intensive, and embedded in place.

While the smart city approach was forged with an impetus towards urban-solution-driven fixes (European Commission, 2016), the experimental city is based on three steps that unpack urban practices (Latour, 1983, p.166): 'first, social scientists must capture the interests of non-scientists outside of the laboratory (in the field); second, they must collect information on real-world problems in the field and introduce this information into the controlled conditions of the laboratory to facilitate experimentation; and third, social scientists must extend the laboratory into wider society by carefully reintroducing the experimental results back into the field'.

Thus, by emphasising the active role of (smart) citizenship, this chapter includes the notion of the Data Commons in this narrative, as the rhetoric of the smart city has been entirely based on the idea of PPP. Regarding the technopolitics and the psychopolitics of data and the transition towards a more experimental city approach, it is important to understand that the debate over the Data Commons (Borch & Kornberger, 2015; Foster & Iaione, 2016) coincides with great technological changes that demand and invite urban scholars and practitioners to work both from a scientific perspective (to increase the capacity for innovation and cross-fertilisation) and from a social perspective (to ensure processes of social change and transformation). The Data Commons thus go beyond state-market relations (Subirats, 2016). As such, at this stage of the chapter, it is important to revisit the final research question. Is another type of city possible, that is, a 'third way' between the state and the market, a city not dominated by PPP? A political debate is gathering around these ever-more-frequent conflicts that do not find an adequate response in the traditional market-state dichotomy (Blanco et al., 2017). What is the answer to this governance challenge?

Bollier and Helfrich (2016) suggest that cities are at crossroads insofar as (smart) citizens could use the ideas of the Data Commons to retain control of the services that matter to them and to ensure that these services work for the people of the city, not just for businesses or the bureaucracy. However, the Data Commons could be abstract in its outcomes (Borch & Kornberger, 2015). At this preliminary stage, the urban governance model should be evolving, which means that there should be a necessary transition from the Triple and Quadruple helixes to the Penta helix (Calzada, 2016a). The prospect that the experimental city can overcome the limitations of the smart city offers a plethora of strategies for including more voices in the governance equation.

According to Lewontin (2000) and Leydesdorff and Fritsch (2006), the Triple helix framework (made up of private/industry, public/government, and academia/university) enabled researchers to study the knowledge base of an urban economy in terms of civil society's support for the evolution of cities. However, dynamic and pervasive SI processes are not included in this analysis insofar as the definition of smart city governance only considers the fixed structure fuelled 'by academia, industry, and government' (Deakin, 2014, p. 7). Even the recurring obsession with developing a full list of indicators using the Triple helix for 'smart city performance' (Lombardi, Giordano, Farouh, & Yousef, 2012;

Michelucci, De Marco, & Tanda, 2016) depicts this narrow vision, which fails to notice any pervasive and interdependent power interactions among stakeholders that ultimately defines the governance outcome.

The experimental city must include methodologically civic society (Quadruple helix) and consider entrepreneurs/activists (Penta helix) as part of the transition from the smart city approach. Deakin (2014, p. 1) considers the Triple helix framework sufficient to 'cultivate the environmental capacity, ecology, and vitality of those spaces which the direct democracy of their participatory governance opens up, add value to, and construct'. However, this chapter examines further connections between entrepreneurship and policy experimentation, as Sabato et al. (2017, p. 18) suggested, by avoiding 'narrow interpretations of SI', which could reinforce ongoing dynamics of welfare state retrenchment instead of its reactivation.

Given the current multi-stakeholder dynamics taking place in European cities and regions under the policy framework of H2020 Smart Cities and Communities, transformative alliances among the public sector, the private sector, academia, and civic society should eventually include the fifth helix, embodied by social entrepreneurs and activists (i.e. intermediaries, bricoleurs, brokers, and/or assemblers), as the main driver of change. Further research is needed to explore the profiles, motivations, modes of interaction, and transformative conditions of this type of invisible but highly influential stakeholder in the socio-economic and cultural life of the city (see Table 2.3 and Fig. 2.1) (Calzada & Cowie, 2017). Chapter 3 elaborates further and operationalises Penta helix in depth on this point.

Recent projects, such as Smart Urban Intermediaries (2018), are clearly exploring this path – complementing the active role of social entrepreneurs and activists in local neighbourhoods as an integral part of the civic society. Nevertheless, it is worth distinguishing them methodologically as social entities. Conflating civic society (fourth helix) and the social entrepreneurs and activists (fifth helix) would leave out a powerful collective intelligence in communities that can nurture socially innovative processes based on local experimentation to tackle social inequalities. Triple helix by itself does not suffice to activate unpredictable and experimental dynamics due to the fixed and technocratic nature of the interplay among stakeholders. Similarly, the Quadruple helix, as it is shown in Table 2.3, cannot leverage any intrinsic transformational reaction by itself since it is based on an institutionalised bottom-up process, where citizens react passively to suggested initiatives.

As processes based on Quadruple helix framework have revealed, the initiatives are pushed by institutions, resulting in poor or even inexistent mobilisation. Furthermore, neither the Triple nor the Quadruple helix frameworks can articulate a deeper transformational democratic disruption entirely led and governed by collective intelligence. However, data-driven sensitive urban environments require the valuable role of intermediaries as social entrepreneurs and activists (i.e. transformers and bricoleurs). Ultimately, it is essential to bring

TABLE 2.3 Rethinking stakeholders' helix strategies.

	Rethinking stakeholders' helix strategies		
	Triple helix (TH)	Quadruple helix (QH)	Penta helix (PH)
Literature	Etzkowitz and Leydesdorff (2000)	Goddard and Kempton (2016)	Ostrom (2010), Anttiroiko (2016), Calzada (2017, 2018b)
Multi-stakeholders	Public Private Academia	Public Private Academia Civic society	Public Private Academia Civic society Assemblers: (social) Entrepreneurs or/ and activists
Paradigms	PPP	Civic universities	Urban/data commons
Governance scheme and citizenship response	Invisible and passive citizenship	Reactive and passive citizenship	Proactive citizenship
Techno-politics of data	Technocratic top-down	Institutionalised bottom-up	Emergent and complex bottom-up

back the social ties that modern hyperconnected societies have dramatically diluted through the spread of data-rich fragmented environments. Therefore, it is vital to rethink multi-stakeholders' helix strategies that rely on the techno-political awareness of data. Yet this cannot occur while taking for granted the valuable role of proactive stakeholders who set up new collective connections based on the interplay among a diverse set of interests, imaginaries, and practices (Lombardi et al., 2011; Poppen & Decker, 2018).

Hence, in the laboratory context, experiments regarding the Data Commons should ensure the complete representation of diverse voices from each helix. This would reflect a wide range of voices in a community without relegating any to institutional settings. The inherent instability of an experimentally driven city provides a mechanism for co-evolution and a capacity to process the transition from the smart city approach. Often, the dynamics of SI (Calzada, 2013b) have been forgotten by those fostering urban change.

2.6.3 Experimenting towards Urban Co-operative Platforms? The city as a platform and (smart) citizens as maker citizens

Ultimately, the third structural element of the experimental city is the understanding of the city as a platform (Anttiroiko, 2016; Anttiroiko et al., 2013) and of (smart) citizens as 'maker citizens' (European Commission, 2017b; Levy, 1968; The Atlantic, 2015). Local authorities provide a wide range of services, including users' involvement in product development and citizens' right to bring up their concerns to open innovation systems. Forms of participation may vary—some are nominal, some are transformative. More transformative modes of participation are associated with opening public data sets for public use free of charge and are related to the open-source and user innovation movements (Smarticipate, 2016). On the whole, these modes reflect the increasing intersection between the Penta helix, driven by (social) entrepreneurs/activists, and the experimental notion of the Data Commons.

The inclusion of the fifth helix, broadly understood as those agents playing the role of transformational intermediaries (i.e. bricoleurs, brokers, or assemblers) in pursuit of social entrepreneurship and activism, connects directly to these early adopters with an ethical awareness of data and social justice. These agents are ultimately the source of the collective and experimental disruption, as Srnicek argued (Srnicek, 2017, p. 128): 'More radically, we can push for post-capitalist platforms that make use of the data collected by these platforms in order to distribute resources, enable democratic participation, and generate further technological development. Perhaps today we must collectivise the platforms'. Additionally, these agents could initiate a new generation of co-operative platforms including (i) co-operatively owned online labour brokerages and market places, (ii) city-owned platform co-operatives, (iii) producer-owned platforms, (iv) union-backed labour platforms, (v) co-operatives from within, and ultimately, (vi) the platform as protocol (Scholz, 2016). Will experimenting with data in cities pushed by the fifth helix mean evolving from 'platform capitalism' (Srnicek, 2017) to 'co-operative platforms' (Scholz, 2016)? Who will begin *this* 'platform revolution' and how will this happen (Parker et al., 2016)?

To some extent, a balance between private and public interests is complemented by other activities that could be considered the seeds of the experimental city in the realm of the Data Commons. As such, there are inherent asymmetries in the levels of engagement of firms and citizens, and these asymmetries are compensated for by welfare structures. Understanding the city as a platform may be a less controversial view of how to legitimise urban laboratories while redistributing capital and reducing inequalities at the neighbourhood level through the 'Robin-Hood effect' (Louail et al., 2016), enabling citizens to build and use the data platforms and make their own decisions based on urban co-operatives, as in Barcelona (Morozov & Bria, 2018; Urban I-Lab, 2018; Digital Social Innovation (DSI), 2018; La Borda, 2015).

In the realm of the experimental city, (smart) citizens should play a transformative role as decision-makers. In addition, the way some cities are evolving towards the power of the maker culture is related to the emergence of citizens as makers. The initiatives Barcelona and Amsterdam are implementing based on the 'decentralised citizens owned data ecosystem' fuelled by 'blockchain' technology through the Decode EU project are remarkable (Decode, 2018). Taking the lead on this experimental strategy, Barcelona has set up Decidim.barcelona as a participatory process allowing data and algorithmic transparency for their (smart) citizens (Decidim, 2018). The offline and online co-operative urban platforms are blended in a new 'Data Commons' strategy through Urban Living Labs, as 'Maker District Poblenou' is illustrating with a network of FabLabs (Maker District Poblenou, 2018). Likewise, other cities, such as London, have established a network of makers in diverse disciplines (Open Workshop Network, 2017), which creates further experimentation in the city. The case of Barcelona will be developed in detail in Chapters 5–7.

Although this type of experimentalism resonates with entrepreneurial models of socio-economic systems, which have been implemented in different parts of the world for decades, some models in the realm of co-operativism have also been heavily researched (Dildorth, 2014; Wanyama, 2014). According to the ILO (ILO, 2002, p. 2), a co-operative is 'an autonomous association of people united voluntarily to meet their 'common' economic, social, and cultural needs and aspirations through jointly owned and democratically controlled enterprises'. This is the case of the Mondragon co-operatives in the Basque Country (Spain) (Calzada, 2013b; Clamp & Alhamis, 2010; Gupta, 2014), a paradigmatic business model far from the capitalistic business-as-usual type that includes the Penta helix multi-stakeholder framework at the city-regional level, thus driving economic efficiency, territorial development, and social cohesion.

Even this model, however, shows some inherent contradictions that require further analysis. Mondragon co-operatives have been facing two complementary crises for a number of years. The pressure of the global markets is undermining the cohesive model based on local employment, as the crisis in the Fagor flagship firm showed some years ago. As a result of the first crisis, the governance model has revealed a hierarchical conflict between the top management and the workers. The most substantial lesson learned (Calzada, 2013b) has also raised an unresolved question: how can regionally rooted co-operative principles and values survive, be updated, and reactivated in the 21st century? By refounding a new type of co-operative entrepreneurship based on start-ups and spin-offs? Could these co-operatives be established by network-driven *millennials/entrepreneurs* under organisational frameworks based on open innovation, which would be sustainable but strongly fixed? To sum up, there is a need for an updated urban co-operative platform version based on interdependent metropolitan inclusiveness and regionally rooted social capital.

In conclusion, this chapter questions whether the establishment of an ecosystem of urban co-operative platforms could begin a movement towards experimental cities. Some of the hypotheses presented in this chapter (including the evolution of citizens as decision-makers, increasing awareness of the smart city's techno-political and psychopolitical implications, growing interdependence among stakeholders, and the trend towards urban laboratories) create pathways towards urban co-operative platforms in energy, mobility, and ICTs—three sectors defined by the Smart City and Communities H2020 policy framework, while the smart city approach is developing increasingly more sophisticated business models in European neighbourhoods (Müller & Rommel, 2010), cities (Calzada, 2018b), and regions (Cooperatives Europe, 2017).

2.7 Conclusion

This chapter examined the ongoing transition of the notion of (smart) citizens from data providers (extracted from the smart city dominant paradigm) to decision-makers (according to the emergent experimental city alternative paradigm). To conclude this chapter, the following three research questions are answered:

1. What prospects exist for alternative funding and alternative business models to move beyond smart cities by establishing the new paradigm of experimental cities?
   In the current experimental realm, the way in which some urban experiments are modifying the ownership of capital—and in parallel, the ownership of data—could offer interesting pathways to establishing alternative funding and business models based on the awareness and ownership of data. Unlike those who argue that data privacy is not an issue because 'people are happy to give away their personal data if it makes their life easier or more fun' (Racounteur, 2017, p. 6), new business models may arise based on community-based and community-controlled data that could follow more democratic socio-economic models, such as co-operative platforms/firms for self-managing urban issues (Blok et al., 2017).
2. What practical/political interventions have been tried or are possible among businesses, local governments, academia, communities, and social entrepreneurs?
   In light of some smart city interventions, Urban Living Lab experiments highlight new interdependencies among stakeholders while fostering ecosystems of entrepreneurial start-ups and SMEs. However, as Foster and Iaione (2016, p. 1) suggest from the perspective of the city as a 'commons', 'collaborative and polycentric governance strategies should recognise that private ownership rights must sometimes yield to the common good or community interest'. Nonetheless, this chapter presents the Penta helix multi-stakeholder framework as a policy tool by pointing out the active role of the fifth helix, which includes social entrepreneurs, activists, bricoleurs, brokers, and assemblers.

3. Ultimately, is another type of (smart) city possible—that is, a 'third way' between the state and market—that could overcome the PPP framework?
   So far, PPP has been the primary model reinforcing the alliance between the state and market. As Hall (2015, p. 3) notes, 'PPP is used to conceal public borrowing, while providing long-term state guarantees for profits to private companies'. However, several cities and regions, such as Barcelona, Amsterdam, Naples, Torino, Bologna, Vienna, Glasgow, Bristol, Helsinki, Utrecht, Dublin, and Brussels, among many others (Calzada, 2017) are currently undertaking experimental approaches that are likely to open up a 'third way', led by urban co-operative platforms in the European city-regional realm (Mazzucato, 2018).

However, smartness may not be appealing after being seen as technocratic, while the experimental approach has yet to be entirely established as a paradigm, so the open question here is how (smart) citizens will be able to decide, control, govern, and manage their urban futures by being both conscious of their rights to the city and aware of their duties in the processes of city making.

References

Access now. (2018). *Human rights in the age of artificial intelligence*. Retrieved from: https://www.accessnow.org/.

Acuto, M. (2018). Global science for city policy. *Science, 359*(6372), 165–166.

Ahlgren, B., Dannewitz, C., Imbrenda, C., Kutscher, D., & Ohlman, B. (2012). A survey of information-centric networking. *Communications Magazine, IEEE, 50*(7), 26–36.

Albino, V., Berardi, U., & Dangelico, R. M. (2015). Smart cities: Definitions, dimensions, performance, and initiatives. *Journal of Urban Technology, 22*(1), 3–21.

Allam, Z., & Jones, S. D. (2020). On the coronavirus (COVID-19) outbreak and the smart city network: Universal data sharing standards coupled with artificial intelligence (AI) to benefit urban health monitoring and management. *Healthcare, 8*(1). https://doi.org/10.3390/healthcare8010046.

Allenby, B., & Sarewitz, D. (2013). *The techno-human condition*. Cambridge, MA: The MIT Press.

Almirall, E., & Wareham, J. (2011). Living Labs: Arbiters of mid-and ground-level innovation. *Technology Analysis & Strategic Management, 23*(1), 87–102.

Amin, A., & Thrift, N. (2016). *Seeing like a City*. Cambridge: Polity.

Anastasiu, I. (2019). Unpacking the smart city through the lens of the right to the city: A taxonomy as a way forward in participatory city-making. In M. De Lange, & M. Wall (Eds.), *The hackable city: Digital media and collaborative city-making in the network society*. Springer Singapore: Singapore.

Angelo, H., & Vormann, B. (2018). Long waves of urban reform. *City*, 1–19. https://doi.org/10.1080/13604813.2018.1549850.

Anttiroiko, A. V. (2016). City-as-a-platform: Towards citizen-centred platform governance. In *Paper presented at RSA winter conference 2016 on new pressures on Cities and regions, London, UK, 24–25 November 2016*.

Anttiroiko, A. V., Valkama, P., & Bailey, J. (2013). Smart cities in the new service economy: Building platforms for smart services. *AI & Society, 29*(3), 323–334.

Arnstein, S. R. (1968). A ladder of citizen participation. *Journal of the American Institute of Planners, 35*(4), 216–224.

As-Fabrik. (2018). Retrieved from: https://www.uia-initiative.eu/en/uia-cities/bilbao.

Asilomar. (2018). *Asilomar AI principles*. Retrieved from: https://futureoflife.org/ai-principles/.

Bable. (2018). Retrieved from: www.bable-smartcities.eu.

Barcelona City Council. (2018). *Ethical digital standards: A policy toolkit—Barcelona*. Retrieved from: https://www.barcelona.cat/digitalstandards/en/init/0.1/index.html.

Bauman, Z. (2000). *Liquid modernity*. Cambridge: Polity.

Bauwens, M., & Pazaitis, A. (2018). *P2P accounting for planetary survival.* Brussels: P2P Foundation, Guerrilla Foundation and Schoepflin Foundation.

BITS (Barcelona Initiative for Technological Sovereignty). (2016). Retrieved from: https://bits.city/.

Blanco, I., Salazar, Y., & Bianchi, I. (2017). *Transforming barcelona's urban model? Limits and potentials for radical change under a radical left government*. Retrieved from: http://www.urbantransformations.ox.ac.uk/blog/2017/transforming-barcelonas-urban-model-limits-and-potentials-for-radical-change-under-a-radical-left-government/.

Blok, A., Courmont, A., Hoyng, R., Marquet, C., Minor, C., Nold, C., et al. (2017). Data platforms and cities. *Technoscienza: Italian Journal of Science & Technology Studies*, *8*(2), 175–219.

BMW Guggenheim Urban Labs. (2017). Retrieved from: http://www.bmwguggenheimlab.org/.

Bollier, D. (2016). *The city as a commons*. Retrieved from: https://www.youtube.com/watch?v=z3itmhDuem8.

Bollier, D., & Helfrich, S. (2016). *Patterns of commoning: The commons strategies group*. Retrieved from: http://bollier.org/blog/spanish-translation-%E2%80%9Cthink-commoner%E2%80%9D-now-published.

Borch, C., & Kornberger, M. (2015). *Urban commons: Rethinking the city*. London: Routledge.

Broadbent, S. (2017). *How smart citizens live*. Retrieved from: https://www.thersa.org/discover/publications-and-articles/rsa-comment/2017/how-smart-citizens-live.

Bumbee Labs. (2020). Retrieved from: www.bumbeelabs.com.

Calzada, I. (2013a). Critical social innovation in the smart city era for a city-regional European horizon 2020. *Journal of Public Policies & Territory P3T*, *2*(6), 1–20.

Calzada, I. (2013b). Knowledge building and organizational behaviour: Mondragon case. In F. Moulaert, D. MacCallum, A. Mehmood, & A. Hamdouch (Eds.), *International handbook of social innovation. social innovation: Collective action, social learning and transdisciplinary research* (pp. 219–229). Cheltenham: Edward Elgar (UK) Publishing. https://doi.org/10.13140/RG.2.2.30748.69766.

Calzada, I. (2015). Benchmarking future city-regions beyond nation-states. *Regional Studies, Regional Science*, *2*(1), 351–362. https://doi.org/10.1080/21681376.2015.1046908.

Calzada, I. (2016a). (Un)plugging smart cities with urban transformations: Towards multistakeholder city-regional complex urbanity? *URBS, Revista de Estudios Urbanos y Ciencias Sociales Journal*, *6*(2), 25–45. Retrieved from http://www2.ual.es/urbs/index.php/urbs/article/view/calzada.

Calzada, I. (2016b). *HERRISMARTIK: Basque Smart City-Regional Strategy in the H2020 European Context/La Estrategia Vasca de Territorio Inteligente en el Contexto Europeo Horizonte 2020: De la Agenda Digital Municipal a la Gobernanza de la Ciudad-Región Vasca Inteligente*. HERRISMARTIK commissioned by EUDEL (Basque Municipalities' Association), LKS Consultancy and the Basque Regional Government, Entrepreneurship, Innovation and Information Society Department Zumaia: Translokal—Academic Entrepreneurship for Policy Making, ISBN:978-84-946385-1-0. https://doi.org/10.13140/RG.2.2.10932.76161.

Calzada, I. (2017). The techno-politics of data and smart devolution in city-regions: Comparing glasgow, bristol, barcelona, and bilbao. *Systems*, *5*(1), 18. https://doi.org/10.3390/systems5010018.

Calzada, I. (2018a). *Data devolution in Europe. ESADE MSc Speaker Series: Big data & smart cities*. Retrieved from https://www.youtube.com/watch?v=iP8LVQWrdJ0.

Calzada, I. (2018b). (Smart) Citizens from data providers to decision-makers? The case study of Barcelona. *Sustainability, 10*(9), 3252. https://doi.org/10.3390/su10093252.

Calzada, I. (2020). Emerging citizenship regimes and rescaling (European) nation-states: Algorithmic, liquid, metropolitan and stateless citizenship ideal types. In S. Moisio, N. Koch, A. E. G. Jonas, C. Lizotte, & J. Luukkonen (Eds.), *Handbook on the changing geographies of the state: New spaces of geopolitics*. Cheltenham: Edward Elgar (UK) Publishing. https://doi.org/10.13140:RG.2.2.17301.6832/1.

Calzada, I., & Almirall, E. (2020). Data ecosystems for protecting European citizens' digital rights. *Transforming Government: People, Process and Policy, 14*(2). https://doi.org/10.1108/TG-03-2020-0047.

Calzada, I., & Cobo, C. (2015). Unplugging: Deconstructing the Smart City. *Journal of Urban Technology, 22*(1), 23–43. https://doi.org/10.1080/10630732.2014.971535.

Calzada, I., & Cowie, P. (2017). Beyond data-driven Smart City-regions? Rethinking stakeholder-helixes strategies. *The Region, 208*(4), 25–28. https://doi.org/10.1080/13673882.2017.11958675.

Calzada, I., & Keith, M. (2018). *Bridging European urban transformations workshop series 2016-2018*. Oxford: University of Oxford. https://doi.org/10.13140/RG.2.2.32474.39365.

Campbell, T. (2012). *Beyond smart cities: How cities network, learn and innovate*. Oxon: Earthscan.

Caprotti, F., & Cowley, R. (2016). Interrogating urban experiments. *Urban Geography*. https://doi.org/10.1080/02723638.2016.1265870.

Caragliu, A., Del Bo, C., & Nijkamp, P. (2011). Smart Cities in Europe. *Journal of Urban Technology, 18*(2), 65–82.

Cardullo, P., & Kitchin, R. (2018). Being a 'citizen' in the smart city: Up and down the scaffold of smart citizen participation in Dublin, Ireland. *GeoJournal, 78*(4). https://doi.org/10.1007/s10708-018-9845-8.

Carrington, D. (2016). *Yinchuan smart city future*. Retrieved from http://edition.cnn.com/2016/10/10/asia/yinchuan-smart-city-future.

Castells, M. (2018). *Democracy in the age of the internet*. Retrieved from: https://llull.cat/IMAGES_175/transfer06-not01.pdf.

Casual Synthesis Report. (2016). *Co-creating attractive and sustainable urban areas and lifestyles: Exploring new forms of inclusive urban governance*. Nordregio & JPI Urban Europe.

Chisnall, M. (2020). Digital slavery, time for abolition? *Policy Studies*, 1–19. https://doi.org/10.1080/01442872.2020.1724926.

City of Things. (2016). *Discover today the possibilities of tomorrow's smart cities*. Retrieved from: https://www.iminds.be/en/succeed-with-digital-research/go-to-market-testing/city-of-thing.

City-to-City Learning Programme. (2018). Retrieved from: https://replicate-project.eu/city2city-learning/.

Clamp, C., & Alhamis, I. (2010). Social entrepreneurship in the Mondragon co-operative corporation and the challenges of successful replication. *The Journal of Entrepreneurship, 19*(2), 149–177.

Coletta, C., Evans, L., Heaphy, L., & Kitchin, R. (2018). *Creating smart cities*. Oxon: Routledge.

Cooperatives Europe. (2017). *The European region of the international co-operative alliance*. Retrieved from: https://coopseurope.coop/about-cooperatives.

Cowley, R., Joss, S., & Dayot, Y. (2017). The smart city and its publics: Insights from across six UK cities. *Urban Research & Practice*, 1–25. https://doi.org/10.1080/17535069.2017.1293150.

Deakin, M. (2014). Smart cities: The state-of-the-art and governance challenge. *Triple Helix, 1*(1), 7.

Decidim. (2018). Retrieved from: https://www.decidim.barcelona/.

Decode. (2018). Retrieved from: https://www.decodeproject.eu/.

Devish, O., Poplin, A., & Sofronic, S. (2016). The gamification of civic participation: Two experiments in improving the skills of citizens to reflect collectively on spatial issues. *Journal of Urban Technology*, *23*(2), 81–102.

Díaz-Díaz, R., Muñoz, L., & Pérez-González, D. (2017). The business model evaluation tool for smart cities: Application to SmartSantander use cases. *Energies*, *10*(3), 262.

Digital Social Innovation (DSI). (2018). Retrieved from: https://digitalsocial.eu/. http://ajuntament.barcelona.cat/digital/en/digital-innovation/digital-economy/digital-social-innovation-programme-dsi4bcn.

Dildorth, R. (2014). Urban cooperatives and economic development. *Drexel Policy Notes*, *1*(2), 1–11.

Eizaguirre, S. (2016). Comparing social innovation initiatives in Barcelona and Bilbao. Looking at associate participation in the governance of citizens' rights. *Revista Catalana de Sociología*, *31*(1), 19–33. https://doi.org/10.2436/20.3005.01.69.

Eizaguirre, S., & Parés, M. (2018). Communities making social change from below. Social innovation and democratic leadership in two disenfranchised neighbourhoods in Barcelona. *Urban Research & Practice*, 1–19. https://doi.org/10.1080/17535069.2018.1426782.

ENoLL (European Network of Living Labs). (2017). Retrieved from: www.openlivinglabs.eu.

Ersoy, A. (2017). Smart cities as a mechanism towards a broader understanding of infrastructure interdependencies. *Regional Studies, Regional Science*, *4*(1), 1–6.

Eticas Consulting. (2020). Retrieved from: www.eticasconsulting.com.

Etzkowitz, H., & Leydesdorff, L. (2000). The dynamics of innovation: From National Systems and "mode 2" to a triple helix of university-industry-government relations. *Research Policy*, *29*, 109–123.

Eubanks, V. (2017). *Automating inequality: How high-tech tools profile, policy, and punish the poor*. NYC: St. Martin's Press.

European Commission. (2016). *Horizon 2020: Two years on*. Brussels: European Commission.

European Commission. (2017a). *The making of a smart city: Replication and scale-up of innovation in Europe*. Brussels: EU Smart Cities Information System.

European Commission. (2017b). *European maker week*. Retrieved from: https://blogs.ec.europa.eu/eupolicylab/european-maker-week-drawing-citizens-to-the-maker-world/.

European Commission. (2018). *EU smart cities information system*. Brussels: EU Smart cities Information System. Retrieved from: http://smartcities-infosystem.eu/sites-projects/projects.

European Data Protection Board. (2018). *Guidelines 3/2018 on the territorial scope of the GDPR (Article 3)—Version for public consultation*.

Evans, J., Karvonen, A., & Raven, R. (2016). *The experimental city*. London and New York: Routledge.

Flamenco (Project: Flanders Mobile Enacted Citizen Observatories). (2016). Retrieved from: www.citizen-observatory.be.

Floridi, L. (2018). Soft ethics and the governance of the digital. *Philosophy & Technology*, *31*(1), 1–8. https://doi.org/10.1007/s13347-018-0303-9.

Foster, S., & Iaione, C. (2016). The city as a commons. *Yale Law & Policy Review*, *34*, 2.

Friedewald, M., & Pohoryles, R. J. (2013). Technology and privacy. *Innovation: The European Journal of Social Science Research*, *26*(1–2), 1–6.

Gaffney, C., & Robertson, C. (2016). Smarter than smart: Rio de Janeiro's flawed emergence as a smart city. *Journal of Urban Technology*, 1–18.

Galparsoro, J. I. (2017). Big Data y Psicopolítica. Vía de escape: de la vida calculable a la vida como obra de arte. *Dilemata*, *24*, 25–43.

Gartner. (2016). *Gartner says Smart Cities will use 1.6 billion connected things in 2016*. Retrieved from: http://www.gartner.com/newsroom/id/3175418.

Gascó, M. (2017). Living labs: Implementing open innovation in the public sector. *Government Information Quarterly*, *34*(1), 90–98.

Goddard, J., & Kempton, L. (2016). *The civic university: Universities in leadership and management of place*. Warwick: University of Warwick.

Goldsmith, S., & Keliman, N. (2017). *A new city O/S: The power of open, collaborative, and distributed governance*. Washington: Brookings.

Google Urbanism. (2018). Retrieved from: www.googleurbanism.com.

Governance of Urban Sustainable Transitions (GUST). (2017). Retrieved from: http://www.urbanlivinglabs.net/.

Gray, J., & Lammerhirt, D. (2017). *Data and the city: How can public data infrastructures change lives in Urban regions*. Cambridge: Open Knowledge.

Guangzhou Award. (2017). Retrieved from: http://www.guangzhouaward.org/.

Guerrini, F. (2016). *Cities cannot be reduced to just big data and IoT: Smart city lessons from Yinchuan, China*. Retrieved from: http://www.forbes.com/sites/federicoguerrini/2016/09/19/engaging-citizens-or-just-managing-them-smart-city-lessons-from-china/#6a5a34392dda.

Gupta, C. (2014). The co-operative model as a living experiment in democracy. *Journal of Co-operative Organization and Management*, 2(2), 98–107.

Habermas, J. (2015). *The lure of technocracy*. New York, USA: Polity Press.

Hackair Project (Collective Awareness for Air Quality). (2016). Retrieved from: www.hackair.eu.

Hacking Inside Black Box. (2018). *Abrir las instituciones desde dentro*.

Hajer, M., & Dassen, T. (2014). *Smart about cities: Visualising the challenge for 21st century urbanism*. Amsterdam: Nai010 Publishers.

Hall, D. (2015). *Why public-private partnerships Don't work: The many advantages of the public alternative*. University of Greenwich, UK: PSIRU. Public Services International Research Unit.

Han, B.-C. (2015). *The transparency society*. Standford, USA: Standford University Press.

Harari, Y.-N. (2016a). *Homo deus: A brief history of tomorrow*. London, UK: Harvill-Secker.

Harari, Y.-N. (2016b). Yuval Noah Harari on big data, Google, and the end of free will. *Financial Times, 2016*. Retrieved from: https://www.ft.com/content/50bb4830-6a4c-11e6-ae5b-a7cc5dd5a28c.

Hemment, D., & Townsend, A. (2013). *Smart citizens*. Manchester: Future Everything Publications.

Herrschel, T., & Dierwechter, Y. (2015). Smart city-regional governance: A 'dual transition'. *Regions Magazine*, *300*(1), 20–21.

Hughes, R. (2016). *The bleeding edge: Why technology turns Toxix in an unequal world*. Canada: New Internationalist Publications Ltd.

IBM. (2018). *IBM everyday ethics for artificial intelligence & trust and transparency in AI*. Retrieved from: https://www.ibm.com/watson/ai-ethics/. https://www.ibm.com/watson/trust-transparency/.

If You Want To. (2017). Retrieved from: https://iywto.com/.

ILO (International Labour Organisation). (2002). *Recommendation 193 concerning the promotion of cooperatives*. Geneva: ILO.

JPI-Urban Europe. (2017). Retrieved from: http://jpi-urbaneurope.eu/.

Karvonen, A., & Van Heur, B. (2014). Urban Laboratories: Experiments in reworking Cities. *International Journal of Urban and Regional Research*, *38*(2), 379–392.

Keith, M., & Calzada, I. (2016). European smart citizens as decision makers rather than data providers. In *Urban transformations ESRC report on 14th November 2016 workshop entitled '(un) plugging data in smart city-regions'*.

Keith, M., & Calzada, I. (2017). European urban living labs as experimental city-to-city learning platforms. In *Urban transformations ESRC report on 13th February 2017 workshop entitled 'experimenting with urban living labs beyond smart city-regions'*.

Keith, M., & Calzada, I. (2018). Back to the 'Urban commons'? Social innovation through new co-operative forms in Europe. In *Urban Transformations ESRC report on 12th February 2018 workshop entitled 'rethinking the Urban commons in European City-regions'*.

Kitchin, R. (2016). *Reframing, reimagining and remaking Smart Cities*. The Programmable City Working Paper 20.

Kitchin, R. (2017). *Urban science: A short primer*. The Programmable City Working Paper 23.

Kontokosta, C. E. (2016). The quantified community and neighborhood labs: A framework for computational urban science and civic technology innovation. *Journal of Urban Technology, 23*(4), 67–84.

Kourtit, K., Elmlund, P., & Nijkamp, P. (2020). The urban data deluge: Challenges for smart urban planning in the third data revolution. *International Journal of Urban Sciences*, 1–17. https://doi.org/10.1080/12265934.2020.1755353.

Kourtit, K., & Nijkamp, P. (2012). Smart Cities in the innovation age. *Innovation: The European Journal of Social Science Research, 25*(2), 93–95.

Krivy, M. (2016). Towards a critique of cybernetic urbanism: The smart city and the society of control. *Planning Theory*, 1–23. https://doi.org/10.1177/1473095216645631.

La Borda. (2015). Retrieved from: https://vimeo.com/143976280.

Lane, J. (2019). *The digital street*. Oxford: Oxford University Press.

Lanier, J. (2018). *Ten arguments for deleting your social media accounts right now*. New York: Henry Holt and Company.

Latour, B. (1983). Give me a laboratory and I will raise the world. In K. Knorr-Cetina, & M. Mulkay (Eds.), *Science observed: Perspectives on the social study of science* (pp. 141–170). London: Sage Publications.

Leao, S., & Izadpahani, P. (2016). Factors motivating citizen engagement in mobile sensing: Insights from a survey of non-participants. *Journal of Urban Technology, 23*(4), 85–103.

Leminen, S. (2015). *Living labs as open innovation networks: Networks, roles and innovation outcomes*. (Doctoral dissertation). (document ID 132).

Leon, J. K. (2017). Global cities at any cost. *City*, 1–19. https://doi.org/10.1080/13604813.2016.1263491.

Levy, S. (1968). *Hackers: Heroes of the computer revolution*. New York: Dell Publishing.

Lewontin, R. C. (2000). *Gene, Organismo E Ambiente*. Cambridge, MA/London: Harvard University Press.

Leydesdorff, L., & Fritsch, M. (2006). Measuring the knowledge base of regional innovation systems in Germany in terms of a triple helix dynamics. *Research Policy, 35*(10), 1538–1553.

Lombardi, P., Giordano, S., Caragliu, A., Del Bo, C., Deakin, M., Nijkamp, P., et al. (2011). *An advanced triple-helix network model for smart cities performance*. Research Memorandum (p. 2011).

Lombardi, P., Giordano, S., Farouh, H., & Yousef, W. (2012). Modelling the smart city performance. *Innovation: The European Journal of Social Science Research, 25*(2), 137–149.

Louail, T., Lenormand, M., Arias, J. M., & Ramasco, J. J. (2016). Crowdsourcing the Robin Hood effect in Cities. *Applied Network Science*. Physics and Society, arXiv: 1604.08394.

Loukissas, Y. A. (2019). *All data are local: Thinking critically in a data-driven society*. Massachusetts: MIT Press.

Poblenou. (2018). Retrieved from: http://ajuntament.barcelona.cat/digital/en/digital-innovation/make-in-bcn/maker-district.

Marvin, S., Luque-Ayala, A., & McFarlane, C. (2015). *Smart urbanism: Utopian vision or false Dawn?*. New York: Routledge.

Marwick, A. E., & Boyd, D. (2010). I tweet honestly, I tweet passionately: Twitter users, context collapse, and the imagined audience. *New Media & Society*, *13*(1), 114–133.

Mazzucato, M. (2018). *The value of everything: Making and taking in the global economy*. London: Penguin.

McClelland, J. (2017). *What being 'smart' means for cities*. Retrieved from: https://www.raconteur.net/technology/what-being-smart-means-for-cities.

McCullough, M. (2013). *Ambient commons: Attention in the age of embodied information*. Cambridge, MA: MIT Press.

Michelucci, F. V., De Marco, A., & Tanda, A. (2016). Defining the role of the smart-city manager: An analysis of responsibilities and skills. *Journal of Urban Technology*, *23*(3), 23–42.

Mistra Urban Futures. (2017). Retrieved from: http://www.mistraurbanfutures.org/en.

MIT Living Labs. (2017). Retrieved from: http://livinglab.mit.edu/.

Moisio, S., & Jonas, A. E. G. (2018). City-regions and city-regionalism. In A. Paasi, J. Harrison, & M. Jones (Eds.), *Handbook on the geographies of regions and territories* (pp. 285–297). Cheltenham: Edward Elgar (UK) Publishing. https://doi.org/10.4337/9781785365805.

Montreal Declaration Responsible AI. (2018). Retrieved from: https://www.montrealdeclaration-responsibleai.com/the-declaration.

Mora, L., Bolici, R., & Deakin, M. (2017). The first two decades of smart-city research: A bibliometric analysis. *Journal of Urban Technology*, 1–25. https://doi.org/10.1080/10630732.2017.1285123.

Morozov, E. (2014). *The rise of data and the death of politics*. Retrieved from: https://www.theguardian.com/technology/2014/jul/20/rise-of-data-death-of-politics-evgeny-morozov-algorithmic-regulation.

Morozov, E. (2017). *So you want to switch off digitally? I'm Afraid that will cost you…*. Retrieved from: https://www.theguardian.com/commentisfree/2017/feb/19/right-to-disconnect-digital-gig-economy-evgeny-morozov.

Morozov, E. (2018). *Will tech giants move on from the internet, now we've all been harvested?*. Retrieved from: https://www.theguardian.com/technology/2018/jan/28/morozov-artificial-intelligence-data-technology-online?CMP=share_btn_tw.

Morozov, E., & Bria, F. (2017). *Roundtable session—A new deal on data: What role for cities? Smart city expo world congress*. Retrieved from: https://www.youtube.com/watch?v=1cakaaip2Vw.

Morozov, E., & Bria, F. (2018). *Rethinking the smart city. Democratising urban technology*. New York: Rosa Luxemburg Stiftung.

Morozov, E., & Eno, B. (2017). *Debat. Brian Eno i Evgeny Morozov Una conversa sobre tecnologia i democràcia. CCCB*. Retrieved from: https://vimeo.com/206060710.

Morozov, E., & Harvey, D. (2016). *Conversation between evgeny morozov and david harvey*. http://davidharvey.org/2016/11/video-conversation-between-david-harvey-evgeny-morozov-on-post-neoliberalism-trump-infrastructure-sharing-economy-smart-city/.

Müller, J., & Rommel, J. (2010). Is there a future role for urban electricity cooperatives? The case of Greenpeace Energy. In *7th Biennial international workshop-advances in energy studies*.

NESTA. (2015). *Data for good: How big and open data can be used for the common good*. London: NESTA.

Noble, S. U. (2018). *Algorithms of oppression: How search engines reinforce racism*. New York: New York University Press.

Noveck, B. S. (2015). *Smart citizens, smarter state: The technologies of expertise and the future of governing*. Cambridge, MA: Harvard University Press.

O'Neill, C. (2008). *Weapons of math destruction: How big data inequality and threatens democracy*. London: Penguin Random House.

OECD/KIPF. (2016). *Fiscal federalism 2016: Making decentralisation work* (p. 2016). Paris: OECD Publishing. Retrieved from: https://doi.org/10.1787/9789264254053-en.

Open Workshop Network. (2017). Retrieved from: www.openworkshopnetwork.com.

Ostrom, E. (2010). Beyond markets and states: Polycentric governance of complex economic systems. *American Economic Review, 100*, 1–33.

Parker, G. G., Van Alstyne, M. W., & Choudary, S. P. (2016). *Platform revolution: How networked markets are transforming the economy and how to make them work for you*. NY: Norton.

Pentland, A. (2014). *Social physics: How social networks can make us smarter* (p. 2014). New York: Penguin.

Platform of Trust. (2020). Retrieved from: www.platformoftrust.net.

Poppen, F., & Decker, R. (2018). The intermediary as an institutional entrepreneur: Institutional change and stability in triple-helix cooperation. *Triple Helix, 5*(1), 9.

PWC. (2016). *From concept to applied solutions: Data-driven Cities*. London: PWC.

Racounteur. (2017). *Smart cities*. Retrieved from: https://raconteur.uberflip.com/i/798678-smart-cities-special-report-2017.

Ratti, C., & Claudel, M. (2016). *The city of tomorrow: Sensors, networks, hackers, and the future of urban life*. Boston: Yale University Press.

Replicate. (2018). Retrieved from: https://replicate-project.eu/cities/san-sebastian/.

RICS. (2017). *Smart Cities, big data and the built environment: What's required?*. Reading: University of Reading.

Rockefeller 100 Resilient Cities. (2017). Retrieved from: http://www.100resilientcities.org/.

Rossi, U. (2016). The variegated economics and the potential politics of the smart city. *Territory, Politics, Governance, 4*(3), 337–353.

Rossi, U. (2018). Fake friends: The illusionist revision of Western urbanology at the time of platform capitalism. *Urban Studies, 57*(5), 1105–1117. https://doi.org/10.1177/0042098018821581.

Sabato, S., Vanhercke, B., & Verschraegen, G. (2017). Connecting entrepreneurship with policy experimentation? The EU framework for social innovation. *Innovation: The European Journal of Social Science Research, 30*(2), 147–167.

Satyam, A., & Calzada, I. (2017). *The smart city transformations*. New Delhi: Bloomsbury Academic and Professional Publishing.

Scholz, T. (2013). *Digital labor: The internet as playground and factory*. New York, London: Routledge.

Scholz, T. (2016). *Platform cooperativism: Challenging the corporate sharing economy*. New York: Rosa Luxemburg Stiftung.

Schuurman, D., De Marez, L., & Ballon, P. (2016). The impact of Living Lab methodology on open innovation contributions and outcomes. *Technology Innovation Management Review, 1*(6), 7–16.

Sharing Cities. (2018). Retrieved from: www.sharingcities.eu.

Shilton, K. (2016). When they are your big data: Participatory data practices as a lens on big data. In C. Sugimoto, H. R. Ekbia, & M. Mattioli (Eds.), *Big data is not a monolith*. Boston: MIT Press.

Shin, Y., & Shin, S. (2016). Modelling community resources and communications mapping for strategic inter-organizational problem solving and civic engagement. *Journal of Urban Technology, 23*(4), 47–66.

Sidewalk Labs. (2018). *Digital governance proposals for DSAP consultation*. Retrieved from https://waterfrontoronto.ca/nbe/wcm/connect/waterfront/41979265-8044-442a-9351-e28ef6c76d70/18.10.15_SWT_Draft+Proposals+Regarding+Data+Use+and+Governance.pdf?MOD=AJPERES.

Smart Urban Intermediaries. (2018). *Connecting people. Changing communities* (p. 2018). Glasgow: European Commission. Retrieved from: http://www.smart-urban-intermediaries.com/.

SmartEnCity. (2018). Retrieved from: https://smartencity.eu/about/lighthouse-cities/vitoria-gasteiz-spain/.

SmarterTogether. (2018). Retrieved from: www.smarter-together.eu.

Smarticipate. (2016). *Open governance in the Smart City—A scoping report*. Brussels: European Commission.

Solon, O. (2018). *George Soros: Facebook and Google a menace to society*. Retrieved from: https://www.theguardian.com/business/2018/jan/25/george-soros-facebook-and-google-are-a-menace-to-society?CMP=share_btn_tw.

Spilhaus, D. (1964). The experimental city. *Daedalus*, *96*(1129–1141).

Srnicek, N. (2017). *Platform capitalism*. Cambridge: Polity.

Stardust. (2018). Retrieved from: https://stardustproject.eu/cities/pamplona/.

Stone, B. (2016). *The upstarts: How Uber, Airbnb, and the killer companies of the new Silicon Valley are changing the world*. NY: Little, Brown and Company.

Stucke, M. E., & Grunnes, A. P. (2017). *Data-opolies*. Retrieved from:. https://doi.org/10.2139/ssrn.2927018. https://ssrn.com/abstract=2927018.

Subirats, J. (2016). *The commons: Beyond the market vs. state dilemma*. Retrieved from: https://www.opendemocracy.net/joan-subirats/commons-beyond-market-vs-state-dilemma.

Subirats, J., & Rendueles, C. (2016). *Los bienes comunes ¿Oportunidad o espejismo?*. Barcelona: Icaria.

Susskind, J. (2018). *Future politics: Living together in a world transformed by tech*. Oxford: Oxford University Press.

Telefónica. (2018). *Manifiesto por un Nuevo Pacto Digital: Una digitalización centrada en las personas*. Madrid: Telefónica.

The Atlantic. (2015). *Why I am not a maker*. Retrieved from: https://www.theatlantic.com/technology/archive/2015/01/why-i-am-not-a-maker/384767/.

Thomas, V., Wang, D., Mullagh, L., & Dunn, N. (2016). Where's Wally? In search of citizen perspectives on the smart city. *Sustainability*, *8*(3), 207.

Tõnurist, P., Kattel, R., & Lember, V. (2017). Innovation labs in the public sector: What they are and what they do? *Public Management Review*, 1–25.

Tranos, E., & Gertner, D. (2012). Smart networked cities? *Innovation: The European Journal of Social Science Research*, *25*(2), 175–190.

UK Government. (2016). *Future of cities: Foresight for cities. A resource for policy-makers*. London: UK Government.

Universidad de Deusto. (2018). *Declaración Deusto Derechos Humanos en Entornos Digitales*. Retrieved from: https://www.deusto.es/cs/Satellite/deusto/es/universidad-deusto/sobre-deusto-0/derechos-humanos-en-entornos-digitales.

Urb@exp (Learning from Urban Experiments). (2017). Retrieved from: http://www.urbanexp.eu/.

Urban I-Lab. (2018). Retrieved from: http://ajuntament.barcelona.cat/digital/en/digital-innovation/urban-i-lab.

Urban Lab+. (2017). Retrieved from: http://www.urbanlab.com/.

Urban Transformations. (2017). *Urban living partnerships*. Retrieved from: http://www.urbantransformations.ox.ac.uk/about/the-urban-living-partnerships/.

Urban Transformations. (2018). *Rethinking the Urban Commons in European City-Regions*. Retrieved from: http://www.urbantransformations.ox.ac.uk/event/rethinking-the-urban-commons-in-european-city-regions/.

Urry, J. (2014). *The future of urban living paper commissioned by the forsight future of cities programme*. Retrieved from: https://futureofcities.blog.gov.uk/2014/07/11/living-in-the-city/.

Van der Zwan, J., Van Doorn, M., Duivestein, S., & Pepping, T. (2018). *Digital happiness: Code we trust*. Brussels: SogetiLabs.

Waag, A. (2016). *A manifesto for smart citizens*. Retrieved from: http://waag.org/en/blog/manifesto-smart-citizens.

Wanyama, F. (2014). *Cooperatives and the sustainable development goals: A contribution to the Post-2015 development debate a policy brief*. ILO—International Labour Organization.

Watcher-Boettcher, S. (2017). *Technically wrong: Sexist apps, biased algorithms, and other threats of toxic tech*. London: W. W. Norton & Company.

Webb, S., & Mills, E. (2016). *User research insights report: Prototyping the future of planning*. London: Future Cities Catapult.

West, J., & Bogers, M. (2016). Open innovation: Current status and research opportunities. *Innovations, 19*(1), 43–50.

Willis, K. S., & Aurigi, A. (2018). *Digital and smart cities*. Oxon: Routledge.

Wired. (2018). *Yuval noah harari and tristan harris intertwined by wired*. Retrieved from: https://www.youtube.com/watch?v=v0sWeLZ8PXg.

Zanouda, T., Al Emadi, N., Abbar, S., & Srivastava, J. (2017). The quantified city: Sensing dynamics in urban setting. *arXiv preprint arXiv:1701.04253*.

Zuboff, S. (2019). *The age of surveillance capitalism: The fight for a human future at the new frontier of power*. London: Profile.

Chapter 3

DEMOCRATISING smart city citizenship: Penta helix multi-stakeholders policy framework from the Social Innovation perspective

Chapter outline

3.1 Democratising the technocratic smart city

Smartness in cities cannot be more technocratic than democratic (Habermas, 2015). Albeit over recent years, *smart city* has become eminently a mainstream technocratic concept in the European policy agendas (Albino, Berardi, & Dangelico, 2015; Caragliu & Del Bo, 2019). These agendas, in turn, have taken for granted the meaning of *stakeholders* without further questioning who the term actually references, which puts at stake both urban democracy and the related political decisions for the city (Desdemoustier, Crutzen, & Giffinger, 2019; Nesti & Graziano, 2019; Nilssen, 2018; Ranchordás, 2019; Trencher, 2018; Vanolo, 2016).

Smart City Citizenship. https://doi.org/10.1016/B978-0-12-815300-0.00003-4

In addition, increasingly autonomous and invisible algorithms have made it even harder for city authorities to detect and scrutinise their impartiality status, resulting in a technocratic governance push of the smart city (Gunkel, 2018; Komninos & Kakderi, 2019; Zuboff, 2019). Kitchin (2014, p. 9) defines *technocratic* governance as the procedure by which 'all aspects of a city can be measured and monitored and treated as technical problems that can be addressed through technical solutions'. Thus, the aggregated use of digital data to monitor, surveil, and nudge citizens has resulted in an intrinsic version of the technocratic smart city (Janssen & Kuk, 2016; Johnson, Robinson, & Philpot, 2019; Madsen, 2018), which pervasively bypasses the democratic accountability to which stakeholders are entitled. Despite these negative side effects, smart cities have remained the focus of urban policy and decision-makers worldwide, as a broad rubric for using the so-called stakeholder and citizen engagement practices oriented toward the management in such techno-deterministic—and more bluntly, less democratic—and thus further *platformised* urban realms (Barns, 2020; Fields, Bissell, & Macrorie, 2020; Stehlin, Hodson, & McMeekin, 2020).

Against this backdrop, the smart cities policy approach has been intensively implemented in several European cities under the policy umbrella of the H2020-Smart Cities and Communities (H2020-SCC) framework funded by the European Commission (EIP-SCC, 2016; European Commission, 2016, 2017a, 2017b, 2019; Mazzucato, 2018; Vandervyvere, 2017). Particularly since 2015, 17 lighthouse projects—involving 46 lighthouses and 71 follower cities—have been laying out the European H2020-SCC policy scheme (SCIS, 2019). These lighthouse projects, according to the related institutional discourse, aim to deliver smart technologies to municipalities by demonstrating that technologies on energy, mobility, and ICT can be a cost-effective way to tackle some of the most profound social, political, *democratic*, economic, institutional, and environmental issues that current and future generations are likely to face.

Nonetheless, until very recently, the hegemonic policy discourse in the European H2020-SCC policy scheme has been reduced to the economic value it generates through technocratic partnerships with powerful public and private actors: public-private-partnerships (PPP) (Forrer, Kee, Newcomer, & Boyer, 2010; Frug, 2017; Goldstein & Mele, 2016; Grossi & Pianezzi, 2017; Hall, 2015; Mazzucato, 2015; Rossi, 2016). Beyond these cost-effective PPP models, which stem from the institutional discourse, little has been questioned about the strategic stakeholders who have been formulating, uniquely and contextually, the smart city priorities (Hall, 2015; Kennedy, Poell, & Van Dijck, 2015; Paskaleva, Cooper, Linde, Peterson, & Götz, 2015). In fact, the European Commission, as part of its European Innovation Partnerships (EIPs) in H2020-SCC, encourages cities, industries, SMEs, and communities—without clarifying which stakeholders constitute these communities and what role they play—to come together to form an alliance consequential enough to build inclusive *citizen-focused* smart cities (Kummitha, 2019).

According to Harvey (1997, p. 2), 'smart city and the new urbanism movements build an image of the community and rhetoric of place-based civic pride and consciousness for those who do not need it while abandoning others in need to their underclass fate'. This statement intertwines with the criticism on the technocratic European smart city model initially advocated by the European Commission's H2020-SCC policy scheme (Borsboom-Van Beurden, Kallaos, Gindroz, Costa, & Riegler, 2019; Hollands, 2008, 2014; Kitchin, Coletta, Evans, Heaphy, & Mac Donncha, 2017). Through the scheme, the democratic representation of stakeholders is reduced to being labelled as '*citizen-focused* smart cities rooted in pragmatic, instrumental, and paternalistic discourses and practices rather than those of social rights, political citizenship, and the common good' (Cardullo & Kitchin, 2018, p. 1).

Furthermore, the perspective of an increase in the already-remarkable amount of data being controlled by artificial intelligence (AI) tools and devices owned by multinational corporations may further exacerbate already-pervasive social inequalities, marginalising the most voiceless and vulnerable stakeholders in smart cities (Engelbert, Van Zoonen, & Hirzalla, 2018; Eubanks, 2017; Hicks, 2017; Kempin Reuter, 2019; Kourtit & Nijkamp, 2012). This reality has aggravated the already-controversial technocratic smart city model and the related debate, raising questions about who benefits and makes such political determinations.

Thus, the point of departure and the aim of this chapter is the willingness to illuminate and clarify the methodological discussion on the helix frameworks from the Social Innovation (SI) perspective via extending the Triple and Quadruple helix frameworks by suggesting an evidence-based ex novo framework called Penta helix (Calzada, 2016, 2018b, 2018c, 2018d, 2018e; Calzada & Cowie, 2017). Penta helix defines as a joint interaction of the four established helixes of the so-called Quadruple helix (the public sector, the private sector, academia, and civil society) being intermediated and activated by the fifth helix (social entrepreneurs/activists) (Fig. 3.1). Accordingly, this chapter responds operationally to two intertwined research questions related to the democratic representation and the always varied power relations among stakeholders: First, how can we map out, comparatively in three cities, the composition of a multi-stakeholder policy framework based on SI (and the resulting business/social models), particularly enhancing the existing Triple and Quadruple helix frameworks. Second, consequently, how can we further incorporate the dynamic and transformational aspect in smart cities through intermediaries as collaborative capacity builders and the essential transformational agency for SI to occur (SUI, 2018)?

In an attempt to shed light on these two research questions, this chapter operationalises the Penta helix framework and explores research avenues on how to further approach broad democratic representation and agency in smart cities. The chapter, in doing so, aims to unfold the unique multi-stakeholder composition through five strategic dimensions by comparing three follower cities of the Replicate H2020-SCC project—Essen (Germany), Lausanne (Switzerland), and Nilüfer (Turkey) (Calzada, 2018a; Replicate, 2018)—based on the results gathered through intensive action research fieldwork undertaken from February 2017 to December 2018. The methodology ensured (i) the inclusion of the widest diversity of potential strategic stakeholders in each city that regularly, actively, and democratically engaged in the formulations of smart city priorities and, consequently, (ii) the mapping out of the multi-stakeholder policy framework using the Penta helix. The assumption lies in the idea that the broader a composition of stakeholders in a given smart city, the better democratic representation that the smart city intervention may achieve. This chapter presents the empirical results obtained by conducting triangulation methodology in three European cities through three intertwined action research techniques deployed in each case: (i) desk research, (ii) 25 in-depth interviews, and (iii) one validation workshop encompassing 25 strategic stakeholders.

The chapter is structured as follows: The next section presents the literature review on SI, the third section discusses the methodology of the Penta helix carried out in the three case studies, and the fourth section compares and examines the empirical results. The final section concludes with the main results and offers an array of research avenues to continue exploring how SI may enhance the democratisation in smart cities (Butzlaff, 2020; European Political Strategy Centre, 2019; Simon, Bass, Boelman, & Mulgan, 2017; Zandbergen & Uitermark, 2019).

3.2 Social Innovation perspective

3.2.1 Social Innovation

Despite the abundant literature about SI, the notion may be blurred too much in the current policy debate (Angelidou & Psaltoglou, 2017; Bartels, 2020; Bund, Gerhard, & Hoelscher, 2015; Christmann, 2020; Engelbrecht, 2018; European Commission, 2010; Keith & Calzada, 2018; Moulaert & MacCallum, 2019; Moulaert, MacCallum, Mehmood, & Hamdouch, 2014; Moulaert, Martinelli, González, & Swyngedouw, 2007; Pel, Wittmayer, Dorland, & Soggard Jorgensen, 2019; Preskill & Beer, 2012; Sabato, Vanhercke, & Verschraegen, 2017; Schubert, 2018; Terstriep, Rehfeld, & Kleverbeck, 2020; Vadrot, 2020). As Mihci (2019, p. 18) highlights, insofar as 'many theoretical approaches, ideas and practices labelled under the category of SI have relatively little in common', such a vagueness and fuzziness might make the intervention process even more complex and challenging.

In this chapter, though, Social Innovation—defined as the capacity to elaborate alternative discourses and actions that are counter-hegemonic in terms of resistance and/or innovative transformations—plays an important role by generating the intermediation conditions for further democratic decision-making processes for urban and technological adoptions in smart cities (Moulaert &

Mehmood, 2020; Poppen & Decker, 2018). SI, thus, offers a critique of the dominance of market-based logics (also embodied through PPP) and data extractivism in the age of liberalism (Van de Broeck, Mehmood, Paidakaki, & Parra, 2019), which consequently opens up a promising field of research to revisit helix frameworks that enable intermediation conditions among stakeholders to better achieve a democratic representation of varied power relations (Domanski, Howaldt, & Kaletka, 2020).

In this context, how can digital technologies transform the relationships between governments, business, and civil society? Which techno-political (power) relations and dynamics exist between these agents, and how do they change? Which roles do innovative applications of digital technologies and the use of newly emerging technologies play in the post COVID-19 society? How do helix frameworks intersect with contact tracing and tracking apps? What role do the public authorities and civic bottom-up initiatives play in addressing the power imbalances of the current data-driven smart cities' landscape (between data providers, data platforms, and ultimately, decision makers)? SI may provide the lenses to better steer changing power-relationships among stakeholders.

Despite that these intermediation conditions need to be thoroughly prepared by incorporating a wider range of stakeholders operating in diverse domains or helixes, we cannot expect that only incorporating several diverse (even marginal) actors to the sociopolitical game of the smart city will generate a democratic outcome (Engelbert et al., 2018). In fact, SI suggests mediation and translation between network actors or helixes (Moulaert & Mehmood, 2020), who may have different interests and understandings of the same urban issues and domains (Harvey, 1997). In this direction, recent projects, such as Smart Urban Intermediaries (2018), are exploring this path—complementing the active role of social entrepreneurs and activists in local neighbourhoods as an integral part of stimulating the civil society in cross-fertilisation with the public sector, the private sector, and even sometimes academia.

Given the current multi-stakeholder dynamics in regional innovation systems taking place in European cities and regions under the policy scheme of H2020-SCC, this chapter argues that transformative alliances among the public sector, private sector, academia, and civil society are increasingly including—consciously but also sometimes unwittingly—the emerging fifth helix. The fifth helix is embodied by social entrepreneurs and activists—who play the role of intermediaries, bricoleurs, brokers, and/or assemblers—acting as the main driver of change and, most importantly, operating in the borders by connecting the four entities encompassing the Quadruple helix as pollinisers and cross-sectoral ambassadors (Baack, 2015). Hence, this chapter—by applying the Penta helix framework to a comparative study—suggests that the Triple helix (Etzkowitz & Leydesdorff, 2000) alone cannot sufficiently activate unpredictable and experimental dynamics owing to the fixed and technocratic nature of the interplay among stakeholders, nor can the Quadruple helix (Deakin, Mora, & Reid, 2018) leverage any intrinsic transformational reaction by itself since it is based on an institutionalised bottom-up process where citizens might react passively to suggested initiatives.

However, acknowledging the novelty and the early stage of this scientific approach, and that helix frameworks methodologically only represent ideal types (Table 3.1; Turner, 2017), this chapter considers that further research is required to explore the profiles, motivations, modes of interaction, and transformative conditions of such intermediation produced by the fifth-helix. This chapter applies the proposed Penta helix framework (Calzada & Cowie, 2017) to the three aforementioned city cases in order to operationalise SI through helix frameworks which essentially result in a diverse set of business/social models. By opening up a plethora of potential interactions among diverse stakeholders, this chapter suggests that cities may be willing to further experiment with adopting one or another business/social model, without necessarily reducing the chances to create hegemonic PPPs.

Thus, to methodologically operationalise stakeholders among helix frameworks and the related interactions among them that result in a diverse set of business/social models—albeit avoiding normative determinism on further assumptions—this section presents two intertwined literature reviews stemming from SI by focusing on the intermediation that enables the Penta helix framework conditions: The first subsection (Table 3.1.) revolves around the literature on rethinking multi-stakeholder helix frameworks by exploring the potential features of Triple, Quadruple, and Penta helix frameworks based on the notion of the urban commons, particularly through Data Commons as an updated timely trend in several smart cities (Calzada & Almirall, 2019). And the second subsection (Table 3.2) examines the literature on the resulting five business/social models that stem from the multi-stakeholder helix frameworks.

3.2.2 Rethinking multi-stakeholder helix frameworks from the Social Innovation perspective: Triple, Quadruple, and Penta helix

The Triple helix framework was developed to conceptualise public innovation and the flow of knowledge in open innovation systems (Etzkowitz et al., 2007). Initially focused on technological innovation that benefits economic development, the Triple helix framework was useful for the interconnectedness among universities, industry, and government (Poppen & Decker, 2018). In those days, it could be seen as an almost *disruptive* idea. Soon, however, the institutional arrangements established in the name of the Triple helix became more separated and conventional. The inventions were supposed to be generated in what has been called the knowledge infrastructure (universities), developed through the support structure (usually tax-financed incubators), and finally commercialised in the production structure (private sector as business-as-usual). Several authors theorised the Triple helix as the framework (made up of private/industry, public/government, and academia/university) that enabled researchers to study the knowledge base of an urban economy (Lawton Smith & Leydesdorff, 2014; Lewontin, 2000; Leydesdorff, 2012; Leydesdorff & Deakin, 2011; Leydesdorff & Fritsch, 2006).

However, neither dynamic and pervasive SI processes nor civil society as an entity or helix was included in this analysis insofar as the definition of smart city governance only considered the fixed structure fuelled 'by academia, industry, and government' (Deakin, 2014, p. 7). The definition also excluded methodologically civil society (Quadruple helix) and further omitted the assemblage role that social entrepreneurs and activists (Penta helix) may play towards further democratic notions of smart cities. In addition, Deakin (2014, p. 1) considers the Triple helix framework sufficient to 'cultivate the environmental capacity, ecology, and vitality of those spaces which the direct democracy of their participatory governance opens up, add value to and construct'. On the other hand, this chapter emphasises the necessary connections among stakeholders through the active role of the pervasive fifth helix between social entrepreneurs/activists in the policy experimentation process by avoiding narrow interpretations under the banner of SI (Sabato et al., 2017). Paradoxically, though, if wrongly employed, SI can seemingly even reinforce ongoing dynamics of welfare state retrenchment instead of its reactivation by reducing the scope to enhance the position of SI as a better-placed paradigm to develop sustainable responses to contemporary societal challenges, compared to free-market solutions (Grimm, Fox, Baines, & Albertson, 2013) and to neoliberal governing strategies (Swyngedouw, 2005) usually embedded in the so-called PPP.

By acknowledging the limited scope of the Triple helix framework (Lombardi et al., 2011; Poppen & Decker, 2018), Goddard and Kempton (2016) describe the Quadruple helix framework as a partnership convened by universities as key civic institutions to shape the future development of their cities. They suggest that global knowledge locked up in universities could be mobilised to anchor the university locally in the city by using urban foresight methodologies. In essence, this approach challenges the traditional linear models of science and technology push approach to city development through research commercialisation, which has been embraced by governments through the support of Triple helix partnerships between the state, universities, and businesses and the creation of urban science parks (Kummitha & Crutzen, 2019; Leydesdorff, 2012). Thus, the 'civic university' is suggested as contrasting the traditional university, insofar as there are strong overlaps between the three domains of teaching, research, and societal engagement and the adoption of a holistic view of city development. Hence, the Quadruple helix framework might include diverse ways that citizens and stakeholders can actually benefit from recent developments in urban technologies (Vallance et al., 2020). Nonetheless, the Quadruple helix framework has sometimes revealed that the initiatives are pushed by institutions, resulting in poor or even inexistent social mobilisation (Afonso et al., 2012; Ahonen & Hämäläinen, 2012; Carayannis & Campbell, 2012; Cavallini et al., 2016).

Furthermore, neither the Triple nor the Quadruple helix frameworks can explain the articulation of a deeper transformational democratic disruption entirely led and governed by an intermediated collective intelligence. In such frameworks, beside the market creation and competitiveness imperatives, little is left for experimenting among entrepreneurial co-operative networks of individuals and civil groups (Sandoval, 2019; Siapera & Papadopoulou, 2016). This fact could be seen as a systemic innovative spark towards tackling the lack of political engagement and democratic representation. The Penta helix framework, thus, suggests the fifth helix, an assemblage, being diluted in the other four helixes while claiming the need to expand the understanding of the data-driven smart city and focusing on the identification of the urban assets as data with full consideration now as a public good or as Data Commons (Calzada, 2018e).

Inevitably, the Penta helix framework resonates with the narratives of the urban commons (Iaione, 2015), which has recently been reinterpreted, most importantly, in the aftermath of the algorithmic disruptive tsunami, as Data Commons (Calzada & Almirall, 2019), in which data are seen as a common infrastructure beyond the PPP hegemony. Regarding Data Commons, Bollier (2015) suggests that citizens could retain control of data related to the smart services that matter to them, instead of data related to businesses or bureaucracy. The Data Commons, thus, go beyond state-market solutions by asking whether another type of city is possible—that is, a third way between the state and the market, a city not dominated by the PPP. Not surprisingly, then, a techno-political debate appears to be gathering around theses ever-more-frequent conflicts that lack an adequate response in the traditional market-state dichotomy. A nondeterministic way to start exploring new socially innovative outcomes could be a transition from the Triple and Quadruple helixes to the Penta helix in order to enhance the scope for resulting business/social models among stakeholders.

In addition, data-driven sensitive urban environments require the valuable role of intermediaries as social entrepreneurs and activists (Barns, 2020; i.e. transformers or bricoleurs). Ultimately, it is essential to bring back the social ties that modern hyper-connected societies have dramatically weakened through the spread of data-rich fragmented environments (Calzada & Cobo, 2015). Therefore, it is vital to rethink multi-stakeholder helix strategies by ensuring the complete democratic representation of diverse voices from each helix. This representation would reflect a wide range of voices in a community without relegating any to institutional settings, yet it cannot occur while taking for granted the valuable roles of proactive stakeholders, who set up new collective connections based on the interplay among a diverse set of interests, imaginaries, and practices (Calzada, 2018c; Carayannis & Campbell, 2010; Halibas et al., 2017; Poppen & Decker, 2018).

Hence, the inclusion of the fifth helix, broadly understood as those agents playing the role of transformational intermediaries (i.e. brokers or assemblers) in pursuit of social entrepreneurship (Kummitha, 2019) and activism, connects directly to these early adopters with an ethical and sociopolitical awareness of social justice and democracy. Penta helix (shown in Fig. 3.1), in contrast to the institutional structuralist Triple and Quadruple helix, is novel as its contribution includes social entrepreneurs, activists, assemblers, or bricoleurs as an additional helix, which emphasises the active role of citizenship as an agency of systemic, bottom-up, and disruptive SI. This fifth helix is the key driver not only to transform and democratise the smart city concept but also to experiment across institutional boundaries in search of the urban commons (Ostrom, 1990).

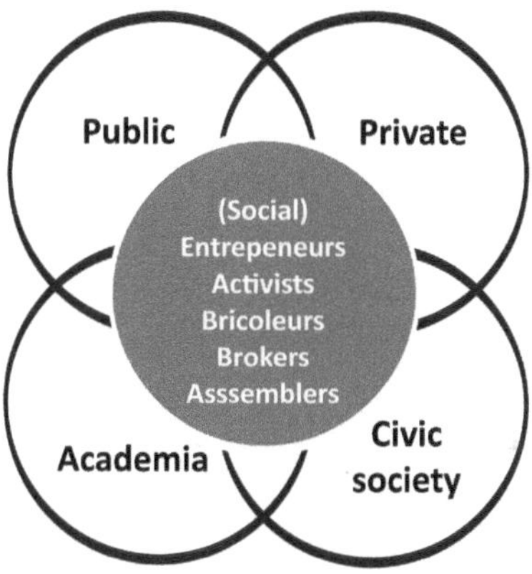

FIG. 3.1 Penta helix multi-stakeholder framework (Calzada & Cowie, 2017).

As a result of the triangulation fieldwork action research conducted, this chapter suggests the Penta helix framework for considering people and/or organisations as playing the key role of connecting the entities of the Quadruple helix by fulfilling the following functions: (i) transfer, receive, and integrate knowledge across helixes in a network; (ii) bring across networks; (iii) nurture the ability to cooperate among stakeholders by gaining support of leadership, structuring transformative alliances, and working under different jurisdictions; (iv) act as 'network builders' by bringing together resources, users, and developers; (v) behave as global carriers of best practices, standards, and institutionalised learning such as lobbying, which are informed by, and in turn inform, concrete local and regional projects; and (vi) ultimately, recognise plural visions by working out societal challenges.

TABLE 3.1 Literature review: rethinking multi-stakeholder helix frameworks from the Social Innovation perspective.

	Multi-stakeholder framework analysis		
	Triple helix (TH)	**Quadruple helix (QH)**	**Penta helix (PH)**
Literature review	Deakin (2014) Etzkowitz and Leydesdorff (2000) Etzkowitz, Ranga, Dzisah, and Zhou (2007) Lewontin (2000) Lawton Smith and Leydesdorff (2014) Leydesdorff (2012) Leydesdorff and Deakin (2011) Leydesdorff and Fritsch (2006) Lombardi et al. (2011) Poppen and Decker (2018)	Afonso, Monteiro, and Thompson (2012) Ahonen and Hämäläinen (2012) Carayannis and Campbell (2012) Cavallini, Soldi, Friedl, and Volpe (2016) Deakin et al. (2018) Goddard and Kempton (2016) Kummitha and Crutzen (2019) Leydesdorff (2012) Vallance, Tewdwr-Jones, and Kempton (2020)	Barns (2020) Bollier (2015) Calzada (2018c, 2018e) Calzada and Almirall (2019, 2020) Calzada and Cowie (2017) Carayannis and Campbell (2010) Halibas, Sibayan, and Maata (2017) Iaione (2015) Masek Tonkovic, Veckie, and Veckie (2017) Ostrom (1990) Sandoval (2019) Siapera and Papadopoulou (2016) SUI (2018)
Stakeholders	Public Private Academia	Public Private Academia Civil society	Public Private Academia Civil society Social entrepreneurs or/and activists
Citizenship response	Invisible and passive	Reactive and passive	Proactive
Governance scheme	Technocratic top-down	Institutionalised bottom-up	Emergent/democratised bottom-up

3.2.3 Resulting business/social models in smart cities

In order to operationalise the multi-stakeholder framework analysis, the conducted research in the three Replicate follower cities—which allow for identifying the strategic priorities by a selected number of strategic stakeholders in each city—links up the composition of stakeholders with the resulting business/social models.

This chapter defines business/social models as the resulting and collective preferences made by the strategic stakeholders—selected by the city representative—of how a city should create economic and social value collectively through the development of urban innovative services that are technically feasible and democratically desirable while reducing the city's overall environmental footprint. This chapter acknowledges, though a potential uncertain precondition and ideological bias exist, a democratic smart city can only be built as long as the strategic stakeholders selected by the city representative in charge of coordinating the smart city strategic formulation are democratically nominated with enough public scrutiny and transparency (Han, 2015).

This chapter operationalises five business/social models (Table 3.2) stemming from the literature review on the multi-stakeholder helix policy framework analysis (Table 3.1). Yet these classifications (Table 3.1 on helixes and Table 3.2 on models, respectively) are neither prescriptive, normative, nor deterministic in essence; instead, these typologies co-exist with each other within a single city's urban environmental strategy (Turner, 2017). The potential of these business/social model typologies is to present their evolution by reaching (and thus testing) the widest version (Penta helix framework) comparatively in three European cities. This premise is a methodological position rather than a normative prescription: amid the Penta helix framework, several business/social models can co-exist in smart city sectors (energy, mobility, and ICT; Fifth Strategic Dimension; Table 3.3) in different cities, as we will observe in the fourth section of this chapter.

Despite the methodology employed to compare and analyse the multi-stakeholder composition in each city, three relevant caveats should be made before discussing each business/social model: (i) first, these business/social models were offered to a group of strategic stakeholders (representing a diverse set of helixes) in each city as suggestions for their strategic preferences; (ii) second—and this caveat is the core aspect of the fieldwork research conducted—each stakeholder prioritised strategic preferences per item presented; and (iii) ultimately, and more importantly, the business/social model resulted in a collective outcome made by the entire representation of stakeholders. Thus, the results presented in the fourth section refer to a triangulation methodology based on 25 in-depth interviews with strategic stakeholders in each city. These interviews were processed collectively through a validation workshop thereafter while being contrasted with appropriate desk research throughout the whole data collection process. Moreover, as we will observe, the plurality of options was visible in all cases of the three cities.

The first model proposed is the Direct Public Provision (DPP). This model is the most straightforward for organising services. For stakeholders, the model can be beneficial in terms of democratic accountability. Under this model, there is a direct link of responsibility between the local government and administration, and their citizens for the design to deploy the service (Forrer et al., 2010). This approach can help, although not guarantee, that citizens' voices will be considered. By establishing its own priorities and working directly with citizens, the municipality can ensure that social interests are not lost to concentrated special and monopolistic interests in the transition to a smart city. Yet the challenges of DPP are related to the financial element of the city management model. Budget restrictions across Europe, especially in southern countries, have made it more difficult for governments to allocate funds to new smart services (Donald et al., 2014). Involving external stakeholders, from private firms to service users and their communities, in the production of smart services can alleviate some of the financial burdens. Service provision with external stakeholders also tends to have greater innovation capacity than direct delivery because of the wider range of ideas and experience they provide (Brogaard, 2017). There is a clear downside of DPP in this regard, however, as some cities might face more difficulties than others when directly financing services.

The second model for service provision that this chapter suggests is the so-called PPP. Forrer et al. (2010, p. 476) define PPP as 'an ongoing agreement between the government and private sector organisations in which the private organisation participates in the decision-making and production of a public good or service that has traditionally been provided by the public sector and in which the private sector shares the risk of that production'. This definition may differ from the interpretation made by Mazzucato (2015), who debunked PPP myths. She is regarded as one of the most influential modern economists and argues that the public sector should not only be perceived as a passive corrector of market failure but also as an entrepreneurial partner with a broader range of roles in stimulating innovation. Further, Forrer et al.'s definition might be problematic after the fieldwork action research conducted in the three case studies. Penta helix somehow makes explicit the critique related to unforeseen negative social impacts when PPP does not even engage citizens or peripheral stakeholders in the smart city strategic formulation (Engelbert et al., 2018; Prainsack, 2019). Therefore, the third and fourth models are variations of the PPP: Triple helix by including academia and Quadruple helix by adding civil society to the Triple helix. The third model is called the Public-Private-Academic Partnership (PPAP), and the fourth model is called the Public-Private-Academic-People Partnership (4PA).

The PPAP model, as an evolution of the traditional PPP, encourages academic partners not only to participate in the delivery of services but also to benefit from the active learning process while the public and private partners benefit from harnessing the research capacity of the university (Murphy et al., 2016). PPAP essentially resonates with the Triple helix multi-stakeholder framework

(Table 3.2). PPAP can offer increased innovation capacity because universities' nonprofit orientation and emphasis on knowledge provide them the ability to explore new ideas that might not be commercially viable yet but might be eventually profitable (Anderson et al., 2012). This model is particularly appropriate for large-scale projects that tend to involve several governments and consortia of private and academic partners (Goddard & Kempton, 2016). Further, the model most likely applies to the ICT sector and smart cities, and particularly to projects like developing an ICT infrastructure and integrated service platforms for firms and users (Fields et al., 2020). The advantage of the PPAP model is that, by including a larger variety of stakeholders around academia, they might be more likely to achieve the social acceptability dimension, albeit far from the democratic requirements such as cases when there is open engagement with communities outside the scientific or business community, which is not always the common trend. As such, PPAP can otherwise create asymmetric power relations in which citizens and their communities are either not given any opportunities to participate in developing scientific solutions (but will nonetheless often provide their data) or are only given the opportunity to provide feedback in an informative fashion at the end of the project, but not throughout (Callon, 1999). Such power relations, in turn, can result in scientific solutions that will not be adopted by citizens or stakeholders for being too far removed from their real needs.

A way to address the previous challenge could be through maximising citizens' engagement in the design and delivery of the service provision. This approach is the fourth model called 4PA, which essentially resonates with the Quadruple helix multi-stakeholder framework (Table 3.2). 4PA emerges in response to some of the challenges inherent to the traditional PPP model, including the accountability challenges discussed above. Specifically, PPP has been critiqued for developing a framework of service or project delivery that overlooks the interests and views of the general public (Ng et al., 2013). The 4PA model, in contrast, aims to provide a framework in which mechanisms to aggregate social concerns are embedded at different stages of the development and delivery process. The civil society domain overseeing a particular project can, therefore, create opportunities for citizens or particular stakeholders around the societal challenge to open up an informative process by providing feedback or getting involved in the project conception and deployment. In smart cities, people living in districts are clearly these strategic stakeholders whose engagement is crucial for the success of the intervention that 'should be exposed to societal deliberation at an earlier stage in their development' Späth and Knieling (2020, p. 1). However, this model is not a panacea for smart cities insofar as conflicts arise if decision-making processes and deliberation are not accurately prepared with the necessary attention and with mediators and ambassadors to curate the whole process without influencing it excessively and directly.

By this sequence, we reach the fifth and the last model, Urban/Data Commons (U/DC), in which the fifth helix may emerge consciously or unwittingly through the interactions between stakeholders and aggregate the necessary agency (Kennedy et al., 2015) to facilitate intermediation conditions among them (Keith & Calzada, 2018). This model has more direct citizen and stakeholder engagement (than previous PPAP and 4PA), also known as co-creation or co-production. Stakeholder engagement is defined as 'the active involvement of end-users and their communities in the various stages of the public service provision' (Voorberg et al., 2015, p. 1335). However, the concept of the commons (both urban and/or data) includes ownership of the outcome beyond the co-created or co-produced involvement of stakeholders in the decision-making process (Allen et al., 2020). Thus, this fifth model essentially resonates with the Penta helix multi-stakeholder framework (Table 3.2.), focusing not only on the delivery side of public services and the initial design process but also on the ownership of such outcomes being delivered (Bollier & Helfrich, 2016; Labaeye, 2017; Prainsack, 2019). Moreover, this model differentiates itself from the 4PA model in how it implies a direct two-way reciprocal relationship between stakeholders involved in representing the entire range of helixes. While one best practice of this could be the project developed by the Barcelona City Council called 'Decidim' (Barcelona City Council, 2018; Calzada, 2018e), by contrast, the absence of any attempt to set up a multi-stakeholder policy framework could be clearly spotted in the so-called and failed case of Toronto, Sidewalk Labs, with critics arguing that this project subverts democracy owing to the monolithic power owned by Google's parent big-tech firm Alphabet. This situation raises questions, in the absence of an alternative Data Commons model, about who will own the smart city's infrastructures and platforms and who will control the access to their services through data ecosystems (Calzada, 2019; Calzada & Almirall, 2020; Domanski et al., 2020; Johnson et al., 2019; Prainsack, 2019; Stehlin et al., 2020).

This fifth business/social model U/DC serves two important purposes. First, individuals represented through any stakeholder helix can be a source of innovation in the production of city-making because they contribute unique experiential knowledge of the service that can lead to significant improvements. Second, this model ensures that the consensus and conflicts of inter-stakeholders are deeply treated by considering antagonist interests (Christmann, 2020), confronted concerns of users, and the whole democratic dimension of the community-building where citizens' ownership of the new services embraces the paradigm of the (urban) commons (Dellenbaugh et al., 2016; Pestoff et al., 2013). Particularly, Data Commons become a sensitive issue insofar as the digital data could be used to monitor and track citizens with or without their consent. Thus, smart city interventions that involve the collection and analysis of data also rely strongly on citizens' decisions. Since it is citizens' data that will be collected, cities are facing pressures to actively engage citizens in their data policy and strategies (Calzada, 2018e).

TABLE 3.2 Literature review: Resulting business/social models in smart cities.

	Resulting business/social models in smart cities				
	Direct public provision (DPP)	**Public-private partnerships (PPP)**	**Public-private-academic partnerships (PPAP)**	**Public-private-academic-people partnerships (4PA)**	**Urban/data commons (U/DC)**
Literature review	Brogaard (2017) Donald, Glasmeier, Gray, and Lobao (2014) Forrer et al. (2010)	Engelbert et al. (2018) Forrer et al. (2010) Mazzucato (2015) Prainsack (2019)	Anderson, Michael, and Peirce (2012) Callon (1999) Fields et al. (2020) Goddard and Kempton (2016) Murphy, Tocher, and Ward (2016)	Ng, Wong, and Wong (2013)	Allen, Tamindael, Bickerton, and Cho (2020) Barcelona City Council (2018) Bollier and Helfrich (2016) Calzada (2018c, 2018e), Calzada (2019) Christmann (2020) Dellenbaugh, Kip, and Bieniok (2016) Domanski et al. (2020) Johnson et al. (2019) Kennedy et al. (2015) Keith and Calzada (2018) Labaeye (2017) Pestoff, Brandsen, and Verschuere (2013) Stehlin et al. (2020) Voorberg, Bekkers, and Tummers (2015)
helix framework	Mono helix	Double helix	Triple helix	Quadruple helix	Penta helix
stakeholders	Public	Public Private	Public Private Academia	Public Private Academia Civil Society	Public Private Academia Civil Society Social Entrepreneurs or/and Activists
Executive summary	Straightforward Democratic accountability Budget restrictions	Private sector participating in the decision-making and production process Debunk PPP myths Other stakeholders excluded	University benefits from the learning process Large-scale projects fit into this suitable model Social acceptability Asymmetric power relations	Social concerns at different stages District level interventions fit into this suitable model	May include the communal ownership of the outcome Stakeholders the source of innovation To ensure inter-stakeholder consensus/conflicts

3.3 Mapping out the Penta helix multi-stakeholder policy framework

This empirical research compares the multi-stakeholder policy framework in three follower cities of the project EU-H2020-SCC-Replicate by employing the Penta helix policy framework. By doing so, the examination focuses on five strategic dimensions—three on multi-stakeholder frameworks and two on resulting business/social models—studied through intensive action research fieldwork conducted from February 2017 to December 2018 in the three cities. This chapter reveals key qualitative observations and mapped out evidence-based empirical results on the five strategic dimensions studied in each follower city: (i) the composition of stakeholders per helix; (ii) the most influential stakeholder helix; (iii) the most proactive stakeholder helix; (iv) knowledge on the PPP; and ultimately, (v) the most suitable business/social model (per smart city sector too) in each follower city. The results were obtained in each city comparatively for the three Replicate follower cities (www.replicate-project.eu/city2citylearning) based on in-depth interviews with a selected group of 25 strategic stakeholders representing the Penta helix framework through in-depth interviews and validated later through a workshop. The five strategic dimensions inferred from the literature review and the results of the empirical research were used to build the comparative methodology of the three cases which addresses the research questions of this chapter, presented in its first section.

3.3.1 Action research fieldwork

The methodology used to apply the Penta helix policy framework included fieldwork research based on action research. Action research encompasses seven features (Higdem, 2014): (i) it stems from SI, which is a significant multidisciplinary approach blending scientific research, business administration, public debate, and ethical controversy (Moulaert, 2009); (ii) it unfolds sociocultural meanings in given territorial contexts through ethnographic fieldwork research; (iii) it aims at generating practical action for stakeholders' betterment; (iv) it is based on participatory research processes that are inclusive of plural ways of knowing in the constitution of theory and practice; (v) it is iterative and heuristic, a continual process of evolving inquiry and action, by learning from reflections on successes and failures; (vi) it is conducted by participants/stakeholders for participants/stakeholders, which addresses the fundamental questions of research; and ultimately, (vii) it is based on democratic ethos, which aims to critique power relations, address grievances of marginalised groups, and achieve smart city-regional empowerment in the face of entrenched institutionalised power.

3.3.2 Triangulation

The research design was based on the mixed-method technique of triangulation via action research (Fig. 3.2), which encompassed (i) desk research (summarised through Table 3.1 and Table 3.2 on the conducted literature reviews), (ii) the findings of 75 in-depth interviews with strategic stakeholders selected by the city representative in each city following the Penta helix framework, and (iii) results corroborated through three validation workshops, one per each case study city. Comparative case study research, as defined by Yin (2011), was identified as the most effective form of mixed-method research. This mixed-method process refers to the practical work conducted by the author to gather evidence-based data through in-depth interviews and validation workshops. The sample consisted of strategic stakeholders selected by the city representative according to his/her criterion aiming to accomplish certain methodological foundations to ensure a minimum degree of representation in the sample.

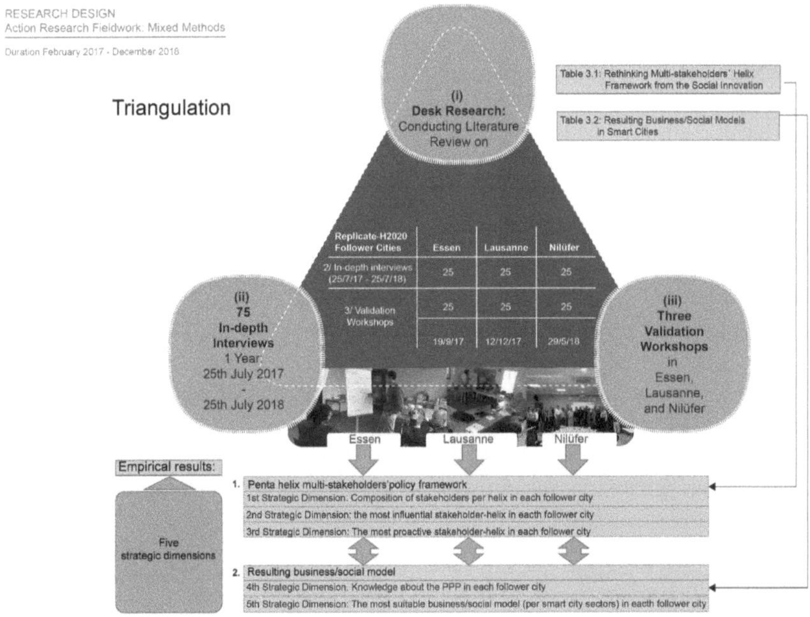

FIG. 3.2 Methodology: Research design based on the mixed-method technique of triangulation via action research.

Data collection through action research was arranged iteratively and paralleled two streams of research while conducting desk research: On one hand, in-depth interviews for the three follower cities took place from 25 July 2017 to 25 July 2018. On the other hand, in each follower city, a validation workshop was conducted on the following dates: 19 September 2017 in Essen, 12 December 2017 in Lausanne, and 29 May 2018 in Nilüfer.

Owing to the language barriers of many stakeholders in the three follower cities, a semi-structured 15-question questionnaire in English was designed from February 2017 to July 2017. The data collection started on 25 July 2017 via in-depth interviews being conducted in parallel in the three cities for 1 year; data collection ended on 25 July 2018, once 25 strategic stakeholders were interviewed in each city. The list of interviewees was meticulously designed and reviewed by each city representative to ensure that the widest level of plurality was reached in their cities. The strategic stakeholders answered the questionnaire; they were encouraged to validate and revise their earlier responses in light of the answers of other members of their validation workshop.

During the fieldwork research process, three validation workshops (one per follower city) were scheduled at different intervals of the data collection. The validation workshops, which ensured that the data collected were not biased or wrongly received, consisted of a selection of five questions (from the semi-structured questionnaire).

It was demonstrated that, during this process, disagreement and conflict were shown among a diverse set of stakeholders. The validation workshop collected these tensions and confrontational dynamics. The role played by the social entrepreneurs/activists as intermediators in the three cities (C RING, Impact Hub Ruhr, and Camp Essen in Essen; Eqlosion, in Lausanne; and Teracy, Mendireck, and Demir Energy facilitators in Nilüfer) was remarkable during this validation process. The final scores stemming from the sum of the interviews was tabulated depending on the discussion and the rearrangement suggested among stakeholders. Again, within this validation process, the role played in clarifying the discussion by those stakeholders who self-identified as fifth helix was substantial to determine the empirical results presented in Table 3.3. The fieldwork fixed 25 responses from strategic stakeholders in each follower city as the average threshold to obtain.

The following subsection briefly presents the profile of the three follower cities and the general composition of stakeholders in each city structured by the Penta helix framework (Calzada & Cowie, 2017).

3.3.3 Comparing three European case studies: Essen (Germany), Lausanne (Switzerland), and Nilüfer (Turkey)

REPLICATE (REnaissance of PLaces with Innovative Citizenship And TEchnologies) is the name of the European research and development project that aims to deploy integrated energy, mobility, and ICT solutions in city districts. The project has a consortium encompassing 38 partners. There are three lead cities (called lighthouses): San Sebastian (Spain), Florence (Italy), and Bristol (UK). The case studies of this chapter encompassed the cities called followers that aimed to look into replicating interventions in their cities: Essen (Germany), Lausanne (Switzerland), and Nilüfer (Turkey) (Fig. 3.3).

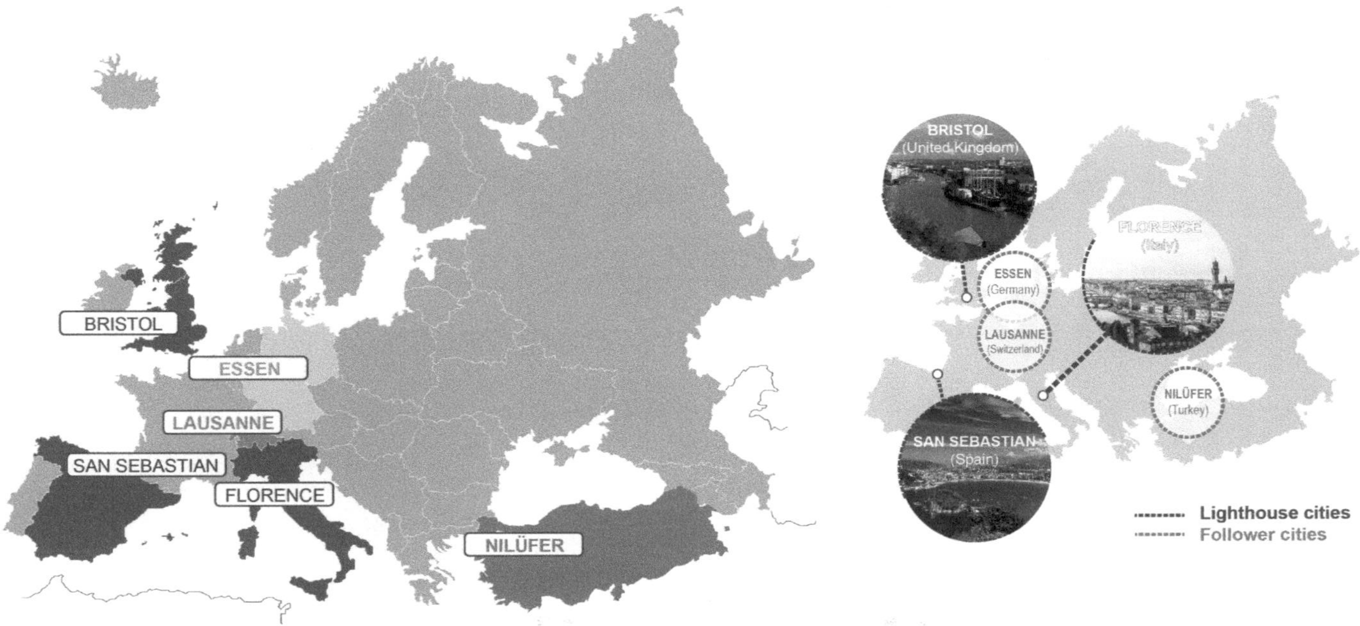

FIG. 3.3 Replicate EU-H2020-SCC project cities: Lighthouses (San Sebastian, Bristol, and Florence) and Followers (Essen, Lausanne, and Nilüfer). *(Source: https://replicate-project.eu/city2citylearning/.)*

The City of Essen is located in the North-Rhine Westphalia in the heart of the Ruhr Area, which encompasses approximately 5.1 million people. Following London and Paris, this metropolitan area constitutes the third-largest urban agglomeration in Europe. Essen is an independent city in the administrative district of Düsseldorf, and its 582,624 inhabitants make it the ninth-largest city in Germany. Essen has made a transition from a coal and steel metropolis to a European Green Capital. The municipal area of 210km per square is divided into 9 districts and 50 neighbourhoods. Further, Essen is an important industrial centre for German enterprises (E.ON SE, Stiftung Mercator, and Westnez GmbH). A combination of big firms, SMEs, and an active craft sector maintains a good economic climate. The composition of stakeholders and their strategic preferences resonate with a new and emerging start-up scene integrally involved in mediating among organisations and projects (Camp-Essen, Impact Hub Ruhr, and Essen 51, among others; Essen, 2019). The European Green Capital 2017 project shares a very comprehensive relationship with Essen's goal to establish a smart city strategy (Fig. 3.4).

During the fieldwork action research process for validation, stakeholders in Essen showed a great level of interaction, particularly by the three stakeholders representing the fifth helix. The level of overlap between academia, the private sector, and social entrepreneurs/activists was high as it was depicted by the strategic project that requires the involvement of several stakeholders having a wide vision of the city.

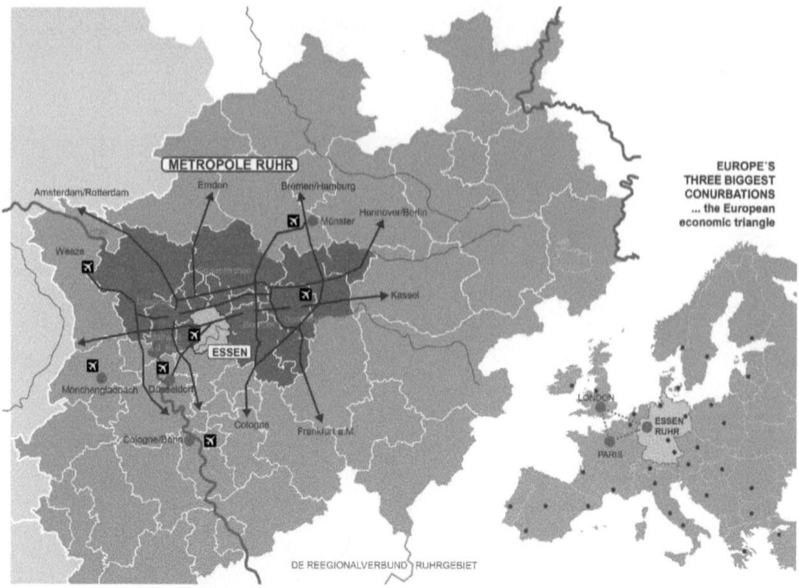

FIG. 3.4 Essen, follower city. *(Source: https://replicate-project.eu/city2citylearning/.)*

Lausanne is the fourth biggest city in Switzerland. It consists of 142,000 inhabitants and is the centre of an urban area with 350,000 inhabitants. Lausanne's main firms are Innobridge Service Sari, Tetrapack, and Logitech.

In 2016, Lausanne launched an energy efficiency programme called Equiwatt, with the objective of saving energy for individuals and businesses, thereby raising awareness regarding energy consumption. In the mobility sector, Lausanne has been striving for many years to limit the overwhelming space taken up by private cars to encourage more access to shops and businesses. By reducing authorised parking times on the streets, the municipality encourages commuters to leave their vehicles at outlying Park & Ride facilities. Private car traffic has been reduced by 6000 vehicles per day. Further, the city stakeholders have been working towards an eco-district called Plaines du Loup, which attempts to promote a public transport axis, a heat production innovative concept based on deep geothermal and heat recovery from wastewater. Strategically speaking, though, ICT seems to be a pending subject for Lausanne (2019).

During the fieldwork action research process for validation, the stakeholders' interaction was clearly dominated by the public sector insofar as it is responsible for the flagship project called Plaines du Loup. However, beyond the widely approved project, clear disagreement existed among stakeholders in terms of how to implement the given project, which demonstrated a need to keep opening a democratic consultation channel intermediated by the fifth helix represented by Eqlosion (Fig. 3.5).

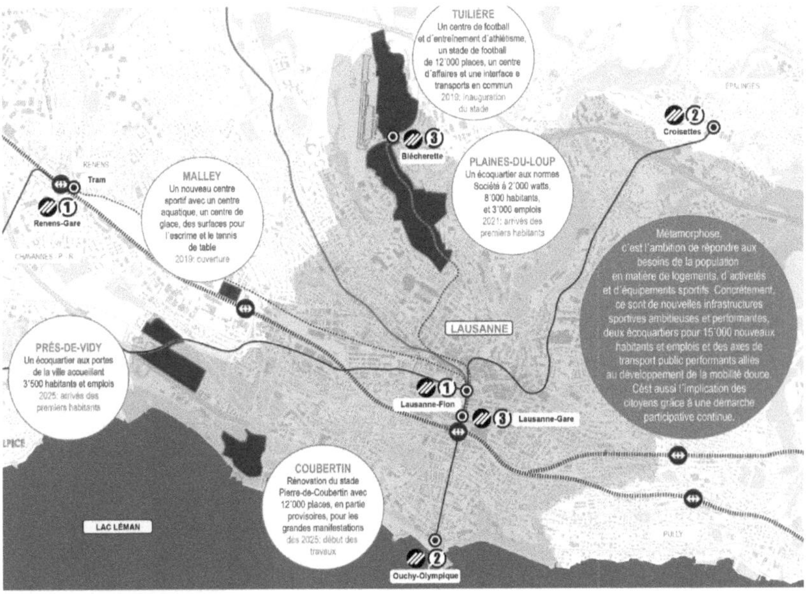

FIG. 3.5 Lausanne, follower city. *(Source: https://replicate-project.eu/city2citylearning/.)*

Nilüfer is one of the 17 districts of Bursa Province. Providing logistics connections for major cities, such as Ankara, İstanbul, and İzmir. Bursa enjoys a key geographic location in Turkey: it is in close proximity to national and global markets. Three universities are offering world-class education. Advanced infrastructure, dynamic entrepreneurs, and a high quality of life and work create an attractive investment and social climate. Moreover, Nilüfer has been established as the main residential development area of Bursa to meet the housing needs of not only the growing city but also industrial and commercial structures. Nilüfer comes first among the districts of Bursa in terms of the economic contributions while providing employment opportunities to 80% of the Bursa population via the Organised Industrial Zones in its border. The population increase in the last 5 years was 35%. This growth is higher than the average of Turkey and Bursa and will probably continue, owing to the attraction of the city to industrial investment and thus the availability of jobs. The population of Nilüfer encompasses 13.98% of the total population of Bursa (2,842,547). Bursa is viewed as one of the fast-growing middle-weight cities projected to account for more than 60% of global GDP growth over the next 15 years. There are 16 organised industrial zones and a free-trade zone with clusters in automotive, textile, machinery, food, and furniture. The multi-stakeholder framework focused on grassroots empowerment through neighbourhood committees and energy cooperatives. The private sector is leading a strong transformation through industry 4.0 and spin-off ecologies (Nilüfer, 2019).

During the fieldwork action research process for validation, the level of participation was remarkably outstanding, which showed the strong deliberative ethos that the city possesses. Particularly, the role played by social entrepreneurs/activists (including Teracity, Mendirek, and Demir Energi facilitation intermediaries) was crucial to spark and guide a constructive debate, particularly when the debate around the understanding of PPP arose (Fig. 3.6).

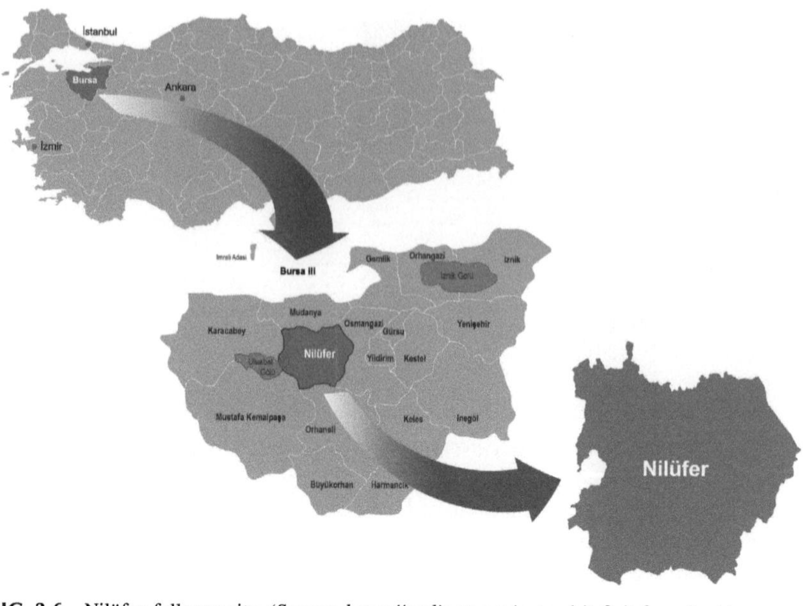

FIG. 3.6 Nilüfer, follower city. *(Source: https://replicate-project.eu/city2citylearning/.)*

3.4 Results: Beyond the PPP

This chapter argues that applying the Penta helix multi-stakeholder framework, albeit adapted to the unique context of urban governance, can support the city councils of the follower cities to manage their own update transitions towards a more democratic smart city approach. The Penta helix framework is intimately connected with the logic of the city business/social models insofar as it provides an understanding of the stakeholder composition while essentially serving as a policy tool for city governments to articulate the smart city strategy.

To operationalise Penta helix, the fieldwork action research was conducted by triangulating desk research, in-depth interviews, and validation workshops (Fig. 3.2), assisted by a semi-structured questionnaire encompassing five strategic dimensions.

The Penta helix framework was conducted by systematising five strategic dimensions through the questionnaire in which each person responded individually to and later validated collectively the following aspects: (i) which helix each stakeholder belonged to (composition), (ii) which was the most influential helix (influence), and (iii) which was the most proactive helix (proactivity). Moreover, regarding the suitability of the resulting the business/social models (DPP, PPP, PPAP, 4PA, and U/DC), each person responded to (iv) whether he/she knew the meaning of PPP and (v) which business/model was the most suitable in general and as per the smart sector (energy, mobility, and ICT).

TABLE 3.3 Empirical results.

Empirical results				
1. Penta helix multi-stakeholder policy framework				
%	ESSEN	LAUSANNE	NILÜFER	GLOBAL
First strategic dimension: COMPOSITION				
1. Public	52	36	20	36
2. Private	12	12	32	18
3. Academia	16	24	20	20
4. Civil society	8	16	12	12
5. Social E/A	12	12	16	14
TOTAL	*100*	*100*	*100*	*100*
Second strategic dimension: INFLUENCE				
1. Public	28	80	44	50
2. Private	44	12	28	28

Continued

TABLE 3.3 Empirical results—cont'd

Empirical results				
3. Academia	8	0	12	7
4. Civil society	0	8	16	8
5. Social E/A	20	0	0	7
TOTAL	*100*	*100*	*100*	*100*
Third strategic dimension: PROACTIVITY				
1. Public	16	21	24	20
2. Private	21	22	23	22
3. Academia	21	21	16	19
4. Civil society	22	16	21	20
5. Social E/A	19	20	16	19
TOTAL	*100*	*100*	*100*	*100*
2. Resulting business/social model				
Fourth strategic dimension: KNOWLEDGE ABOUT PPP				
1. YES	92	60	76	76
2. MAYBE	4	40	12	20
3. NO	4	0	12	4
TOTAL	*100*	*100*	*100*	*100*
Fifth strategic dimension: BUSINESS/SOCIAL MODELS SUITABILITY				
1. DPP	18	17	15	17
2. PPP	21	23	21	22
3. PPAP	20	23	21	21
4. 4PA	19	19	21	19
5. U/DC	22	18	22	21
TOTAL	*100*	*100*	*100*	*100*
ENERGY				
1. DPP	12	34	16	21
2. PPP	36	6	28	23
3. PPAP	16	20	40	25
4. 4PA	20	20	4	15
5. U/DC	16	20	12	16
TOTAL	*100*	*100*	*100*	*100*

TABLE 3.3 Empirical results—cont'd

Empirical results				
MOBILITY				
1. DPP	24	20	20	21
2. PPP	24	34	28	29
3. PPAP	4	13	16	11
4. 4PA	28	20	16	21
5. U/DC	20	13	20	18
TOTAL	*100*	*100*	*100*	*100*
ICT				
1. DPP	8	20	0	9
2. PPP	28	27	27	28
3. PPAP	24	27	52	34
4. 4PA	8	13	13	11
5. U/DC	32	13	8	18
TOTAL	*100*	*100*	*100*	*100*

Regarding the first strategic dimension, amid the global picture of the three follower cities, the most represented helix was the public sector. However, it is remarkable that the profile of stakeholders following this hegemonic helix respectively is academia, the private sector, social entrepreneurs and activists, and civil society. Strikingly, though, the composition in the three follower cities varies considerably: While Essen and Lausanne (with a strong academic presence) were highly represented by people from the public sector, Nilüfer was represented by the private sector, owing to the great interest in developing a new economic model for the metropolitan area as a consequence of the demographic boost. However, in the three cases, we could highlight the regular presence of stakeholders representing the fifth helix, which this chapter refers to as intermediaries.

Examining the second strategic dimension, the fieldwork enquired about the most influential helix and found that, globally, the public sector still overcomes the private influence. However, from case to case, the most influential helix varies: Lausanne overwhelmingly (and consistently with its current publicly owned flagship district intervention, Plaines du Loup) selected the public sector and underscored academia as the most represented helix in the composition of its framework, which entirely contrasts the results obtained in the other two follower cities. In Essen, the strategic alliance between the private and the social entrepreneurs/activists appears to be the most influential helix with strong public support. On the other hand, in Nilüfer, owing to the institutional boundaries and politically fragile situation, the triad between the public-private-civil society still appears to influence the multi-stakeholder policy framework.

The third strategic dimension related to the level of proactivity in each helix per city illustrates a rather regular picture with almost similar distribution in each city per helix (between 16% and 24%). In line with the rationale of this chapter, the fifth helix reveals itself as part of the ecosystem of proactive stakeholders in the three follower cities. Case by case, in Essen, it seems inspiring and hopeful that the leading proactive role of the civil society contrasts with the low level of influence provided to this helix. Similarly, in Lausanne, the proactivity level observed in the private sector differs from the low level of influence regarding this helix. Ultimately, in Nilüfer, the public sector seems to be leading in both its level of influence and proactivity.

After examining the three strategic dimensions related to the multi-stakeholder framework regarding composition, influence, and proactivity, the fieldwork focused on the resulting business/social models. Notably, the fourth dimension asking about the understanding of the PPP sparked a deep discussion in the validation workshops of the three follower cities, which in itself demonstrates the openness of stakeholders in the three cities to go beyond, or at least question, the internal arrangements of the PPP. Furthermore, responding to the two intertwined research questions of this chapter, the debate in the validation workshop invited further exploration of how SI can occur through intermediating smart city initiatives among stakeholders by establishing ad-hoc business/social models. This aspect was responded to operationally through the fifth strategic dimension.

The fourth strategic dimension entirely focused on the knowledge of PPP. Despite the expected affirmative answer being a generic answer, the level of debate in the validation workshops among stakeholders, particularly in Lausanne and Nilüfer, explains and illustrates the doubts, as many responded with *Maybe* and directly with *No:* While 40% in Lausanne responded with *Maybe*, and 12% in Nilüfer opted for *No*. These findings clearly reveal that PPP could have entirely different interpretations and positions, which contrasts the idea of it being the only business/social model in the multi-stakeholder framework, as this chapter elucidates.

Ultimately, the fifth strategic dimension depicts an interesting comparative result for each city, despite that the most suitable model (not the only one, though), generically speaking, was the PPP. Lausanne predominantly and collectively selected PPP and PPAP, but Essen and Nilüfer appeared to show an experimental strategic willingness when selecting U/DC. A reason that could explain these results is the openness and willingness for a further experimental approach insofar as cities seemed to embrace further complex business/social models that result in interdependencies among stakeholders and the related decision-making processes. From the current DPP in Lausanne, stakeholders clearly and collectively pointed out PPP and PPAP as a suitable step forward. In the case of Essen, the alliance between the private sector and the entrepreneurial ecosystem presumably derives to a model with intermediaries, bricoleurs, assemblers, and brokers for transforming the regional economic model as a whole, supported by a strong public sector. Finally, Nilüfer, being dependent on the current DPP model but with resilient leadership in the public sector, may be keen to further exploring PPP, PPAP, and even 4PA by gradually including social innovators in their transformational processes, as is the case with the strategic endeavour of the city council of Nilüfer to establish the Centre for Social Innovation.

However, the suitability of business/social models clearly differs from city to city when focusing on specific sectors, which clearly validates the rationale of this chapter suggesting to going beyond the PPP hegemonic model. The debate on the validation workshop was conducted through specific initiatives and projects related to ongoing implementations in the energy, mobility, and ICT sectors. The detailed analysis of such interventions goes beyond the scope of this chapter. Nonetheless, the emergency of a plethora of actions subject to be openly discussed among a wide range of stakeholders clearly indicates the potential of the variation of such models for democratic deliberation in smart cities.

As such, starting with energy, follower cities selected their current position as the most suitable one. In Lausanne, the model on DPP for the district heating fits consistently with the flagship project Plaines du Loup and apparently well into the expectations of the stakeholders. In Essen, PPP appears to work so far due to the ongoing collaboration among the municipality and the local corporation (E.ON SE), by paving a path for 4PA with the potential proactive role of academia and civil society. In Nilüfer, PPAP appears to be a suitable option as a result of several ongoing energy co-operatives jointly established with the university.

Considering mobility, another different business and social rationale from the perspective of stakeholders determine the strategic selection: the PPP model for Lausanne and Nilüfer, while 4PA is the most suitable model for Essen. According to the stakeholders' validation workshop, Lausanne shows great dependency on its DPP model in the city. The next step to revert this logic was the PPP, yet simply as an evolution on the business/social model of the city for this sector. Consequently, Lausanne aspires to include further involvement of stakeholders, as Eqlosion attempted in the workshop, by establishing further links and interactions. In Nilüfer, the situation was a bit more divided: the lack of sustainable mobility demands clearly signal a shift towards a PPP model, although several key stakeholders could see the potential of U/DC as well insofar as an informal, socially rooted, and highly networked transport system called *dolmuş*—share taxis—works efficiently (Özbilen, 2016). This informal mobility system would require a sharing economy platform based on Data Commons to enhance its socioeconomic impact in the metropolitan area of Bursa (Calzada & Almirall, 2020; Yakowitz, 2011). Essen was already implementing several mobility systems integrating citizens through parking and public transport apps. In the next chapter, Chapter 4, REPLICATING, the way smart cities interact between each other and, most importantly, learn from each other, will be shown. In this chapter, several specific smart city actions will be detailed. Chapter 3, DEMOCRATISING, focuses on the broad picture and the multi-stakeholder policy framework analysis.

Finally, in the ICT sector, Essen chose U/DC, whereas Lausanne and Nilüfer preferred PPP and PPAP, respectively. This sector witnessed the marginal selection of the DPP, acknowledging a weak potential to absorb the investment in data governance and regulation, while Essen embraced new initiatives on Data Commons (U/DC) as a way to take the lead in the post-GDPR context instead. Lausanne admitted its clear weakness in this field, and Nilüfer demonstrated its preliminary smart city platform project led by the university.

3.5 Conclusion

This chapter aimed to shed light on the helix frameworks from the SI perspective by extending the Triple- and Quadruple helix frameworks via suggesting an evidence-based ex novo framework called Penta helix, which has been comparatively operationalised in three case studies. Based on the Penta helix framework, this chapter showed the following for each case study: (i) a unique multi-stakeholder composition, degree of influence, and proactivity per helix; (ii) a diverse set of strategic preferences on business/social models per smart city sector; and (iii) a constant presence of the fifth helix as intermediaries, by concluding that (iv) there is a willingness among stakeholders to increasingly experiment with additional diverse democratic arrangements (beyond the PPP).

Although extant literature on the European model of smart cities presents a detailed illustration of the multi-stakeholder policy frameworks (Späth & Knieling, 2020), there has been little research to compare the helix frameworks and even less evidence-based data on analysing the stakeholders' compositions and strategic preferences in specific urban contexts (Yigitcanlar, Foth, & Kamruzzaman, 2019). One of the major reasons for the lack of evidence might be the hegemonic assumptions around the self-referential PPP model. Considering the newness of opening up towards a wider approach, we can assume the consequences for this absence of rich approaches, which could be seen in the way the term stakeholder adopts a vacuum and apolitical significance (Cardullo & Kitchin, 2018). This does not reflect the reality full of complex and intertwined interactions among stakeholders. In addition, it underestimates the agency and the transformational role that several stakeholders pervasively may take by germinating SI as an iterative joint multi-stakeholder process. Therefore, smart cities by themselves do not necessarily lead to greater democracy, as envisaged by advocates of the term long ago, but rather to a potential risk for generalising pervasive forms of algorithmic extractivism and surveillance capitalism (Gekker & Hind, 2019; Milanovic, 2019; Zuboff, 2019), whose substantial aim is to monetise all bits of citizens' lives. Building on this, this chapter—by comparing three cities—provided evidence for demonstrating how their multi-stakeholder composition brings about a diverse set of strategic priorities resulting in different business/social models.

The literature review on the helix multi-stakeholder framework and the resulting business/social models helped in discussing various selected dimensions, which then opened up avenues to raise further findings that can inform future empirical research on this topic. In the prospects of future research addressing democratic legitimacy-related questions smart cities face, this chapter shed light on a further nuanced empirical demonstration regarding the Penta helix framework playing a role in creating less technocratic smart cities. Apart from addressing the research questions, this chapter encourages scholars to follow the methodological rationale that was suggested by taking up comparative case study research approach that highlights novel analytical practices carried out in the broad SCC H2020 European framework bringing together not less than 117 European smart cities, which, in itself, is an opportunity to further explore the research questions elucidated. Especially when a field is in the emergent stage, case studies offer rich comparative understanding and allow researchers to adopt exploratory approaches to describe novel frameworks like the suggested Penta helix.

In summary, this chapter, acknowledging the preliminary exploratory findings stemming from this intensive fieldwork action research study conducted in three European cities encourages critical scholars working in the SI field to engage in applied research pertaining to democratic smart city-building through the Penta helix framework. Consequently, the private sector, the public sector, academia, and civil society can come together—assisted by the fifth helix, the intermediaries, social entrepreneurs, or/and activists, who can have the capacity to enhance the plurality towards a democratic smart city—and fulfil ambitions of a wide multiplicity of stakeholders who co-exist and act in the city. The research questions established in this chapter serve as a trigger for a much-needed push in influencing the H2020-SCC policy framework programme in augmenting the role that SI—stemming from the renowned European social market economy approach—plays in smart cities. Other researchers can actively reuse this research to match the growing contribution that SI makes at the grassroots level in building democratic smart cities in Europe. This chapter was a direct invitation to do so: there is plenty of opportunities to foster SI through the intermediation produced by a wide range of plural agents. This chapter referred to them as the 'fifth helix', sometimes visible but not always. Instead, their contribution might produce opportunities to democratise the smart city by protecting citizens' digital rights and helping the most vulnerable ones in our communities.

References

Afonso, O., Monteiro, S., & Thompson, M. (2012). A growth model for the quadruple helix. *Journal of Business Economics and Management, 13*(5), 849–865. https://doi.org/10.3846/16111699.2011.626438.

Ahonen, L., & Hämäläinen, T. (2012). CLIQ: A practical approach to the quadruple helix and more open innovation. In S. Macgregor, & T. Carleton (Eds.), *Sustaining innovation. Collaboration models in a complex world.* Cham: Springer.

Albino, V., Berardi, U., & Dangelico, R. M. (2015). Smart cities: Definitions, dimensions, performance, and initiatives. *Journal of Urban Technology, 22*(1), 3–21. https://doi.org/10.1080/10630732.2014.942092.

Allen, B., Tamindael, L. E., Bickerton, S. H., & Cho, W. (2020). Does citizen coproduction lead to better urban services in smart cities projects? An empirical study on e-participation in a mobile big data platform. *Government Information Quarterly, 37*(1), 101412. https://doi.org/10.1016/j.gig.2019.101412.

Anderson, T. S., Michael, E. K., & Peirce, J. J. (2012). Innovative approaches for managing public-private academic partnerships in big science and engineering. *Public Organization Review, 12*(1), 1–22. https://doi.org/10.1007/s11115-010-0142-3.

Angelidou, M., & Psaltoglou, A. (2017). An empirical investigation of social innovation initiatives for sustainable urban development. *Sustainable Cities and Society, 33*, 113–125. https://doi.org/10.1016/j.scs.2017.05.016.

Baack, S. (2015). Datafication and empowerment: How the open data movement re-articulates notions of democracy, participation, and journalism. *Big Data & Society, 2*(2), 1–11. https://doi.org/10.1177/2053951715594634.

Barcelona City Council. (2018). *Decidim.* Retrieved from: https://www.decidim.barcelona/.

Barns, S. (2020). *Making sense of platform intermediation. Platform urbanism: Negotiating platform ecosystems in connected cities.* Singapore: Springer.

Bartels, K. (2020). Transforming the relational dynamics of urban governance: How social innovation research can create a trajectory for learning and change? *Urban Studies.* https://doi.org/10.1177/0042098019889290.

Bollier, D. (2015). *Commoning as a transformative social paradigm. The next system project.* Retrieved from: http://www.thenextsystem.org/commoning-as-a-transformative-social-paradigm/.

Bollier, D., & Helfrich, S. (2016). *Patterns of commoning: The commons strategies group.* Levellers Press.

Borsboom-Van Beurden, J., Kallaos, J., Gindroz, B., Costa, S., & Riegler, J. (2019). *Smart city guidance package: A roadmap for integrated planning and implementation of smart city projects.* Brussels: EIP-SCC.

Brogaard, L. (2017). The impact of innovation training on successful outcomes in public–private partnerships. *Public Management Review, 19*(8), 1184–1205. https://doi.org/10.1080/14719037.2016.1272710.

Bund, E., Gerhard, U., & Hoelscher, M. (2015). A methodological framework for measuring social innovation. *Historical Social Research, 40*, 48–78.

Butzlaff, F. (2020). Between empowerment and abuse: Citizen participation beyond the post-democratic turn. *Democratization, 27*(3), 477–493. https://doi.org/10.1080/13510347.2019.1707809.

Callon, M. (1999). The role of lay people in the production and dissemination of scientific knowledge. *Science, Technology and Society, 4*(1), 81–94. https://doi.org/10.1177/097172189900400106.

Calzada, I. (2016). (Un)plugging smart cities with urban transformations: Towards multistakeholder city-regional complex urbanity? *URBS, Revista de Estudios Urbanos y Ciencias Sociales, 6*(2), 25–45.

Calzada, I. (2018a). *D.8.4. Report on conclusions of the interviews and the validation workshops.* Oxford: University of Oxford.

Calzada, I. (2018b). Deciphering smart city citizenship: The techno-politics of data and urban co-operative platforms. *Revista International de Estudios Vascos, RIEV, 63*(1-2), 42–81. https://doi.org/10.13140/RG.2.2.24498.35524/6.

Calzada, I. (2018c). From smart cities to experimental cities? In V. M. B. Giorgino, & Z. Walsh (Eds.), *Co-designing economies in transition: Radical approaches in dialogue with contemplative social sciences.* Cham: Springer. https://doi.org/10.1007/978-3-319-66592-4_11.

Calzada, I. (2018d). Local entrepreneurship through a multistakeholders' tourism living lab in the post-violence/peripheral era in the Basque Country. *Regional Science Policy & Practice, 11*(3), 1–16. https://doi.org/10.1111/rsp3.12130.

Calzada, I. (2018e). (Smart) Citizens from data providers to decision-makers? The case study of Barcelona. *Sustainability, 10*(9), 3252. https://doi.org/10.3390/su10093252.

Calzada, I. (2019). Data spaces and democracy. *RSA Journal, 2*, 40–43. https://doi.org/10.13140/RG.2.2.35392/89601/1.

Calzada, I., & Almirall, E. (2019). Barcelona's grassroots-led urban experimentation: Deciphering the 'data commons' policy scheme. In *Zenodo. Data for Policy 2019, 11-12 June, London, UCL.* https://doi.org/10.5281/zenodo.2604618.

Calzada, I., & Almirall, E. (2020). Data ecosystems for protecting European citizens' digital rights. *Transforming Government: People, Process and Policy (TGPPP), 14*(2). https://doi.org/10.1108/TG-03-2020-0047.

Calzada, I., & Cobo, C. (2015). Unplugging: Deconstructing the smart city. *Journal of Urban Technology, 22*(1), 23–43. https://doi.org/10.1080/10630732.2014.971535.

Calzada, I., & Cowie, P. (2017). Beyond smart and data-driven city-regions? Rethinking stakeholder-helixes strategies. *Regions Magazine, 308*(4), 25–28. https://doi.org/10.1080/13673882.2017.11958675.

Caragliu, A., & Del Bo, C. F. (2019). Smart innovative cities: The impact of smart city policies on urban innovation. *Technological Forecasting and Social Change, 142*, 373–383. https://doi.org/10.1016/j.techfore.2018.07.022.

Carayannis, E. G., & Campbell, D. F. J. (2010). Triple helix, quadruple helix and quintuple helix and how do knowledge, innovation and the environment relate to each other? A proposed framework for a trans-disciplinary analysis of sustainable development and social ecology. *International Journal of Social Ecology and Sustainable Development (IJSESD), 1*(1), 41–69. https://doi.org/10.4018/978-1-4666-0882-5.ch3.8.

Carayannis, E. G., & Campbell, D. F. J. (2012). Mode 3 knowledge production in quadruple helix innovation systems. *SpringerBriefs in Business: vol. 7.* https://doi.org/10.1007/978-1-4614-2062-0_1.

Cardullo, P., & Kitchin, R. (2018). *Smart urbanism and smart citizenship: The neoliberal logic of 'citizen-focused' smart cities in Europe.* The programmable city working paper. Paper 39. Maynooth.

Cavallini, S., Soldi, R., Friedl, J., & Volpe, M. (2016). *Using the quadruple helix approach to accelerate the transfer of research and innovation results to regional growth.* Brussels: European Union Committee of the Regions.

Christmann, G. B. (2020). Introduction: Struggling with innovations. Social innovations and conflicts in urban development and planning. *European Planning Studies, 28*(3), 423–433. https://doi.org/10.1080/09654313.2019.1639396.

Deakin, M. (2014). Smart cities: The state-of-the-art and governance challenge. *Triple Helix, 1*(1), 1–16. https://doi.org/10.1186/s40604-014-0007-9.

Deakin, M., Mora, L., & Reid, A. (2018). The research and innovation of smart specialisation strategies: The transition from the triple to quadruple helix. In *27th international scientific conference on economic and social development, 1-2 March 2018, Rome*.

Dellenbaugh, M., Kip, M., & Bieniok, M. (2016). *Urban commons: Moving beyond state and market*. Basel/Berlin/Boston: Birkhäuser.

Desdemoustier, J., Crutzen, N., & Giffinger, R. (2019). Municipalities' understanding of the Smart City concept: An exploratory analysis in Belgium. *Technological Forecasting and Social Change*, *142*, 129–141. https://doi.org/10.1016/j.techfore.2018.10.029.

Domanski, D., Howaldt, J., & Kaletka, C. (2020). A comprehensive concept of social innovation and its implicationns for the local context - on the growing importance of social innovation ecosystems and infrastructures. *European Planning Studies*, *28*(3), 454–474. https://doi.org/10.1080/09654313.2019.1639397.

Donald, B., Glasmeier, A., Gray, M., & Lobao, L. (2014). Austerity in the city: Economic crisis and urban service decline? *Cambridge Journal of Regions, Economy and Society*, *7*(1), 3–15. https://doi.org/10.1093/cjres/rst040.

EIP-SCC. (2016). *Towards a joint investment programme for European smart cities: A consultation paper to stimulate action*. Brussels: European Commission.

Engelbert, J., Van Zoonen, L., & Hirzalla, F. (2018). Excluding citizens from the European smart city: The discourse practices of pursuing and granting smartness. *Technological Forecasting and Social Change*, *142*, 347–353. https://doi.org/10.1016/j.techfore.2018.08.020.

Engelbrecht, H. J. (2018). The (social) innovation—Subjective well-being nexus: Subjective well-being impacts as an additional assessment metric of technological and social innovations. *Innovation: The European Journal of Social Science Research*, *31*(3), 317–332. https://doi.org/10.1080/13511610.2017.1319262.

Essen. (2019). Retrieved from: https://replicate-project.eu/2nd-session-the-new-smelters-of-the-coal-heartland/.

Etzkowitz, H., & Leydesdorff, L. (2000). The dynamics of innovation: From national systems and mode 2 to a triple helix of university–industry–government relations. *Research Policy*, *29*, 109–123.

Etzkowitz, H., Ranga, M., Dzisah, J., & Zhou, C. (2007). University-industry-government interaction: The triple helix model of innovation. *Asia Pacific Tech Monitor*, *24*(1), 14–23.

Eubanks, V. (2017). *Automating inequality: How high-tech tools profile, police, and punish the poor*. NYC: St. Martin's Press.

European Commission. (2010). *Social innovation research in the European Union. Approaches, findings, and future directions*. Luxembourg: Publications Office of the European Union.

European Commission. (2016). *Creating the links for scaling smart cities solutions*. Eindhoven: H2020.

European Commission. (2017a). *The making of a smart city: Best practices across Europe*. Brussels: European Commission.

European Commission. (2017b). *The making of a smart city: Policy recommendations*. Brussels: European Commission.

European Commission. (2019). *Co-creating innovative public services for citizens and businesses*. Luxembourg: European Commission.

European Political Strategy Centre. (2019). *10 trends: Shaping democracy in a volatile world*. Brussels: EPSC.

Fields, D., Bissell, D., & Macrorie, R. (2020). Platform methods: Studying platform urbanism outside the black box. *Urban Geography*, 1–8. https://doi.org/10.1080/02723438.2020.1730642.

Forrer, J., Kee, J. E., Newcomer, K. E., & Boyer, E. (2010). Public-private partnerships and public accountability question. *Public Administration Review*, *70*(3), 475–484. https://doi.org/10.1111/j.1540-6210.2010.02161.x.

Frug, G. E. (2017). *The city: Private or public?*. London: LSE Cities Working Papers.

Gekker, A., & Hind, S. (2019). Infrastructural surveillance. *New Media & Society*. https://doi.org/10.1177/1461444819879426.

Goddard, J., & Kempton, L. (2016). *The civic university: Universities in leadership and management of place. RR2016/01*. Warwick: University of Warwick. https://doi.org/10.13140/RG.2.2.18136.29448.

Goldstein, B. T., & Mele, C. (2016). Governance within public–private partnerships and the politics of urban development. *Space and Polity*, *20*(2), 194–211. https://doi.org/10.1080/13562576.2016.1157968.

Grimm, R., Fox, C., Baines, S., & Albertson, K. (2013). Social innovation, an answer to contemporary societal challenges? Locating the concept in theory and practice. *Innovation: The European Journal of Social Science Research*, *26*(4), 436–455. https://doi.org/10.1080/13511610.2013.848163.

Grossi, G., & Pianezzi, D. (2017). Smart cities: Utopia or neoliberal ideology? *Cities*, *69*, 79–85. https://doi.org/10.1016/j.cities.2017.07.012.

Gunkel, D. J. (2018). *Robots rights*. Boston: The MIT Press.

Habermas, J. (2015). *The lure of technocracy*. London: Polity Press.

Halibas, A. S., Sibayan, R. O., & Maata, R. L. R. (2017). The penta helix model of innovation in Oman: An HEI perspective. *Interdisciplinary Journal of Information, Knowledge, and Management*, *12*, 159–172.

Hall, D. (2015). *Why public-private partnerships don't work: The many advantages of the public alternative*. Greenwich/UK: University of Greenwich/PSIRU (Public Services International Research Unit).

Han, B.-C. (2015). *The transparency society*. Standford: Standford University Press.

Harvey, D. (1997). The new urbanism and the communitarian trap. *Harvard Design Magazine*, *1*(3), 68–69.

Hicks, M. (2017). *Programmed inequality: How Britain discarded women technologists and lost its edge in computing*. Boston: The MIT Press.

Higdem, U. (2014). The co-creation of regional futures: Facilitating action research in regional foresight. *Futures*, *57*, 41–50. https://doi.org/10.1016/j.futures.2014.01.006.

Hollands, R. G. (2008). Will the real smart city please stand up? *City*, *12*(3), 303–320. https://doi.org/10.1080/13604810802479126.

Hollands, R. G. (2014). Critical interventions into the corporate smart city. *Cambridge Journal of Regions, Economy and Society*, *8*(1), 61–77. https://doi.org/10.1093/cjres/rsu011.

Iaione, C. (2015). *Governing the Urban Commons*. IJPL ISSUE 1/2015.

Janssen, M., & Kuk, G. (2016). The challenges and limits of big data algorithms in technocratic governance. *Government Information Quarterly*, *33*(3), 371–377. https://doi.org/10.1016/j.giq.2016.08.011.

Johnson, P. A., Robinson, P. J., & Philpot, S. (2019). Type, tweet, tap, and pass: How smart city technology is creating a transactional citizen. *Government Information Quarterly*. https://doi.org/10.1016/j.giq.2019.101414.

Keith, M., & Calzada, I. (2018). Back to the 'urban commons'? Social innovation through new co-operative forms in Europe. In *Bridging European urban transformations*. Brussels: ESRC. https://doi.org/10.13140/RG.2.2.22227.27688/1.

Kempin Reuter, T. (2019). Human rights and the city: Including marginalized communities in urban development and smart cities. *Journal of Human Rights*, 1–21. https://doi.org/10.1080/14754835.2019.1629887.

Kennedy, H., Poell, T., & Van Dijck, J. (2015). Data and agency. *Big Data & Society*, *2*(2). https://doi.org/10.1177/2053951715621569.

Kitchin, R. (2014). The real-time city? Big data and smart urbanism. *GeoJournal*, *79*, 1–14. https://doi.org/10.1007/s10708-013-9516-8.

Kitchin, R., Coletta, C., Evans, L., Heaphy, L., & Mac Donncha, D. (2017). *Smart cities, urban technocrats, epistemic communities and advocacy coalitions*. The Programmable City Working Paper. Paper 26. Maynooth.

Komninos, N., & Kakderi, C. (2019). *Smart cities in the post-algorithmic era: Integrating technologies, platforms, and governance*. Chentelham: Edward Elgar.

Kourtit, K., & Nijkamp, P. (2012). Smart cities in the innovation age. *Innovation: The European Journal of Social Science Research*, *25*(2), 93–95. https://doi.org/10.1080/1351610.2012.660331.

Kummitha, R. K. R. (2019). Smart cities and entrepreneurship: An agenda for future research. *Technological Forecasting and Social Change*, *149*. https://doi.org/10.1016/j.techfore.2019.119763.

Kummitha, R. K. R., & Crutzen, N. (2019). Smart cities and the citizen-driven internet of things: A qualitative inquiry into an emerging smart city. *Technological Forecasting and Social Change*, *140*, 44–53. https://doi.org/10.1016/j.techfore.2018.12.001.

Labaeye, A. (2017). *Sharing cities: Using urban data to reclaim public space as a commons*. Retrieved from: http://www.shareable.net/blog/sharing-cities-using-urban-data-to-reclaim-public-space-as-a-commons.

Lausanne. (2019). Retrieved from: https://replicate-project.eu/4th-session-roadmap-for-the-realization-of-an-eco-district-including-development-of-medium-depth-geothermal-energy-in-urban-areas/.

Lawton Smith, H., & Leydesdorff, L. (2014). The triple helix in the context of global change: Dynamics and challenges. *Prometheus*, *32*(4), 321–336. https://doi.org/10.1080/08109028.2014.972135.

Lewontin, R. C. (2000). *The triple Helix: Gene, organism, and environment*. Cambridge, MA/London: Harvard University Press.

Leydesdorff, L. (2012). The triple helix, quadruple helix, …, and an N-tuple of helices: Explanatory models for analyzing the knowledge-based economy? *Journal of the Knowledge Economy*, *3*(1), 25–35. https://doi.org/10.1007/s13132-011-0049-4.

Leydesdorff, L., & Deakin, M. (2011). The triple-helix model of smart cities: A neo-evolutionary perspective. *Journal of Urban Technology*, *18*(2), 53–63. https://doi.org/10.1080/10630732.2011.601111.

Leydesdorff, L., & Fritsch, M. (2006). Measuring the knowledge base of regional innovation systems in Germany in terms of a triple helix dynamics. *Research Policy*, *35*(10), 1538–1553.

Lombardi, P., Giordano, S., Caragliu, A., Del Bo, C., Deakin, M., Nijkamp, P., et al. (2011). An advanced triple-helix network model for smart cities performance. In *Research memorandum 2011–45*. Amsterdam: Vrije Universiteit.

Madsen, A. K. (2018). Data in the smart city: How incongruent frames challenge the transition from ideal to practice. *Big Data & Society*, *5*(2), 1–13. https://doi.org/10.1177/2053951718802321.

Masek Tonkovic, A., Veckie, E., & Veckie, V. W. (2017). Applications of Penta Helix Model in economic development. *Economy of Eastern Croatia Yesterday, Today, Tomorrow*, *4*, 385–393.

Mazzucato, M. (2015). *The entrepreneurial state: Debunking public vs. private sector myths*. London: Anthen Press.

Mazzucato, M. (2018). *Mission-oriented research & innovation in the European Union: A problem-solving approach to fuel innovation-led growth*. Brussels: European Commission.

Mihci, H. (2019). Is measuring social innovation a mission impossible? *Innovation: The European Journal of Social Science Research*. https://doi.org/10.1080/13511610.2019.1705149.

Milanovic, B. (2019). *Capitalism, alone: The future of the system that rules the world*. Cambridge and London: Harvard University Press.

Moulaert, F. (2009). Social innovation: Institutionally embedded, territorialy (re)produced. In D. MacCallum, F. Moulaert, J. Hillier, & S. V. Haddock (Eds.), *Social innovation and territorial development*. London: Routledge.

Moulaert, F., & MacCallum, D. (2019). *Advanced introduction to social innovation*. Cheltenham, UK: Edward Elgar.

Moulaert, F., MacCallum, D., Mehmood, A., & Hamdouch, A. (2014). *The international handbook on social innovation: Collective action, social learning and transdisciplinary research*. Cheltenham, UK: Edward Elgar.

Moulaert, F., Martinelli, F., González, S., & Swyngedouw, E. (2007). Introduction: Social innovation and governance in European cities. *European Urban and Regional Studies*, *14*(3), 195–209. https://doi.org/10.1177/0969776407077737.

Moulaert, F., & Mehmood, A. (2020). Towards a social innovation (SI) based epistemology in local development analysis: Lessons from twenty years of EU research. *European Planning Studies*, *28*(3), 434–453. https://doi.org/10.1080/09654313.2019.1639401.

Murphy, G. B., Tocher, N., & Ward, B. (2016). An examination of public private academic partnerships: Does program success enhance university performance outcomes? *Public Organization Review*, *16*(1), 95–115. https://doi.org/10.1007/s11115-014-0298-3.

Nesti, G., & Graziano, P. R. (2019). The democratic anchorage of governance networks in smart cities: An empirical assessment. *Public Management Review*, 1–20. https://doi.org/10.1080/14719037.2019.1588355.

Ng, S. T., Wong, J. M. W., & Wong, K. K. W. (2013). A public private people partnerships (P4) process framework for infrastructure development in Hong Kong. *Cities*, *31*, 370–381. https://doi.org/10.1016/j.cities.2012.12.002.

Nilssen, M. (2018). To the smart city and beyond? Developing a typology of smart urban innovation. *Technological Forecasting and Social Change*, *142*, 98–104. https://doi.org/10.1016/j.techfore.2018.07.060.

Nilüfer. (2019). Retrieved from: https://replicate-project.eu/6th-session-socio-economic-development-from-below/.

Ostrom, E. (1990). *Governing the commons: The evolution of institutions for collective action*. Cambridge, UK: Cambridge University Press.

Özbilen, B. (2016). *Integration of Dolmus as a paratransit mode to the existing public transport network: Ankara example*. The Middle East Technical University.

Paskaleva, K., Cooper, I., Linde, P., Peterson, B., & Götz, C. (2015). *Stakeholder engagement in the Smart City: Making living labs work. Transforming City governments for successful smart cities*. Cham: Springer.

Pel, B., Wittmayer, J., Dorland, J., & Soggard Jorgensen, M. (2019). Unpacking the social innovation ecosystem: An empirically grounded typology of empowering network constellations. *Innovation: The European Journal of Social Science Research*. https://doi.org/10.1080/13511610.2019.1705147.

Pestoff, V., Brandsen, T., & Verschuere, B. (2013). *New public governance, the third sector, and co-production*. Oxon: Routledge.

Poppen, F., & Decker, R. (2018). The intermediary as an institutional entrepreneur: Institutional change and stability in triple-helix cooperation. *Triple Helix*, *5*(1), 1–22. https://doi.org/10.1186/s40604-018-0063-7.

Prainsack, B. (2019). Logged out: Ownership, exclusion and public value in the digital data and information commons. *Big Data & Society*, *6*(1), 1–15. https://doi.org/10.1177/2053951719829773.

Preskill, H., & Beer, T. (2012). *Evaluating social innovation*. Center for Evaluation Innovation.

Ranchordás, S. (2019). Nudging citizens through technology in smart cities. *International Review of Law, Computers & Technology*, 1–23. https://doi.org/10.1080/13600869.2019.1590928.

Replicate, E. U. (2018). *City-to-city learning programme*. Brussels: European Commission. Retrieved from: www.replicate-project.eu/city2citylearning.

Rossi, U. (2016). The variegated economics and the potential politics of the smart city. *Territory, Politics, Governance*, *4*(3), 337–353. https://doi.org/10.1080/21622671.2015.1036913.

Sabato, S., Vanhercke, B., & Verschraegen, G. (2017). Connecting entrepreneurship with policy experimentation? The EU framework for social innovation. *Innovation: The European Journal of Social Science Research*, *30*(2), 147–167. https://doi.org/10.1080/13511610.2017.1282308.

Sandoval, M. (2019). Entrepreneurial activism? Platform cooperativism between subversion and co-optation. *Critical Sociology*, 1–17. https://doi.org/10.1177/0896920519870577.

Schubert, C. (2018). Social innovation. A new instrument of social change? In W. Rammert, A. Windeler, M. Hutter, & H. Knoblauch (Eds.), *Innovation society today. Perspectives, fields, and cases*. Wiesbaden: Springer VS.

SCIS. (2019). *Lighthouse projects*. Retrieved from: https://smartcities-infosystem.eu/scc-lighthouse-projects.

Siapera, E., & Papadopoulou, L. (2016). Entrepreneurialism or cooperativism? *Journalism Practice*, *10*(2), 178–195. https://doi.org/10.1080/17512786.2015.1125760.

Simon, J., Bass, T., Boelman, V., & Mulgan, G. (2017). *Digital democracy: The tools transforming political engagement*. London: NESTA.

Späth, P., & Knieling, J. (2020). How EU-funded smart city experiments influence modes of planning for mobility: Observations from Hamburg. *Urban Transformations*, *2*(1), 1–17. https://doi.org/10.1186/s42854-020-0006-2.

Stehlin, J., Hodson, M., & McMeekin, A. (2020). Platform mobilities and the production of urban space: Toward a typology of platformization trajectories. *Economy and Space*, 1–19. https://doi.org/10.1177/0308518X19896801.

SUI (Smart Urban Intermediaries). (2018). *Smart cities, social innovation, and smart urban development*.

Swyngedouw, E. (2005). Governance innovation and the citizen: The janus face of governance-beyond-the-state. *Urban Studies*, *42*(11), 1991–2006. https://doi.org/10.1080/00420980500279869.

Terstriep, J., Rehfeld, D., & Kleverbeck, M. (2020). Favourablee social innovation ecosystem(s)—An explorative research. *European Planning Studies*, 1–25. https://doi.org/10.1080/09654313.2019.1708868.

Trencher, G. (2018). Towards the smart city 2.0: Empirical evidence of using smartness as a tool for tackling social challenges. *Technological Forecasting and Social Change*, *142*, 117–128. https://doi.org/10.1016/j.techfore.2018.07.033.

Turner, B. S. (2017). Contemporary citizenship: Four types. *Journal of Citizenship and Globalisation Studies*, *1*(1), 10–23. https://doi.org/10.1515/jcgs-2017-0002.

Vadrot, A. B. M. (2020). Re-thinking the conditions for social change and innovation. *Innovation: The European Journal of Social Science Research*, *33*(1), 1–3. https://doi.org/10.1080/13511610.2020.1713455.

Vallance, P., Tewdwr-Jones, M., & Kempton, L. (2020). Building collaborative platforms for urban innovation: Newcastle City futures as a quadruple helix intermediary. *European Urban and Regional Studies*, 1–7. https://doi.org/10.1177/0969776420905630.

Van de Broeck, P., Mehmood, A., Paidakaki, A., & Parra, C. (2019). *Social innovation as political transformation through for a better world.* Cheltenham, UK and Northampton, MA, USA: Edward Elgar Publishing.

Vandervyvere, H. (2017). *Recommendations on EU R&I and regulatory policies: Why may replication (not) be happening?.* EU Smart Cities Information System. D32. 3A Retrieved from: https://smartcities-infosystem.eu/newsroom/news/scis-policy-analysis-%E2%80%93-why-may-rcplication-not-be-happening.

Vanolo, A. (2016). Is there anybody out there? The place and role of citizens in tomorrow's smart cities. *Futures*, *82*, 26–36. https://doi.org/10.1016/j.futures.2016.05.010.

Voorberg, W. H., Bekkers, V. J. J. M., & Tummers, L. G. (2015). A systematic review of co-creation and co-production: Embarking on the social innovation journey. *Public Management Review*, *17*(9), 1333–1357. https://doi.org/10.1080/14719037.2014.930505.

Yakowitz, J. (2011). Tragedy of the data commons. *Harvard Journal of Law & Technology*, *25*(1), 1–68.

Yigitcanlar, T., Foth, M., & Kamruzzaman, M. (2019). Towards post-anthropocentric cities: Reconceptualizing smart cities to evade urban ecocide. *Journal of Urban Technology*, *26*(2), 147–152. https://doi.org/10.1080/10630732.2018.1524249.

Yin, R. K. (2011). *Applications of case study research.* London: SAGE.

Zandbergen, D., & Uitermark, J. (2019). In search of the smart citizen: Republican and cybernetic citizenship in the smart city. *Urban Studies*. https://doi.org/10.1177/0042098019847410.

Zuboff, S. (2019). *The age of surveillance capitalism: The fight for a human future at the new frontier of power.* London: Profile.

Chapter 4

REPLICATING smart city citizenship: City-to-city learning programme

Chapter outline

4.1 Replication may not be happening

In the recent years, the concept of smart cities has gained momentum among policymakers in Europe (Borsboom-van Beurden, Kallaos, Gindroz, Costa, & Riegler, 2019; Coletta, Evans, Heaphy, & Kitchin, 2018; EIP-SCC, 2016; Johnson, Robinson, & Philpot, 2019; Kitchin, Coletta, Evans, Heaphy, & Mac Donncha, 2017; Nesti & Graziano, 2019; Trencher, 2018). Moreover, smart cities have certainly reached the post-General Data Protection Regulation (GDPR) algorithmic era (Calzada, 2019a, 2019b; Janssen & Kuk, 2016; Komninos & Kakderi, 2019), where a truly smart city in Europe could be established, in which citizens can move in relative anonymity and be identified only when needed and under conditions that allow for a significant control over what can be done with their own data (Zuboff, 2019).

Hence, against the backdrop of this self-demanding scenario, city representatives in Europe are not solely in charge of co-ordinating funded lighthouse projects under the European Commission's Horizon 2020: Smart Cities and Communities (EC-H2020-SCC) framework programme (European Commission, 2016, 2017a, 2017b, 2017c, 2017d; SCIS, 2019). This group must also engage in joint and continuous conversations with diverse and numerous groups of city-regional stakeholders, as well as consider a generation of smart technologies (including the increasingly autonomous machine intelligence that

Smart City Citizenship. https://doi.org/10.1016/B978-0-12-815300-0.00004-6

can gather and analyse granular and real-time 'Big Data') if it is to effectively tackle the most pressing economic, technologic, ethical, and social issues that face European cities (Aurigi & Odendaal, 2020; Caragliu, Del Bo, & Nijkamp, 2011; Cardullo & Kitchin, 2018; European Commission, 2017a). The smart cities that prosper in the future will likely be those that are best equipped at learning from other cities—and directly from their stakeholders—for replicating, adapting, and scaling up initiatives by adopting a complex and socially innovative constellation of post-GDPR smart technologies predicated upon artificial intelligence (AI) and reflexive autonomous machine learning, digital innovation and the Internet of Things (enhanced by 5G and new sensor technologies), and quantum leaps in data infrastructure and capacities (Bartels, 2020; Heinelt & Terizakis, 2020; Potjer & Hajer, 2017). Additionally, city representatives should be equally prepared to identify the risks associated with the techno-politics of data and the democratic misalignment that the gig economy generates through disruptions and power imbalances among stakeholders (Barns, 2020; Dyer-Witheford, 2020; Graham, 2020; Graham, Kitchin, Mattern, & Shaw, 2019; Sadowski, 2020; Woodcock & Graham, 2019; Zuboff, 2019).

In the EC-H2020-SCC policy framework, replication is defined as 'the possibility of transporting or copying results from a pilot case to other geographical areas, albeit potentially different boundary conditions', thus slightly recommending that 'if a pilot was proven to work in one community or region, it could be exported to other communities or regions (indigenously or abroad), but taking into account that the boundary conditions could be quite different from those in piloted community or region' (European Commission, 2017c, p. 8).

However, far from being prepared for such a complex techno-political scenario, the policy framework design by the EC-H2020-SCC explicitly encourages cities and their representatives to apply pure replication without deeply considering the examination of further contextual elements characterising the uniqueness, singularity, adaptability, and scalability of the projected urban interventions (European Commission, 2016, 2017a, 2017b, 2017c). Actually, in these replicated interventions, ecosystems of stakeholders and their related power interdependencies ultimately seem to define the adoption of one or another technology more than their mere rational and mechanic cost-value analysis (Grimmelikhuijsen & Porumbescu, 2017; Jilke, Petrovsky, Meuleman, & James, 2017; Kitchin, 2017; Riegler, 2017; Walker, James, & Brewer, 2017).

In contrast, a report also published by the European Commission (Vandervyvere, 2017, p. 1) strikingly confirms the hypothesis in line with the research question of this chapter: 'replication may not be happening' among smart cities of the EC-H2020-SCC framework programme, as the policy designers extrapolated. As such, the notable conclusion of this report is the point of departure of this chapter when it refers to replication as 'a quest for the Holy Grail: everyone is searching, but no one seems to be able to find it' (Vandervyvere, 2017, p. 6). The report clearly states that the replication of smart urban energy, mobility, and Information Communication Technologies (ICT) solutions for a clean energy future is challenging. The report reveals that 70% of the currently existing smart city pilot interventions are undermined due to very 'specific solutions that are difficult to adapt to local contexts' (Vandervyvere, 2017, p. 8). To some extent, this report resonates with the rebuttal statement formulated by the urban scholar, Ayona Datta, and with this chapter, thereby making sense of the replication panacea deadlock in the policymaking of smart cities, as formulated so far by the European Commission: 'The "urban" is not "science". It cannot be measured, *replicated*, and forecast like other sciences. The urban is an imaginary, a relationship between multiple spaces and scales from the personal to the global, a site of politics and governance. The urban is much more than "science"' (Datta, 2018, p. 1).

Thus, to shed light on this discussion, this chapter considers the main findings of the fieldwork action research (Forester, Kuitenbrouwer, & Laws, 2019; Higdem, 2014), undertaken in the specific EU-H2020-SCC Replicate project from February 2016 to December 2019. This action was operationally embodied in the *City-to-City Learning Programme* during the entirety of 2019, with the direct involvement of the six Replicate cities, without making any hierarchical distinction among the three lighthouse cities (San Sebastian in Spain, Florence in Italy, and Bristol in the United Kingdom), as well as the three follower or fellow cities (Essen in Germany, Lausanne in Switzerland, and Nilüfer in Turkey), as established explicitly by the programme. The term used to refer to the latter has been changed during the implementation of the EC-H2020-SCC framework programme from follower cities to fellow cities, which may slightly show the potential misalignment and the subsequent gradual fix in the understanding of the replication function among different cities, regardless of their hierarchical position. Furthermore, from the start, the replication nature appeared to be even more challenging in the EC-H2020-SCC Replicate project, as follower cities were relegated to a passive role in processes for being unidirectional, hierarchical, mechanistic, solutionist (Morozov, 2013), and technocratic. Local stakeholders in each fellow city were depicted only as developers of solutions already prepared and packed in the lighthouse cities. This replication-driven policy design took for granted the assumption that the three lighthouse cities could be the only ones spelling out urban solutions, without considering whether, first, the urban implementations in the lighthouse cities were appropriate for the fellow cities, and, second, the fellow cities already had ongoing replicable models worth considering. Instead, this chapter offers an alternative from the Social Innovation (SI) perspective (Bartels, 2020; Mihci, 2019; Moulaert & MacCallum, 2019; Pel, Wittmayer, Dorland, & Jørgensen, 2019; Terstriep, Rehfeld, & Kleverbeck, 2020), which is an inversion of Morozov's description. That is, interaction and learning among cities and their related stakeholders would be multidirectional, radial, dynamic, iterative, and democratic.

The chapter contributes to the literature on the replication problem among smart cities by revealing the research findings and results from the Replicate EC-H2020-SCC project and challenging the given institutional, technocratic (as described by Morozov) policy guidelines applied in lighthouse cities to follower-fellow cities. It, instead, examines the alternative, more diverse, and democratic process of interaction and learning in the six Replicate cities. The action research intervention took the form of a webinar series, *City-to-City Learning Programme* (ReplicateEU, 2019), in two phases.

First, it employed the active direct engagement of the wide range of EU-Replicate project's stakeholders (150 registered participants and almost 300 offline views). Second, it employed broad dissemination among the network of stakeholders of the 17 lighthouse projects by reaching the entire H2020-SCC targeted audience (SCIS, 2020). The resulting programme was operationalised through the leading role of the six-city Replicate representatives, who acted as intermediaries and bricoleurs of the replication-learning process (SUI, 2018; Poppen & Decker, 2018; Calzada & Cowie, 2017; see Chapter 3). In the proposed programme, the concept replication was channelled through a learning loop characterised by singularity, adaptability, and scalability.

The chapter proceeds as follows. The next section examines the policy context until 2019, encompassing 17 lighthouse projects (46 lighthouse cities and 71 fellow cities) with their related replication strategies, city composition, networks, and stakeholders' involvement (Bryson, 2004). The third section reviews the literature from the SI perspective in response to the research question (Mihci, 2019; Moulaert & MacCallum, 2019; Pel et al., 2019; Schubert, 2018; Terstriep et al., 2020; Voorberg, Bekkers, & Tummers, 2015). The fourth section describes how the *City-to-City Learning Programme* was established and implemented among the six Replicate cities. The fifth section presents the potential content for the replication plans of the fellow cities stemming from the *City-to-City Learning Programme*. The chapter concludes by suggesting five potential transitions to enhance replication among smart cities' stakeholders and outlines directions for the future research on SI.

4.2 Benchmarking EC-H2020-SCC lighthouse projects' replication strategies

This section analyses policy documents of the EC-H2020-SCC framework programme (SCIS, 2019) and, in particular, conducts a generic benchmarking about the explicit replication strategies mentioned through the websites and materials provided by each of the 17 ongoing lighthouse projects (Atelier, 2020; City Exchange, 2020; MakingCity, 2020; Matchup, 2020; Pocityf, 2020; Ruggedised, 2020; Sparcs, 2020; Stardust, 2020; Triangulum, 2020; Growsmarter, 2019; Smarter Together, 2019; IRIS, 2020; ReplicateEU, 2019; MySmartLife, 2017; SmartenCity, 2017; Remourban, 2016; Sharing Cities, 2016). However, it is worth clarifying that this section comparatively identifies general traces and policy evidence on the EC-H2020-SCC policy context by focusing somewhat on the specific strategic formulation about replication in the ongoing 17 lighthouse projects. It is, therefore, outside the scope of this chapter to offer an exhaustive and in-depth analysis of each project's replication strategy and process.

17 Lighthouse Projects (up to 2019)	City-Network-Composition		Round/Period/Budget/ Website	Replication Strategy: (LC=Lighthouse Cities; FC=Follower-Fellow Cities)
	Lighthouse Cities (46)	Follower-Fellow Cities (71)		
1. **Growsmarter**	**Stockholm, SE** Barcelona, ES Koln, DE	Cork, IE Graz, AT Porto, PT Suceava, RO Valetta, MT	SCC1-2014 2015-2019 34M € https://grow-smarter.eu/home/	Based on "twelve groups of smart solutions entirely developed by the LC to be, thereafter, tested and adopted by the FC" (Growsmarter, 2019, p. 3).
2. **Remourban**	**Nottingham, UK** Tebebasi, TR Valladolid, ES	Miskolc, HU Seraing, BE	SCC1-2014 2015-2019 23M € http://www.remourban.eu/	Based on LC supply to FC demands' being entirely separated procedures (Remourban, 2016, p. 4).
3. **Triangulum**	**Stavanger, NO** Eindhoven, NL Manchester, UK	Tianjin, CHN Leipzig, DE Prague, CZ Sabadell, ES	SCC1-2014 2015-2019 29M € http://www.triangulum-project.eu/	Based on "a replication tool shown as a smart city decision-making tool, which stores the smart solutions achieved by the LC" (Triangulum, 2020, p. 1).
4. **Replicate**	**San Sebastian-Donostia, ES** Bristol, UK Florence, IT	Essen, DE Lausanne, CH Nilüfer, TR	SCC1-2015 2016-2021 29M € www.replicate-project.eu	Based on the *City-to-City Learning Programme* adopting a multidirectional approach jointly among the LC and FC' from the early beginning of 2016 (ReplicateEU, 2018). www.replicate-project.eu/city2citylearning
5. **Sharing Cities**	**London, UK** Lisbon, PT Milan, IT	Bordeaux, FR Burgas, BG Warsaw, PL	SCC1-2015 2016-2020 28M € http://www.sharingcities.eu/	Based on "the ambition being not less than making each follower city to be treated and make them act as a fellow city" (Sharing Cities, 2016, p. 6).
6. **SmartenCity**	**Vitoria-Gasteiz, ES** Sonderborg, DK Tartu, EE	Asenovgrad, GB Lecce, IT	SCC1-2015 2016-2021 32M € https://smartencity.eu/	Based on "capacity building workshops and thematic webinars from the LC to FC" (SmartenCity, 2017, p. 51).
7. **Smarter Together**	**Lyon, FR** Munich, DE Vienna, AT	Santiago de Compostela, ES Sofia, BG Venice, IT Yokohama, JP Kiev, UA	SCC1-2015 2016-2021 29M € https://www.smarter-together.eu/	Based on "enablers, key problems and challenges and solutions of the LC to be reproduced in the FC by gradually engaging them in the process" (Smarter Together, 2019, p. 7).
8. **My Smart Life**	**Nantes, FR** Hamburg, DE Helsinki, FI	Bydgoszcz, PL Palencia, ES Rijeka, HR Varna, BG	SCC1-2016 2016-2021 21M € https://www.mysmartlife.eu/	Based on "stage 2, after LC interventions, where FC will be involved, which are going to be learning during the project from the LC, and will apply their replication plans" (MySmartLife, 2017, p. 8; Späth & Knieling, 2020).
9. **Ruggedised**	**Rotterdam, NL** Glasgow, UK Umea, SE	Brno, CZ Gdansk, PL Parma, IT	SCC1-2016 2017-2021 19M € https://ruggedised.eu/	Based on "32 smart solutions in the LC and 27 follower solutions in the FC being entirely autonomous procedures" (Ruggedised, 2020, p. 1).
10. **IRIS**	**Nice, FR** Gothenburg, SE Utrecht, NL	Alexandroupolis, GR Focsani, RO Santa Cruz de Tenerife, ES Vaasa, FI	SCC1-2016 2017-2022 20M € https://irissmartcities.eu/	Based on "processes for scaling the solutions both inside and outside of the consortium" (IRIS, 2020, p. 38).
11. **Matchup**	**Valencia, ES** Antalya, TR Dresden, DE	Herzliya, IL Kerava, FI Ostend, BE Skopje, MA	SCC1-2016 2017-2022 19M € https://www.matchup-project.eu/	Based on "active involvement organising events" (Matchup, 2020, p. 1).
12. **Stardust**	**Pamplona-Iruñea, ES** Tampere, FI Trento, IT	Derry, UK Kozani, GR Cluj-Napoca, RO Litomerice, CZ	SCC1-2016 2017-2022 21M € http://stardustproject.eu/	Based on "FC will take into consideration the actions carried in the LC". (Stardust, 2020)
13. **Making City**	**Groningen, NL** Oulu, FI	Vidin, BG Bassano del Grappa, IT Lublin, PL Poprad, SK León, ES Kadikoy, TR	SCC1-2017 2018-2023 20M € http://makingcity.eu/	Based on "the concept of Positive Energy District (PED) that will be tested and validated in two LC, and later will be replicated in 6 FC' (MakingCity, 2020).
14. **City Exchange**	**Limerick, IE** Trondheim, NO	Smolyan, BG Pisek, CZ Voru, EE Alba Iulia, RO Sestao, ES	SCC1-2018 2018-2023 24M € https://cityxchange.eu/	Based on "the demonstration projects [that] are developed in the LC and will be replicated in five FC" (City Exchange, 2020)
15. **Atelier**	**Bilbao, ES** Amsterdam, NL	Copenhagen, DK Budapest, HR Riga, LV Krakow, PL Matosinhos, PT Bratislava, SK	SCC1-2018 2019-2024 21M € http://www.smartcity-atelier.eu/	No information provided on replication strategy yet (Atelier, 2020).
16. **Pocityf**	**Evora, PT** Alkmaar, NL	Hvidovre, DK Ioannina, GR Ujpest, HU Bari, IT Celje, SI Granada, ES	SCC1-2018 2019-2024 22M € https://pocityf.eu/	No information provided on replication strategy yet (Pocityf, 2020).
17. **Sparcs**	**Espoo, FI** Leipzig, DE	Kladno, CZ Kifissia, GR Reykjavik, IS Maia, PT Lviv, UA	SCC1-2018 2019-2024 23M € https://www.sparcs.info/	Based on "LC proving the urban energy transformation while FC demonstrates the smooth transferability of this transformation model" (Sparcs, 2020).

FIG. 4.1 Benchmarking EC-SCC-H2020 Lighthouse Projects' replication strategy (SCIS, 2019). *Source: www.replicate-project.eu/city2citylearning.*

Based on the analysis shown in Fig. 4.1, there are three takeaways for benchmarking the process of replication among smart cities, which this chapter highlights (European Commission, 2020).

First, the EC-H2020-SCC framework programme is based on the rationale that cities achieve more when they collaborate. The lighthouse projects share technical learning, spread the risk of investing in new technology, and use their scale to drive down costs through joint procurement. Technologies tested as a part of the EC-H2020-SCC framework programme can then be implemented on a wider scale at a vastly reduced cost per unit. Evidence suggests that joint procurement can generate massive cost savings for cities bold enough to embrace inter-city co-operation. For instance, following a 2001 reorganisation of regional procurement in Austria, city authorities achieved savings of 30% and an administrative workload reduction of 60% (European Commission, 2017c).

Second, during the 2014–2019 period, 17 lighthouse projects—Growsmarter, Remourban, Triangulum, Replicate, Sharing Cities, SmartenCity, Smarter Together, My Smart Life, Ruggedised, IRIS, Matchup, Stardust, Making City, City Exchange, Atelier, Pocityf, and Sparcs (SCIS, 2019)—have been funded under the EC-H2020-SCC framework programme encompassing 46 lighthouse cities and 71 follower-fellow cities with the direct involvement of their related stakeholders. An overarching benchmarking analysis shows a wide range of city networks, compositions, and budget allocations. Nonetheless, the rationale behind the formulation of replication strategy seems to follow the institutional discourse, where the lighthouse cities command and entirely determine the replication procedure with very little active decision-making by follower-fellow cities. It is also true that there are nuanced differences among lighthouse projects. Whereas the first round of lighthouse projects (GrowSmarter, Remourban, and Triangulum) depicts a rather mechanistic and unidirectional managerial understanding in how to proceed with replication, the rounds after SCC1-2014 have gradually evolved towards a more iterative or dynamic approach by (i) including follower-fellow cities much earlier in the process (City Exchange, 2020; MySmartLife, 2017; Ruggedised, 2020; Sharing Cities, 2016; Smarter Together, 2019; Sparcs, 2020; Stardust, 2020) and (ii) allowing their active involvement in the replication planning and outcomes through knowledge exchange activities such as workshops, thematic webinars, and interaction activities (IRIS, 2020; MakingCity, 2020; Matchup, 2020; SmartenCity, 2017). It is worth paying attention to a recent network called 'Cities Coalition for Digital Rights' encompassing global cities worldwide (Calzada & Almirall, 2020): this network seems to be heading to the right direction in terms of learning among cities rather than replicating solutions.

Third, beyond the ongoing technical implementations and because they are hypothetical and not mentioned in lighthouse projects' replication-related formulations analysis, this chapter highlights that, sooner than later, innovative technological solutions in the lighthouse projects will require attention to the inevitable consequences of data disruption of existing platforms (Gillespie, 2010; Graham et al., 2019). As a result of the GDPR taking effect from May 2018, lighthouse and follower-fellow cities are required to include particular protocols by allowing citizens to avoid complicated (and often obscure) extractive algorithmic governance practices (Chisnall, 2020). Failure to do so may mean bypassing the role of city stakeholders in filtering urban solutions from the techno-ethical perspective of data beyond complying with privacy standards, as requested by the GDPR (Calzada, 2019a, 2019b). There are already clear consequences for replication activities in terms of the current European digital economy that is being increasingly characterised by pervasive processes of datafication, with 'big data' on citizens' behaviour collected by private companies without further democratic accountability (Sadowski, 2020). However, the benchmarking conducted did not find any evidence yet of such harvesting in the replication strategies carried out by the lighthouse projects (Calzada, 2019a, 2019b).

4.3 Why might replication (not) be (mechanistically) happening among smart cities?

One of the most important challenges in implementing smart city policies is grasping the nature and procedure for replication dynamics in the current post-algorithmic smart city (Komninos & Kakderi, 2019). As such, while evidence, as analysed in the previous section, from the lighthouse projects suggests that the devil is often in the details, it is, at the same time, possible to identify common mechanisms that appear to hamper replication. According to Vandervyvere (2017, p. 7), replication is not happening as smoothly as anticipated by the EC-H2020-SCC because of the following five factors. First, there is a lack of connection between the replicating technology and the local stakeholders' interest. Second, the simplistic business-as-usual approach of the profit-driven private and the public sectors focused excessively on the short term (Timeus, Vinaixa, & Pardo-Bosch, 2020). Third, unique contexts are not seriously considered. Fourth, regulatory bottlenecks are still sustained by vested private interests and systemic inertia. Fifth, there is a lack of commitment from politicians in realising urban transformations. Of these, context is particularly important as the secret to effective replication lies in the proper combination of context-specific measures, on the one hand, and uniformity for scaling up, on the other. Thus, what should be treated as context specific? Moreover, where can (should) the local context be transcended?

Replication has been broadly researched through different perspectives focusing on public management practices (Grimmelikhuijsen & Porumbescu, 2017; Jilke et al., 2017; Walker et al., 2017). According to Walker, James, and Brewer (2017, p. 1221), 'replication is increasingly recognised as an important part of knowledge production in the social sciences, especially for experimental approach'. However, replication is also discussed and undertaken, sometimes controversially, in many other disciplines. For instance, Jilke et al. (2017) clearly argue that there are good reasons to believe that replication may not always work as anticipated or designed by policy frameworks due to the difficulty in measuring a comprehensive equivalence in replications of experiments.

More specifically, it is noteworthy that replication methodologies applied in the EC-H2020-SCC framework programme by lighthouse projects, such as the one by Remourban (2016), resonate with the idea of designing a list of indicators that pre-define the main features of cities through data sources, where to find this information, and the statistical procedures to be conducted to obtaining a classification of cities typologies (García-Fuentes et al., 2017). Similarly, the Triangulum project acknowledges that their focus is only on the lighthouse cities (Triangulum, 2020), thus remaining relatively non-committal about the adoption by the follower-fellow cities (von Radecki, 2018; von Radecki, Tcholtchev, Lämmel, & Schaj, 2020). Based on this technocratic-mechanistic approach, several replication techniques are suggested, including best practices, common cross-domain use cases, capability models, benchmarking and key performance indicators (KPIs), interoperability, platform approach, standard (vertical and horizontal), and profiling. As such, the replication function in the EC-H2020-SCC was initially expected to increase innovation and technological transfer. It required finding suitable financing that was allied with innovative business models, while sharing knowledge, good practices, and lessons learned to achieve a successful replication. The complexity of such a task makes simple copy-paste replication rare and difficult.

In light of the brief benchmarking of the EC-H2020-SCC framework programme's lighthouse projects to overcome their failures and provide a readjustment to its initial approach, this chapter suggests that replication may be well redesigned as a blend of elements consisting of a learning process that includes the following: (i) examine in-depth the technological solution and, even, prototyping to assess its potential for replication by local stakeholders (as a whole or partially); (ii) adapt the intervention to local regulatory and socio-economic conditions; (iii) include non-technical aspects that could be hindering replication, such as financing opportunities, the economic situation, regulatory regimes, social acceptability, business and social model adoption, algorithmic disruption, and data ownership and privacy; and (iv) ultimately, offer an operational framework where city representatives could well co-ordinate their learning process by including a wide range of stakeholders that could directly interact with other stakeholders operating within the same EC-H2020-SCC lighthouse project.

Thus, to provide not only a critical but also a constructive alternative to the given institutional definition of replication, as designed by the EC-H2020-SCC, this chapter justifies this approach by suggesting a transition from the former approach to the one implemented in the Replicate project by using the SI perspective (Fig. 4.2). Thus, the function of replication seemed to have been projected, from the policy designers and practitioners simulating such a unidirectional, hierarchical, mechanistic, solutionist, and, even, technocratic procedure among smart cities, as Morozov described (Bable, 2018; Janssen & Kuk, 2016; Riegler, 2017; von Radecki, 2018). Instead, the *City-to-City Learning Programme* operated by following a SI perspective, thus considering the unique combination of

From (pure) replicationion	To city-to-city learning
Unidirectional	Multidirectional
Hierarchical	Radial
Mechanistic	Dynamic
Solutionist	Iterative
Technocratic	Democratic

Bartels, 2020; Terstriep, Rehfeld, & Kleverbeck, 2020; Mihci, 2019; Moulaert & MacCallum, 2019; Pel et al., 2019.

FIG. 4.2 Conceptual evolution of replication from the Social Innovation perspective: five transitions. *Source: www.replicate-project.eu/city2citylearning.*

multiple stakeholders in each Replicate city (regardless of being a lighthouse or follower-fellow) and, more importantly, the way replication could be effectively facilitated through a city network's multidirectional, radial, dynamic, iterative, and democratic learning process (Engelbrecht, 2018; Grimm, Fox, Baines, & Albertson, 2013; Potjer & Hajer, 2017; ReplicateEU, 2019).

According to Mihci (2019, p. 1), given the problem of the SI perspective and, also, the function of replication, 'it is the difficulty to obtain reliable results through metrics that could be extended to the statistical, methodological, and, even, conceptual spheres'. Nonetheless, this chapter adopts the SI perspective of empowering networks of stakeholders suggested by Pel et al. (2019) for the conceptual evolution of replication, as conducted in the EC-H2020-SCC Replicate project's *City-to-City Learning Programme*. The replication function actually has proven the requirement to be connected with local contextual ecosystems of stakeholders to better adopt the suggested and agreed upon urban interventions (Terstriep et al., 2020). In line with the DNA of the resulting *City-to-City Learning Programme* in the Replicate EC-H2020-SCC lighthouse project, Bartels (2020) argues that SI now can play an active role in bolstering transformative change and create a trajectory for learning for smart cities and their urban governance (Calzada & Cobo, 2015). This chapter offers an operational alternative through a conceptual evolution of the understanding and implementation of replication in the given institutional corpus of EC-H2020-SCC in the specific Replicate project through five transitions stemming from a multiple stakeholder-driven, socially innovative perspective. The key transitions are (i) from a unidirectional to a multidirectional perspective, where six Replicate cities shared their best practices and lessons learned at the same level; (ii) from a hierarchical logic to a radial one; (iii) from a mechanistic understanding of replication to a dynamic, flexible, and agile one; (iv) from the almost obligatory requirement to finding urban solutions to an ongoing iterative process of pinpointing causes and alternative prototypes for solutions; and, (v) ultimately, creating a more democratic ecosystem realised with a wide range of stakeholders, unlike a technocratically directed outcome.

4.4 City-to-city learning programme in the EC-H2020-SCC Replicate project

The design of the *City-to-City Learning Programme* as the main replication strategy of the EC-H2020-SCC Replicate project was initiated from the beginning of the project in February 2016. Since then, the three lighthouse cities (San Sebastian, Florence, and Bristol) and the three fellow cities (Essen, Nilüfer, and Lausanne)—replacing the former nomenclature and the hierarchical position of the follower cities—closely collaborated in the definition of the contents and the methodological activities involved. In doing so, the function of replication within the project intensively encouraged a fertile dialogue, thus connecting stakeholders (regardless of their lighthouse or fellow city consideration) working either in one or, sometimes, several smart policy sectors (energy, mobility, and ICT). Furthermore, this experimental approach resulted in a productive conversation among stakeholders in the six cities (Späth & Knieling, 2020). The replication strategy previously examined the unique multiple stakeholder framework in each fellow city through the Penta helix (including actors interacting in the public, private, civil society, academic, and entrepreneur-activist domains of smart cities; Calzada, 2018; Calzada & Cowie, 2017).

Wisely influenced by the research and policy findings piloted by the Urban Transformations ESRC (Economic and Social Research Council) Programme at the University of Oxford (Calzada & Keith, 2018), the fieldwork action research conducted until December 2019 allowed the researchers to anticipate the cleavage between the smart city as a mobile policy understood as 'glossy stories, fragmented processes, and a random process' (Wathne & Haarstad, 2020, p. 133), and the early entrepreneurial research findings at the beginning of the Replicate project by deconstructing a somewhat techno-deterministic smart city policy agenda. Consequently, the Replicate project's strategy primarily focused on putting methodological advancements into action to foster learning in and among cities by avoiding (and presumably overcoming) replicability dependent on techno-deterministic principles based on so-called solutionism (Morozov, 2013). Smart cities are not machines (Amin & Thrift, 2017). Moreover, their internal initiatives are directly and proportionally dependent on the stakeholders interacting uniquely with a dense set of power relationships (Bryson, 2004). How should such a complex strategy called Replication be approached (European Commission, 2017c)?

Within the first 3 years of the project, covering the 2016–2018 period, the three lighthouse cities focused entirely on their pilot initiatives in the three smart city sectors (energy, mobility, and ICT). Alongside these initiatives, the Replication strategy suggested reverting the rationale for the mainstream approach (preliminarily designed by European Commission policymakers), stemming from a unidirectional and mechanistic logic. By contrast, the Replicate project was gradually empowering the former follower cities (now already officially and institutionally fellow cities) by putting them at the same level as the lighthouse cities through a multidirectional learning cycle. Until 2019, an intense fieldwork action research process alongside the lighthouse cities' initiatives in three fellow cities for those early 3 years was carried out, including (i) critical factors' assessment and (ii) mapping out the unique composition of stakeholders by following the Penta helix policy framework (Calzada & Cowie, 2017). Essentially, the programme was based on the following methodological steps: (i) the singularity of each city (strategic aim and contextual factors) was examined through a critical factors' assessment methodology, with (ii) the scalability depending on the composition of the multiple stakeholders' policy scheme, such as their interdependence and power relations (examined through the Penta helix policy framework). Moreover, (iii) the adaptability of the given smart action (contrasting feasibility and potential impact) was facilitated through this *City-to-City Learning Programme;* and, ultimately, (iv) the replicability after the multidirectional learning loop among stakeholders through each fellow city's action-driven formulation was established, completing their own replication plans tailored to their strategic and operational needs.

As a result, the *City-to-City Learning Programme* set the scene to establish a prolific common ground among the six Replicate cities without any hierarchical or functional distinctions. The stakeholders fostered a shared participatory agora and a co-operative platform directly among Replicate stakeholders (regardless of their city of reference). Funnily enough, and most importantly, the Replicate project curated and warmed-up this programme with the active participation of the representative and strategic stakeholders of the six Replicate cities by experimenting with the complex task of replication through a multidirectional learning loop stemming from an approach using SI.

Ultimately, this programme was designed to assist fellow cities in formulating their own replication plans, outlined in the fifth section of this chapter. Drawing on the experience and objective results achieved and publicly available at www.replicate-project.eu/city2citylearning—more than 150 registered participants and almost 300 offline views—this section addresses how this replication strategy and intervention, stemming from a perspective of SI, developed new forms of policy incentives for more participatory policy design, as well as monitoring, feedback, assessment, and learning loops that utilise the characteristics of digital transformations in smart cities among a vast and nuanced democratic representation of stakeholders' plurality and diversity.

This section provides an analytical summary of the fieldwork action research conducted for the elaboration of the *City-to-City Learning Programme* encompassing a series of six webinar sessions in which each Replicate city elaborated on its smart city strategic actions (organised through three slots per city by including a diverse range of stakeholders). It was presented and discussed directly among Replicate stakeholders, thus ensuring a multidirectional, radial, dynamic, iterative, and intentionally more democratic learning process by bypassing the given pure mechanistic approach suggested by the EC-H2020-SCC framework programme.

San Sebastian, as the leading lighthouse city of the Replicate project, was the first city to participate in the webinar programme. The session led by the city representative of San Sebastian, entitled *Excellence of service provision based on data monitoring and smart management,* took place on 5 February 2019 (San Sebastian, 2020).

The city profile and characterisation of San Sebastian in the context of the Replicate project can be summarised as follows: the municipality of Donostia-San Sebastian is the capital of the Province of Gipuzkoa in the autonomous Basque community in the northern region of Spain. It has a population of 186,000 people. Within the context of the Replicate project, several pilot projects were planned in the area of the Urumea river district. The district has the city's largest green park, Ametzagaña Park, and a large industrial park, Poligono 27, which houses over 300 companies employing almost 4500 people. More dramatically though, it has also been a district in the city vulnerable to flooding from the river, which is a problem that has gradually been addressed through the Replicate project. One challenge the Replicate project attempted to tackle in this neighbourhood was improving the district's connectivity to the rest of the city through public transport, public lighting, Internet connectivity via a high-speed network, and the energy efficiency of its buildings. This district was the target of many measures to improve the quality of life, including the construction of approximately 1500 new homes in a new neighbourhood, building a district heating plant, and installing a smart lighting system.

The *City-to-City Learning Programme* session for San Sebastian consisted of three smart city presentations subject to be replicated by the fellow cities involving a diverse set of stakeholders—representing primarily the public, private, and academic sectors applying the Penta helix framework (Calzada & Cowie, 2017). The first presentation revolved around the transition from traditional infrastructures to intelligent-connected solutions for smart lighting implemented by the local small and medium enterprise (SME), Leycolan (2020, SS.1). This urban intervention allowed for communication between luminaries. The second presentation aimed at exploiting the city's information by linking data to other cities through the semantic web executed by the ICT firm, Eurohelp (2020, SS.2). The information is a part of the Linked Open Data Cloud, published as open data under the linked data paradigm. Finally, the third presentation showed a smart platform developed by the local firm, Ikusi (2020, SS.3), that aimed at integrating the city's mobility data sources.

The second session of the programme, *The new smelters of the coal heartland,* was led by the city representative of the fellow city of Essen and took place on 21 March 2019 (Essen, 2020).

The city profile and characterisation of Essen in the context of the Replicate project was introduced in Section 3.3.3.

The *City-to-City Learning Programme* session for Essen was represented primarily by the public, private, academic, and entrepreneurial and start-up sectors. The first presentation described how the support of start-ups could help blend the smart and sustainable agendas of cities, as in the case of Camp-Essen (2020, E.1). Camp-Essen was presented as a platform for collaboration and co-innovation among start-ups, corporations, SMEs, business angels, and academia in line with the Penta helix policy scheme (Calzada & Cowie, 2017) employed for the whole replication strategy. The second presentation presented by the socially driven entrepreneurial non-governmental organisation (NGO), Impact Hub Ruhr (2020, E.2), aimed at connecting communities for change and how the start-up scene can help blend the smart and sustainable agendas of cities. Impact Hub Ruhr complemented Camp-Essen by connecting social entrepreneurs with a broadband of active citizens. Impact Hub Ruhr was actually presented as a global network focused on building entrepreneurial communities out of innovators, social entrepreneurs, and urban intermediaries (SUI, 2018). The final action elaborated on how a brownfield could turn into a showcase for the smart and sustainable future of cities by presenting the flagship project, Essen 51, led by a private firm called Thelen Gruppe (Essen 51, 2020, E.3). This new district is being built with a forecast of 1500 new homes and 500,000 m^2 of new business space.

The third session of the programme, *Go fast, go green, get connected: That's smart!,* was led by the city representative of the lighthouse city of Florence and took place on 7 May 2019 (Florence, 2020).

Florence, the capital of the Italian region of Tuscany, is the region's most populous city. It has approximately 383,000 and over 1 million inhabitants in the core and greater metropolitan area. Due to its historical and cultural heritage, tourism is its most important industry. However, production and commercial activities remain important economic drivers, especially in the greater metropolitan area. The city is often in the top 10 most visited cities in the world, with approximately 10 million tourists staying in local accommodation. About two million more visitors arrive through cruise ships and day tours. This high number of visitors presents a significant challenge for the city's administration. While it represents the main source of income for the city, it is also increasingly seen as a threat to its services and management, as well as the quality of life for those who live in the highly congested central urban zones. Within the context of the Replicate project, the smart city pilot projects were implemented in the district of Novoli, northwest of Florence.

The *City-to-City Learning Programme* session for Florence was represented primarily by the public, private, civil society, academic, and entrepreneurial sectors. The first presentation revolved around the fast recharge and e-taxi examples of e-mobility initiatives to deploy sustainable mobility presented by the company, e-distribuzione (eDistribuzione, 2020, F.1). Florence has been undertaking transport network modernisation from 2016 to 2020, thus increasing the number of electric vehicles, doubling the number of hybrid-electric vehicles, and reducing the number of pure internal combustion engine vehicles to as low as zero. The second presentation covered an e-recharge system, facilitating the move towards a sustainable community (F.2). Florence aimed at promoting the development of electric mobility through the realisation of a recharging network for electric vehicles. Finally (F.3), the third presentation was primarily developed by the University of Florence around the smart city platform and the control room.

The fourth session of the programme, *Roadmap for the realisation of an eco-district, including the development of medium-depth geothermal energy in urban areas,* was led by the city representative of the fellow city of Lausanne and took place on 9 July 2019 (Lausanne, 2020).

The city profile and characterisation of Lausanne in the context of the Replicate project was introduced in Section 3.3.3.

The *City-to-City Learning Programme* session for Lausanne was represented primarily by the public, private, and academic sectors: the first presentation covered a roadmap for the realisation of the eco-district, called Plaines-du-Loup (L.1). This district promotes the attractiveness by introducing a functional mix (30% activity and 70% housing) and the creation of a public transport axis. The second presentation covered the development of medium-depth geothermal energy in the Plaines-du-Loup district (L.2). In this district, heat production was based on deep geothermal and heat recovery from wastewater. Finally, the third presentation was devoted to the energy programme called Equiwatt (L.3).

The fifth session of the programme, *Collaborating with communities: Creating the future cities we need,* was led by the city representative of the lighthouse city of Bristol on 26 September 2019 (Bristol, 2020).

A performance assessment framework on Bristol's smart city strategy (Calzada, 2017) stated that the strategy was formed in 2011 to lead the digital innovation agenda within the city. Two main landmark projects are detailed as the key performance of this city: the Bristol is Open and Replicate project. Research and policy findings reveal two main and optimistic conclusions for the case of Bristol (Calzada, 2017, p. 6). First, 'Bristol presents an increasing effort to experiment with the citizen-centric approach, [considering] (smart) citizens as decision-makers rather than pure data providers'. Second, 'Bristol is ultimately amalgamating a large number of smart projects in a complex network of interactions with citizens. The prospect for the future will be fostering decision-makers' interplay, [thus] portraying the city as an open platform'.

The *City-to-City Learning Programme* session for Bristol was represented primarily by the public, academic, and civil society sectors. The first presentation delivered Bristol's methodological approach to co-design urban interventions with citizens (B.1; Allen, Tamindael, Bickerton, & Cho, 2020). According to its strategic stakeholder, KWMC (2020), Bristol's approach put local needs at the heart of innovation: that is, tech is pulled in, not pushed onto citizens. The second presentation revolved around technology, data, and governance. Particularly, how we make it accessible for citizens embodied by the flagship project Bristol is Open. Data that could affect a city planning project—such as air quality, traffic rates and patterns, energy consumption, and crime statistics—were shown through open data platforms of the city (B.2). Finally, the third presentation emphasised the ongoing project called the One City Approach and Inclusive Futures. The presentation was, essentially, a shared city vision by 2050 based on six prioritised themes: health and well-being, economy, homes and communities, environment, learning and skills, and connectivity (B.3).

The final session of the programme, *Socio-economic development from below,* was led by the city representative of the fellow city of Nilüfer and took place on 20 November 2019 (Nilüfer, 2020).

The city profile and characterisation of Nilüfer in the context of the Replicate project was introduced in Section 3.3.3.

The *City-to-City Learning Programme* session for Nilüfer was represented primarily by the public, private, academic, civil society, and emergent entrepreneurial activities and sectors. The first presentation addressed grassroots empowerment through neighbourhood committees that were created in 2009 to reach disadvantaged segments in the society (N.1; Nilüfer Kent Konseyi, 2020). The second presentation covered bottom-up energy efficiency, including initiatives for energy co-operatives, grey water treatment and compost facilities, and a social entrepreneurship centre (N.2). Finally, the third presentation covered emerging industrial spin-off ecologies related to the paradigm of industry 4.0 and advanced manufacturing (N.3).

4.5 Shaping replication plans

As a result of the *City-to-City Learning Programme*, a broad amalgamation of smart city actions interdependently touching upon smart sectors, such as energy, mobility, ICT, and citizens' engagement, and, more importantly, deeply discussed among a wide range of Replicate stakeholders was offered to fellow cities to formulate their own replication plans. Fig. 4.3 summarises the outcome of the learning process among stakeholders, resulting in a strategic replication formulation framed by the general context of the *City-to-City Learning Programme,* which finished in December 2019.

Essen concluded by considering the lessons learned for replicating the following smart city initiatives, organised by sectors involving both lighthouse or fellow cities and the related stakeholders. (i) In energy, smart public lighting, intelligent LED systems, and an e-taxi system would be adopted directly, learning from stakeholders in San Sebastian and Florence. Improvements to the public lighting infrastructure would include innovative solar thermal seasonal storage (for social housing). Moreover, Essen will attempt to incorporate the energy planning of an eco-district for Essen 51, learning directly from the Plaines-du-Loup district carried out by the fellow city of Lausanne. (ii) In the case of mobility, Essen expressed its interest in adopting electric buses and an e-bike sharing system, as deployed by the smart mobility platform of the lighthouse city of San Sebastian. Additionally, the info-mobility system developed by the lighthouse city of Florence offers a comprehensive information system across services, full electric taxi vehicles, fast recharging systems, and a sustainable

City-to-City Learning Programme as a Multidirectional, Radial, Dynamic, Iterative, and Further Democratic Replication Strategy among EC-H2020-SCC Replicate Project's Cities																					
Replicate cities	**L/F (*)**	**Smart city action**	**Impact (**)**		**Stakeholders directly involved: Identified through Penta Helix Multiple Stakeholders' Policy Framework (***)**					**Potential fellow cities' replication plans (****): Selected actions to be replicated, scaled up, and adapted**											
			P	V	1	2	3	4	5	**Essen**				**Lausanne**				**Nilüfer**			
					Public	Private	Academia	Civil Society	Entrepreneurs/ Activists	E	M	I	C	E	M	I	C	E	M	I	C
(SS) San Sebastian	L	SS.1.	30	149	X	X				X				X							
		SS.2.			X	X															
		SS.3.			X	X					X				X						
(E) Essen	F	E.1.	22	33	X	X	X		X									X			
		E.2.			X	X			X												
		E.3.			X	X			X					X							
(F) Florence	L	F.1.	35	40	X	X	X		X	X											
		F.2.			X	X	X				X				X						
		F.3.			X	X	X		X												
(L) Lausanne	F	L.1.	10	20	X	X		X	X	X											
		L.2.			X				X												
		L.3.						X	X												
(B) Bristol	L	B.1.	23	40	X		X		X		X					X			X		
		B.2.					X		X			X								X	
		B.3.			X		X	X					X				X	X			X
(N) Nilüfer	F	N.1.	30	18	X		X	X													
		N.2.			X		X	X	X				X								
		N.3.			X	X			X												
			150	300																	

* L represents lighthouse cities and F does fellow cities.
** P represents the number of participants during the session and V represents the number of offline views.
*** The Penta Helix framework (Calzada & Cowie, 2017) distributes stakeholders in five categories: 1 represents the public sector, 2 represents the private sector, 3 represents academia, 4 represents the civil society, and 5 represents social entrepreneurs and activists.
**** This column depicts the identification made by fellow cities' representatives in the General Assembly that took place in Florence on 30 October 2019. The potential fellow cities' replication plans have effectively selected these smart city initiatives in close collaboration with stakeholders of the Replicate cities, regardless of being lighthouse or fellow cities. E represents smart city initiatives related to energy, M represents mobility, I represents ICT, and C represents citizens' engagement.

FIG. 4.3 Replication plans: scalability, adaptability, and singularity. *Source: www.replicate-project.eu/city2citylearning.*

public taxi fleet. Finally, the journey planner and parking apps (including payment), developed by the lighthouse city of Bristol, was decided to be an appropriate model. (iii) In the area of ICT, Essen may adopt the model of Bristol is Open, which would drive social collaboration, knowledge, data sharing, and analytics management across the digital landscapes to deliver services to the public authorities, residents, business, students, and visitors. (iv) Finally, in the area of citizens' engagement, Essen showed a particular interest in emulating the One City Approach and Bristol is Open (particularly through its Citizen Sensing initiative), and the bottom-up energy efficiency measures adopted in Nilüfer, which directly connects with the approach of involving multiple stakeholders in Essen.

Lausanne concluded with its own list of potential actions after being matched with several interventions conducted by the following Replicate cities. (i) In energy, in line with the core value proposition put forth by Lausanne around the district heating intervention, the demand-side platform developed in the St. Sebastian and Essen 51 interventions drew special attention in combination with the public smart lighting system deployed in St. Sebastian. (ii) In mobility, Lausanne may be adapting the smart transport management system developed in St. Sebastian and showed interest in learning from the experience in Florence regarding the taxi fleet with electric vehicles and the superfast recharging system. (iii) In the ICT sector, the Bristol is Open approach could be adapted in Lausanne, (iv) as well as for citizens' engagement with the One City Approach of Bristol.

Ultimately, Nilüfer is likely to implement the following initiatives. (i) In energy, it aims to expand the renewable energy co-operatives (also called as energy communities), led by Camp-Essen. In addition to this, Nilüfer showed interest in adapting the smart homes model related to the smart residential demand response that was implemented in the One City Approach in Bristol. (ii) In mobility, Nilüfer learned about the ParkUS parking model that is related to the Open Data Movement in Bristol. Additionally, an adaptation of smart e-bike rental solutions developed by the SME Co-Wheels could be well attempted in Nilüfer by re-contextualising methodologies to co-design mobility alternatives through informal transport systems with citizens (see Section 3.4). (iii) In the ICT sector, Nilüfer requested information to scale up the policy framework known as Bristol is Open. (iv) Finally, the intensive investment that is being made in Nilüfer in citizen engagement may be reinforced through the lessons from the Bristol One City Approach concerning offering a systemic and strategic intervention.

4.6 Conclusions

This chapter constructively contributes to the research on replication among smart cities in the EC-H2020-SCC framework programme by suggesting an alternative strategy to the one implemented by the Replicate project. The chapter concludes that under the umbrella of the EC-H2020-SCC institutional framework, replication may not be mechanistically happening as it was intended. Thus, shedding light on this issue, this chapter presents the main results of the *City-to-City Learning Programme* undertaken by the EC-H2020-SCC Replicate project for 2019 and proposes the application of five transitions as a conceptual evolution of replication stemming from the SI perspective. These five transitions—multidirectional, radial, dynamic, iterative, and more democratic—have, respectively, been suggested as an alternative policy pathway to revert the unidirectional, hierarchical, mechanistic, solutionist, and technocratic rationale behind the given institutional framework. Essentially, these five transitions have a common the core role played in the *City-to-City Learning Programme* by the multiple stakeholders' policy scheme, which resonates with Bryson's (2004, p. 21) following statement: 'A wise use of stakeholders can help frame issues that are solvable in ways that are technically feasible and politically acceptable and that advance the common good'.

The first finding of this research is that technocratic unidirectional replication strategies may not be readily adopted by follower-fellow cities primarily because of the lack of adaptability to local contexts and possibly due to the fact that they require more complex and elaborated interventions to achieve broad social acceptance. During the *City-to-City Learning Programme*, stakeholders from different Replicate cities engaged in conversations tailored not only to solutions but also to their specific problems. This situation was particularly noteworthy for the cases of Essen and Nilüfer, where, despite their clear differences, they actively exchanged their ideas about energy regulations and organisational forms of co-operatives (Cuesta-Fernandez, Belda-Miquel, & Calabuig Tormo, 2020; Wiese, 2020) and, even, came up with solutions different from those already experimented in other cities, regardless of whether they were lighthouse or follower-fellow cities.

Consequently, the second finding is that the policy design of the EC-H2020-SCC framework programme advocating a hierarchical model from the lighthouse to the follower-fellow cities may be the source of the lack of adoption of strategies for replication. Put differently, the given selection of smart city initiatives in the lighthouse cities, subject to be replicated by the follower-fellow, may well be misaligned. This situation includes the selection of the sector, specific actions deployed, and, more importantly, stakeholders who are directly or indirectly affected (Eubanks, 2017). The given hierarchical model can 'exclude the perspectives and interests of citizens' and particular groups of stakeholders (Engelbert, van Zoonen, & Hirzalla, 2018, p. 1).

Thus, how can replication be implemented among smart cities? This chapter, by contrasting several conclusions extracted by Vandervyvere (2017) through intense and continuous fieldwork action research from 2016, and more particularly for 2019 with 150 stakeholders participating actively in the *City-to-City Learning Programme*, suggests (as a third finding) a dynamic vision of replication by which stakeholders adopt and adapt their particular interventions to their own circumstances. During the webinar sessions, stakeholders from fellow cities further asked specific questions about adapting, tailoring, prototyping, or scaling up certain tested interventions.

Judging from the potential replication plans of fellow cities (as shown in Fig. 4.3), the fourth finding is related to the iterative nature of the decision-making process in each fellow city rather than copy-pasting solutions (European Commission, 2016; Morozov, 2013). After a comprehensive benchmarking that generically analysed the replication strategies of the 17 lighthouse projects (as shown in Fig. 4.1), the *City-to-City Learning Programme* in the Replicate project has anticipated debates around the GDPR, algorithmic disruption, data privacy, and ownership that generate increasingly even more timely techno-political issues than sectoral technical interventions have so far identified (Bigo, Isin, & Ruppert, 2019; Calzada, 2019a, 2019b; Madsen, 2018; van Dijck, 2014), which makes the function of replication from the ethical and social standpoints even more complicated.

The final finding concerns the narrative that underpins the smart city. Habermas (2015) argues that smartness in cities cannot be more technocratic than democratic. Above all, smartness postulates that problems and their solutions are presented as being interlinked only with a technical nature. This chapter attempted to focus on the learning process among cities and, therefore, their stakeholders, by overlooking the neutral vision of technology, led by policymakers, to disregard equality and diversity issues, although the smart city—and its products and services—is not similarly accessible to every stakeholder. In line with the argument by Nesti and Graziano (2019) by which the technical nature of urban problems is required to be reframed in (techno-)political terms, this chapter showed and opened up directions for future replication research from the SI perspective: there is a significant room for manoeuvre for local stakeholders in their ability to pick and choose, adapt, and prototype between innumerable intervention models and networks. Their capacity to produce insightful narratives while learning from each other may also mean that cities and their stakeholders can seize the current pathway and fashion new alternatives for the future (Wathne & Haarstad, 2020).

References

Allen, B., Tamindael, L. E., Bickerton, S. H., & Cho, W. (2020). Does citizen coproduction lead to better urban services in smart cities projects? An empirical study on e-participation in a mobile big data platform. *Government Information Quarterly*, *37*(1), 101412. https://doi.org/10.1016/j.giq.2019.101412.

Amin, A., & Thrift, N. (2017). *Seeing like a city*. Cambridge: Polity.

Atelier. (2020). Retrieved from: http://www.smartcity-atelier.eu/.

Aurigi, A., & Odendaal, N. (2020). From 'smart in the box' to 'smart in the city': Rethinking the socially sustainable smart city in context. *Journal of Urban Technology*, 1–16. https://doi.org/10.1080/10630732.2019.1704203.

Bable. (2018). Retrieved from: www.bable-smartcities.eu.

Barns, S. (2020). *Platform urbanism: Negotiating platform ecosystems in connected cities*. Palgrave Macmillan Singapore: Springer. https://doi.org/10.1007/978-981-32-9725-8.

Bartels, K. (2020). Transforming the relational dynamics of urban governance: How social innovation research can create a trajectory for learning and change. *Urban Studies*, 1–17. https://doi.org/10.1177/0042098019889290.

Bigo, D., Isin, E., & Ruppert, E. (2019). *Data politics*. London: Routledge.

Borsboom-van Beurden, J., Kallaos, J., Gindroz, B., Costa, S., & Riegler, J. (2019). *Smart city guidance package: A roadmap for integrated planning and implementation of smart city projects*. Brussels: EIP-SCC.

Bristol. (2020). Retrieved from: https://replicate-project.eu/5th-session-collaborating-with-communities-creating-the-future-cities-we-need/.

Bryson, J. M. (2004). What to do when stakeholders matter. *Public Management Review*, *6*(1), 21–53. https://doi.org/10.1080/14719030410001675722.

Calzada, I. (2017). The techno-politics of data and smart devolution in city-regions: Comparing Glasgow, Bristol, Barcelona, and Bilbao. *Systems*, *5*(1), 18. https://doi.org/10.3390/systems5010018.

Calzada, I. (2018). Deciphering smart city citizenship: The techno-politics of data and urban cooperative platforms. *Revista International de Estudios Vascos, RIEV*, *63*(1–2), 42–81. https://doi.org/10.13140/RG.2.2.24498.35524/6.

Calzada, I. (2019a). Technological sovereignty: Protecting citizens' digital rights in the AI-driven and post-GDPR algorithmic and city-regional European realm. *Regions eZine*, (4). https://doi.org/10.1080/13673882.2018.00001038.

Calzada, I. (2019b). Data spaces and democracy. *RSA Journal*, (2), 40–43. https://doi.org/10.13140/RG.2.2.35392/89601/1.

Calzada, I., & Almirall, E. (2020). Data ecosystems for protecting European citizens' digital rights. *Transforming Government: People, Process and Policy*, *14*(2). https://doi.org/10.1108/TG-03-2020-0047.

Calzada, I., & Cobo, C. (2015). Unplugging: Deconstructing the smart city. *Journal of Urban Technology*, *22*(1), 23–43. https://doi.org/10.1080/10630732.2014.971535.

Calzada, I., & Cowie, P. (2017). Beyond smart and data-driven city-regions? Rethinking stakeholder-helixes strategies. *Regions Magazine*, *308*(4), 25–28. https://doi.org/10.1080/13673882.2017.11958675.

Calzada, I., & Keith, M. (2018). *Bridging European Urban transformations workshop series 2016–2018. @utconnect digest*. Oxford: University of Oxford/ESRC.

Camp-Essen. (2020). Retrieved from: www.camp-essen.de.

Caragliu, A., Del Bo, C., & Nijkamp, P. (2011). Smart cities in Europe. *Journal of Urban Technology*, *18*(2), 65–82. https://doi.org/10.1080/10630732.2011.601117.

Cardullo, P., & Kitchin, R. (2018). Smart urbanism and smart citizenship: The neoliberal logic of 'citizen-focused' smart cities in Europe. *Environment and Planning C: Politics and Space*, 1–17. https://doi.org/10.1177/0263774x18806508.

Chisnall, M. (2020). Digital slavery, time for abolition? *Policy Studies*, 1–19. https://doi.org/10.1080/01442872.2020.1724926.

City Exchange. (2020). Retrieved from: https://cityxchange.eu/demo-projects/.

Coletta, C., Evans, L., Heaphy, L., & Kitchin, R. (2018). Creating smart cities. *Series regions and cities*. Oxon: Routledge.

Cuesta-Fernandez, I., Belda-Miquel, S., & Calabuig Tormo, C. (2020). Challengers in energy transitions beyond renewable energy cooperatives: Community-owned electricity distribution cooperatives in Spain. *Innovation: The European Journal of Social Science Research*, 1–20. https://doi.org/10.1080/13511610.2020.1732197.

Datta, A. (2018). *The 'urban' is not 'science' [Tweet]*. Retrieved from: https://twitter.com/AyonaDatta/status/1014186757187874817.

Dyer-Witheford, N. (2020). Left populism and platform capitalism. *Triple C: Journal for a Global Sustainable Information Society*, *18*(1), 116–131.

eDistribuzione. (2020). Retrieved from: www.e-distribuzione.it.

EIP-SCC. (2016). *Towards a joint investment programme for European smart cities: A consultation paper to stimulate action*. EC: Brussels.

Engelbert, J., van Zoonen, L., & Hirzalla, F. (2018). Excluding citizens from the European smart city: The discourse practices of pursuing and granting smartness. *Technological Forecasting and Social Change*, *142*, 347–353. https://doi.org/10.1016/j.techfore.2018.08.020.

Engelbrecht, H.-J. (2018). The (social) innovation—Subjective well-being nexus: Subjective well-being impacts as an additional assessment metric of technological and social innovations. *Innovation: The European Journal of Social Science Research*, *31*(3), 317–332. https://doi.org/10.1080/13511610.2017.1319262.

Essen. (2020). Retrieved from: https://replicate-project.eu/2nd-session-the-new-smelters-of-the-coal-heartland/.

Essen 51. (2020). Retrieved from: www.thelen-gruppe.com/essen51.

Eubanks, V. (2017). *Automating inequality: How high-tech tools profile, police, and punish the poor*. NYC: St. Martin's Press.

Eurohelp. (2020). Retrieved from: www.eurohelp.es.

European Commission. (2016). *Creating the links for scaling smart cities solutions*. Eindhoven: H2020.

European Commission. (2017a). *EU research & innovation for and with cities*. Brussels: European Commission.

European Commission. (2017b). *The making of a smart city: Policy recommendations*. Brussels: European Commission.

European Commission. (2017c). *The making of a smart city: Replication and scale-up of innovation in Europe*. Brussels: European Commission.

European Commission. (2017d). *The making of a smart city: Best practices across Europe*. Brussels: European Commission.

European Commission. (2020). Retrieved from: http://www.smartcities-infosystem.eu/scc-lighthouse-projects.

Florence. (2020). Retrieved from: https://replicate-project.eu/3rd-session-go-fast-go-green-get-connceted-thats-smart/.

Forester, J., Kuitenbrouwer, M., & Laws, D. (2019). Enacting reflective and deliberative practices in action research. *Policy Studies*, 1–20. https://doi.org/10.1080/01442872.2019.1618445.

García-Fuentes, M. A., Quijano, A., de Torre, C., García, R., Compere, P., Degard, C., et al. (2017). European cities characterization as basis towards the replication of a smart and sustainable urban regeneration model. *Energy Procedia*, *111*, 836–845. https://doi.org/10.1016/j.egypro.2017.03.246.

Gillespie, T. (2010). The politics of "platforms". *New Media & Society*, *12*(3), 347–364. https://doi.org/10.1177/1461444809342738.

Graham, M. (2020). Regulate, replicate, and resist—The conjunctural geographies of platform urbanism. *Urban Geography*, 1–5. https://doi.org/10.1080/02723638.2020.1717028.

Graham, M., Kitchin, R., Mattern, S., & Shaw, J. (2019). *How to run a city like Amazon, and other fables*. London: MeatSpacePress.

Grimm, R., Fox, C., Baines, S., & Albertson, K. (2013). Social innovation, an answer to contemporary societal challenges? Locating the concept in theory and practice. *Innovation: The European Journal of Social Science Research*, *26*(4), 436–455. https://doi.org/10.1080/13511610.2013.848163.

Grimmelikhuijsen, S., & Porumbescu, G. A. (2017). Reconsidering the expectancy disconfirmation model. Three experimental replications. *Public Management Review, 19*(9), 1272–1292. https://doi.org/10.1080/14719037.2017.1282000.

Growsmarter. (2019). *Road to replication—Guiding cities on smart Urban development: Process and lessons learned in Growsmarter*. Retrieved from: www.grow-smarter.eu/home.

Habermas, J. (2015). *The lure of technocracy*. London: Polity Press.

Heinelt, H., & Terizakis, G. (2020). Innovative cities: How to explain differences between cities? An answer based on an interpretive approach. *Urban Research & Practice*, 1–15. https://doi.org/10.1080/17535069.2020.1723032.

Higdem, U. (2014). The co-creation of regional futures: Facilitating action research in regional foresight. *Futures, 57*, 41–50. https://doi.org/10.1016/j.futures.2014.01.006.

Ikusi. (2020). Retrieved from: www.ikusi.com.

Impact Hub Ruhr. (2020). Retrieved from: www.ruhr.impacthub.net.

IRIS. (2020). *Transition strategy, commissioning plan for the demonstration and replication*. Retrieved from: https://irissmartcities.eu/system/files/private/irissmartcities/d1.7_transition_strategy_commissioning_plan_for_the_demonstration_replication_v1.2.pdf.

Janssen, M., & Kuk, G. (2016). The challenges and limits of big data algorithms in technocratic governance. *Government Information Quarterly, 33*(3), 371–377. https://doi.org/10.1016/j.giq.2016.08.011.

Jilke, S., Petrovsky, N., Meuleman, B., & James, O. (2017). Measurement equivalence in replications of experiments: When and why it matters and guidance on how to determine equivalence. *Public Management Review, 19*(9), 1293–1310. https://doi.org/10.1080/14719037.2016.1210906.

Johnson, P. A., Robinson, P. J., & Philpot, S. (2019). Type, tweet, tap, and pass: How smart city technology is creating a transactional citizen. *Government Information Quarterly*. https://doi.org/10.1016/j.giq.2019.101414.

Kitchin, R. (2017). Urban science: A short primer. In *The programmable city working paper 23*. Maynooth: National University of Ireland.

Kitchin, R., Coletta, C., Evans, L., Heaphy, L., & Mac Donncha, D. (2017). Smart cities, Urban technocrats, epistemic communities and advocacy coalitions. In *The programmable city working paper 26*. Maynooth: National University of Ireland.

Komninos, N., & Kakderi, C. (2019). *Smart cities in the post-algorithmic era: Integrating technologies, platforms and governance*. Chentelham: Edward Elgar.

KWMC. (2020). Retrieved from: https://kwmc.org.uk/.

Lausanne. (2020). Retrieved from: https://replicate-project.eu/4th-session-roadmap-for-the-realization-of-an-eco-district-including-development-of-medium-depth-geothermal-energy-in-urban-areas/.

Leycolan. (2020). Retrieved from: www.leycolan.com.

Madsen, A. K. (2018). Data in the smart city: How incongruent frames challenge the transition from ideal to practice. *Big Data & Society, 5*(2), 1–13. https://doi.org/10.1177/2053951718802321.

MakingCity. (2020). Retrieved from: http://makingcity.eu/city-profiles/.

Matchup. (2020). Retrieved from: https://www.matchup-project.eu/news/when-a-follower-takes-the-floor.

Mihci, H. (2019). Is measuring social innovation a mission impossible? *Innovation: The European Journal of Social Science Research*, 1–31. https://doi.org/10.1080/13511610.2019.1705149.

Morozov, E. (2013). *To save everything, click here: The folly of technological solutionism*. New York: PublicAffairs.

Moulaert, F., & MacCallum, D. (2019). *Advanced introduction to social innovation*. Cheltenham: Edward Elgar.

MySmartLife. (2017). *D.6.14 mySMARTLife cities network replication activities planning.* Retrieved from: https://www.mysmartlife.eu/fileadmin/user_upload/Deliverables/D6.14_mySMARTLife_Cities_Network_replication_activities_planning.pdf.

Nesti, G., & Graziano, P. R. (2019). The democratic anchorage of governance networks in smart cities: An empirical assessment. *Public Management Review*, 1–20. https://doi.org/10.1080/14719037.2019.1588355.

Nilüfer. (2020). Retrieved from: https://replicate-project.eu/6th-session-socio-economic-development-from-below/.

Nilüfer Kent Konseyi. (2020). Retrieved from: http://www.niluferkentkonseyi.org.

Pel, B., Wittmayer, J., Dorland, J., & Jørgensen, M. S. (2019). Unpacking the social innovation ecosystem: An empirically grounded typology of empowering network constellations. *Innovation: The European Journal of Social Science Research*, 1–26. https://doi.org/10.1080/13511610.2019.1705147.

Pocityf. (2020). Retrieved from: https://pocityf.eu/.

Poppen, F., & Decker, R. (2018). The intermediary as an institutional entrepreneur: Institutional change and stability in triple-helix cooperation. *Triple Helix*, *5*(1), 1–22. https://doi.org/10.1186/s40604-018-0063-7.

Potjer, S., & Hajer, M. (2017). *Learning with cities, learning for cities: The golden opportunity of the Urban agenda for the EU*. Utrecht: Utrecht University.

Remourban. (2016). *D.5.2. Model for replication potential*. Retrieved from: www.remourban.eu.

ReplicateEU. (2019). *City-to-city-learning programme*. Retrieved from: www.replicate-project.eu/city2citylearning.

Riegler, J. (2017). *Scaling up & replication of smart city and community plans*. JPI Urban Europe.

Ruggedised. (2020). Retrieved from: https://ruggedised.eu/project/about/.

Sadowski, J. (2020). Cyberspace and cityspaces: On the emergence of platform urbanism. *Urban Geography*, 1–5. https://doi.org/10.1080/02723638.2020.1721055.

San Sebastian. (2020). Retrieved from: https://replicate-project.eu/1st-session-excellence-of-service-provision-based-on-data-monitoring-and-smart-management.

Schubert, C. (2018). Social innovation. A new instrument of social change? In A. Windeler, W. Rammert, M. Hutter, & H. Knoblauch (Eds.), *Innovation society today. Perspectives, fields, and cases* (pp. 371–391). Wiesbaden: Springer VS.

SCIS. (2019). Retrieved from: https://smartcities-infosystem.eu/scc-lighthouse-projects.

SCIS. (2020). *REPLICATE #City2CityLearning*. Retrieved from: https://smartcities-infosystem.eu/newsroom/news/replicate-city2citylearning.

Sharing Cities. (2016). Retrieved from: http://nws.eurocities.eu/MediaShell/media/Onereplication-strategy.pdf.

SmartenCity. (2017). Retrieved from: https://smartencity.eu/news/detail/?rx_call=124.

Smarter Together. (2019). Retrieved from: https://www.smarter-together.eu/file-download/download/public/1177.

Sparcs. (2020). Retrieved from: https://www.sparcs.info/objectives.

Späth, P., & Knieling, J. (2020). How EU-funded smart city experiments influence modes of planning for mobility: Observations from Hamburg. *Urban Transformations*, *2*(1), 1–17. https://doi.org/10.1186/s42854-020-0006-2.

Stardust. (2020). Retrieved from: http://stardustproject.eu/all-cities/.

SUI (Smart Urban Intermediaries). (2018). *Smart Cities, social innovation and smart urban development*. Edinburgh: University of Edinburgh.

Terstriep, J., Rehfeld, D., & Kleverbeck, M. (2020). Favourable social innovation ecosystem(s)?—An explorative approach. *European Planning Studies*, 1–25. https://doi.org/10.1080/09654313.2019.1708868.

Timeus, K., Vinaixa, J., & Pardo-Bosch, F. (2020). Creating business models for smart cities: A practical framework. *Public Management Review*, 1–20. https://doi.org/10.1080/14719037.2020.1718187.

Trencher, G. (2018). Towards the smart city 2.0: Empirical evidence of using smartness as a tool for tackling social challenges. *Technological Forecasting and Social Change*, *142*, 117–128. https://doi.org/10.1016/j.techfore.2018.07.033.

Triangulum. (2020). Retrieved from: https://www.triangulum-project.eu/?page_id=3576.

van Dijck, J. (2014). Datafication, dataism and dataveillance: Big data between scientific paradigm and ideology. *Surveillance and Society*, *12*(2), 197–208. https://doi.org/10.24908/ss.v12i2.4776.

Vandervyvere, H. (2017). *Recommendations on EU R&I and regulatory policies: Why may replication (not) be happening?*. Brussels: EU SCIS.

von Radecki, A. (2018). *Triangulum: Demonstrate-disseminate-replicate. D.6.2. Smart City replication framework*. European Commission.

von Radecki, A., Tcholtchev, N., Lämmel, P., & Schaj, G. (2020). *Building data ecosystems to unlock the value of Urban (big) data: A good practices reference guide*. Liverpool: Heseltine Institute.

Voorberg, W. H., Bekkers, V. J. J. M., & Tummers, L. G. (2015). A systematic review of co-creation and co-production: Embarking on the social innovation journey. *Public Management Review*, *17*(9), 1333–1357. https://doi.org/10.1080/14719037.2014.930505.

Walker, R. M., James, O., & Brewer, G. A. (2017). Replication, experiments and knowledge in public management research. *Public Management Review*, *19*(9), 1221–1234. https://doi.org/10.1080/14719037.2017.1282003.

Wathne, M. W., & Haarstad, H. (2020). The smart city as mobile policy: Insights on contemporary urbanism. *Geoforum*, *108*, 130–138. https://doi.org/10.1016/j.geoforum.2019.12.003.

Wiese, K. (2020). Energy 4 all? Investigating energy justice implications of community-based micro-hydropower cooperatives in Ethiopia. *Innovation: The European Journal of Social Science Research*, 1–24. https://doi.org/10.1080/13511610.2020.1745059.

Woodcock, J., & Graham, M. (2019). *The gig economy: A critical introduction*. London: Polity.

Zuboff, S. (2019). *The age of surveillance capitalism: The fight for a human future at the new frontier of power*. London: Profile.

Chapter 5

DEVOLVING smart city citizenship: Smart city-regions, data devolution, and technological sovereignty

Chapter outline

5.1 Techno-politics of data

The politics of urban digital data are discussed infrequently in smart city events worldwide (Forbes, 2016). Consequently, the smart city technologies and initiatives are generally portrayed and positioned as technical, pragmatic, commonsensical, and non-ideological—that is, as rational interventions designed to improve social, economic, and governance systems. They are inherently politically and ideologically loaded in vision and application, reshaping in particular ways how cities are managed and regulated (Kitchin, 2015, p. 17).

Given the context of hyperconnected societies (Floridi, 2015; Morozov, 2014), how can the politics of data be unpacked to be used actively to design and deliver the effective public policy to tackle global urban sustainability issues? (Vinuesa et al., 2020). How can we design and implement open data platforms that will not only guarantee citizen engagement, privacy, and security but also strike a new, broader balance between democracy, politics, and real-time public deliberation? (Taylor, 2020). How can we alter the data politics by considering

Smart City Citizenship. https://doi.org/10.1016/B978-0-12-815300-0.00005-8

citizens as decision-makers rather than data providers by devolving their rights to own their data? (Calzada, 2018a; Calzada & Almirall, 2020).

Habermas argued that smartness cannot be more technocratic than democratic (Habermas, 2015). However, these days, the development of smart urban governance is being based increasingly on the conception that smart cities are merely systems of systems, systems of data, or systems of algorithms. The term *techno-politics* thus illustrates that it is never possible to make clear distinctions between technology and politics (Kurban, Peña-López, & Haberer, 2016; Smith & Pietro Martín, 2020). Politics uses technical standards because they can be more effective than laws, at the same time that technical expertise is acquiring a political power that was not intended (Grasseger & Krogerus, 2017).

Hence, despite the abundant critical literature espousing a techno-deterministic view of smart cities (Campbell, 2012; Davies, 2017; Harari, 2015; Hughes, 2016; Marvin, Luque-Ayala, & McFarlane, 2015; Noveck, 2015), this chapter suggests that what is required for comparative purposes is a critical review of the smart city itself (European Union, 2016). Meanwhile, what is needed for a more comprehensive democratic interpretation of the usage of data and a socially progressive policy agenda of smartness in cities and regions is a socially constructive approach called *Commoning* (Bollier & Helfrich, 2013, 2017; Borch & Kornberger, 2015). This approach will be elaborated in Chapter 6 regarding the term *Data Commons* (Yakowitz, 2011).

By exploring the side effects of the hyperconnected societies (Calzada & Cobo, 2015; Floridi, 2015), critical techno-politics views, such as those advocated by Morozov (2014) and Harari (2016), have gained momentum in criticising and altering the course of some ongoing smart city initiatives. For Morozov (2014, p. 1), despite the plethora of technological solutions to social problems, the following key questions remained unanswered: 'Who gets to implement data?' and 'What kinds of politics of data do technological solutions smuggle through the back door?' Others, like Rossi (2016, p. 12), promulgate the urban governance perspective when arguing that 'the contemporary smart city cannot be reduced to the economic value generated by partnerships involving powerful public and private actors, such as multinational corporations and the state'.

Another reason that the current interest in citizens' participation and interaction is at the centre of the debate about smart cities is because too many times technological solutions have been proposed without considering needs and usability by citizens or the sociotechnical misalignment within the city (Almirall, Lee, & Majchrzak, 2014; Anttiroiko, 2016). This chapter elaborates on the idea that favourable conditions exist for a potential politics of progressive smart city policy agendas based on urban transformations driven by Social Innovation (SI) and experimentation (Moulaert & MacCallum, 2019). However, some city-regions may be better equipped than others to this aim: data as an asset should be brought back to citizens through data devolution (Loukissas, 2019), which suggests remarkable rearrangements in multilevel governance models by considering technological sovereignty as the main post-GDPR EU digital policy principle (Brabham, 2009; Calzada, 2015, 2019a; Davies, 2014, 2015). Cities represent powerful places for detecting emerging processes and observing spontaneous urban transformations (Cohen, Almirall, & Chesbrough, 2016; Grau-Solés, Íñiguez-Rueda, & Subirats, 2011). The technology-oriented pathways of smart cities offer still unexplored opportunities for experimenting as long as we would be able to liberate data of citizens from big tech giants through tailored and unique forms of technological sovereignty at the city-regional level such as data altruism, donation, or more globally, data and platform co-operatives (Borkin, 2019; Calzada, 2019b; Saunders & Baeck, 2015; Seltzer & Mahmoudi, 2012; Taylor, 2014).

Having said that, we should face the reality when Gartner predicts billions connected devices (and consequently humans controlled as a result of the post COVID-19 aftermath) will be hooked up to the larger smart city infrastructure by the end of 2020. According to Harari (2016), in the era of data in the post COVID-19, the authority has already shifted from humans to computer algorithms (Dyer-Witherford, Kjosen, & Steinhoff, 2019). What is the role of the state in this context? How can regions and cities regain data ownership? This chapter sheds light on these questions.

From academia, urban studies have a long tradition of critically examining the interface between space and digital technologies, and information studies have targeted the city as one of its principal domains of study. However, narratives and practices around notions of *smartness* have been largely absent regarding citizenship and the territorial rescaling with the nation-state (Alizadeth, 2016; Calzada, 2015, 2018b, 2020a). This chapter aims to rethink the dominant technocratic and technology-centric smart city discourse—not by imagining cities beyond or before technologies, but by accepting that city-regions are already fundamentally shaped by networked and mobile ICTs and by acknowledging that city-regions as techno-political assemblages will inevitably revolve around generating large amounts of data, which will lead to new governance strategies (Calzada, 2018b). In reality, city-regions are much more complex, as the report by the European Commission and UN-Habitat shows (Calzada, 2015; European Union and UN-Habitat, 2016). They are shaped by a large variety of different actors and organisations with often conflicting positions. All this makes truly smart city-regional governance exceedingly difficult but at the same time a fascinating and rewarding scale for investigating the various meanings and usages of smartness (Herrschel & Dierwechter, 2016). Here are three general questions to start working with these meanings:

(i) How can smart cities and urban data ecosystems be designed, built, and governed to enable city leaders and municipal representatives to exploit more fully the powerful digital and data revolution and effectively tackle critical economic, social, and environmental challenges in a way which is democratic and ethical, and which maintains ongoing stakeholder and public trust? (Van Noordt, Misuraca, Mortati, Rizzo, & Timan, 2020)

(ii) How can city leaders and municipal authorities increase access to and enable better harvesting of smart tech, digital assets, and urban big data while maintaining buy-in from stakeholders and citizens? (Misuraca et al., 2020)

(iii) Ultimately, how might metropolitan and city-regional authorities build smart cities in collaboration with citizens and for citizens, dedicated to the cause of enabling public, private, and third sector actors to capitalise on Big Data while also delivering public good, including through accelerating inclusive and clean local growth? (Lee, Woods, & Kong, 2020)

In the context of this chapter, the hypothesis is that we need to harness a new generation in algorithms which will enable machines to engage unprecedented scales of data so as to mimic aspects of human consciousness, reach reflexive decisions, undertake cognitive and sentient reflection, and perhaps even arrive at moral judgements (Kuziemski & Misuraca, 2020). And thus, the aim would be to better understand the efficacy and ethics of the institutional machinery at the metropolitan and city-regional level currently being used to govern a progressive smart city. But, what would such a metropolitan smart city-region look like?

In order to provide qualitative, evidence-based comparatives of smart city-regional governance, this chapter will examine research results obtained during fieldwork research conducted between September 2015 and June 2016 in four European city-regions (Fricke, 2017), two in Spain—Bilbao and Barcelona—and two in the UK—Glasgow and Bristol. In the next subsection, further details about the research process, case studies, and methodology will be provided (Fig. 5.1).

This chapter will first emphasise the transition of their smart city initiatives, especially regarding the techno-politics of data. Second, it will stress the increasingly substantial importance of a multilevel governance about data devolution scheme (Calzada, 2017a; Khanna, 2016; Scott & Copeland, 2016) by guaranteeing *smart* allocation of territorial autonomy, social, and technological sovereignty (Couture & Toupin, 2017; DiEM25, 2018; Galdon, 2017; Maurer, Skierka, Morgus, & Hohmann, 2015) in owning, managing, and being responsible for their data in relation to their smart city projects.

Hence, this chapter examines smart transitions going on in comparatively in Glasgow, Bristol, Barcelona, and Bilbao by pointing out differences in their city-regional governance. The analysed cases combine in a novel manner the three domains that, according to Kitchin (2015), smart cities encompass: regulation and efficiency, economic development, and SI and civic engagement.

These aspects suggest the need to elaborate on the key component of the debate: what we mean when we talk about *smart citizens*. This chapter focuses on two critical factors of the smartness in cities and regions to capture the way in which the smart citizens' discussion is taking place in the presented case studies. The first factor refers to the requirement for a techno-politics of data by providing transparent business and social models including a wide range of stakeholders in the decision-making process. The second factor suggests that smarter use of technology and data are vital to the success of city-regional data devolution processes, and vice versa (European Commission, 2020).

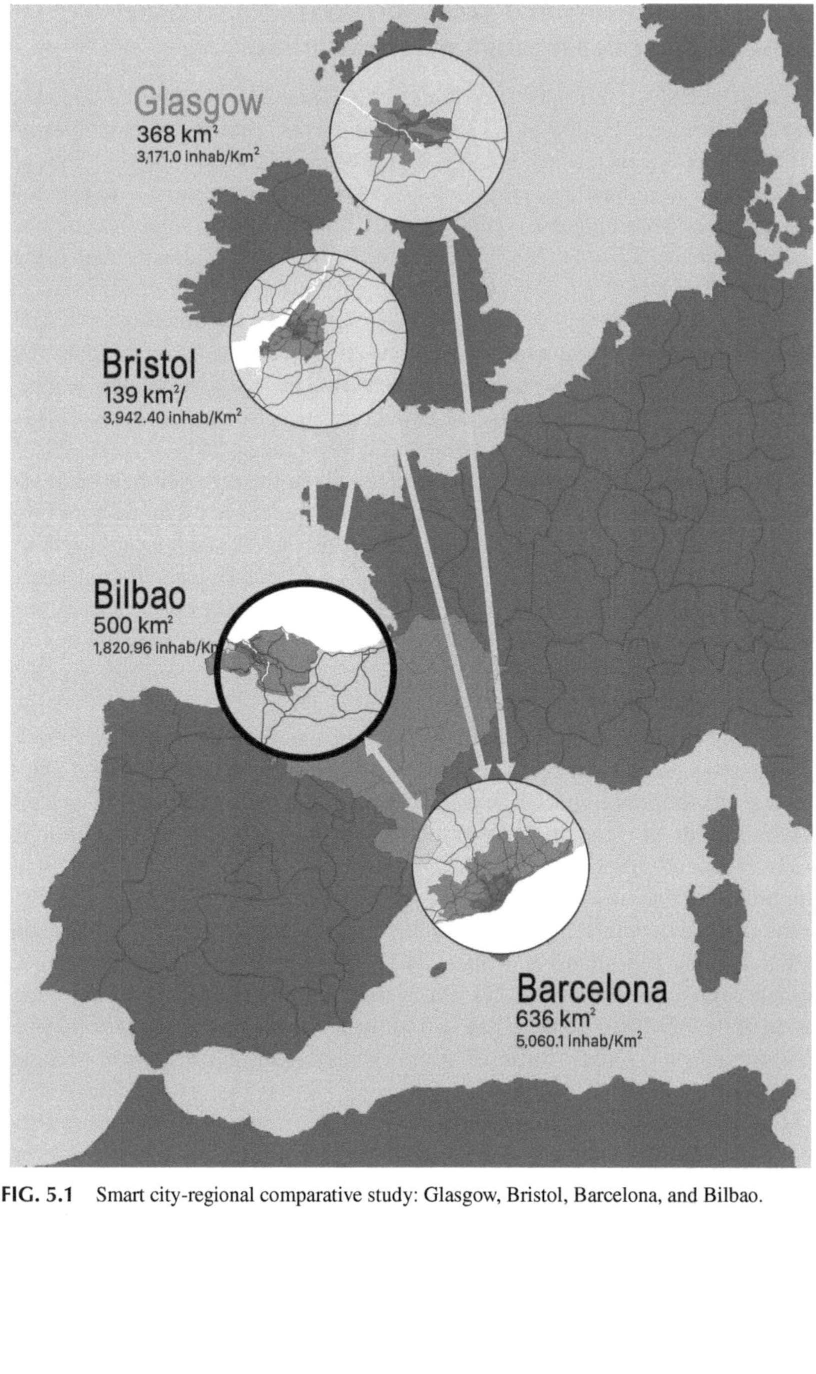

FIG. 5.1 Smart city-regional comparative study: Glasgow, Bristol, Barcelona, and Bilbao.

5.2 Problematising and politicising transitional smart city-regional scales through data devolution

In recent years, the European Commission's Horizon 2020 Smart Cities and Communities (EC-H2020-SCC) policy framework (European Commission, 2017) has led an increasing number of European cities and metropolitan areas—as well as *natural* but less obvious extensions, city-regions—to promote the benefits of becoming smart (European Parliament, 2014), regardless of what the term means (Calzada, 2015; Calzada & Cobo, 2015; Caragliu, Del Bo, & Nijkamp, 2011).

Alongside this trend, according to the European Commission and UN-Habitat (European Union and UN-Habitat, 2016), addressing municipal, metropolitan, and regional governance fragmentation across urban realms is a key strategic and smart challenge in the emerging European system of multilevel governance (Henderson, Jeffery, Wincott, & Wyn Jones, 2013; Klinke, 2016). Having said that, this issue is rather complex given the different historical and political path dependencies of nation-states and the uneven dynamics of city-regions in Europe towards a more democratic, distributed, and bottom-up smartness approach (Habermas, 2015). Thus, this chapter introduces the unspoken but remarkable role that data devolution is already playing in smart city-regional strategies and policies by problematising the techno-political implications for citizens and stakeholders in some European city-regions (Cardullo & Kitchin, 2017; Keith & Calzada, 2016).

Despite the different city-regional dynamics and particularities of diverse nation-states, such as the UK, Spain, and Italy (Giordano & Roller, 2003), we see city-regional spaces beyond nation-states (Calzada, 2015) as constitutive fields of 'tensions between different spatial policy representations, discourses, and practices, embodied by different action rationales and with potentially different scalar effects' (Fricke & Gualini, 2017, p. 6). In regards to the diverse devolution schemes in the UK, Spain, and Italy, Giordano and Roller argued, (Giordano & Roller, 2003, pp. 911–912) it 'is imperative to compare the experiences of other European countries which share longer histories of devolution (…) have had difficulties in their respective processes of state formation (…) have suffered from a sometimes fragile sense of national identity'.

Furthermore, the fashionable discourse of smartness has emphasised the need to make explicit and thus unpack its techno-political implications at different scales, including which among them resonate with the data devolution of complex governance problems (such as healthcare anonymised personal data to react to the COVID-19 global outbreak; Krutzinna & Floridi, 2019) and, consequently, with politicisation understood as political decentralisation with nation-states. Thus, scaling smart city initiatives and projects up to or down from the metropolitan and city-regional scales, provokes frictions, overlaps, related ambiguities, and contradictions (Calzada, 2017b), ultimately affecting the daily lives of (smart) citizens (Gardner & Hespanhol, 2017). These associated problems are common because of the sheer multiplicity of stakeholders shaping complex urbanity, the divergent levels of power, and their sometimes-conflicting agendas. Hence, some European city-regions are experimenting with how best to govern urban structures that encompass several municipalities and with transcalar city-regional governance schemes by drawing from different government traditions, constitutional frameworks, and policy cultures related to data.

Paralleling this desire for smartness and referring directly to metropolitan and city-regional transcalar overlaps and contradictions, this chapter highlights the fact that ongoing territorial and political reforms of administrative borders and competences of local governments strongly encourage that special attention is paid to a phenomenon that is always overlooked in smart city mainstream political rhetoric, media dissemination, official policy discourses, and research agendas (Albino, Berardi, & Dangelico, 2015): devolution (Rodríguez-Pose & Gill, 2003; Scott & Copeland, 2016; Travers, 2017) and its relation to data belonging to citizens (Loukissas, 2019).

Thus, the availability of data and its ownership will be part of the new condition of cities, which will require new governance mechanisms of connectivity, collaboration, and collective intelligence (Saunders & Mulgan, 2017) as core elements that rely on platforms, social media, data analytics and literacy, crowdsourcing, SI and engagement (De Koning, Jaffe, & Koster, 2015), and ultimately, digital democracy (Simon, Bass, Boelman, & Mulgan, 2017). By assuming that citizens, regardless of their geolocalised position in a wide city-regional spatial dimension, will be increasingly considered decision-makers rather than mere data providers, we favour the use of a more complex, democratic, distributed, and devolved governance framework for data ecosystems' management (Calzada, 2019b). Ultimately, the chapter finds that whether devolution will be smart in each city-region depends not only on how efficient but also on how democratic and transparent the use of technology and data will substantially be.

5.3 Comparing four smart city-regions: Glasgow, Bristol, Bilbao, and Barcelona

5.3.1 Fieldwork research

On the one hand, the data discourse is transforming not only the way cities understand and thus implement their governance roles but also how they should deal with techno-political issues (Neff & Nafus, 2016; Sugimoto, Ekbia, & Mattioli, 2016). On the other hand, the allocation of resources at the local and regional levels seems to be a pervasive trend for some city-regional governance issues, based on real data institutional settings, that has been taking place unevenly in some European city-regions' strategies (Calzada & Almirall, 2020; Scott & Copeland, 2016).

In Europe, shifts in metropolitan policies are taking place regarding spatial development such as polycentricity, competitiveness, or integrated development (Fricke, 2017). Previous research findings advocate that despite similarities between the main definitions of metropolitan city-regions, which refer to underlying concepts of city-regional co-operation and their relevance for spatial and economic development, metropolitan policies in the four cases have taken various forms and have focused on different governance instruments (Muñoz, 2020). As such, the comparison of two national cases, the UK and Spain, can thereby contribute to a better and more systemic understanding of the *smart city-region* beyond national perspectives and methodological nationalism. These aspects resonate with the current version of data ecosystems that are emerging as a result of the digital innovation hubs deployed by the European Commission (Calzada, 2019b).

Particularly, the UK has been facing this policy debate in an open and constructive manner by considering that city-regional economic and territorial scales should meet regionally diverse urban transformations, as the Brexit vote on 23 June 2016 clearly depicted (Penny, 2016). Thus, the devolution debate has been entirely connected with data and smart strategies. With some remarkable differences, this has been the case in Glasgow and Bristol after both had been noted as leading cities in the smart policy field (McClelland, 2017). Likewise, in Spain, Bilbao and Barcelona took diverse path dependency routes towards devolution, having different impacts on their data and smart policies' current evolution. The chapter thus will resonate with these differences and path dependencies.

In order to provide an evidence-based, empirical research comparison of case studies of smart city-regions, qualitative fieldwork research was conducted in four cases—Glasgow, Bristol, Barcelona, and Bilbao—from September 2015 until June 2016. This period of qualitative action research fieldwork was funded by the European Commission, Marie Curie Actions-MSCA-COFUND-2015-Regional Programmes under the Grant AYD-000-268. The host and beneficiary institutions and local partners of the fieldwork research were Bizkaia Talent (Talentia Network, 2017) and Bilbao Metrópoli 30 (2017). Both are strategic institutions of the Biscay province in the Basque Country (Spain). Thus, the selection of the cases followed the funding institutions and the host and beneficiary institutions' criteria. As such, the study aims to focus on the potential pervasive governance linkage between data devolution and techno-politics of data in the way the two Spanish (Bilbao and Barcelona) and the two British (Glasgow and Bristol) cities implemented their current smart city strategies. Although data devolution term was not even used in the policy domain, this study determined a plethora of aspects worth considering to when anticipating the protection required by the European citizens' digital rights in the post-GDPR era (after May 2018) (see Chapter 7).

The research method employed was action-based qualitative research by examining strategic and ethnographic factors in each location. This comparative study was based on triangulation techniques such as interviews, policy paper analyses, and ethnographic research. As such, 20 interviews were carried out in each location. The aim of the fieldwork research was to cover the most diverse and heterogeneous range of stakeholders. Actually, this research design was based on the Penta helix framework driven by multi-stakeholders' interdependencies (Calzada, 2016; Foster & Iaione, 2016). Thus, instead of suggesting the Triple helix or Quadruple helix model, this chapter follows the Penta helix framework in order to capture the widest governance narrative to inform how each location has been carrying out its data and devolution policies and strategies. The broader picture that this research covered, the better and richer research outcomes could be achieved. The scientific principle leading this research and the Penta helix framework is based on the idea that stakeholders' interdependencies and their social and culturally rooted practices are as important as the data and technical knowledge itself. Indeed, the role of data institutions seems to be strategically substantial in order to foster ecosystems of experimentation engaging not only the public sector, private sector, and academia but also civic society and social entrepreneurs and/or activists. As the last type of stakeholder, social entrepreneurs and/or urban activists represented the initial spark in the ecosystem of urban experimentation by acting as intermediators, brokers, and assemblers (as explained in Chapters 2 and 3). Given the different configurations in each location, the interviews followed the same semi-structured form by interviewing policymakers and civil servants (public sectors), practitioners (private sector), civic group representatives (civic society), academics/researchers/scientists (academia), and social entrepreneurs/urban activists (change-makers). In this sense, despite the wide literature in the field of open innovation (West & Bogers, 2016), as we are going to observe in the following subsections, this comparative study emphasises particular features in each location by comparing both ethnographic and strategic perspectives.

5.3.2 Smart citizens from (just) data providers to decision-makers

When Habermas (2015) confronted technocratic and democratic smartness, he made it possible to generalise a category called *smart citizens*. But could smartness be a possible answer based on Ostrom's idea of the *commons* requiring reconciliation between the conflicting interests of individualism and collectivity (Ostrom, 1990, 2010)? Yet, there is a shift that the mainstream literature has pervasively addressed. For a full understanding of the techno-political implications of the term *smart citizens* and to put into practice the whole capacities of citizens as the main driver in urban transformations, this chapter underlines the requirement of a transition in the term itself. When citizens are considered users or data providers, it is assumed that personal data comprise a raw material that the citizens take for granted as another element of the market. This fact should draw the attention of policymakers insofar as there are underlying value issues and political decisions involved.

FIG. 5.2 Smart city-regional case study: Barcelona.

According to the interviews conducted, the policy chapters analysed, and the ethnographic research carried out, the current status of the smart citizens understanding in each location is as follows.

In Barcelona (Fig. 5.2), according to Capdevilla and Zarlenga (2015) and Bakici, Almirall, and Wareham (2013), *smart citizen* projects served as illustrative examples of how grassroots initiatives could be gradually adopted by citizens and public institutions. In 2012, the concept of the smart citizen was launched. It was the result of many technological and cognitive experiments developed over the years at the Fab Lab Barcelona at IAAC and was inspired by the work of entrepreneurs such as Arduino and Pachube. But, at that time, it was quite adventurous to imagine a smart city model that was different than the landscape painted by large technology corporations, which were hegemonic by selling worldwide as an IT-based, urban playground where citizens were seen as mere consumers, data providers. Since then, the www.smartcitizen.me project has deployed more than 1200 sensors around the world. This process has employed working with more than 20 universities and has been used as a case study in many academic chapters and books (Noveck, 2015). Now, cities are using the term smart citizen as a standard for defining citizen participation in the smart city agenda. The founders advocate for making technology valuable for people's lives not as a consumer good, but as a tool that empowers citizens and takes their roles in their cities to a new level, and we feel this has only just begun. In 2013, the 'Smart Citizen Kit' project won the World Smart Cities Awards. According to Bakici et al. (2013) particularly, the overall transformation of Barcelona into a smart city was progressing successfully, and it was already widely recognised as a leading case of smart city initiatives all over Europe (Calzada, 2020b).

Nevertheless, as we will observe later, after some changes in the City Council of Barcelona and the Regional Government of Catalonia (Generalitat de Catalunya, 2016), *smart citizens* initiatives have been evolving. On the one side, the City Council of Barcelona launched the Barcelona Initiative for Technological Sovereignty smart strategy (BITS, 2017), which was absolutely a political manifesto in favour of fighting for the digital rights and sovereignty of data, contrasting with the previous governmental period in both ideology and scope (Calzada, 2020b). This is a notion that crosses with the factor of the techno-politics of data and will be elaborated further in Chapter 6 and particularly Chapter 7. On the other hand, projects such as *Data-Driven Cities* (PwC, 2016) and *Making Sense* (Digital Social Innovation, 2017) have engaged much more with data literacy and citizen sensing.

Thus, as we can observe from recent research results, projects deploying the preliminary idea of smart citizens as decision-makers rather than data providers vary from the previous institutional period (Adjuntament de Barcelona, 2013; Barcelona Institute of Technology, 2015) by introducing new elements insofar as sociopolitical and ethical challenges are surfacing. As such, techno-politics of data is rather present in the policy debate in Barcelona, a debate that is not entirely linked (thus far) with devolution but paradoxically related to technological sovereignty (Galdon, 2017). Although paradoxically, devolution (macro)-political debate exists permanently among those interviewed and in the diagnosis of Barcelona as a global smart city beyond its borders (Blanco, Salazar, & Bianchi, 2020; Jordana, 2019).

Regarding Bilbao (Fig. 5.3), the interviews with the public authorities, private companies, local social entrepreneurs, managers in academia, and some civic associations located in certain renewed areas in Bilbao, such as Zorrozaurre (UIA, 2016), have shown pervasive transitions towards smart citizens as decision-makers rather than data providers. The main conclusion could be the dichotomic narrative analysed from the SI perspective in the city (Moulaert & MacCallum, 2019) by some local managers (Aldekoa, 2014a, 2014b) on the one hand and by grassroots urban movements on the other hand (Calvo, 2015; Calzada, 2011; Eizaguirre, 2016; González, 2004, 2011; Larrea, 2012). Despite the Guggenheim effect—highly studied by many authors (Alayo, 2013; Alayo, Henry, & Plaza, 2016; KPMG, 2014; Martinez Cearra, 2014a, 2014b; Plöger, 2007)—representing the opening of the new Guggenheim Museum in 1997 and characterising this beginning with the redevelopment of the old port and waterfront into a post-industrial, trendy, urban landscape with distinct international references in architecture and design, the urban political divide was rather pervasive, according to some authors (Gonzalez, 2006; Rodriguez & Martinez, 2003; Rodríguez, Martínez, & Guenaga, 2001). In fact, the interviews clearly showed a divide in the understanding of who were *smart citizens*. There is an *industrial* business version of how the city should encourage *just* competitiveness

FIG. 5.3 Smart city-regional case study: Bilbao.

as a main driving force of the smart strategy (Bilbao City Hall and Ekintza, 2012; Bilbao Lan Ekintza, 2012; Bilbao Urban Solutions, 2012). Even the narrative around data and its techno-politics simply reproduce a technical infrastructure of information without considering any experimental, deliberative processes so far (Cimubisa, 2015). However, some initiatives led by academia and social entrepreneurs emerged (Calzada, 2018d, 2019d; WeLive, 2017). Those could be seen as seeds for upcoming less technocratic approaches to smart cities by opening up the experimental policy scope towards *smart citizens* as decision-makers. Actually the new Master courses designed to take place from 2020 onwards in Bilbao by the University of Deusto in Urban Sustainable Development and the new Bachelor's degree by the University of Mondragon in Global Digital Humanities could be seen as a clear turning point in this strategic pathway (University of Deusto, 2020; University of Mondragon, 2020).

According to a recent performance assessment framework on Bristol's smart city strategy (Henley, 2017; Fig. 5.4), this strategy was formed in 2011 to lead the digital innovation agenda within the city with the initial focus areas of smart energy, smart mobility, and smart data. Two main landmark projects are detailed as the key performance of this city: Bristol Is Open (2015a, 2015b) and Replicate EU-funded H2020 project (broadly examined in Chapters 3 and 4). Actually, Bristol's smart strategy (Bristol City Council, 2011a, 2011b, 2012, 2014; Bristol Smart City Delegation, 2016) according to the assessment, has

FIG. 5.4 Smart city-regional case study: Bristol.

already implemented interactive, inclusive, and continuous engagement methods to practice transparency and has made the best of the feedback (Caprotti, 2019; Cowley & Caprotti, 2019; Hambleton, 2020).

After conducting interviews in Bristol, the first institutional feature that modified the governance strategy regarding the smart city was the appointment of the new mayor, Mr. Marvin Rees. Despite landmark projects such as Connect Bristol (Future Cities Demonstrator), funded via a £3 million grant from the UK government's Technology Strategy Board (TSB); Gigabit Bristol; Bristol Is Open; 3-E Houses; Bristol Data Dome; Knowle West Media Centre; and Replicate, some commentators asked whether the smart city strategy and projects being rolled out in Bristol were sufficiently ambitious and systemic to compete with London. By contrast, others note that Bristol was expected to increase its population by over 20% by the end of the 2020s.

Considering the information provided in the policy reports and the interview results, Bristol presents an increasing effort to experiment with smart citizens as decision-makers rather than data providers. As it has been regularly shown in the VentureFest event, the technology produced in Bristol (VentureFest, 2017) depicts a singular notion of citizens as those taking part in deliberation processes. As such, Bristol is ultimately amalgamating a large number of smart projects in a complex network of interactions with citizens in a prospect of the

FIG. 5.5 Smart city-regional case study: Glasgow.

future that will be held on the challenge to foster decision-makers' interplay, portraying the city as an open innovation platform (Fig. 5.5) (Caprotti, Cowley, Flynn, Joss, & Yu, 2016).

Finally, Glasgow (Cowley, Joss, & Davot, 2017) has been portrayed as a city trying to reinvent itself through competition and awards, including Glasgow European Capital of Culture 1990, Glasgow City of Science, Glasgow City of Music, and, the smart-city-related Future City Glasgow, awarded by the Technology Strategy Board, now Innovate UK, since 2013 (Boyle & Rogerson, 2013; Caprotti, 2019; Clark, 2016; Leleux & Webster, 2018; Rogerson, Nicholson, Reid, & Sly, 2019). Despite long-standing social problems, the high level of commitment to transforming the city points to an inclusive highly networked city with a commitment to partnership. The partnership infrastructure in Glasgow resonates with urban governance institutionalised settings. On top of the urban governance partnership, Glasgow flags its commitment clearly with the quality of citizens' lives as central. As well, the city branding fuelled by the motto 'People

Make Glasgow' speaks for itself. However, after analysing what the Future City Glasgow demonstrator project proposed, we can assess that the ideas of transformation, of what is to be transformed, and by whom could appear vague. After conducting interviews on this issue, despite the good urban governance partnership, the direct benefits of making data public were not clear. Thus, there was an assumption that providing data/evidence will directly lead to action. Since these interviews, more recently, in addition to the existing leading institutions (Glasgow City Council, Scottish Cities Alliance, and the Urban Big Data Centre), the data landscape has been very fertile with the creation of new data infrastructures and institutions (Calzada & Almirall, 2020) such as Scotland 5G Centre, Scottish Tech Army, Data-Driven Innovation, Edinburgh International Data Facility, Economic Development Association Scotland (EDAS), The DataLab, Creating the Data Capital of Europe, Scotland's AI Strategy, DataFest2020, John Smith Centre, and Edinburgh Futures Institute, among many others.

Hence, despite the rich and comprehensive smart data and strategy in Glasgow showing an outstanding interplay between institutions and organisations, some discussants pointed out the lack of specific deployment of strategic actions, which contrasts with the reports provided at the city-regional level by the Scottish Cities Alliance (Scottish Cities Alliance, 2015a, 2015b, 2016). In a report of the Scottish Cities Alliance, there is a remarkable claim of establishing a city-regional collaborative environment to develop, deploy, and scale smart city solutions in Scotland's seven cities. The challenge now would be how to organise data ecosystems and more importantly how to regain technological sovereignty for citizens at a collective level.

To sum up, citizens own data as the intrinsic part of their urban experience and their *right to the city* (Morozov & Harvey, 2016; Shaw & Graham, 2017). Why then do we not naturally consider *smart citizens* pure decision-makers rather than passive data providers? Despite the willingness to pursue more democratic than technocratic sustainable futures, there is strong inertia resisting this alternative path. 'The current round of urban experimentation differs from previous incarnations, representing a specific kind of governance fix for a broadly neoliberal system struggling to move towards more sustainable forms of urban development' (Evans, Karvonen, & Raven, 2017, p. 10). Perhaps it is worth noting Subirats' (2016) interesting reflection that, based on Ostrom's influential thoughts on the *commons*, suggests breaking with the individualistic vision conceived by the capitalist tradition. Subirats (Subirats & García Bernardos, 2015) notes that this vision has progressively transferred the idea of rights to individual people; the new prevailing view is that only privatisation leads to growth (Milanovic, 2019).

In a serious attempt to show a transition towards smart city strategies in the four cases presented, a deeper analysis of the techno-politics of data will be required to interpret the role of *smart citizens* as decision-makers rather than data providers. This notion is likely to be influenced by new conceptual explorations and empirical analyses carried out under the broad umbrella of the *urban commons* or the *data commons*.

5.3.3 Comparing smart city-regional governance strategies

European cities (European Parliament, 2014; European Union & UN-Habitat, 2016; Fricke, 2017) in many countries have expanded beyond their municipal borders and commuting distances have increased, further extending the reach of these economies. To better reflect this new urban reality, more and more countries have established metropolitan governments and/or merged municipalities. According to the European Commission and UNHabitat joint report (European Union & UN-Habitat, 2016), the keys to good urban governance are high levels of trust, efficient service delivery, and good stakeholder and citizen involvement. This improves policy effectiveness, which, in turn, inspires more trust and involvement, thus creating a virtuous cycle.

However, establishing metropolitan governments themselves could be the first step towards a forward-looking politics of smartness in cities and regions (Calzada, 2017b). According to Herrschel and Dierwechter (2016, pp. 20–22), the fluid, complex, and fuzzy socio-territorial configuration of city-regions (Calzada, 2015) requires a governance approach using innovative transitions to address two aims. The first of these is to establish powers and policymaking tools, including collaborative networks across institutional and territorial divisions between metropolitan and regional stakeholders. The second is to experiment with new ideas about democratic legitimacy and political inclusion.

In the current smart city universe, technologies generally enact algorithmic and KPI-driven governance and forms of automated management. In this direction, Harari states (Harari, 2015, p. 367), '[…] Dataism says that the universe consists of data flows, and the value of any phenomenon or entity is determined by its contribution to data processing'. These facilitate and produce instrumental, functionalist, technocratic, top-down forms of governance and government, including planning, which are underpinned by an ethos of civic paternalism (what's the best for *smart citizens* without considering them). They often provide *sticking plaster* or *work around* solutions, rather than tackling root and structural causes. By contrast, a smart city-regional governance model that would foster, co-create, and co-produce citizen engagement should be open and transparent in its formulation and operation. Furthermore, it should be used in conjunction with a suite of aligned interventions, policies, and investments that seek to tackle issues in complementary ways and need to be set within a wider long-term plan/vision for the city by the city. However, city-regions could be presented as fractured landscapes with respect to the city-regional geography itself and also with respect to stakeholders. City-regional actors are supposed to play an important role due to the vagueness of the policy concept of metropolitan regions as Fricke advocates (Fricke, 2017, p. 13).

After the qualitative fieldwork based on action research in the aforementioned four cases of Glasgow, Bristol, Bilbao, and Barcelona, this chapter concludes that any smart city-regional governance model must answer to this question that Kitchin posed (Kitchin, 2016, p. 7): For whom and what purpose is the smart city in our location being developed? Thus, three intertwined options are at stake when smart cities primarily are or should be about:

(i) creating new markets and profit,
(ii) facilitating state control and regulation, and
(iii) improving the quality of life in citizens.

This chapter reflects the governance transitions and the broader difficulties in grasping the smart cities' systemic urban transformation (Osborne Clarke, 2015) at the metropolitan and the city-regional scale. It is noteworthy that the scales of multilevel governance pluralise with intensifying patterns of European connectivity and accelerating economic restructuring. This trend gives rise to the notion of city-regional governance in nation-states. In this chapter, smartness should be taken as an outcome of regional urban transformations in governance. This reconciles seeming contradictions between established growth agendas and a rising concern with a broader range of qualitative parameters, such as societal and territorial cohesion. These are aspects that increasingly are being included in smart city policy agendas as an outcome of the ongoing transition in the researched city-regions.

Regarding the comparison of the metropolitan scale of the four cases (see Table 5.1), these are noteworthy: the abundance of municipalities in Bilbao and Barcelona, the slightly higher population in Barcelona and Glasgow, and the prominent economic context in Bristol.

Table 5.2 provides information about the city-regional scale in each of the cities. In Bilbao, it is evident that the absolute fiscal autonomy of the city-region as a consequence of the Economic Agreement with the nation-state (*Concierto Económico*) and the control of revenue-raising powers has allowed the province of Bizkaia to design a tax system that promotes investment and responds to economic changes (Uriarte, 2016). The most paradigmatic landmark is the

TABLE 5.1 Metropolitan scale.

	Bilbao	Barcelona	Bristol	Glasgow
	Metropolitan			
Municipalities	35	31	4	5
Surface (km^2)	500	636	139	368
Density (Inhabit/km^2)	1820	5060	3942	3171
Population (Inhabit)	910,480	3,218,223	547,993	1,166,928
GDP *per capita* ($)	38,708	36,157	42,326	37,753

Source: European Commission. (2017). Retrieved from www.ec.europa.eu/eurostat.

TABLE 5.2 City-regional scale.

	Bilbao	Barcelona	Bristol	Glasgow
	City-regional			
City-region	Basque	Catalonia	West of England	Scotland
City-constellations/network	Bilbao, San Sebastian, Vitoria, Pamplona & BAB (Biarritz-Anglet-Bayonne)	Barcelona, Tarragona, Lleida & Girona (Paisos Catalans)	Bristol, Bath & NESomerset, SGloucester & NSomerset	Glasgow, Aberdeen, Dundee, Edinburgh, Inverness, Perth & Stirling
Nation-states	ES		UK	
General devolution context: How would this general context affect data devolution and technological sovereignty?	Fiscal autonomy/Potential recentralisation by the nation-state (Calzada, 2018c)	Post-referendum secession crisis (Calzada, 2019c)	Commitment to form a Combined Authority Post-Brexit	Post-Brexit Indyref-2? (Calzada, 2018c)

Guggenheim Museum although the metro system and the water sanitation project should also be mentioned. Since the Basque autonomy is equipped with the power to decide on local and regional policies, Bilbao combines determined public sector leadership and existing entrepreneurial culture.

In Barcelona, Catalonia's elected parliament after regional elections in September 2015 announced the beginning of the secession process within Spain. It could be argued that this announcement took place after a long period of no communication with the Spanish Central Government. It is evident that this situation provokes uncertainty, both at the city-regional level in Catalonia and in Spain, where the Spanish government has not been found the way of this secession crisis (Calzada, 2019c).

In Bristol, the West of England's city-region is already the UK's most economically productive area. In September 2015, the city-region proposed a devolution deal worth £2bn Pounds with a commitment to form a Combined Authority and a £1bn investment. This could triple the level of spending on major projects—such as transport, flood defence, and housing—over the next 10 years.

In Glasgow, finally, the smart city debate is not separated from the city devolution discussion either. The devolution debate is focused on the disagreement with the rest of the favourable vote for *de facto* Brexit in the rest of the UK by demanding a direct interlocution between the Scottish government and Brussels in order to remain in the EU as a direct way to achieve the devolution of powers on welfare and tax policy. At present, after the UK has already left the EU, the debate has not disappeared.

The conclusion is that in the Spanish cities, infrastructure regimes are organised at an urban or city-regional scale, at least in Bilbao. Barcelona will seemingly allow itself to have financial resources by altering the territorial model and confronting the nation-state. In contrast, in the UK cities, after UK Innovate demonstrator projects in the two cities, Glasgow and Bristol will face, sooner or later, the city-regional data devolution debate. This is after years of multilevel centralised government in the UK, regarding policy direction, funding, and infrastructure investment (Arup, 2011, 2014a, 2014b; BIS, 2013).

The hypothesis of this chapter suggests that, on the one hand, the techno-politics of data's social awareness and, on the other hand, devolution policy in the four cases mentioned will mutually reinforce one another. How would this general context on devolution affect data devolution and technological sovereignty in the post-GDPR European realm (Calzada, 2019a)? We could observe this potential correlation in the four cases in rather different ways though very difficult so far to quantify or to assess in numeric terms how much this influences the formulation of smart city-regional policies.

Hence, in order to operationalise this hypothesis and provide some preliminary research results for further future exploration, a comparative analysis in Table 5.3 describes nine dimensions that blend and intertwine, whether or not and how the cases are considering the techno-politics of data and the influence of data devolution in their policy implementations and potentialities. After policy papers of each case were analysed and interviews were carried out, the analysis of the four smart city-regional governance cases-in-transition will describe:

(i) The Smart City-Regional Governance Analyses
(ii) Multi-Stakeholder Interdependencies' Analyses
(iii) Current Smart City-Regional Transitions
(iv) Current Smart Metropolitan Transitions
(v) Degrees of Devolution, *per se*
(vi) Degrees of Civic Engagement (Karvonen & van Heur, 2014)
(vii) Smart Policy Formulations
(viii) Collective Intelligence (NESTA, 2017)
(ix) Techno-Politics of Data Approaches

As a systemic outcome, the chapter will conclude by deducing one strategic implicit typology per case.

Bilbao depicts an outstanding city to be rebranded as a new, modern icon of the smart urban renaissance. Its strategy has been led by public-private-partnerships (PPP) without any explicit strategy, but with implicit corporate procedures. However, we should point out that civic groups, social entrepreneurs, and academics have been absent in this strategy so far (see Chapter 3). Therefore, Bilbao requires well-funded, interconnected, niche experiments in a limited range of urban contexts by mobilising a multi-stakeholder approach (Karvonen & van Heur, 2014).

By focusing on the table, the smart city-regional governance context shows a strong metropolitan institutional model, although it is fragmented in a highly dense fabric of actors regarding the three-scale institutional structure (regional, provincial, and local). Metropolitan Bilbao's historic renewal has been a model in noticing the consistent PPP employed during the last 20 years. Nevertheless, civic engagement has been largely absent, accompanied by a weak urban interdisciplinary collaboration between universities and civic society. Ultimately, the landmark niche project titled *Zorrozaurre* seems to concentrate the highest expectations of the post-Guggenheim era on the city-region. Regarding multi-stakeholder interdependencies, Bilbao has thus far been dominated by a top-down model labelled as Industry 4.0 (De Popris & Bailey, 2020). Thus, the Zorrozaurre pilot project could be presented as a linkage with citizenship in a more experimental and wider, platform-based project, which was funded by the EU under the acronym AS FABRIK (and potentially amplified a recently granted new EU lighthouse project where Bilbao acts as lighthouse city alongside with Amsterdam; https://smartcity-atelier.eu/). Paradoxically, the high degree of devolution contrasts with the elite-driven, low degree of citizen engagement. However, around academic and social entrepreneurial urban spaces, new collective intelligence initiatives are flourishing with a strong awareness of the techno-politics of data and alternative urban models for economic development and social cohesiveness. For instance, a new degree on global digital humanities being now setting up in site by the University of Mondragon may well serve this function. As such, we could deduce that Bilbao is having a transitioning from a corporate urban governance model. Thus, this chapter calls this case 'Corporate-In-Transition'.

For a long time, Barcelona has been investing and promoting itself as the first smart city in Spain, the fourth in Europe, and the 10th in the world. Presently, the current city mayor—Ada Colau, who represents a radical new citizen platform called 'Barcelona in Common'—shifted the smart city policy agenda towards an 'open source' strategy. Nonetheless, after interviewing key stakeholders in the city, we can conclude that Barcelona has digested the new city strategy called the Barcelona Initiative for Technological Sovereignty (BITS) influenced by renowned scholars such as Harvey, Morozov, and Subirats, among others. Since 2015, this transition moved from the hegemonic position of the private sector that aimed to produce universal solutions that could be applied globally with minimal adaptation in order to maximise profit, to local authorities' interests now that co-produced and place-specific smart city solutions are required (Calzada, 2020b). Now the challenge for Barcelona is how to establish data infrastructures and institutions in a co-ordinated fashion as well as leading the European digital policy realm stemming from technological sovereignty and humanism.

By focusing on the results of Table 5.3, this chapter concludes that there is actually a transition occurring after the new mayor, Ms. Ada Colau, was appointed in 2015 as the grassroots leader from the civilian platform Barcelona in Common. In fact, the new smart city branding is 'Technological Sovereignty', or an explicit governance model to encourage public debates on the implications, rights, and techno-politics of all that the digital revolution affects. Although a clear evolution is taking place since then in Barcelona from a top-down to a bottom-up approach, there are still inherent conflicts between the regional government (*Generalitat*) and the local authority led by Mayor Ada Colau. In addition, both devolution claims are increasingly progressing, and the civic engagement initiatives are being popularised by diverse local actors. In this sense, both the smart city policy formulation and the collective intelligence initiatives reinforce each other in new exploitation of projects and strategies embracing 'data-driven cities' (NESTA, 2016) by particularly considering smart citizens as those central to decision-making processes. Nonetheless, the engagement of the private sector (which is highly substantial regarding the international IT corporate sector located in the metropolitan area) needs to be seriously considered in the plans of the local authority in combination with the regional government. Thus, this chapter calls this case 'Anti-Corporate-Uncertain'.

In April 2013, Bristol received £3 million from UK Innovate. Bristol has followed 'open innovation' principles led by its flagship operational organisation; Bristol is Open, driven by the Triple helix. Bristol has been described by some discussants as the 'rebel' of the UK's smart city agenda. The new mayor, Mr. Marvin Rees, altered from the early beginning the smart agenda towards more social cohesiveness and inequality policy principles. However, considering its diverse funding model, there may be a need for the city council to engage the smart city agenda with the city-regional's ongoing process of data devolution.

Judging from Table 5.3, Bristol presents a prominent context in which to experiment with new models of urban governance. Considering the high degree of citizen engagement, Bristol is undoubtedly a city leading in smart citizens' roles as decision-makers. In contrast, the current data devolution context may evolve due to Bristol having voted to move forward with the West of England devolution deal. Already in June 2016, three councils—Bristol, South Gloucestershire, and Bath and Northeast Somerset—agreed to form a new authority headed by a 'metro mayor'. Thus, the new West of England Mayoral Combined Authority has sat above the existing councils to decide how to spend an increased budget and what to do with its new powers. Thus, this chapter calls this case 'Open-Innovation-Alternative'.

By contrast, in January 2013, Glasgow won £24 million in funding from the UK Innovate. Why was Glasgow so successful? Glasgow was distinct in its ambition and the framing of its intervention around the city's social and health priorities. The question here is whether or not its broad infrastructural and institutional support and its urban governance model have integrated into a broader, city-regional scale, as suggested by either the Scottish Cities Alliance or by Core Cities, two city-networks with entirely different city-regional political directions.

By analysing Table 5.3, Glasgow has been investing in a smart partnership structure and establishing data infrastructures and institutions. However, further strategic interventions will be required to consolidate technological investment towards higher degrees of communitarian participation and technological sovereignty, even in the current stage of being officially out of the EU. We could already say that there is a mismatch between the data discourse and the willingness of the Glaswegian participatory atmosphere. Thus, this chapter argues that increasingly a techno-political debate on data devolution and technological sovereignty has begun among stakeholders regarding self-tracking systems and the 'big data-ism' concerns. Thus, this chapter calls this case 'Urban-Governance-Transformative'.

5.4 Towards techno-politics of data devolution?

The availability of data is and will be part of the new conditions in cities (Nasa, 2016). Yet, unpacking the ownership of data and its governance structure and dynamics within their citizenries will be as important as the collection, storage, and usage of data in AI-driven cities and regions. Why is smarter use of technology and data vital to the success of city devolution and vice versa? On the one hand, city data devolution could deal with data deficit or Big Data's surveillance capitalism approach. But, on the other hand, it will be worth using existing public sector data ecosystems to effectively deliver devolved powers to local and regional authorities.

TABLE 5.3 Analysing Bilbao, Barcelona, Bristol, and Glasgow Smart City-regional governance cases in transition: Towards techno-politics through data devolution?

	Bilbao	Barcelona	Bristol	Glasgow
	Smart city-regional governance cases in transition: towards techno-politics through data devolution?			
Executive summary: Implicit Strategies	Corporate-In-Transition	Anti-Corporate-Uncertain	Open-Innovation-Alternative	Urban-Governance-Transformative
1. Smart city-regional governance analyses	Dense and fragmented. Strong metropolitan governance model Driven just by consistent PPP model Absent civic engagement Weak urban interdisciplinary collaboration between universities Niche experiments required: Zorrozaurre	Ongoing transition New mayor: • Ms. Ada Colau: grassroots leadership • 'BCN in common' • Technological sovereignty Place specific	£3 m UK Innovate/TSB New mayor: Mr. Marvin Rees Triple helix 'Rebel' Citizen Sensing	£24 m UK Innovate/TSB. Social and health priorities. Scottish Cities Alliance vs Core Cities
2. Multi-stakeholder interdependencies' analyses	Top-down led by the province council/Basque regional government. Limited strategy focussed just on the advanced manufacturing called Industry 4.0. Wider sectorial long-term vision about the city of Bilbao/the district of Zorrozaurre as a lab/platform needed and opened to citizenship	Evolving from top-down to bottom-up Still an inherent conflict/mistmach between the regional (*Generalitat*) with SmartCat brand and the local authority (city council led by Ms. Ada Colau with the new brand, BITS)	Bottom-up with a networked-driven collaboration between organisations. Changing the mayor has altered the 'smart' strategy in Bristol by prioritising social inequality projects	Top-down led by the Triple helix (Private, Public, and Academia). However, city-regional implementation presents some shortcomings. Scottish Cities Alliance and Core Cities city-network confronted in their city-regional and techno-political view

Continued

TABLE 5.3 Analysing Bilbao, Barcelona, Bristol, and Glasgow Smart City-regional governance cases in transition: Towards techno-politics through data devolution?—cont'd

	Bilbao	Barcelona	Bristol	Glasgow
3. Current smart city-regional transitions	After long time without any comprehensive implentation, 'As Fabrik' (an urban innovative action-funded EU project) is presented as the flagship project now	After a large investment in the Smart City Strategy (iBarcelona) disseminated with the smart city expo well-known international event, BITS has been recently launched based on the idea of technological sovereignty	A strategic smart city portfolio was developed: Bristol is Open, Replicate, Smart City Operations Centre, Bristol Brain, Green Capital, Open Data, Playable Cities … Citizen Sensing	Glasgow Future City strategy entails a set of interconnected three work streams: Glasgow Operations Centre (GOC), City System Integration Demonstrator Projects and Open Glasgow
4. Current Smart Metropolitan Transitions	From the corporate to Industry 4.0 district in Zorrozaurre	From the private-sector-driven Smart City (iBarcelona) to Barcelona Initiatives in Technological Sovereignty	From Multi-stakeholder approach to citizen sensing	From Glasgow Smart City to Scottish Smart City-Region
5. Degrees of Devolution, *per se*	High	In-progress	Low	In-progress
6. Degrees of Civic Engagement	Low	Very active	Highly considered	Considered but not sufficiently exploited

7. Smart Policy Formulations	Industry 4.0 /Advanced Manufacturing Smart Specialisation Competitiveness Knowledge Intense Business Services Citizen Makers Global Digital Humanities BilbaoDataLab	Smart Citizen Digital Social Innovation Making Sense City in Common Democratic City Circular City Creative City Fab Labs DECODE DECIDIM METADECIDIM	Bristol Is Open Replicate—H2020-EU Steep-7FP-EU Censored technologies Sharing data	Scottish Cities Alliance vs Core Cities (Nationalistic vs Centralistic Strategies) Data Community Code for Scotland Open Data Scotland Data-Driven Innovation Edinburgh International Data Facility Urban Big Data Centre EDAS The DataLab DataFest2020 Scotland's AI Strategy Edinburgh Futures Institute John Smith Centre Data Capital of Europe Scotland 5G Centre and Scottish Tech Army

Continued

TABLE 5.3 Analysing Bilbao, Barcelona, Bristol, and Glasgow Smart City-regional governance cases in transition: Towards techno-politics through data devolution?—cont'd

	Bilbao	Barcelona	Bristol	Glasgow
8. Collective Intelligence	• http://www.bm30.es/ • www.welive.eu • http://www.zorrotzaurre.com/en/ • http://www.uia-initiative.eu/en/uia-cities/bilbao • http://www.zawp.org/en/oos-origin-of-spaces/ • http://urbanbat.org/2016/09/29/humancities/ • https://www.fablabs.io/deustofablab	• www.bit.barcelonamodel.com • www.smartcity.bcn.cat • www.barcelona.cat/digital • www.smartcat.gencat.cat • www.bits.city • http://making-sense.eu/ • www.smartcitizen.me • https://fablabbcn.org/ • https://ec.europa.eu/digital-single-market/en/news/dsi4eu-shaping-future-digital-social-innovation-europe • www.cityprotocol.org	• www.bristolisopen.com • www.cityfibre.com/gigabit-bristol • www.connectingbristol.org • www.kwmc.org.uk/projects/bristolapproach • www.kwmc.org.uk/projects/3ehouses/ • www.futurecities.catapult.org.uk/project/bristol-data-dome/ • https://www.venturefestbristolandbath.com	• www.futurecity.glasglow.gov.uk/ops-data/ • www.futurecity.glasgow.gov.uk/intelligent-street-lighting/ • www.futurecity.glasgow.gov.uk/pdfs/future%20maps%20final%20report.pdf • www.open.glasgow.gov.uk • www.oascities.org • www.scottishcities.org.uk • www.corecities.com
9. Techno-Politics of Data Devolution Approaches	Not specified. The focus is on the economic activity. Lack of the vision regarding the sociotechnical misalignments and the role of the citizenship. Pre-Data Provider. However, FabLab could mean considering students/entrepreneurs as Citizen Makers as an opportunity	A whole strategy defined to consider citizens as decision-makers. Very early stage of the policy formulation. Institutions should follow this innovative approach. Work in progress. Particularly active through the triad DECODE+ DECIDIM+ METADECIDIM	Evolving from data provider to decision-maker. Early stage and inspiring sociotechnical path that should be followed-up	Institutions very aware of the importance of the value of data but without considering the ethical and techno-political debate in reference to the implications for the well-being of citizens. Not implemented at Glasgow level. Some interesting initiatives at the city-regional level that should be connected. Data provider towards decision-maker, with different level of achievement from hub to hub

In this chapter, four European city-regional cases show diverse path dependencies when it comes to their strategic approaches to smart city policy formulations regarding two intertwined aspects:

(i) The consideration and social awareness of the techno-politics of data in each case.
(ii) The influence of current devolution schemes on smart policy formulation and implementation.

After presenting the comparative analysis and results of the qualitative research of the four cases, and given the interest of devolution as it is related to data, software applications for user engagement, bottom-up decision-making processes, and user-driven or citizen-centric open innovation platforms, this chapter concludes that in all of the analysed cases, pervasive devolution will make the difference insofar as:

(i) It could determine the financial and institutional infrastructures to implement smart city initiatives in diverse fields, not only energy, mobility, and ICT, but also welfare and social fields (i.e. education, healthcare, tourism, culture, and social policy).
(ii) As a consequence, data debate will sooner or later combine with devolution debate insofar as collectively deciding will mean facing changes in city government, new political leadership profiles, innovative financial schemes, establishing a level of autonomy in relation to the central government, and a degree of devolution and powers to be devolved, which would modify the interplay of stakeholders and their interdependencies.

In summary, this chapter has compared four cases by drawing attention to the weakened capacities of urban governments to control their data infrastructural destinies and the constraints on the public and private sectors' abilities to innovate. Based on the results presented, this chapter has, by comparing four smart city-regional governance strategies, concluded the following: At present, Bilbao is driven by a corporate-*in-transition* strategy, Barcelona by an anti-corporate-*uncertain* strategy, Bristol by an open-innovation-*alternative* strategy, and Glasgow by an urban-governance-*transformative* strategy.

The conclusion of this chapter lies in the notion that smart strategies in city-regions are being modified as a result of a transition in the understanding and application of the techno-politics of data and of the increasing significance for their benefitting from some devolution scheme. As long as a city or a region facilitates the ownership and the self-responsibility of investment in the smart infrastructures and resources, the data-issue awareness will be shared among different stakeholders, even by encouraging them to collaborate having different visions and aims.

From a broad perspective, data devolution is a phenomenon that will be affecting cities and regions in their governance structures and forms. According to Khanna (2016, p. 64), 'the growing power and connectivity of provinces and cities are driving devolution in the 21st century as significantly as decolonisation did in the 20th century'. In fact, cities no longer need their national capitals neither to filter paradiplomatic relations with the world nor prioritise their smart initiatives and data ecosystem projects. Every location can compete/co-operate as an investment destination, and central governments will no longer control and decide how the money will be spent or how data must be used on behalf of their citizens. Data belongs to citizens and citizens are very much reliant on their city-regional data ecosystems (Loukissas, 2019).

To conclude, as we are recently observing and noticing in the UK, a notion of 'data devolution' is required to better implement a test of devolution, understood as technological sovereignty, legitimacy, authority, and also responsibility directly derived from the right to the city but retaining autonomy to pursue each city or region's own interests.

As such, the future will show us an increasing number of cities rolling out and deploying their metropolitan data strategies in co-ordination with a broader region to achieve further democratic developments in which the will of citizens is likely to be at the centre of the decision-making process. Thus, three questions, related to current transitions in some city-regions like those four presented, could be suggested at the end of this chapter to open the floor for further discussion on the techno-politics of data devolution in city-regions:

(i) What prospects are there for alternative funding and business/social models for smart city-regions?
(ii) What are the practical/political interventions needed within a multi-stakeholder pent-helix scheme (business, government, communities, academia, and entrepreneurs)?
(iii) Is another smart city-region paradigm possible—one that is connected with some experimental advancements related to the urban 'commons' and data devolution, a third way between state and market and beyond the so-called public-private-partnership (PPP)? Chapter 6 responds to these questions by examining in-depth the case study of Barcelona.

5.5 Conclusion: Is data devolution smart? Technological sovereignty

To conclude, judging from the four cases analysed, a policy agenda tailored to data devolution seems to be required for and beneficial to encompassing issues such as technological sovereignty; the political legitimacy of stakeholders without external interventions; the full capacity to self-govern, enabling distributed power networks and data literacy; and the responsibility directly derived from the right of the city-region to retain autonomy to pursue its own interests.

The way in which technological sovereignty in the EU will be shaped is uncertain despite the fact that the European Commission's data strategy clearly indicates this mandate (European Union, 2016; more recently Gaia-X project has shown and exemplified a potential pathway). How would city-regional data ecosystems as these four presented in this chapter be interrelated with this policy mandate? Europe is focusing on the need to start from the bottom-up to build a truly European model that is sustainable, locally driven, regionally rooted, and inclusive. Thus, GDPR has been politically speaking timely when considering the technological, sovereignty-minded debate over controversies related to algorithmic disruption, privacy, and ownership of data, fuelled by big corporations, along with hegemonic rhetoric about the benefits of technocentric smart cities.

Hence, the future will probably show an increasing number of city-regions rolling out smart city-regional strategies in co-ordination with more complex and varied data devolution schemes stemming from technological sovereignty to achieve further democratic developments in which the will of (smart) citizens is likely to be at the centre of the decision-making processes. This is one possible way to ensure that problematising and politicising smartness through devolution is contributing democratically to city-making and, in fact, the only way to ensure that devolution is smart.

References

Adjuntament de Barcelona. (2013). *Barcelona smart city: Vision, approach and projects of the Barcelona city to smart cities (Executive version)*. Barcelona: Barcelona City Council.

Alayo, J. (2013). Re-positioning the post-industrial city in the Global economy: Case study summary. In *Paper given at 2013 remaking cities congress*.

Alayo, J., Henry, G., & Plaza, B. (2016). Bilbao case study. In D. K. Carter (Ed.), *Book remaking post-industrial cities: Lessons from North American and Europe*. New York, NY, USA: Routledge.

Albino, V., Berardi, U., & Dangelico, R. M. (2015). Smart cities: Definitions, dimensions, performance, and initiatives. *Journal of Urban Technology*, *22*(1), 3–21. https://doi.org/10.1080/10630732.2014.942092.

Aldekoa, A. (2014a). *The vision of Bilbao*. Presentation Jakiunde.

Aldekoa, A. (2014b). *El caso de Bilbao. La reinvención de una ciudad basada en su tradición industrial*. Jakiunde: Academia de las Ciencias del País Vasco.

Alizadeth, T. (2016). An investigation of IBM's smarter cities challenge: What do participating cities want? *Cities*, *63*, 70–80.

Almirall, E., Lee, M., & Majchrzak, A. (2014). Open innovation requires integraded competition-community ecosystems: Lessons learned from civic open innovation. *Business Horizons*, *57*, 391–400.

Anttiroiko, A. (2016). City-as-a-platform: Towards citizen-centre platform governance. In *Paper presented at the RSA winter conference 2016 on new pressures on cities and regions, 24–25 November 2016, London, UK*.

Arup. (2011). *Smart cities: Transforming the 21st city via the creative use of technology*. London.

Arup. (2014a). *Future cities: UK capabilities for urban innovation*. London.

Arup. (2014b). *Delivering the smart city: Governing cities in the digital age*. London.

Bakici, T., Almirall, E., & Wareham, J. (2013). Smart city initiative: The case of Barcelona. *Journal of the Knowledge Economy*, *4*, 135–148. https://doi.org/10.1007/S13132-012-0084-9.

Barcelona Institute of Technology. (2015). Retrieved from. https://bithabitat.barcelona/.

Bilbao City Hall, & Ekintza, B. (2012). *Bilbao urban solutions*.

Bilbao Lan Ekintza. (2012). *Diagnóstico de Competitividad Comarcal.*

Bilbao Metrópoli 30. (2017). *Bilbao Metropolitano 2035: Una mirada al futuro. Reflexión Estratégica.* Retrieved from: www.bm30.es.

Bilbao Urban Solutions. (2012). *Solutions for the future: Arteche, BBVA, CAF, factor Co2, Gamesa, Gerdau, Iberdrola, Ibermática, Idom, Ikusi, Inbisa, Ingeteam, Lks, Mesa, Ormazabal, Orona, Saitec, Sener, Tecnalia and Vicinaymarine.*

BIS. (2013). *Smart cities. Report.* London: Department for Business Innovation and Skills.

BITS (Barcelona Initiative for Technological Sovereignty). (2017). Retrieved from: http://bits.city.

Blanco, I., Salazar, Y., & Bianchi, I. (2020). Urban governance and political change under a radical left government: The case of Barelona. *Journal of Urban Affairs*, *42*(1), 18–38. https://doi.org/10.1080/07352166.2018.1559648.

Bollier, D., & Helfrich, S. (Eds.). (2013). *The wealth of the commons. A world beyond market and state.* Amherst, MA: Levellers Press.

Bollier, D., & Helfrich, S. (2017). *Patterns of commoning, the commons strategies group.* Retrieved from: http://bollier.org/blog/spanish-translation-%E2%80%9Cthink-commoner%E2%80%9D-now-published.

Borch, C., & Kornberger, M. (2015). *Urban commons: Rethinking the city.* London: Routledge.

Borkin, S. (2019). *Platform co-operatives: Solving the capital conumdrum.* London: NESTA.

Boyle, M., & Rogerson, R. (2013). "Third way" urban policy and the new moral politics of community: Conflicts over the virtuous community in Ballymun in Dublin and the Gorbals in Glasgow. *Urban Geography*, *27*(3), 201–227. https://doi.org/10.2747/0272-3638.27.3.201.

Brabham, D. C. (2009). Crowdsourcing the public participation process for planning projects. *Planning Theory*, *8*(3), 242–262.

Bristol City Council. (2011a). *Smart city Bristo—Final report.*

Bristol City Council. (2011b). *Smart city benchmark.*

Bristol City Council. (2012). *Connect bristol feasibility study.*

Bristol City Council. (2014). *The population of Bristol.*

Bristol Is Open. (2015a). *FAQ.*

Bristol Is Open. (2015b). *Creating the World's first open programmable city.*

Bristol Smart City Delegation. (2016). *Information pack.*

Calvo, N. (2015). *Building the Basque City: The political economy of nation-building. Reno: UNR-CBS.*

Calzada, I. (2011). Hacia una Ciudad Vasca? Aproximación desde la Innovación Social. *Vitoria-Gasteiz: Servicio de Publicaciones del Gobierno Vasco.* ISBN: 978-84-457-3180-2. https://doi.org/10.13140/RG.2.2.20682.36801. 978-84-457-3180-2.

Calzada, I. (2015). Benchmarking Future City-regions beyond nation-states. *Regional Studies, Regional Science*, *2*(1), 350–361. https://doi.org/10.1080/21681376.2015.1046908.

Calzada, I. (2016). (Un)plugging smart cities with urban transformations: Towards multistakeholder city-regional complex urbanity? *Revista de Estudios Urbanos y Ciencias Sociales Journal*, *6*(2), 25–45. ISSN: 2014-2714. Retrieved from: http://www2.ual.es/urbs/index.php/urbs/article/view/calzada.

Calzada, I. (2017a). Invited keynote speaker on smart cities: Data devolution in Europe, data, analytics & cloud. In *Speaker series in the MSc Programmes in Management at the ESADE Business School, Barcelona (Catalonia/Spain), 23rd November.*

Calzada, I. (2017b). Metropolitan and city-regional politics in the urban age: Why does '(smart) devolution' matter? *Palgrave Communications*, *3*(17094), 1–17. In the special issue 'politics of the urban age'(ISSN: 2055-1045) https://doi.org/10.1057/palcomms.2017.94.

Calzada, I. (2018a). From smart cities to experimental cities? In M. B. G. Vincenzo, & Z. D. Walsh (Eds.), *Co-designing economies in transition: Radical approaches in dialogue with contemplative social sciences* (pp. 191–217). Cham: Palgrave Macmillan. https://doi.org/10.1007/978-3-319-66592-4_11.

Calzada, I. (2018b). Algorithmic nations: Seeing like a city-regional and techno-political conceptual assemblage. *Regional Studies, Regional Science*, *5*(1), 267–289. https://doi.org/10.1080/21681376.2018.1507754.

Calzada, I. (2018c). Metropolitanising small European stateless city-regionalised nations. *Space and Polity*, *22*(3), 342–361. https://doi.org/10.1080/13562576.2018.1555958.

Calzada, I. (2018d). *AUZOLABS: Recomendaciones Estratégicas desde la Innovación Social para la Regeneración Urbana Integral mediante Barrios-Laboratorio (Urban Living Labs) – NEIGHBOURHOODLABS: Neighbourhood laboratories for the urban integral regeneration through strategic recommendations from the social innovation.* Zumaia: Translokal – Academic Entrepreneurship for Policy Making & University of Oxford. https://doi.org/10.13140/RG.2.2.36311.11686.

Calzada, I. (2019a). Technological sovereignty: Protecting citizens' digital rights in the AI-driven and post-GDPR algorithmic and city-regional European realm. *Regions eZine*, (4). https://doi.org/10.1080/13673882.2018.00001038.

Calzada, I. (2019b). Data spaces and democracy. *RSA Journal*, (2), 40–43. https://doi.org/10.13140/RG.2.2.35392/89601/1.

Calzada, I. (2019c). Catalonia rescaling Spain: Is it feasible to accommodate its "stateless citizenship"? *Regional Science Policy and Practice*, *11*(5), 805–820. https://doi.org/10.1111/rsp3.12240.

Calzada, I. (2019d). *HERRISMARTIK: Activating the Basque network of smart municipalities through 2018-2019 implementation of the strategic programme (Basque smart city-regional strategy in the H2020 European context)/Activando la Red Vasca de Municipios Inteligentes mediante la Implementación 2018-2019 del Programa (Estrategia Vasca de Territorio Inteligente en el Contexto Europeo Horizonte 2020)*. Zumaia: Translokal – Academic Entrepreneurship for Policy Making & University of Oxford. https://doi.org/10.13140/RG.2.2.14382.97606.

Calzada, I. (2020a). Emerging citizenship regimes and rescaling (European) Nation-States: Algorithmic, liquid, Metropolitan and stateless citizenship ideal types. In S. Moisio, N. Koch, A. E. G. Jonas, C. Lizotte, & J. Luukkonen (Eds.), *Handbook on the changing geographies of the state: New spaces of geopolitics*. Cheltenham, UK and Northampton, MA, USA: Edward Elgar Publishing. https://doi.org/10.13140/RG.2.2.17301.6832/1.

Calzada, I. (2020b). Review of the book smart city Barcelona: The Catalan Quest to improve future urban living, by A. Vives. *International Journal of Iberian Studies*, *33*, 103–104.

Calzada, I., & Almirall, E. (2020). Data ecosystems for protecting European citizens' digital rights. *Transforming Government: People Process and Policy (TGPPP)*, *14*(2). https://doi.org/10.1108/TG-03-2020-0047.

Calzada, I., & Cobo, C. (2015). Unplugging: Deconstructing the smart city. *Journal of Urban Technology*, *22*(1), 23–43. https://doi.org/10.1080/10630732.2014.971535.

Campbell, T. (2012). *Beyond smart cities: How cities network, learn and innovate*. London: Earthscan.

Capdevilla, I., & Zarlenga, M. I. (2015). Smart city or smart citizens? The Barcelona case. *Journal of Strategy and Management*, *8*(3), 266–282.

Caprotti, F. (2019). Spaces of visibility in the smart city: Flagship urban spaces and the smart urban imaginary. *Urban Studies*, *56*(12), 2465–2479. https://doi.org/10.1177/0042098018798597.

Caprotti, F., Cowley, R., Flynn, A., Joss, S., & Yu, L. (2016). *Smart-eco cities in the UK: Trends and city profiles 2016*. Exeter: University of Exeter (SMART-ECO Project).

Caragliu, A., Del Bo, C., & Nijkamp, P. (2011). Smart cities in Europe. *Journal of Urban Technology, 18*(2), 65–82. https://doi.org/10.1080/10630732.2011.601117.

Cardullo, P., & Kitchin, R. (2017). *Being a 'citizen' in the smart city: Up and down the scaffold of smart citizen participation*. Maynooth: The Programmable City.

Cimubisa. (2015). *Ciudades Inteligentes: Los datos como base para la toma de decisiones*.

Clark, G. (2016). *Cities, global cities and Glasgow: Some reflections*. Glasgow: International Public Policy Institute.

Cohen, B., Almirall, E., & Chesbrough, H. (2016). The city as a lab: Open innovation meets the collaborative economy. *California Management Review, 59*(1), 5–13.

Couture, S., & Toupin, S. (2017). What does the concept of 'sovereignty' mean in digital, network, and technological sovereignty? In *Giganet 2017 conference*.

Cowley, R., & Caprotti, F. (2019). Smart city as anti-planning in the UK. *Environment and Planning D: Society and Space, 37*(3), 428–448. https://doi.org/10.1177/0263775818787506.

Cowley, R., Joss, S., & Davot, Y. (2017). *The smart city and its publics: Insights from across six UK cities*. Working document, smart eco cities.

Davies, R. (2014). *Civic crowdfunding: Participatory communities, entrepreneurs and the political economy of place*. Master Thesis MIT.

Davies, R. (2015). Three provocations for civic crowdfunding. *Information, Communication & Society, 18*(3).

Davies, W. (2017). *How statistics lost their power—And why we should fear what comes next*. Retrieved from: https://www.theguardian.com/politics/2017/jan/19/crisis-of-statistics-big-data-democracy. (Accessed 10 January 2017).

De Koning, A., Jaffe, R., & Koster, M. (2015). Citizenship agendas in and beyond the nation-state: (En)countering framings of the good citizen. *Citizenship Studies, 19*(2), 121–127. https://doi.org/10.1080/13621025.2015.1005940.

De Popris, L., & Bailey, D. (2020). *Industry 4.0 and regional transformations*. Oxon: Routledge.

DiEM25. (2018). *Technological sovereignty: Democratising technology and innovation*.

Digital Social Innovation. (2017). *Making sense EU-funded project*. Retrieved from: https://digitalsocial.eu/case-study/14/making-sense.

Dyer-Witheford, N., Kjosen, M., & Steinhoff, J. (2019). *Inhuman power artificial intelligence and the future of capitalism*. London: Pluto Press.

Eizaguirre, S. (2016). Comparing social innovation initiatives in Barcelona and Bilbao. Looking at associative participation in the governance of citizens' rights. Revista Catalana de Sociología. *31*(1), 19–33.

European Commission. (2017). *The making of a smart city: Policy recommendations*. Brussels: European Commission.

European Commission. (2020). *A European strategy for data*. Brussels: European Commission.

European Parliament. (2014). *Mapping smart cities in the EU*. Strasbourg: EU.

European Union. (2016). *Mapping smart cities in the EU*. Luxembourg: EU.

European Union & UN-Habitat. (2016). *The state of European cities 2016: Cities leading the way to a better future*.

Evans, J., Karvonen, A., & Raven, R. (2017). *The experimental city*. London and New York: Routledge.

Floridi, L. (2015). *The onlife manifesto: Being human in a hyperconnected era*. Cham: Springer.

Forbes. (2016). *Cities cannot be reduced to just big data and IoT: Smart city lessons from Yinchuan, China*. Retrieved from: http://www.forbes.com/sites/federicoguerrini/2016/09/19/engaging-citizens-or-just-managing-them-smart-city-lessons-from-china/#6a5a34392dda.

Foster, S. R., & Iaione, C. (2016). The city as a commons. Yale Law & Policy Review. *34*(2), 281.

Fricke, C. (2017). Metropolitan regions as a changing policy concept in a comparative perspective. *Raumforschung und Raumordnung Spatial Research and Planning*, *75*(3), 291–305. https://doi.org/10.1007/s13147-016-0450-3.

Fricke, C., & Gualini, E. (2017). Metropolitan regions as contested spaces: The discursive construction of metropolitan space in comparative perspective. *Territory, Politics, Governance*, 1–23. https://doi.org/10.1080/21622671.2017.1351888.

Galdon, G. (2017). *Technological sovereignty? Democracy, data and governance in the digital era*. Barcelona: CCCB.

Gardner, N., & Hespanhol, L. (2017). SMLXL: Scaling the smart city, from metropolis to individual. *City, Culture and Society*. https://doi.org/10.1016/j.ccs.2017.06.006.

Generalitat de Catalunya. (2016). *SmartCATALONIA: Catalonia's smart strategy*.

Giordano, B., & Roller, E. (2003). A comparison of city region dynamics in the UK, Spain and Italy: More similarities than differences? *Regional Studies*, *37*(9), 911–927. https://doi.org/10.1080/0034340032000143913.

González, S. (2004). The role of the Guggenheim Museum in the development of urban entrepreneurial practices in Bilbao. *International Journal of Iberian Studies*, *16*(3), 177–186. https://doi.org/10.1386/ijis.16.3.177/1.

Gonzalez, S. (2006). Scalar narratives in Bilbao: A cultural politics of scales approach to the study of urban policy. *International Journal of Urban and Regional Research*, *30*(4), 836–857. https://doi.org/10.1111/j.1468-2427.2006.00693.x.

González, S. (2011). Bilbao and Barcelona 'in motion'. How urban regeneration 'models' travel and mutate in the global flows of policy tourism. *Urban Studies*, *48*(7), 1397–1418. https://doi.org/10.1177/0042098010374510.

Grasseger, H., & Krogerus, M. (2017). *The data that turned the world upside down*. Retrieved from: http://motherboard.vice.com/read/big-data-cambridge-analytica-brexit-trump.

Grau-Solés, M., Íñiguez-Rueda, L., & Subirats, J. (2011). How to govern the complexity? Invitation to a hybrid and relational urban governance. *Athenea Digital*, *11*(1), 63–84.

Habermas, J. (2015). *The lure of technocracy*. New York, USA: Polity Press.

Hambleton, R. (2020). The Bristol One City Approach to city governance: New Civic Leadership in action. *Urban Research & Practice*, *13*(2), 228–237. https://doi.org/10.1080/17535069.2020.1752055.

Harari, Y. N. (2015). *Homo Deus: A brief history of tomorrow*. London: Harvill-Secker.

Harari, Y. N. (2016). *Noah Harari on big data, Google and the end of free will*. Retrieved from: https://www.ft.com/content/50bb4830-6a4c-11e6-ae5b-a7cc5dd5a28c.

Henderson, A., Jeffery, C., Wincott, D., & Wyn Jones, R. (2013). Reflections on the 'devolution paradox': A comparative examination of multilevel citizenship. *Regional Studies*, *47*(3), 303–322. https://doi.org/10.1080/00343404.2013.768764.

Henley, R. (2017). *Evaluating the performance of Bristol's smart city programme*. Presentation, Bristol City Council, Bristol.

Herrschel, T., & Dierwechter, Y. (2016). Smart city-regional governance: A dual transition. *The Region*, *300*(4), 20–21. https://doi.org/10.1080/13673882.2015.11668693.

Hughes, B. (2016). *The bleeding edge: Why technology turns toxic in an unequal world*. Oxford: New Internationalist.

Jordana, J. (2019). *Barcelona, Madrid y el Estado*. Madrid: Catarata.

Karvonen, A., & van Heur, B. (2014). Urban laboratories: Experiments in reworking cities. *International Journal of Urban and Regional Research*, *38*(2), 379–392.

Keith, M., & Calzada, I. (2016). European smart citizens as decision makers rather thank data providers. In *Urban transformations ESRC report on 14th November 2016 workshop entitled '(un) plugging data in Smart City-regions'*. https://doi.org/10.13140/RG.2.2.11175.14240.

Khanna, P. (2016). *Connectography: Mapping the global network revolution*. London: Orion Books.

Kitchin, R. (2015). Smart cities and the politics of urban data. In S. Marvin, A. Luque-Ayala, & C. McFarlane (Eds.), *Smart urbanism: Utopian vision or false dawn?* (pp. 16–33). Oxon: Routledge.

Kitchin, R. (2016). *Reframing, reimaging, and remaking smart cities*. The programmable city working paper 20.

Klinke, A. (2016). Dynamic multilevel governance for sustainable transformation as postnational configuration. *Innovation: The European Journal of Social Science Research*, *30*(3), 1–27. https://doi.org/10.1080/13511610.2016.1205969.

KPMG. (2014). *Magnet cities: Decline, fightback, victory*. London, UK.

Krutzinna, J., & Floridi, L. (2019). *The ethics of medical data donation*. Cham: Springer One.

Kurban, C., Peña-López, I., & Haberer, M. (2016). What is technopolitics? A conceptual scheme for understanding politics in the digital age. In J. Balcells, R. Borge, A. M. D. García, M. Fiori, M. Julià, C. M. Raventós, … M. Vilasau (Eds.), *Building a European digital space Proceedings of the 12th international conference on internet, law & politics. Universitat Oberta de Catalunya, Barcelona, 7–8 July* (pp. 499–519). Barcelona: UOC-Huygens Editorial.

Kuziemski, M., & Misuraca, G. (2020). AI governance in the public sector: Three tales from the frontiers of automated decision-making in democratic settings. *Telecommunications Policy*. https://doi.org/10.1016/j.telpol.2020.101976.

Larrea, A. (2012). *Euskal Hiria: Reflexión sobre la Ciudad y las Ciudades Vascas*. Bilbao: ex-Liburuak.

Lee, J. Y., Woods, O., & Kong, L. (2020). Towards more inclusive smart cities: Reconciling the divergent realities of data and discourse at the margins. *Geography Compass*. https://doi.org/10.1111/gec3.12504.

Leleux, C., & Webster, W. (2018). Delivering smart governance in a future city: The case of Glasgow. *Cogitatio*, *6*(4). https://doi.org/10.17645/mac.v6i4.1639.

Loukissas, Y. A. (2019). *All data are local: Thinking critically in a data-driven society*. Massachusetts: MIT Press.

Martinez Cearra, A. (2014a). *Hacia la smart city*. Bilbao: El Mundo.

Martinez Cearra, A. (2014b). *Smart Cities un urbanismo más sostenible, amable e inteligente*. Bilbao: El Correo.

Marvin, S., Luque-Ayala, A., & McFarlane, C. (2015). *Smart urbanism: Utopian vision or false dawn?*. Oxon: Routledge.

Maurer, T., Skierka, I., Morgus, R., & Hohmann, M. (2015). Technological sovereignty: Missing the point? In M. Maybaum, A. M. Osula, & L. Lindström (Eds.), *2015 7th international conference on cyber conflict: Architectures in cyberspace*. Tallinn: NATO CCD COE Publications.

McClelland, J. (2017). *Why Bristol's a city of the future*. Retrieved from: http://www.raconteur.net/technology/why-bristols-a-city-of-the-future.

Milanovic, B. (2019). *Capitalism, alone: The future of the system that rules the world*. Cambridge and London: Harvard University Press.

Misuraca, G. (2020). Assessing the impacts of digital government transformation in the EU – Conceptual framework and empirical case studies. In C. Codagnone, G. Liva, E. Barcevičius, G. Misuraca, & L. Klimavičiūtė (Eds.), *EUR 30230 EN*. Luxembourg: Publications Office of the European Union, ISBN:978-92-76-19005-9. https://doi.org/10.2760/40285. JRC 120865.

Morozov, E. (2014). *The rise of data and the death of politics*. Retrieved from: https://www.theguardian.com/technology/2014/jul/20/rise-of-data-death-of-politics-evgeny-morozov-algorithmic-regulation.

Morozov, E., & Harvey, D. (2016). Retrieved from: http://davidharvey.org/2016/11/video-conversation-between-david-harvey-evgeny-morozov-on-post-neoliberalism-trump-infrastructure-sharing-economy-smart-city/.

Moulaert, F., & MacCallum, D. (2019). *Advanced introduction to social innovation*. Cheltenham: Edward Elgar.

Muñoz, O. (2020). *Barcelona redefine su futuro omo metrópoli de 5 millones*. Retrieved from https://www-lavanguardia-com.cdn.ampproject.org/c/s/www.lavanguardia.com/local/barcelona/20200623/481924058712/barcelona-plan-estrategico-2030-area-metropolitana-habitantes.html.

Nasa. (2016). *Open city smart—The open platform for smart cities*. Retrieved from: https://www.youtube.com/watch?v=aWuMfMMPfPw.

Neff, G., & Nafus, D. (2016). *Self-tracking*. Boston: MIT Press.

NESTA. (2016). *Wise council: Insights from the cutting edge of data-driven local government*. London: NESTA.

NESTA. (2017). *Governing with collective intelligence*. London: NESTA.

Noveck, B. S. (2015). *Smart citizens, smarter state: The technologies of expertise and the future of governing*. Cambridge: Harvard University Press.

Osborne Clarke. (2015). *Smart cities in Europe: Enabling innovation*. White Paper.

Ostrom, E. (1990). *Governing the commons: The evolution of institutions for collective action*. Cambridge: Cambridge University Press.

Ostrom, E. (2010). Beyond markets and states: Polycentric governance of complex economic systems. *American Economic Review*, *100*, 1–33.

Penny, L. (2016). *I want my country back*. Retrieved from: http://www.newstatesman.com/politics/uk/2016/06/i-want-my-country-back.

Plöger, J. (2007). *Bilbao city report. CASEreport 43, Centre for analysis of social esclusion*. An ESRC Research Centre.

PwC. (2016). *Data-driven cities: From conceptual to applied solutions*. Paris: PwC.

Rodriguez, A., & Martinez, E. (2003). Restructuring cities: Miracles and mirages in urban revitalization in Bilbao. In F. R. Moulaert, & A. E. Swyngedouw (Eds.), *The Globalized city*. Oxford: OUP.

Rodríguez, A., Martínez, E., & Guenaga, G. (2001). Uneven redevelopment—New urban policies and socio-spatial fragmentation in metropolitan Bilbao. *European Urban and Regional Studies*, *8*(2), 161–178.

Rodríguez-Pose, A., & Gill, N. (2003). The global trend towards devolution and its implications. *Environment and Planning. C, Government & Policy*, *21*(3), 333–351. https://doi.org/10.1068/c0235.

Rogerson, R. J., Nicholson, F., Reid, F., & Sly, B. (2019). Using major events to increase social connections: The case of the Glasgow Host city volunteer programme. *Journal of Policy Research in Tourism Leisure and Events*, 1–13. https://doi.org/10.1080/19407963.2019.1696351.

Rossi, U. (2016). The variegated economics and the potential politics of the smart city. *Territory, Politics, Governance*, *4*(3), 337–353. https://doi.org/10.1080/21622671.2015.1036913.

Saunders, T., & Baeck, P. (2015). *Rethinking smart cities from the ground up*. London: NESTA.

Saunders, T., & Mulgan, G. (2017). *Governing with collective intelligence*. London: Nesta.

Scott, C., & Copeland, E. (2016). *Smart devolution: Why smarter use of technology and data are vital to the success of city devolution*. London: Policy Exchange.

Scottish Cities Alliance. (2015a). *City investment plans: Aberdeen, Dundee, Edinburgh, Inverness, Perth and Stirling.*

Scottish Cities Alliance. (2015b). *Smart cities readiness: Smart cities maturity model and self-assessment tool. Guidance note for competion of self-assessment tool.*

Scottish Cities Alliance. (2016). *Smart cities Scotland blueprint.*

Seltzer, E., & Mahmoudi, D. (2012). Citizen participation, open innovation, and crowdsourcing: Challenges and opportunities for planning. *Journal of Planning Literature*, 1–16. https://doi.org/10.1177/0885412212469112.

Shaw, J., & Graham, M. (2017). An informationl right to the city? Code, content, control, and the urbanization of information. *Antipode, A Radical Journal of Geography*. https://doi.org/10.1111/anti.12312.

Simon, J., Bass, T., Boelman, V., & Mulgan, G. (2017). *Digital democracy: The tools transforming political engagement.* London: NESTA.

Smith, A., & Prieto Martín, P. (2020). Going beyond the smart city? Implementing technopolitical platforms for urban democracy in Madrid and Barcelona. *Journal of Urban Technology, Forthcoming.*

Subirats, J. (2016). *The commons: Beyond the market vs. state dilemma.* Retrieved from: https://www.opendemocracy.net/joan-subirats/commons-beyond-market-vs-state-dilemma. (Accessed 10 November 2016).

Subirats, J., & García Bernardos, A. (Eds.). (2015). *Innovación Social y Políticas Urbanas en España: Experiencias significativas en las grandes ciudades.* Barcelona: Icaria.

Sugimoto, C. R., Ekbia, H. R., & Mattioli, M. (2016). *Big data is not a monolith.* Massachussets: MIT.

Talentia Network. (2017). *Zorrozaurre: Smart and sustainable system for the future Zorrozaure Island.* Retrieved from: www.bizkaiatalent.org/en/talentiasareafinala/.

Taylor, A. (2014). *The people's platform: Taking back power and culture in the digital age.* London: Metropolitan Books.

Taylor, A. (2020). *The people's platform: Taking back power and culture in the digital age.* New York City: Metropolitan Books.

Travers, T. (2017). *The power to the regions: Why more devolution makes sense.* Retrieved from: https://www.theguardian.com/public-leaders-network/2017/feb/08/power-regions-more-devolution-cities-brexit?CMP=ema-1704&CMP.

UIA (Urban Innovative Actions). (2016). *Call 1: Selected cities taking-off.*

University of Deusto. (2020). *Master Universitario en Gobernanza para el Desarrollo Urbano Sostenible.* Retrieved from https://www.deusto.es/cs/Satellite/deusto/es/masteres/estudios-masteres/master-universitario-en- -gobernanza-para-el-desarrollo-urbano-sostenible/programa.

University of Mondragon. (2020). *Bachelor's degree in global digital humanities.* Retrieved from https://www.mondragon.edu/en/bachelor-degree-global-digital-humanities.

Uriarte, P. L. (2016). *Nuestro Concierto: Claves Para Entenderlo.* Concierto Plus, Bilbao.

Van Noordt, C., Misuraca, G., Mortati, M., Rizzo, F., & Timan, T. (2020). *AI watch – Artificial Intelligence for the public sector – Report of the "1st Peer Learning Workshop on the use and impact of AI in public services", Brussels 11–12 February.* JRC120315 Luxembourg: Publications Office of the European Union, ISBN:978-92-76-19438-5. https://doi.org/10.2760/25756.

VentureFest. (2017). Retrieved from: www.venturefestbristolandbath.com.

Vinuesa, R., Azizpour, H., Leite, I., Balaam, M., Dignum, V., & Domisch, S. (2020). The role of artificial intelligence in achieving the Sustainable Development Goals. *Nature Communications, 11*(1), 233–243. https://doi.org/10.1038/s41467-019-14108-y.

WeLive. (2017). *EU H2020 funded project, addressing ICT-enabled open government—INSO1 topic, about a new concept of public administration based on citizen co-created mobile urban services*. Retrieved from: http://welive.eu/.

West, J., & Bogers, M. (2016). Open innovation: Current status and research opportunities. *Innovation: Organization & Management, 19*(1). https://doi.org/10.1080/14479338.2016.1258995.

Yakowitz, J. (2011). Tragedy of the data commons. *Harvard Journal of Law & Technology, 25*(1), 1–68.

Chapter 6

COMMONING smart city citizenship: Data Commons through (smart) citizens

Chapter outline

6.1 From smart cities to experimental cities?

In recent years, European city authorities started claiming that (smart) citizens are as important to a successful smart city programme as data and technology, and must be convinced of the benefits and security the initiatives offer to them (Bria, 2018; Morozov & Bria, 2018; Xnet, 2017). As such, the main argument of this chapter is that European cities like Barcelona (among others like Amsterdam) are already restoring privacy and empowering citizens with data through a diverse set of policies and strategies (Andrews, 2018; Bass, Sutherland, & Symons, 2018). In doing so, Barcelona seems to be leading a new digital transformation agenda called Data Commons Barcelona (2018). This works alongside the European Union (EU)'s General Data Protection Regulation (GDPR) (Edwards, 2016; GDPR, 2018; Schiek & Gideon, 2018), which mandates the ethical use of data to protect (smart) citizens from risks inherent in new, data-intensive technologies (Bridle, 2018; Buttarelli, 2018; Evenstad, 2018; Finn, 2017; Hintz, Dencik, & Wahl-Jorgensen, 2017; Nelson, 2016; O'Neill, 2008; Taplin, 2017; Van Dijck, 2014; Wyly, 2014). Hence, this

Smart City Citizenship. https://doi.org/10.1016/B978-0-12-815300-0.00006-X

chapter, through a case study of Barcelona, explores the problem of how city authorities can proactively set up policies, strategies, and initiatives based on the *commoning* to locally enhance digital rights, and give citizens more control over personal data by protecting them from discrimination, exclusion, and the erosion of their privacy (Eubanks, 2017; Noble, 2018).

Amid the clamour for smart city rhetoric in Europe (European Commission, 2017a, 2017b, 2017c), a deep debate about digital ethics and rights emerged in cities such as Barcelona (Kitchin, 2014; Trencher, 2018). Thus, the chapter aims at elucidating whether Barcelona is marking a departure from the so-called smart city paradigm (Karvonen, Cugurullo, & Caprotti, 2018; Marvin, Luque-Ayala, & McFarlane, 2015; Sadowski & Pasquale, 2015; Willis & Aurigi, 2018) to a newly emerging paradigm called experimental cities (Evans, Karvonen, & Raven, 2016; Karvonen, 2018; Marvin, Bulkeley, Mai, McCormick, & Palgan, 2018). This case study is examined through the systematic articulation and response to three operational research questions that concern:

(i) the existence of alternative data ownership regimes in the ongoing smart city model of Barcelona;
(ii) the practical consequences of the grassroots innovation initiatives implemented so far in the city; and
(iii) the searching for evidence of another experimental type of smart city.

Methodologically speaking, this chapter deconstructs Barcelona's Digital Plan 2017–2020 through qualitative fieldwork research carried out from September 2017 to March 2018 (Barcelona City Council, 2017; Calzada, 2020a; Calzada & Almirall, 2020). The methodology was based on the mixed-method technique of triangulation via action research (Fielding, 2012), which encompasses a deep literature review; the findings of 20 in-depth interviews with key stakeholders, following the Penta helix framework (private sector, public sector, academia, civil society, and social entrepreneurs/activists) (Calzada & Cowie, 2017); and result validation through participation in three key symposiums organised in Barcelona and related to the smart city renewed strategic digital agenda formulation (Barcelona City Council, 2016b).

In the EU, the debate on data privacy, transparency, and ultimately ownership gained momentum as the GDPR, based on codes such as *privacy by design* and *data portability*, took effect in May 2018 (European Commission, 2020; Wallace & Castro, 2018). The GDPR have directly influenced how city authorities implement their data policies and strategies, and foster potential transitions to allow citizens a more active role in decision-making processes. The GDPR may have already shifted the conversations that city authorities have with smart city solution providers, particularly in relation to their business models, monetisation strategies, and their data-processing procedures. Thus, a deal among developers, companies, citizens, and governments on the ethics of the underlying decisions in the application of digital technology of data seems to be at stake in the post-GDPR future at present (Reuter, 2020).

With the backdrop of this regulation, on 24 January 2018 at the World Economic Forum in Davos, Angela Merkel announced 'data will be the raw material of the 21st century' and then added 'the question "who owns that data?" will decide whether democracy, the participatory social model, and economic prosperity can be combined' (Chu, 2018, p. 1). This declaration comes at a time when data and technological sovereignty is becoming increasingly important to colocation providers, and citizens' data rights in smart cities is attracting attention from many scholars and practitioners (Almirall et al., 2016; Calzada, 2019a, 2019b; Caragliu & Del Bo, 2018; Cardullo & Kitchin, 2018; Christl & Spiekermann, 2016; Christl, 2017).

Also, in Early 2018, Cambridge Analytica and Facebook were in the spotlight due to circumstances in which Facebook data may have been illegally obtained and used by the firm (Bucher, 2012; Morozov, 2014, 2017, 2018; Solon, 2018; Stucke, 2018; Stucke & Grunes, 2017). This episode had enormous influence on the techno-political debate and the critical perception of how data analytics could have been used for political purposes without the informed consent of users. Overall, this incident highlighted the idea that political parties, data analytics companies, and social media platforms view citizens and social media users as no more than data providers (Cadwalladr & Graham-Harrison, 2018; Lupton, 2016; Lupton & Michael, 2017).

The GDPR is timely when considering the debate over controversies related to algorithmic disruption and fuelled by big corporations, along with hegemonic rhetoric about the benefits of technocentric smart cities; an aspect that has been entirely revised from scratch in the post COVID-19 societies (Baeck & Reynolds, 2020). According to Richard Sennett (2020), the pandemic may, finally, humanise the use of smart cities. What is emerging in this pandemic crisis could be good programmes and protocols which create community, which contrasts with the early days' definition on smart cities. These programmes may include: (i) open sharing with citizens about the spread and management of COVID-19; (ii) mobilising community-led responses; (iii) collaborative economy steps up to meet new social and economic needs and models such as platform co-operatives and data co-operatives (Calzada, 2020b); (iv) urban citizen makers' ecosystems for rapidly developing medical equipment; and (v) finding new ways to make social isolation less isolating. This pandemic disruption now requires collaboration between cities and inevitably will need an alternative data governance model to interact with citizens and communities (Taylor, 2020). However, the smart city may not be what it has been so far. West (2013) argued that we would think by now all the urban planners would have an operational definition of a city that we just could look up. According to him, this definition does not simply exist as such. Another standpoint is needed more urgently after COVID-19.

Hence, a critical perspective on data ownership blended with a socially constructed and citizen-centric smart city approach emerges as the context for this chapter (Hatuka, 2020). Furthermore, over the last 5 years, certain cities, such as Barcelona, started implementing digital policy frameworks and programmes intended to strategically overcome the side effects of the techno-deterministic emphasis on smart cities (Calzada & Cobo, 2015; Coletta & Kitchin, 2017; Danaher et al., 2017). So far, this emphasis meant understanding the city just from a dispassionate, scientific perspective—purely as solutionist, predictable, replicable, linear, and normative urban machinery fed by citizens as pure user/data providers (see Chapter 4). Moreover, citizens' data are pervasively owned by private big data firms. As such, it becomes a mechanical entity solely governed through the market logic stemming from the public-private partnership (PPP) scheme, and occasionally and slightly including stakeholders' engagement through helix strategies such as the Triple or Quadruple helix (see Chapter 3). By contrast, and consciously in response to this techno-deterministic approach (Nilssen, 2018), a critical and evolutionary transition known as experimental cities recently surfaced in cities such as Barcelona. It is characterised by initiatives encompassing (i) the awareness of the techno-politics of data for citizens (Calzada, 2017a); (ii) potential alternative economics for city policies (Caragliu & Del Bo, 2018); (iii) citizen engagement as a democratic practice (Joss, 2018; Shin, 2009; Shin & Shin, 2016; Thomas, Wang, Mullagh, & Dunn, 2016); (iv) multi-stakeholder schemes as a pervasive governance logic; and (v) living-lab initiatives as sites devised to design, test, and learn from social and technical innovation in real time (Almirall & Wareham, 2011; Bulkeley et al., 2015; Evans, 2016; Evans et al., 2016; Kronsell & Mukhtar-Landgren, 2018; Marvin et al., 2018; Scholl & Kemp, 2016; Schuurman, De Marez, & Ballon, 2016; Von Wirth, Fuenfschilling, Frantzeskaki, & Coenen, 2018). This emergent amalgamation of initiatives surrounding the experimental urbanism trend regards urban transformations as inherently interdisciplinary, data intensive, and embedded in place. However, it remains to be seen whether the top-down (see Chapter 1), hegemonic approach to the smart city is effective in transitioning to the new paradigm, which is characterised by considering (smart) citizens as decision-makers rather than data providers.

According to Evans et al. (2016, p. 3), while the hegemonic smart city discourse has hitherto focused on 'trialling technological solutions' in real cities and benefitting multinational corporations as urban actors, the experimental cities approaches—embodied by grassroots movements, living labs, and cooperative platforms—consistently position local communities as the designers and proactive instigators of urban experiments (Karvonen et al., 2018; Marvin et al., 2018, 2015; Trencher, 2018). The smart city approach is being driven by market-based urban solutions and deconstructed from many angles after recently saturating policy agendas as a concept with very little reflexivity. In response, a new smart-citizen-centric paradigm is being tested in the experimental city. This real-world urban experiment matters because it produces 'a different type of city by offering novel modes of engagement, governance, and politics that both challenge and complement conventional strategies such as ongoing smart city strategies' (Evans et al., 2016, p. 9). Therefore, new techniques explored in the experimental city approach should rethink the smart city approach from the ground up (De Jong, Joss, Schraven, Zhan, & Weijnen, 2015; Mora, Bolici, & Deakin, 2017; Morozov & Bria, 2018; Saunders & Baeck, 2015). Reframing urban development to utilise the experimental city approach seems to shift the balance of power between stakeholders, empowering some while disempowering others, and enables new forms of coproduced knowledge by raising a fundamental academic debate (Kitchin, 2016).

Since the GDPR took effect in the EU, the transition to data and technological sovereignty inevitably sparked a debate regarding the role of citizens and their relationship with data in their own context (Andrews, 2013; Ashton, Weber, & Zook, 2017; Atkin, 2018; Burns, Daltan, & Thatcher, 2018; Cherry, 2016; Hardin, 1968; Kelleher & Tierney, 2018; Levy & Barocas, 2018; Lightfoot & Wisnieski, 2014; Lohr, 2015; Manzerolle & Smeltzer, 2011; Morozov & Bria, 2017; Niederer & Priester, 2016; Ojo, Curry, & Zeleti, 2015; Ostrom, 2010; PWC, 2016; Scholz, 2016; Shilton, 2016; Subirats & Rendueles, 2016; Waag, 2016). As such, two general questions frame this debate in relation to implementing the transition towards (smart)-citizen-centric, data-driven urban environments (Acuto, Steenmans, Iwaszuk, & Ortega-Garza, 2018; Aragón et al., 2018; Baeck, 2015; Coletta, Heaphy, Perng, & Waller, 2017; Gray & Lämmerhirt, 2017; Harari, 2016; Hemment & Townsend, 2013; Noveck, 2015; The Royal Society, 2017):

(i) Can European cities build alternatives that put citizens back in the driver's seat as decision-makers rather than relegating them to the role of data provider (Alosi, 2016; Bianchi, 2018; Bull & Azennoud, 2016; Capdevilla & Zarlenga, 2015; Gerlitz & Helmond, 2013; Gutiérrez-Rubí, 2017; Kitchin, 2017a; Replicate EU Project, 2018)?
(ii) Should European cities focus on building decentralised infrastructures based on blockchain to prevent extractive data practices by large technological corporations, where these practices violate citizens' digital rights (Jun, 2018)?

In particular, the following three operational research questions about the examination of the transition of Barcelona from the smart city to the experimental city paradigm constitute the core strands of this chapter (Almirall et al., 2016; Calzada, 2017a; Calzada & Cobo, 2015; Morozov & Bria, 2018):

(i) What prospects exist for an alternative data ownership regime in the current smart city model used in Barcelona?
(ii) What are the practical consequences of the grassroots innovation initiatives implemented in Barcelona for businesses, local governments, academia, civil society, and social entrepreneurs/activists?
(iii) Is another experimental type of smart city driven by co-operative service provision models based on Social Innovation (SI) possible in Barcelona? That is, does a *third way* exist between the state and the market that overcomes the PPP?

To respond to these three operational research questions, the chapter is organised as follows:

(i) the introduction addressed the conceptual transitions from smart cities to experimental cities;
(ii) a literature review on the term *(smart) citizens*;
(iii) the results of the chapter elaborate on (smart) citizens as decision-makers;
(iv) Barcelona's (smart) citizens' policy framework is deconstructed through its Digital Plan 2017–2020;
(v) Data Commons (Morozov, 2019; Yakowitz, 2011) policy framework is examined from the grassroots-led policy urban experimentation standpoint; and
(vi) conclusions are presented in response to each of the three operational research questions.

6.2 (Smart) citizens

6.2.1 A systematic state of the art

Many attempts were made to conceptualise smart citizens. While a variety of researchers focused on contextually bound definitions, there seems to be a lack of agreement regarding the significance of smart citizens in practice (Bull & Azennoud, 2016; Cardullo & Kitchin, 2018; De Waal & Dignum, 2017; Hemment & Townsend, 2013; Niederer & Priester, 2016; Noveck, 2015; Thomas et al., 2016; Vanolo, 2016). Expanding on prior works, some authors fiercely countered the techno-deterministic and/or neoliberal smart city rhetoric from policymakers and technology vendors by pointing out the absence of benefits from citizen-centred smart cities (Greenfield, 2017; Hollands, 2014; Milanovic, 2019), whereas others more took a constructive approach to consider and elaborate upon the alternatives offered by experimentalism (Calzada, 2018a; Evans, 2016; Evans et al., 2016; Kronsell & Mukhtar-Landgren, 2018).

Back in 1969, Arnstein's ladder—a widespread conceptual frame used to examine citizen participation in place-making and city governance—offered a valuable heuristic to start integrating the role of (smart) citizens in the city (Arnstein, 1969). Arnstein detailed three forms (citizen power, tokenism, and nonparticipation) and seven levels of participation (citizen control, delegated power, partnership, placation, consultation, informing, choice, therapy, and manipulation). This conceptual framework should strongly resonate in the current European context, where the citizen's data debate coincides with the significant weakening of citizens' right to privacy and information self-determination. Likewise, a 1969 paper might provoke a profound debate on the real meaning of participation and democracy after more than 30 years of neoliberalism (Cardullo & Kitchin, 2018; Habermas, 2015). Despite the glossy citizen-centric institutional discourse, the framework of that paper analytically enhanced the evidence-based analysis by presenting a wide range of participation levels at which smart citizens' representation and involvement may find many modalities for deliberation. These included not participating, only consuming, providing feedback, suggesting ideas, negotiating between stakeholders with conflicting visions, and leading ownership regimes. These findings are particularly relevant when cities become expanded laboratories—with special efforts to equip (smart) citizens with information and skills to enable access beyond merely supplying data. In this way, different, sustainable, prosperous, and liveable urban futures can be tested in real time (Kitchin, 2017b). Coletta et al. (2017, p. 8) argue that 'Singapore, Barcelona, Dublin, and San Francisco are (currently) but a few examples of cities undertaking experimental modes of development'.

Ratti argued that municipalities in these timely transitional examples 'are starting to understand the importance that citizens, in particular, should have a key role through "bottom-up" dynamics' (in Almirall et al., 2016, p. 142). Therefore, instead of concentrating on the installation and control of hardware, the (smart) citizens approach highlights the importance of governments getting people enthusiastic about creating apps and exploiting data themselves. Thus, an understanding of this novel paradigm of data—which involves algorithmic analysis of unrelated datasets within presently under-examined situations and social interactions—exists in the recent literature. It suggests that the notion of (smart) citizens should be associated with the idea that governments, regardless of governance scale, should act as data facilitators rather than as providers of services (see Chapter 5). This notion connects directly with the aim of this chapter insofar as (smart) citizens interact (often unwittingly) with an increasing volume of data, encounter pervasive and unethical extractive data practices, face an increasing number of privacy issues, and remain unaware of the value of their data in terms of ownership; addressing these issues opens new avenues to engage citizens with government digital policy and strategic frameworks through specific initiatives and projects (Datacity Numa, 2018; Knowledge Society Forum, 2019).

Over the last few years, the idea of smart citizens profoundly influenced smart city literature (Capdevilla & Zarlenga, 2015; De Waal & Dignum, 2017; Gutiérrez-Rubí, 2017; Hemment & Townsend, 2013; Niederer & Priester, 2016; Noveck, 2015; Waag, 2016). In summary, scholars such as Cardullo and Kitchin (2018) interestingly argue that the concept of the smart citizen is often synonymous with 'choice' in the market, with the following predominant roles: a 'consumer' or 'user'—who selects the services acquired from the marketplace of providers; 'resident'—who can afford the exclusivity offered by a 'smart district'; and 'data provider'—who creates data through the use of smart city technologies that companies can incorporate into products and extract value from. For instance, Cardullo and Kitchin's study revealed that citizens in smart cities are 'consistent with neoliberal citizenship and its emphasis on personal autonomy and consumer choice' (Cardullo & Kitchin, 2018, p. 12). This remarkable interpretation may lead us to reflect upon individuals performing certain roles and taking responsibility for opportunities in their private life (entrepreneurial self), and for the marketisation and privatisation of amenities and infrastructures. Despite citizen participation being potentially varied, it is frequently framed in a post-political fashion that provides feedback, participation, negotiation, and creation within an instrumental frame—rather than a normative or political one. That is to say, citizens are stimulated to assist in providing solutions to everyday issues, for example, by producing an app, giving an opinion on a progress plan, or performing certain functions/responsibilities that do not contest or substitute the fundamental political rationalities affecting an issue or plan. Very often, citizens are empowered by devices that consider them as consumers or testers—people to be steered, controlled, and nudged to behave in certain ways—or as raw material for algorithms that can be turned into commodities—i.e., passive data providers. In other words, citizens in the smart city act within the constraints of predictable and acceptable patterns 'rather than transgressing or resisting social and political norms' or simply becoming active decision-makers (Cardullo & Kitchin, 2018, p. 12).

Literature on smart citizens reached broad consensus that technological solutions are often proposed under the sponsorship of the smart city buzzword, while neither considering citizens' needs nor socio-technical misalignment between mechanical urban solutions and the citizens' decision-making processes (Calzada & Cobo, 2015; Campbell, 2012; Hajer & Dassen, 2014). Moreover, the literature review of reports published by the European Commission, analysing the implementation of a wide range of H2020 lighthouse projects and covering developments on smart citizens, illustrates that smart city initiatives only foster limited forms of citizen engagement and citizen power (European Commission, 2017a, 2017b, 2017c; Replicate EU Project, 2018). Although some European cities are allegedly being used as experimental testbeds or living laboratories for super-connected, technologically mediated smart districts, they must continue providing common resources and benefits to all citizens. Thus, the expectations that (smart) citizens participate in these experimental laboratories should be grounded in a much more politically active discourse of rights, data, and urban commons (Bianchi, 2018; Yakowitz, 2011). This previous dimension resonates with the 'commoning' as Bollier (2015) and Bauwens, Kostakis, and Pazaitis (2019) define. In other words, is it possible to reassemble the driving ethos for smart cities beyond a market rooted in data ownership? Consequently, could we convert data into a 'commons' (Yakowitz, 2011)? Consequently, Data Commons?

6.2.2 (Smart) citizenship at stake in European cities

Hence, (smart) citizenship appears to be at stake. In response, European smart cities such as Barcelona (Mora & Bolici, 2015) and Amsterdam (Mora & Bolici, 2017) (Barcelona's partner city in EU project Decode) are leading an alternative movement by following experimental city policy framework practices that rely on democratic data ownership regimes establishing municipal data offices, grassroots innovation, and co-operative service provision models (Bulkeley et al., 2015; Caprotti & Cowley, 2016; Decode, 2018; Evans, 2016; Evans et al., 2016; Kronsell & Mukhtar-Landgren, 2018). These cities are implementing pervasive transitions to cope with the disruption to the techno-politics of data, and address concerns that include privacy, literacy, awareness, and ownership issues while empowering local communities to avoid the side effects of the predatory sharing economy and extractive practices (Morozov & Bria, 2018; Sassen, 2017).

According to Cardullo and Kitchin (2018, p. 13), Barcelona 'is presently attempting to formulate and implement a different vision of a smart city and smart citizenship'. While under a right-wing and neoliberal government in the early 2010s, the city became an iconic smart city through its abundant initiatives and self-promotion events within the programme 'Smart City Barcelona' (March & Ribera-Fumaz, 2016). However, since the May 2015 election of Ada Colau—the mayor, representing the left-wing, green, social movement coalition—Barcelona gradually experimented with its vision and policy framework via the Digital Plan 2017–2020, deployed as 'Barcelona Ciutat Digital: A Roadmap Toward Technological Sovereignty' (Barcelona City Council, 2016b, 2017). Colau has since been effectively advised by Francesca Bria to revert to a less technocratic approach in smart city discourse and practices (Calzada, 2020a). In this period, Barcelona has shown how much strategic and techno-political light is shedding on how to challenge ideological and strategic political positions in the contemporary smart city. Practitioners and academics alike found the case of Barcelona a good source for practical examples and a retrospective analysis of the city's turn towards a more avant-garde policy agenda driven by data, techno-politics, and citizenship.

In October 2016, the new vision for Barcelona was fixed as an 'open, fair, circular, and democratic city' with a special emphasis on its mission to promote citizens' data ownership and technological sovereignty (Barcelona City Council, 2016a). This was a conscious strategy to overcome the excesses of data extractivism. Since then, the Barcelona City Council implemented a new policy framework entitled the Barcelona Data Commons programme (Barcelona City Council, 2018), which parallels an EU-funded experimental project titled Decode (Decode, 2018; Roio, 2018). The latter project functioned as a test-bed and flagship project to repoliticise the smart city and shift its creation and control towards grassroots, civil movements, and SI, and away from private interests and the state (Calzada, 2017b; Islar & Irgil, 2018; Mazzucato, 2015). As an amalgamation of strategic initiatives, the policy framework established under the Barcelona City Council Digital Plan 2017–2020 is analysed in the Section 6.4 of this chapter.

Based on this new shift, Barcelona explicitly brands itself as an inclusive, democratic, and participative smart city by promoting accordingly (Blanco, Salazar, & Bianchi, 2017; Bria, 2018; Eizaguirre, 2016): 'If you would rather have smart citizens than smart cities ... BITS, "Barcelona Initiative for

Technological Sovereignty", will be in your interest' (Barcelona City Council, 2016a, p. 1). Likewise, in Amsterdam, those advocating for smart citizens suggest that (smart) citizens should be guided by the following principles (Hajer & Dassen, 2014; Mora & Bolici, 2017; Ojo et al., 2015; Waag, 2016): take responsibility for the environment they live and work in, and the places they like; value access over ownership and involvement over power; ask for tolerance, not authorisation; ethical algorithms rather than extractive algorithms; and offer assistance to less technologically savvy individuals. This set of ethics underlies the notion of a still-limited consideration of the interconnections between hard and soft smart infrastructures, as well as those between political, institutional, economic, and social systems on the metropolitan and regional scales. Moreover, this new paradigm advocates the significance of overcoming the often-failed smart-city-in-a-box strategy, by keeping the loop with the various stakeholders.

By examining the Digital Plan 2017–2020 of Barcelona (Barcelona City Council, 2017), in particular, it is evident that the notion of the commons and the *commoning* extensively influenced the three experimental strategies of Barcelona's renewed smart city plan that were put into effect since September 2016 (Bollier, 2016; Borch & Kornberger, 2015; Foster & Iaione, 2016). Three main strategic components were identified as experimental strategies during the fieldwork research (and are explained in greater detail in the following section):

(i) a Data Commons through three strategic initiatives;
(ii) local democracy through two intertwined grassroots innovation initiatives; and
(iii) political economic co-operative platforms in relation to three initiatives built around Digital Social Innovation, Barcelona Urban Commons, and a 'social economy' municipal framework.

Thus, this plan opened a new path for action in Barcelona based on Ostrom's prominent thinking on the commons (Bass et al., 2018; Bianchi, 2018; Ostrom, 2010; Subirats & Rendueles, 2016). For example, one of the strategic initiatives, entitled Data Commons Barcelona (Bria, 2018; Barcelona City Council, 2018, p. 1), is defined as 'a shared resource that enables citizens to contribute, access, and use the data—for instance about air quality, mobility, or health—as a common good, without intellectual property rights restrictions', which clearly resonates with Ostrom's assertion that nonprofit and voluntary actions should govern the collective resources that many citizens use as data (including free software, Wikipedia, and Open Street Map). However, as Hardin (and more recently Yakowitz, 2011) warned (Hardin, 1968), the 'tragedy of the commons' could occur when data extractive practices conquer the urban metabolism. A notion of the commons, updated by Bollier, argues that historically embedded individualisation procedures gradually shape the communal settings such that they require experimental interventions as a corrective (Bollier, 2016).

In a bold attempt to transition from a smart city to an experimental city, conceptual explorations around the commons are likely to influence a more profound examination of the techno-politics of data. Thus, because this chapter emphasises the active role of (smart) citizenship; the conception of the commons should be encompassed in the narrative, because the rhetoric of the hegemonic smart city is uniquely based on the idea of PPPs (Rossi, 2016). Bollier (2016) suggests that cities are at an intersection insofar as (smart) citizens could use the ideas of the commons to retain control of the services that matter to them and safeguard the functions of these services for the people of the city, and not only for businesses or bureaucracy. However, the idea of the commons could also be argued to be rather abstract with regards to policy implementation (Bauwens et al., 2019).

One possible solution to the issues above is offered by the hypothesis of this chapter: the notion of (smart) citizens as decision-makers is being explicitly included in the policy formulation of Barcelona by addressing the three main operational research questions of this chapter. The fieldwork research process identified three experimental strategies that directly relate to the debate on the implications of the GDPR for citizens and on the governance structures required to critically tailor the techno-politics of these data:

- **(i)** alternative data ownership alternative regime initiatives;
- **(ii)** grassroots innovation initiatives; and
- **(iii)** co-operative service provision models, such as urban co-operative platforms (Scholz, 2016), living-lab initiatives (Almirall & Wareham, 2011; Schuurman et al., 2016; Tõnurist, Kattel, & Lember, 2017), and proactive social economy policy frameworks.

Ultimately, this chapter aims to examine whether the rhetoric of the experimental city is followed by an evidence-based impact in the case of Barcelona. The exact definition of more citizen-centred approaches is often left unstated; therefore, this chapter aims to unravel the meaning from the Barcelona case to provide evidence-based insights into the city's experimental strategies. Within the scope of some approaches to experimental cities, the extent to which citizens play a more active role as co-producers rather than as mere data providers remains to be seen, although the techno-politics of data (i.e. ownership and governance) is an under-explored area of research (Baeck, 2015; Gray & Lämmerhirt, 2017).

After a rigorous literature review covering the case of Barcelona and its transition from the 'Smart City Barcelona' strategic period in 2011–2014, led by former mayor Xavier Trias (Bakıcı, Almirall, & Wareham, 2013; Degen & García, 2012; Gascó-Hernandez, 2018), to the current 'Barcelona Data Commons' strategic period led by current mayor, Ada Colau (Blanco et al., 2017; Calzada, 2017a, 2017b; Capdevilla & Zarlenga, 2015; Eizaguirre, 2016; Eizaguirre & Parés, 2018; Gutiérrez-Rubí, 2017; Jones, 2015; March & Ribera-Fumaz, 2016; Tieman, 2017; Timeus & Gascó, 2018), this chapter offers the hypothesis that the existing smart city cannot simply be reduced to the economic trade-off of the data it generates through partnerships with powerful public and private actors (Rossi, 2016). A key element of this shift in discourse is the need to embrace a multi-stakeholder approach by broadening the representation of social actors in decision-making processes in order to overcome the new religion of data. Coined 'dataism' by Harari (2016), over-reliance on data is understood as a logic oversimplifying a city's metabolism as a mere assemblage or system of data and algorithms (Kelleher & Tierney, 2018; Lohr, 2015; Morozov, 2014; Morozov & Bria, 2017; Morozov & Eno, 2017; Morozov & Harvey, 2016; O'Neill, 2008; Van Dijck, 2014), rather than an ecosystem of citizens (Calzada, 2018a).

6.3 Decision-makers

Citizens' personal data are a fundamental part of their urban experience, and their digital rights should be based on a logic of solidarity, social co-operation, and collective rights to the city (Gago-Fernandez, 2020; Morozov & Harvey, 2016). Why, then, do we not naturally consider (smart) citizens as pure decision-makers rather than simply passive data providers? Despite the willingness to pursue sustainable futures that are more democratic than technocratic futures, strong inertia obstructs this alternative path. If the government offers greater data accessibility, better public services will be delivered (Ashton et al., 2017; Joss, 2018). Thus, alternative policy paths explore city government policies that could require large corporations to share data collected from their users to preserve full digital rights for citizens by developing decentralised, privacy-enhancing alternative data infrastructures based on blockchain and attribute-based cryptography (Decode, 2018; Jun, 2018; Martens & Duch Brown, 2019). In fact, the current round of urban experimentation differs from previous incarnations (Evans et al., 2016, p. 10), indicating a 'specific type of governance fix for a neoliberal system that is struggling to move toward more sustainable forms of urban development'. In Barcelona, this ongoing experimentalism addresses new business and social models that also demand previously accepted legal frames and procurement regimes be revisited. According to Francesca Bria, the Chief Technology Officer (CTO) of Barcelona (Almirall et al., 2016, p. 145), the techno-politics of data in Barcelona are articulated in response to an explicit strategy to 'disrupt these data accumulation, making data available across vertical silos experimenting with decentralised data infrastructures through distributed ledgers such as blockchain, and proposing new frameworks and business models that reward and incentivise openness, enabling data discovery, transactions, and secure data sharing'. This citizen-centric approach to the techno-political policy scheme of Barcelona is called Barcelona Data Commons (Barcelona City Council, 2018); it is influenced by the experimental EU-funded project Decode (2018), which is centred around strategic initiatives regarding technological sovereignty and data transparency.

This section underlines how data-driven and algorithmic issues open up novel challenges for implementing policy in cities all over the world. In terms of the ethical, institutional, and political dimensions of the ownership of data, urban experiments—Barcelona in particular—are gaining traction as a strategy to stimulate alternatives and steer change (Caprotti & Cowley, 2016), as suggested by the Digital Plan 2017–2020. The idea of experimentation feeds on the appealing notions of innovation and creativity (both individual and collective) while also shifting the focus of sustainability from distant targets and government policies to concrete and feasible actions that can be undertaken by a wide variety of urban stakeholders in particular locations. The ability of urban experiments to be radical in ambition while limited in geographical scope underpins a challenging debate in both the policy and academic domains with respect to the potential for such experiments to initiate genuine transformation. Are these experiments simply extensions of business as usual, spatially limited, and captured by a familiar cast of dominant interests? Or, can they engender genuine alternatives and stimulate profound transformation?

6.4 Deconstructing Barcelona's (smart) citizens' digital policy framework case study

This section examines the case of Barcelona in depth by deconstructing the Digital Plan 2017–2020 and analyses the promises and hazards of experimentation as an alternative mode of urban governance that moves beyond the structural mistakes of the so-called smart city, which is the dominant mode thus far (Hughes, 2016; Marvin et al., 2018; Nilssen, 2018; Willis & Aurigi, 2020). This section is divided into three subsections that examine the three experimental strategies of Barcelona's Digital Plan through an analysis of fieldwork material: policy documents, interviews, and symposiums:

- **(i)** The first subsection examines the first operational research question presented in the introduction, situating (smart) citizens within the context of the data ownership and technological sovereignty experimental strategy; three initiatives illustrate the ways in which experimentation is occurring within Barcelona.
- **(ii)** In the second subsection, this chapter investigates the experimental strategy of grassroots innovation in response to the chapter's second operational research question; two intertwined initiatives are presented to allow dissection of the practical consequences for stakeholders (interviewed following the Penta helix framework).
- **(iii)** In the third subsection, the chapter explores the extent to which considering decision-makers could achieve a potential ecosystem of co-operative service provision models as alternatives to capital-based forms of business.

According to the Barcelona City Council's Digital Plan 2017–2020 (Barcelona City Council, 2017, p. 3), 'in September 2016, Barcelona City Council embarked on an important digital transformation process, announcing that public services must be provided through digital channels from the outset, following new guidelines oriented towards citizens and the use of open standards and open-source software, and in accordance with an ethical data strategy that puts privacy, transparency and digital rights at the forefront'. The smart-citizen concept at the core of this strategic formulation suggests that cities should implement new legal, economic, and governance schemes to nurture collaborative behaviours from citizens to contribute to the digital commons, including commons involving personal data (Yakowitz, 2011). It is not yet clear the extent to which this move in strategic formulation is merely lip service to the critics of the term smart city versus an initiative that will actually lead to implementing real consideration of (smart) citizens. Thus, this section aims to provide empirical evidence-based insights to scrutinise the nature and intensity of this transition via the three operational research questions.

To begin, the Barcelona case study will deconstruct the Digital Plan 2017–2020 by applying three methodological techniques based on triangulation. Case study research, as defined by Yin (1984), was identified as the most effective form of mixed-method research:

(i) First, an analysis of its most recent policy documents related to the three experimental strategies was identified in the Digital Plan 2017–2020.

(ii) Second, a qualitative study of 20 semi-structured interviews was conducted in Barcelona from September 2017 to March 2018. The interviewees were identified following the Penta helix multi-stakeholders' framework and included representatives from each helix (see Fig. 2.1/3.1; Calzada & Cowie, 2017). The purpose of the interview study was to validate the mixed-method action-research process with a broad representation of opinions and evidence.

(iii) To reinforce the mixed-method technique of triangulation via action research (Fielding, 2012), the author participated in three symposiums directly related to the smart city strategic formulation in Barcelona during the fieldwork timeframe (September 2017–March 2018):

- **(a)** the celebration of the Smart City Expo World Congress 2017;
- **(b)** the ESADE Business School Smart Cities and Data Speaker Series; and
- **(c)** a presentation of the Barcelona Data Commons programme in January 2018.

The case of Barcelona was selected using a theoretical sampling approach. With slightly more than 3.2 million citizens in the metropolitan area, the city of Barcelona falls into the category of urban areas experiencing a deep transition connected to the dynamic devolution debate and vibrant bottom-up initiatives. Furthermore, its success in the smart-cities field makes the analysis of its strategic transition an ideal sample for the study; this assertion is easily demonstrated by considering the multiple smart city awards Barcelona received, in addition to its geographical location (European Commission, 2017a).

Barcelona's smart city strategy experienced two distinct periods. In 2011, the mayor, Xavier Trias, and his municipal administration decided to transform

Barcelona into a smart city through an approach slightly biased towards top-down management and with a focus on technological capacity. However, since Ada Colau's election as mayor in May 2015, the strategy reached a clear turning point. In October 2016, the publication of 'Barcelona Ciutat Digital: A Roadmap Toward Technological Sovereignty' kicked off the implementation of the new smart-citizen policy framework disseminated through the Barcelona Initiative for Technological Sovereignty (BITS) by Commissioner Francesca Bria (Barcelona City Council, 2016a, 2016b; Bria, 2018).

In the extensive evaluation of the literature discussing Barcelona, considerable consensus can be found regarding the strategic shift in the smart city pathway (Almirall et al., 2016; Bakıcı et al., 2013; Blanco et al., 2017; Calzada, 2017a; Capdevilla & Zarlenga, 2015; Degen & García, 2012; Eizaguirre, 2016; Eizaguirre & Parés, 2018; Gascó-Hernandez, 2018; Gutiérrez-Rubí, 2017; Jones, 2015; March & Ribera-Fumaz, 2016; Mora & Bolici, 2015; Tieman, 2017; Timeus & Gascó, 2018).

- First, during the 2011–2014 period and based on the corporative technocratic vendor push, the Barcelona Smart City strategy was driven more by deliberate components than by emergent and experimental components.
- Second, the current transition, called Technological Sovereignty, gained momentum. Almirall et al. (2016, p. 152) highlight 'tensions in smart cities regarding efforts in the provision of services' during the current period, while Bakıcı et al. (2013) identify five components (smart districts, living-lab initiatives, infrastructures, new services for the citizen, and open data) that were clearly updated with the launch of the City Data Analytics Office.
- Overall, this period was characterised by a critical and proactive social context formed through transversal initiatives that merge distinct municipal datasets.

Regarding the political economy resulting from the increasing influence of grassroots initiatives on the city, Eizaguirre and Parés (2018) and Degen and García (2012) studied several neighbourhoods in Barcelona. They found great significance in the role of collective leadership practices, creative social strategies, and political dissent in the founding and the social impact of local initiatives. Likewise, Almirall and Wareham (2011), Gascó-Hernandez (2018), and Timeus and Gascó (2018) examined the degree of efficiency in living labs in Barcelona at different periods (Acuto et al., 2018; Bulkeley et al., 2015; Kronsell & Mukhtar-Landgren, 2018; Schuurman et al., 2016; Tõnurist et al., 2017). Although the findings are primarily related to public and private organisations, they suggest that it may be worth exploring the contribution of living labs as intermediaries that mediate between multiple stakeholders in highly political environments such as Barcelona.

For several authors, the changing urban governance model over the two periods became the most important factor in Barcelona. At the time of the switch between the two institutional periods, Capdevilla and Zarlenga (2015) suggested a combined approach by merging top-down and bottom-up dynamics. This approach is already included in the political agenda of the current smart city strategy, despite the problematic so-called smart contradictions noted by March and Ribera-Fumaz (2016, p. 825): 'it is unclear now how interests of citizens are to be made compatible with the interests of private capital and of the urban political elites in Barcelona'. Their underlying critique relies on the idea that there is little exploration of the inner contradictions in how smart interventions are inserted into a wider political economy of urban transformation. As such, in this section, this chapter pays special attention to the central role (smart) citizens hypothetically play in the collective production and administration of the city, by identifying three experimental strategies included in the Digital Plan 2017–2020.

6.4.1 Establishing the Data Commons

Fieldwork research revealed that the data ownership and technological sovereignty experimental strategies comprise three intertwined initiatives (Barcelona City Council, 2017).

The first initiative, Data Commons Barcelona, focused on ethical data ownership and technological sovereignty principles achieved by opening the public procurement process, and ensuring that 70% of investments in new software development go towards free and open-source software in municipal systems. Barcelona attempted to include small and medium-sized enterprises (SMEs) in the public procurement process, generating a virtuous cycle where any SME, co-operative, or self-employed citizen could work under equal conditions while avoiding vendor lock-in and path dependency. Interviews revealed that the procurement process was opening promising pathways, based on the upcoming creation of an open digital marketplace for small-scale providers designed to meet the needs of the 13,000 existing technological companies, and to offer employment increases of 26.3% in the digital sector compared to 2016. This initiative implemented services such as a help for new citizens and an information portal, mobile phone services for citizens, a new calendar of city events and facilities, an open city dashboard for citizens, a technology-provider portal, and a new mobile digital identity service. Likewise, a main principle of the technopolitics of data involves explicitly improving access to the authority's data, respecting privacy, and evaluating the ethical risks of smart cities and large databases by establishing a code of ethical technological practices, including legal compliance with data protection regulation and defining a data strategy. Thus, Barcelona was experimenting with socialising previously collected data via sensors operated by citizens, with the city taking the lead in aggregating and acting upon such data to promote new co-operative approaches that solve common urban issues, such as tackling noise levels and improving air quality. The plan was to keep this common data infrastructure open to local companies, co-operative platforms, and social organisations, allowing them to build data-driven services and create long-term public value. The strategy was leading the transition to the GDPR by motivating initiatives creating a Data Commons that incorporated self-determination and the digital right of citizens to use municipal data for the public good of all citizens and stakeholders (Barcelona City Council, 2018).

Second, the city council opened the City Data Analytics Office on 13 February 2018. The office housed a Chief Data Officer and 40 staff members from different departments. They offered new privacy-related data improvement and analysis capabilities and can make predictions covering all areas related to managing the city. This research revealed that civil servants seemed to understand the challenge of breaking down data 'silos' (energy, noise, housing, garbage, meteorological, parking, air quality, water, bicycle flow, people flow, vehicle flow, and gentrification, among others) to manage 3 million data records per day. Despite that, it remained to be seen whether the external agile entrepreneurial culture and the bureaucratic public culture will find common ground (Wiseman, 2017). Furthermore, the office created an Open Data Challenge programme (Datacity Numa, 2018) to include SMEs in solving the city's challenges and to successfully position the Data Protection Delegate in line with the GDPR. The Data Protection Delegate was in charge of coordinating data protection policy within and across departments.

Third, the Decode project was an EU-funded experimental project led by Barcelona (in partnership with Amsterdam) to develop a blockchain-based architecture for data sovereignty in parallel with the operational activity of the city council. It was attempting to build new foundations for data sharing on the internet, drawing inspiration from decentralised technologies such as Bitcoin, Blockstack, and Sovrin. The project enabled a system whereby all interactions involving any citizen's data were fully auditable on a public ledger (though raw data itself remained hidden). Decode was testing how people could allow their data to be used for specific social purposes, such as informing local policymaking, and could overcome the municipalities' failure to foster local alternatives to certain services (such as Uber and Airbnb) due to the lack of raw data (Roio, 2018). However, interviews revealed that, despite this remarkable, cutting-edge initiative, citizens and even some stakeholders believed that the initiative was too abstract and experimental, and questioned the feasibility of business models based on that scheme.

To summarise this subsection, the fieldwork research revealed that Barcelona is motivated by compliance with EU legislation, particularly the GDPR. Business models that rely on the collection and commercial exploitation of personal data based on neoliberal data extractivist practices will face clear boundaries. GDPR seemed to offer to Barcelona a way to build alternative digital infrastructures that enhance privacy and can guarantee data sovereignty for citizens, giving them back control over their data. Data Commons Barcelona could have been seen as a custodian of the digital rights of citizens and a milestone in the strategic formulation of Barcelona stemming from GDPR, since it was based on the remarkable principles such as privacy by design, data portability, and the right to be forgotten or 'unplugged' (Calzada & Cobo, 2015). The city authorities proactively advocated application of the GDPR. For them, 'it represents an opportunity to create a city data infrastructure that puts citizens' right to data at the center of the game'. Another interviewee described the situation as follows: 'We have created a new City Data Analytics Office, appointed a Chief Data Officer, and introduced a new data directive that is implemented across city hall that includes transparency, ethics, security, and privacy as fundamental principles'. Moreover, other interviewees representing the private sector, academia, and (social) entrepreneurship/activism agreed upon the following visionary statement: 'We need to make sure that GDPR does not hinder social and technological innovation, but foster data-driven innovation while making sure citizens' rights are respected. The competitive advantage of Europe in the future world of AI and data should be this rights-based democratic framework, a new deal on data that can shape a people-centric digital future and make GDPR an international standard'.

6.4.2 Experimenting within grassroots innovation

According to Aragón et al. (2018, p. 277), Decidim Barcelona was an 'online participatory-democracy platform launched by the City Council of Barcelona' on 1 February 2016 as the main grassroots innovation experimental strategic initiative (Decidim Barcelona, 2018). In parallel fashion, Metadecidim Barcelona (2018) was launched in November 2017 as a watchdog, techno-political research community positioned to monitor Decidim Barcelona and reflect on its work. During its short tenure, Decidim Barcelona achieved the active participation of 40,000 citizens. Overall, 12 participatory processes were initiated and 11,873 proposals were analysed, with 70% of proposals approved as public policy for a wide range of urban issues. Interviews revealed the difficulties of integrating representative participation from the private sector, particularly from large companies with a stake in city making. Including the multi-stakeholders' framework suggested further challenges regarding representation and the constitution of socioeconomic digital co-operative firms and platforms stemming from data altruism and donation beyond the civilian volunteer activism (Mondragon Corporación Cooperativa, 2018; Scholz, 2016; Warren, 2016).

6.4.3 Fostering platform co-operatives

The third identified experimental strategy centres around the emergence of three urban co-operative platform initiatives. According to Scholz (2016, p. 1), these initiatives 'encompass new ownership models for the internet in the urban realm'.

The first initiative, Digital Social Innovation (Digital Social Innovation, 2018), is an EU-funded project to map and support cases of digital Social Innovation in Europe (Stokes, Baeck, & Baker, 2017). In Barcelona, this initiative was established as the 'Barcelona Maker District' around the FabLabs in the Poblenou neighbourhood. FabLabs aimed to develop and expand new educational models and skills by democratising access to fabrication through work with targeted segments, such as women, elderly people, and children.

Similarly, the second initiative, the Barcelona Urban Commons (2018), was established in the broader metropolitan area of Barcelona in 2010 (Cámara, 2017; Observatorio Metropolitano de Barcelona, 2018). A wide range of economic activities affecting citizens and communities was identified, including 'Guifi.net', 'Som Energia', and 'Coop57', among many others. Thus, over the last decade, these example activities offered digital connectivity, energy, and financial services, respectively, in a socioeconomic model that comprises 10% of the city economy. However, interviews revealed that some participants do not consider these initiatives as having successfully scaled up due to the shortcomings in transitioning from a grassroots communitarian movement driven by voluntarism to entrepreneurial co-operatives driven by professionalism.

The third initiative corresponds to the social economy policy framework, which consisted of 4718 socioeconomic projects and 861 co-operative firms (Barcelona City Council, 2016c). This policy framework aimed to support transformation of these projects from serving local economies to inclusion in the socioeconomic model of the entire city. Interviews pointed out the gap between the modus operandi of the corporate private sector and the initiatives conducted at the neighbourhood level by the city council. One example was the digital local currency called 'rec', promoted by the EU-funded project B-Mincome (2018), that addressed guaranteed minimum income in deprived urban areas of the city.

Despite the strong efforts of the council, the EU funds received to foster urban co-operative platforms, and the rapid pollination of projects, findings suggested that the metropolitan ecosystem still needed to mature, particularly because scaling up an alternative socioeconomic model seemed to be a process that takes longer than one institutional period. Although the strategic formulation attempted to line up a large number of initiatives in a transversal fashion, in the short term, it was likely to require further corrective measures.

To summarise this policy analysis and integrate it with the fieldwork research findings, Table 6.1 illustrates the responses to each research question proposed in this chapter. The identified experimental strategies and the strategic initiatives respond directly to the initiatives that connect the three operational research questions. Despite the individual identification of initiatives, I must acknowledge the vast amalgamation of intertwined initiatives, confirmed through interviews, which made the fieldwork complex. Thus, Table 6.1 does not provide a deep analysis of each initiative but instead serves to deconstruct Barcelona's digital policy framework to examine strategic evidence-based insights by providing the main findings grouped through the coding system of interviews/interlocutors accordingly.

TABLE 6.1 Deconstructing Barcelona's (smart) citizen digital policy framework. GDPR—General Data Protection Regulation.

	Policy/scientific analysis		Qualitative analysis
			Based on 20 interviews of key stakeholders in Barcelona from September 2017 to March 2018
Three operational research questions	**Experimental strategies**	**Strategic initiatives**	**Summary of key responses structured through the Penta helix framework (Calzada & Cowie, 2017): private sector (2); public sector (9); academia (2); civil society (3); (social) entrepreneurs/activists (3)**
1. What prospects exist for an alternative data ownership regime in the ongoing smart city model of Barcelona?	Establishing the Data Commons (Section 6.4.1)	1. Barcelona Data Commons 2. City Data Analytics Office 3. Decode	1. The majority of interlocutors clearly addressed the positive and irreversible transition as Barcelona is already adapting to the GDPR 2. The feedback was very positive in relation to the public procurement reform 3. The transition to open-source software presented remarkable obstacles 4. Despite the positive initiatives and irreversible transition towards GDPR, Decode created overly high expectations, as the initiative was perceived as too experimental
2. What are the practical consequences of the grassroots innovation initiatives implemented in Barcelona for businesses, local governments, academia, civil society, and social entrepreneurs/activists?	Experimenting with Grassroots Innovations (Section 6.4.2)	1. Decidim Barcelona 2. Metadecidim Barcelona	1. Interlocutors argued that these initiatives lacked an overall degree of representation because they omit stakeholders' power relation interdependencies 2. Others asked: How is the private sector represented in these initiatives? 3. The established channel could have been seen as a seed to scale up a broader deliberative governance model based on multi-stakeholder representation
3. Is another experimental type of smart city driven by co-operative service provision models based on Social Innovation possible in Barcelona? That is, does a *third way* exist between the state and the market that overcomes the PPP?	Fostering Platform Co-operatives (Section 6.4.3)	1. Digital Social Innovation 2. Barcelona Urban Commons 3. Social Economy	1. Interlocutors revealed the lack of a critical mass for co-operative platforms 2. Although Barcelona was shifting its smart city model, co-operative niche experiments were having difficulties scaling up 3. Setting up a *third way* required moving on from volunteer grassroots initiatives to professional entrepreneurial co-operatives

6.5 Grassroots-led urban experimentation: Deciphering the Data Commons policy scheme

To conclude, after the previous section deconstructed the Digital Plan 2017–2020, this section examined it from the grassroots-led policy urban experimentation standpoint to address how remarkable is *commoning* smart city citizenship (Bollier, 2015) particularly to enable platform and data co-operatives in the urban realm (see Chapter 7).

Since the newly elected mayor, Ada Colau—representing the left-wing, green, social movement coalition called *Barcelona en Comú* (*Barcelona in Common*)—was appointed in May 2015, Barcelona was significantly shifted its smart policy agenda towards a less technocratic approach headed for citizens' digital rights, in pursuit of data and technological sovereignty (Almirall et al., 2016; Bakıcı et al., 2013; Calzada, 2017a; Calzada & Cobo, 2015; Coletta et al., 2017; Karvonen et al., 2018; Marvin et al., 2015). This policy transition was shaped through grassroots innovation strategies and implemented using the Digital Plan 2017–2020, called 'Barcelona Ciutat Digital: A Roadmap Toward Technological Sovereignty'. Considering the timely implementation of this new, smart, urban experimental framework called 'Data Commons', this subsection questions whether the ongoing transition that began in 2015 is sustainable and solid enough (Blanco, Salazar, & Bianchi, 2019), and furthermore, the past events revealing an structural urban contestation between the *Elite Taxi BCN* association and the big tech giants *Cabify* and *Uber*.

This struggle illuminated a conflicted and unresolved data policy debate in cities like Barcelona, while opening up a plethora of alternatives for discussion of negotiated data policy among urban stakeholders (Calzada & Cowie, 2017; Keymolen & Voorwinden, 2019; Sommobilitat, 2020).

Technological developments such as data analytics and individual profiling have raised the level of awareness (and criticism) of the increasing power asymmetries between big digital players, civil society, and governments, which leave behind important invisible actors. Rarely is it acknowledged how such technological tendencies might actually do good for citizens by innovating policymaking and improving the public sector (Mazzucato, 2015). Moreover, the increasing attention worldwide to artificial intelligence (AI) makes this claim crucial to ensuring high-quality data to audit new algorithms and develop new applications. It seems that there is a pressing need for city-regional and sovereign strategies at the European level, as Barcelona has implemented, to promote ethical, citizen-centric, data-driven policymaking (Gruber, 2019; Micheli, Blakemore, Ponti, & Craglia, 2018). The Ethics Advisory Board of the European Commission (2018) defines *digital ethics* of a certain innovation territorial ecosystem through seven intertwined values: dignity, freedom, autonomy, solidarity, equality, democracy, justice, and trust.

In this general policy context, and acknowledging a certain degree of ambition in the steps laid out by Barcelona in 2015, Data Commons is presented as a policy scheme to negotiate the techno-politics of the smart city as a process that is contentious and dynamic among several stakeholders. Consequently, this subsection aims to respond to the following research question: as an alternative and transitional strategic pathway, will Barcelona's grassroots-led urban experimentation through the 'Data Commons' policy remain given the ongoing aftermath of the decision to allow *Cabify* and *Uber* to operate in Barcelona and current tensions between the two antagonistic business models of 'platform capitalism' and 'platform co-operativism'?

Barcelona's shifting discourse about smart cities is a direct reaction to a remarkable amount of data being controlled by AI tools and devices owned by multinational corporations like *Cabify* and *Uber*—as well as *Airbnb* provoking serial *tourismophobia* in the city (Calzada, 2018b). This elevates the question of how a smart city can ensure the privacy, identity, and security of its citizens while experimenting with intertwined representative and deliberative democratic public expressions. Closely following the contours of the smart city citizenship debate via the Data Commons policy scheme, this question has prompted a counter-reaction worldwide fuelled by the interplay of certain multi-stakeholders, highlighting the need for an ethically transparent data-driven society that reinforces the digital rights of citizens through accountable data ethics. A wide range of manifestos, declarations, and institutional frameworks have endorsed this paradigm turn, led by Barcelona (Barcelona City Council, 2019): Access Now, Montreal Declaration Responsible AI, and even the tech giants, Telefónica and IBM. By contrast, due to a so-called lack of transparency and democratic accountability, the case study of the Sidewalk Labs in the Quayside, Toronto (Sidewalk Labs, 2018), an operation led by *Alphabet Inc.*, has gathered the most severe criticisms and finally, the project has been cancelled. The tech giants' ambition seemed to be to control and exploit as much of the urban environment as possible, regardless of the consent of citizens. They invested highly in broadening and deepening their surveillance techniques, and even in building their own cars.

As a way not only of reverting *dataism* and surveillance capitalism, but also of leading a global movement of activism campaigning in favour of technological sovereignty through the Data Commons, in 2018, Barcelona undertook another step in this strategic direction: the declaration of Cities Coalition for Digital Rights was signed by Barcelona, Amsterdam, and NYC (Cities Coalition for Digital Rights, 2019; www.citiesfordigitalrights.org). This event showed the global leadership of the Barcelona City Council in advocating digital rights and promoting the transparent use of data through open-source digital practices (Barcelona City Council, 2019). The Declaration was rooted in the idea that digital technologies draw on a hacker ethic, working with decentralised forms of online participation and open-source devices, and committed to democratic digital rights. Therefore, the Declaration espoused five digital rights and principles, signed by the three global cities in collaboration with the United Nations Human Settlements Programme (UN-Habitat):

1. Universal and equal access to the Internet and to digital literacy.
2. Privacy, data protection, and security.

3. Transparency, accountability, and nondiscrimination of data, content, and algorithm.
4. Participatory democracy, diversity, and inclusion.
5. Open and ethical digital service standards.

In a broader examination, De Hoop, Smith, Boon, Macrorie, Marvin, and Raven (2018, p. 3) argue that the case of Barcelona shows clearly 'how digital projects can be disrupted, reconceived and reclaimed—or complemented and replaced by new digital projects—through urban politics that interact across elite and grassroots settings, and in ways that suggest more plural and hopeful possibilities'. Furthermore, Cardullo, Di Feliciantonio, and Kitchin (2019) similarly argue that urban agencies in smart city development increasingly underline that further hybrid, less-conventional data policy schemes are emerging, each nevertheless involving an inescapable knowledge politics. Cardullo and Kitchin (2018, p. 13) agree with Hoop et al. that Barcelona has attempted to do something *different*: 'Barcelona is presently attempting to formulate and implement a different vision of a smart city and smart citizenship'.

In analysing this transitional data policy momentum, these attempts clearly 'overlap with the importance of including multi-stakeholder frameworks to counter-balance the lack of attention apparently paid to local users of the services established under the former mayor Trias' (De Hoop et al., 2018, p. 10). As a result, the Data Commons policy scheme opened up by dynamic and contradictory initiatives between different stakeholders for redefining and redistributing power relations that in the past were fixed and taken for granted, exclusively following the private-public-partnership scheme. As such, the Data Commons policy scheme was a way to negotiate the techno-politics of the smart city as a contentious and dynamic process among several stakeholders, reconfiguring sociopolitical and power interrelations through conflicting trade-offs as well as ownership of the data, and ultimately, of the technology itself (Ranchordás, 2019). Negotiating the smart city means fulfilling three conditions: 're-subjectivation, transparency, and vulnerability' (Keymolen & Voorwinden, 2019, p. 16). As such, multi-stakeholder frameworks could be imagined as contexts in which conflicts arise and norms emerge through collective regulation of social interactions and political relationships in the city. Data infrastructure thus impacts the interplay among stakeholders and the city it builds, simply because data are never politically neutral (Calzada & Cobo, 2015). Different platforms' techno-political architectures could then articulate the data infrastructure and associated policy schemes depending on the inner principles of those architectures, as it is the case with the 'platform capitalism' (*Cabify* and *Uber)* and 'platform cooperativism' (*Som Energia*; Pellicer-Sifres, Belda-Miquel, Cuesta-Fernandez, & Boni, 2018; https://www.somenergia.coop/).

Consequently, Barcelona's policy discourse has gradually been influenced by a critical agenda (Eubanks, 2017; Lane, 2019; Morozov, 2018) while being translated into novel policy initiatives (Morozov & Bria, 2018) with diverse degrees of success. In this regard, initiatives implemented under the label 'platform co-operativism' are worth emphasising (Borkin, 2019; Fuster & Espelt, 2018; Parker, Van Alstyne, & Choudary, 2016; Scholz, 2016; Scholz & Schneider, 2017; Srnicek, 2017; Stone, 2016). This is the case for the remarkable renewable energies co-operative called *Som Energia*, which was officially founded in 2010 in Girona (Catalonia). In January 2019, the co-operative had over 54,300 members, had invested over 13 million euros in renewable energy production projects, and employed 47 people.

In order to look into Barcelona's grassroots-led urban experimentation, the following issue was identified: a potential implementation of 'platform cooperativism' in taxis—a severe labour problem in Barcelona—providing a path for its evolution towards a more competitive, locally owned co-operative business model, an alternative to the hegemonic, disruptive, and extractive private operations such as Uber (Gramano, 2019; Wired, 2019). Thus, despite being hypothetical, this subsection sheds light on the synergies for the feasibility and resilience between both initiatives: (i) the established co-operative *Som Energia* and (ii) the potential co-operative platform for local taxis.

There was a beneficial and broad consensus regarding the direction and suitability of this transformational paradigm of the smart city paradigm into a further negotiable arena reconsidered through a techno-political lens, and digital urbanism in the city reoriented through a policy of technological sovereignty; ambition in terms of awareness, though, seemed not to match the concrete results. However, stakeholders highlighted the novelty of using municipal institutions to spur a wide debate on digital rights and data ownership, and most of the interviewees agreed with the need for such a debate. The multi-stakeholder approach, as in the Penta helix, should mean negotiating throughout the whole life cycle of a smart city implementation, entailing more involvement of citizens than current citizen-centred smart city initiatives. Without the full interplay and negotiation of the multiple parties involved, a new mindset of municipality or private parties is not sufficient. Instead, a new orchestration of an active multi-stakeholder democratisation push is essentially needed to reassert the validity of this grassroots-led urban experimentation.

In this policy scheme, the role of social entrepreneurs and activists (the fifth helix of the Penta helix) was clearly encouraged to develop alternative digital practices like DECODE, DECIDIM, and METADECIDIM, among many other initiatives. Grassroots-led urban experimentation was demonstrably based on principles of openness, accessibility, collaboration, decentralisation, and sharing.

In the broader contours of Barcelona's data policy discussions, Catalonia (see Chapter 5; Calzada, 2018c, 2019b) is surrounded by a vibrant political tension invigorated by debates on devolution and independence, which directly affects the extent to which Barcelona, as a European city-regional hub, may claim technological sovereignty and a particular data policy fuelled by city-regional projects led by the regional government such as *Smart Catalonia* and by the motto and hashtag *#DigitalRevolutionaries*. Political sovereignty is not detached from technological sovereignty: both are extremely intertwined with democracy, governance, and the right to the city/to decide, on which Barcelona's future may rest.

Against this backdrop, the struggle between *Elite Taxi BCN* and *Cabify* and *Uber,* and the lack of (social) entrepreneurship to experiment with a co-operativised and locally/regionally rooted 'platform co-operative' for local taxi drivers seems to show the way forward. How should the new local government deal with this debate (Vesnic-Alujevic, Stoermer, Rudkin, Scapolo, & Kimbell, 2019)? This subsection suggests that examples like *Som Energia* or *Mondragon Co-operative Corporation* (www.mondragon-corporation.com; through its recently launched course on Platform Co-operatives) in the Basque Country could illuminate the experimental pathway towards a more democratic and data-driven fair platform environment (see Fig. 6.1). Drawing from SI and techno-political studies, this chapter delves into questions regarding the 'platform revolution' (Parker et al., 2016). Whilst its analysis will not be exhaustive, this chapter aims to contribute to the existing body of work with an original perspective on data policy schemes and the related platform discussion. Recently, the popular academic activist and advocate of the brand 'platform co-operatives' based at the New School in NYC, Trebor Scholz, has launched in collaboration with Mondragon Co-operative Corporation an online course to incubate platform co-ops (Platform Cooperativism Consortium, 2020).

Colau's government (Blanco et al., 2019), and particularly Barcelona's CTO Francesca Bria, managed to open a profound European debate on digital rights and to bring together a coalition of very relevant European cities (including London, Paris, Amsterdam, Milan, and Helsinki), effectively renewing part of the European discourse about smart cities around new key ideas: technological sovereignty, Data Commons, algorithmic disruption, open source in cities, and collaboration in software development.

What is particularly remarkable is the way Barcelona is leading towards a new conception of smart cities as well as strategic priorities centred on 16 digital rights by influencing the launch of a diverse set of manifestos and declarations of digital rights and its consequences for urban data policies (Barcelona City Council, 2019). Even more impressive is how these priorities have spread through Europe and became an integral part of the European discourse for deciphering citizenship in smart cities (see Chapter 2).

Smart cities is a *fuzzy* concept that translates to each territory according to its needs and priorities, as well as the prevailing political views in power. The tension between these two opposing sides resolves with the creation of a diversity of smart city discourses and the implementation of a multiplicity of solutions, either market based (Visnjic, Neely, Cennamo, & Visnjic, 2016) or nonmarket based. Europe, until now, has somehow lacked its own voice, reproducing policy ideas and paradigms created in other regions, as has been the case with 'Open Data' or the 'City as a Platform'. This is perhaps the first time that Europe has spoken with its own voice by blending *avant-garde* research and policy formulations.

However, this subsection concludes by suggesting that data used for policy formulation and data policy are not neutral. Cities as Barcelona reveal this from a techno-political standpoint: it is not just one data strategy that makes the city. As such, platforms inevitably involve designing business models. This subsection

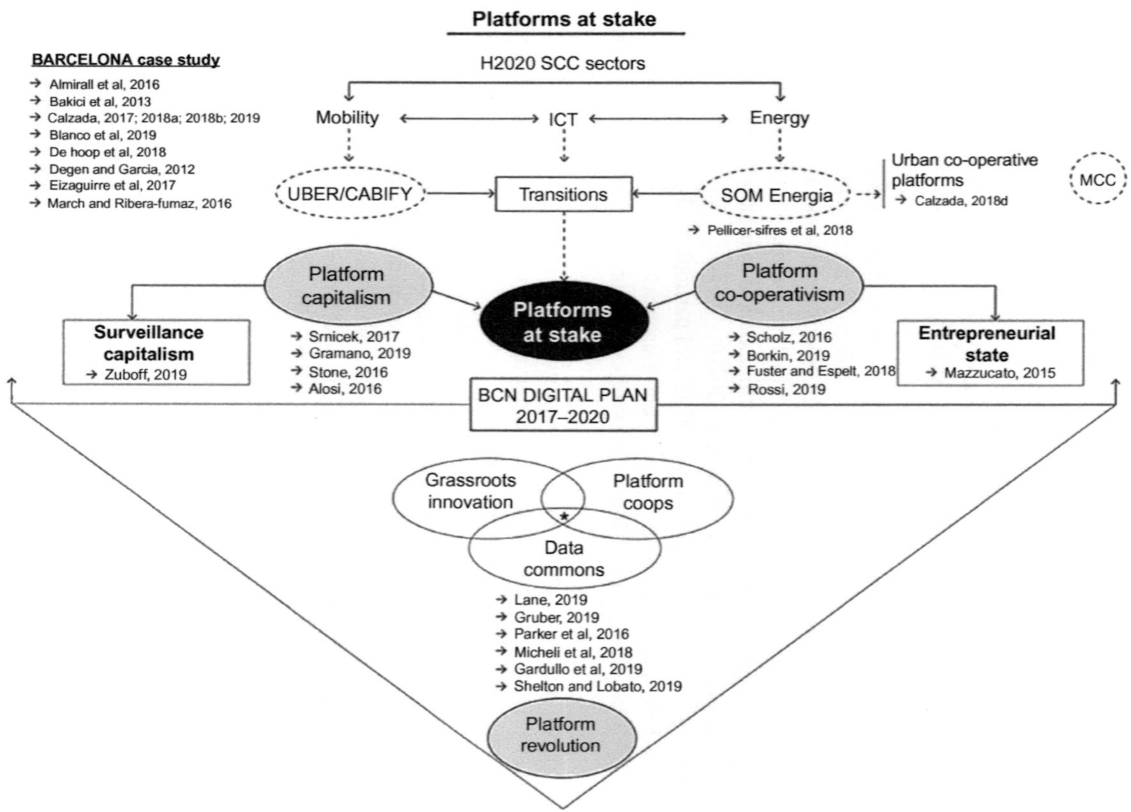

FIG. 6.1 Platforms at stake.

has raised the inner, unresolved conflict in the taxi service both for traditional taxi drivers operating for *Elite Taxi BCN* and for *precarised Uber* or *Cabify* operators in Barcelona, amidst the broad contour of the grassroots-led urban experimentation via the Data Commons policy scheme. Alternatives based on locally rooted 'platform co-operatives' may emerge by referencing cases such as *Som Energia.*

Hence, this subsection has attempted to open up a debate on the way the 'platform metropolis' (Rossi, 2019) is evolving and on conflicting common-seeking claims involving high-tech corporations, on the one hand, and *commoditised* or *precarised* workers (in this case, ridesharing workers or taxi drivers) on the other (Alosi, 2016). Beyond critical standpoints on how to collectively resist 'platform capitalism' (Rossi, 2019), this subsection has suggested that the taxi service in Barcelona might benefit from the Data Commons policy scheme and establish an experimental solution among stakeholders based on 'platform co-operatives' such as *Som Energia* (Fuster & Espelt, 2018; Senabre & Espelt, 2016). The taxi service conflict depicts, in conclusion, that another metropolis in Barcelona is not only possible but also already exists, waiting to be experimented with and recast as a common and co-operative good for the (smart) city itself, and, ultimately, more fundamentally, for its citizens (Shelton & Lodato, 2019; Vesnic-Alujevic et al., 2019).

6.6 Conclusions

This chapter argues that deconstructing the policy's framework provides further research directions to expand understanding of the ongoing urban challenges arising from the direct techno-political implications of these initiatives for (smart) citizens. As a result, this chapter concludes by highlighting these future research directions potentially shaped as follows:

(i) post-GDPR privacy, technological sovereignty, and Data Commons alternative regimes in the establishment of more tailored, human-centred, and context-aware algorithmic governance platforms for new co-operative socioeconomic models within and among European cities and regions;
(ii) publicly scrutinised new bottom-up democratic mechanisms through blockchain infrastructure to conduct decentralised and networked decision-making and deliberation processes on integrated sectorial urban policies (energy, mobility, health, entrepreneurship, voting, taxation, residency, migration, etc.); and
(iii) practical urban experiments through living labs at the neighbourhood and district level using blockchain technology to foster open SI ecosystems among a broad representation of agents through the Penta helix multi-stakeholders' framework.

The research findings from the fieldwork articulated and validated responses to the three operational research questions presented in the introduction, as summarised below.

In response to the first question, in the experimental phase in Barcelona, the degree to which strategic initiatives modify techno-political awareness of who owns data could offer interesting pathways for establishing an alternative data ownership regime. In addition, Barcelona City Council's new procurement process was designed to incentivise responsible innovation and respect for privacy, and was undergoing complete internal migration to open-source software by spring 2019. Furthermore, by the end of 2019, the city government planned to launch new online tools allowing people to selectively disclose the information they desire to share when using the council's official e-participation platform, Decidim Barcelona, while preserving citizens' anonymity. Nonetheless, the fieldwork revealed that, despite the positive transition reforming public procurement service provisions, technological sovereignty—citizens' ability to have a voice in surrounding technological infrastructure operation and end results—still has growth opportunities regarding integrating open-source software and emerging blockchain data architecture in the new EU context, characterised by the GDPR. As such, employing infrastructures such as blockchain is likely to require a new interpretation from the urban and data science perspective, which will be key to future experiments and predicting alternative data ownership regimes in cities. Likewise, technologies such as blockchain could improve access to data held by authorities while respecting privacy. Ultimately, this can also lead to proper evaluation of the ethical and political risks of smart cities with large databases by establishing a code of ethics for technological practices, including legal compliance with data protection regulations such as the GDPR and a defined data strategy benefitting citizens.

In response to the second question, in light of the grassroots initiatives examined, interdependencies among stakeholders have a thorough policy focus while fostering ecosystems of entrepreneurial starts-ups and SMEs. However, despite the effort to bring together a wide range of stakeholders, interviews revealed that initiatives based on a collaborative, polycentric, and deliberative governance model may need to evolve towards a more integrated, multi-stakeholder framework through further collaboration with the private sector (potentially by living labs bringing in entrepreneurial academics and enthusiastic civil servants). These initiatives might also need to foster the active role of social entrepreneurs, activists, 'bricoleurs', brokers, and assemblers to further explore the opportunities of an emerging and open SI ecosystem in Barcelona.

Ultimately, in response to the third question, thus far, PPPs were the leading smart city model underpinning the alliance between the state and market in many cities. Yet, these deals may have been driven by neoliberal and extractivist data policy implementation. Questions such as 'who controls the data?' are still rarely subject to any public oversight and scrutiny. Thus, to revert this situation, Barcelona could implement two steps:

(i) build a critical mass of locally rooted co-operative platforms based on the Data Commons to scale-up initiatives, while taking back control of citizens' data and

(ii) explore alternative, professional, entrepreneurial, co-operative business cultures to complement the volunteer grassroots seeds already flourishing (Calzada, 2013; Mondragon Cooperative Corporation, 2018).

Regarding the lessons learnt from the Barcelona case study and policy implications of the field of interdisciplinary and global smart cities research (Lytras & Visvizi, 2018), this chapter, drawing from detailed policy analysis and fieldwork study, suggests that Barcelona, in the post-GDPR context, appears to be leading a cutting-edge digital transformation agenda that may soon influence other European or international cities and regions on data techno-political implications for (smart) citizens. The next chapter will elaborate further in this dimension.

Whereas, generally, the pervasive algorithmic disruption consciously or unwittingly reveals the lack of critical reflective smart city policymaking, or indicates the hegemonic mainstreamed position of the PPPs, cities like Barcelona are challenging, and thus, embarked in experimenting an alternative policy route. Hence, it is likely the interdisciplinary and global smart cities research focus may gradually evolve towards the increasing study of a typology of (smart) citizens, defined as decision-makers and concerned users not only about data protection and security issues (Visvizi & Lytras, 2018), but also data ownership and technological sovereignty policy implications directly related to digital rights to the city.

In summary, whether Barcelona's current strategy is little more than a declaration of intentions of a progressivist smart city policy agenda remains to be seen. Having said that, it is noteworthy that Barcelona is leading a new paradigm as we are going to observe in the following Chapter 7. Therefore, this chapter concludes that, in the ongoing algorithmic disruptive context characterised by extractive data practices, smartness may not be appealing in cities such as Barcelona, although the experimental approach has yet to be firmly fixed as an alternative paradigm. Recognising that smartness may not be appealing and having been viewed as technocratic, the experimental approach has yet to be entirely established. Thus, an open question remains: how will (smart) citizens decide, control, govern, manage, and ultimately, own their data by being both conscious of digital rights to the city and aware of duties in the techno-political processes of city making?

References

Acuto, M., Steenmans, K., Iwaszuk, E., & Ortega-Garza, L. (2018). Informing urban governance? Boundary-spanning organisations and the ecosystem of urban data. *Area*, 1–10. https://doi.org/10.1111/area.12430.

Almirall, E., & Wareham, J. (2011). Living labs: Arbiters of mid-and ground-level innovation. *Technology Analysis & Strategic Management*, *23*(1), 87–102. https://doi.org/10.1080/09537325.2011.537110.

Almirall, E., Wareham, J., Ratti, C., Conesa, P., Bria, F., Gaviria, A., et al. (2016). Smart cities at the crossroads: New tensions in the city transformation. *California Management Review*, *59*(1), 141–152. https://doi.org/10.1177/0008125616683949.

Alosi, A. (2016). Commoditized workers: Case study research on labor law issues arising from a set of on-demand/gig economy platforms. *Comparative Labor Law & Policy Journal, 37*(653).

Andrews, L. (2013). *I know who you are and I saw what you did: Social networks and the death of privacy*. New York, NY, USA: Free Press.

Andrews, J. (2018). *How will Europe's new data laws affect cities?*. Retrieved from: https://cities-today.com/how-will-europes-new-data-laws-affect-cities/.

Aragón, P., Kaltenbrunner, A., Calleja-López, A., Pereira, A., Monterde, A., Barandiaran, X., et al. (2018). Deliberative platform design: The case study of the online discussions in Decidim Barcelona. In G. L. Ciampaglia, A. Mashhadi, & T. Yasseri (Eds.), *Social informatics*. Cham: Springer International Publishing.

Arnstein, S. R. (1969). A ladder of citizen participation. *Journal of the American Institute of Planners, 35*(4), 216–224. https://doi.org/10.1080/01944366908977225.

Ashton, P., Weber, R., & Zook, M. (2017). The cloud, the crowd, and the city: How new data practices reconfigure urban governance. *Big Data & Society, 4*(1), 1–5. https://doi.org/10.1177/2053951717706718.

Atkin, R. (2018). *Stop replacing London's phone boxes with corporate surveillance*. Retrieved from: https://www.wired.co.uk/article/linkuk-bt-google-free-wifi-and-calls-london.

Baeck, P. (2015). *Data for good: How big and open data can be used for the common good*. London, UK: NESTA.

Baeck, P., & Reynolds, S. (2020). *Smart cities during COVID-19*. Retrieved from: https://www.nesta.org.uk/blog/smart-cities-during-covid-19/.

Bakıcı, T., Almirall, E., & Wareham, J. (2013). A smart city initiative: The case of Barcelona. *Journal of the Knowledge Economy, 4*(2), 135–148. https://doi.org/10.1007/s13132-012-0084-9.

Barcelona City Council. (2016a). *BITS, Barcelona initiative for technological sovereignty*. Retrieved from: https://bits.city/.

Barcelona City Council. (2016b). *Barcelona Ciutat digital: A roadmap toward technological sovereignty*. Retrieved from: http://ajuntament.barcelona.cat/estaregiadigital/upload_Digital.pdf.

Barcelona City Council. (2016c). *Plan de Impulso Economía Social y Solidaria*. Retrieved from: http://ajuntament.barcelona.cat/economia-social-solidaria/es/objectivos-generales.

Barcelona City Council. (2017). *Barcelona City council digital plan 2017–2020: A government measure for open digitization: Free software and agile development of public administration services*. Retrieved from: http://ajuntament.barcelona.cat/digital/en/blog/barcelona-digital-government-open-agile-and-participatory.

Barcelona City Council. (2018). *Plan Digital de Ayuntamiento de Barcelona: Medida de Gobierno de Gestión Ética y Responsable de Datos: Barcelona Data Commons*. Retrieved from: http://ajuntament.barcelona.cat/digital/en/blog/ethical-and-responsible-data-management-barcelona-data-commons.

Barcelona City Council. (2019). *Manifesto in favour of technological sovereignty and digital rights for cities*. Retrieved from: https://www.barcelona.cat/digitalstandards/manifesto/0.2/.

Barcelona Urban Commons. (2018). Retrieved from: www.bcncomuns.net.

Bass, T., Sutherland, E., & Symons, T. (2018). *Reclaiming the Smart City: Personal data, trust and the new commons*. London, UK: NESTA.

Bauwens, M., Kostakis, V., & Pazaitis, A. (2019). *Peer to peer: The commons manifesto*. London, UK: University of Westminster Press.

Bianchi, I. (2018). The post-political meaning of the concept of commons: The regulation of the urban commons in Bologna. *Space & Polity*, 1–20. https://doi.org/10.1080/13562576.2018.1505492.

Blanco, I., Salazar, Y., & Bianchi, I. (2017). Transforming Barcelona's urban model? In *Limits and potentials for radical change under a radical left government*. Retrieved from: http://www.urbantransformations.ox.ac.uk/blog/2017/transforming-barcelonas-urban-model-limits-and-potentials-for-radical-change-under-a-radical-left-government/.

Blanco, I., Salazar, Y., & Bianchi, I. (2019). Urban governance and political change under a radical left government: The case of Barcelona. *Journal of Urban Affairs*, 1–21. https://doi.org/10.1080/07352166.2018.1559648.

B-Mincome. (2018). *Combining guaranteed minimum income and active social policies in deprived urban areas*. Retrieved from: http://www.uia-initiative.eu/en/uia-cities/barcelona.

Bollier, D. (2015). *The Commoning as a transformative social paradigm*. The Next System Project.

Bollier, D. (2016). *The city as a commons*. Retrieved from: https://www.youtube.com/wtch?v=z3itmhDuem8.

Borch, C., & Kornberger, M. (2015). *Urban commons: Rethinking the city*. London, UK: Routledge.

Borkin, S. (2019). *Platform co-operatives—Solving the capital conumdrum*. London: NESTA.

Bria, F. (2018). *Our data is valuable. Here's how we can take that value back*. Retrieved from: https://www.theguardian.com/commentisfree/2018/apr/05/data-valuable-citizens-silicon-valley-barcelona.

Bridle, J. (2018). *New dark age*. London, UK: Verso.

Bucher, T. (2012). Want to be on top? Algorithmic power and the threat of invisibility on facebook. *New Media & Society*, *14*(7), 1164–1180. https://doi.org/10.1177/1461444812440159.

Bulkeley, H., Breitfuss, M., Coenen, L., Frantzeskaki, N., Fuenfschilling, L., Grillitsch, M., et al. (2015). Working paper on urban living labs and urban sustainability transitions. In *GUST governance of urban sustainability transitions*. Retrieved from: http://www.urbanlivinglabs.net/p/publications.html.

Bull, R., & Azennoud, M. (2016). Smart citizens for smart cities: Participating in the future. *Proceedings of the Institution of Civil Engineers: Energy*, *169*(3), 93–101. https://doi.org/10.1680/jener.15.00030.

Burns, R., Daltan, C. M., & Thatcher, J. E. (2018). Critical data, critical technology in theory and practice. *The Professional Geographer*, *70*, 126–128. https://doi.org/10.1080/00330124.2017.1325749.

Buttarelli, G. (2018). *Big tech is still violating your privacy*. Retrieved from: https://www.washingtonpost.com/news/theworldpost/wp/2018/08/14/gdpr/?utm_term=.9e9ddd6cf937.

Cadwalladr, C., & Graham-Harrison, E. (2018). *Revealed: 50 million facebook profiles harvested for Cambridge Analytica in Major Data Breach*. Retrieved from: https://www.theguardian.com/news/2018/mar/17/cambridge-analytica-facebook-influence-us-election.

Calzada, I. (2013). Knowledge building & organizational behaviour: Mondragon case. In F. Moulaert, D. Maccallum, A. Mehmood, & A. Hamdouch (Eds.), *International handbook of social innovation. Social innovation: Collective action, social learning and transdisciplinary research* (pp. 219–229). Cheltenham, UK: Edward Elgar Publishing.

Calzada, I. (2017a). The technopolitics of data and smart devolution in city-regions: Comparing Glasgow, Bristol, Barcelona, and Bilbao. *Systems*, *5*(1), 1–18. https://doi.org/10.3390/systems5010018.

Calzada, I. (2017b). Problematizing and politicizing smart city-regions: Is devolution smart? *Territorio*, *83*(2017), 37–47. https://doi.org/10.3280/TR2017-083005.

Calzada, I. (2018a). From smart cities to experimental cities? In V. M. B. Giorgino, & Z. D. Walsh (Eds.), *Co-designing economies in transition: Radical approaches in dialogue with contemplative social sciences* (pp. 191–217). Cham, UK: Palgrave Macmillan.

Calzada, I. (2018b). Local entrepreneurship through a multistakeholders' tourism living lab in the post-violence/peripheral era in the Basque Country? *Regional Science Policy and Practice*, *11*(3), 451–466. In the special issue 'local entrepreneurship and tourism: Policies and practices in peripheral areas' https://doi.org/10.1111/rsp3.12130.

Calzada, I. (2018c). Metropolitanising small European stateless city-regionalised nations. *Space and Polity*, *22*(3), 342–361. https://doi.org/10.1080/13562576.2018.1555958.

Calzada, I. (2019a). Technological sovereignty: Protecting citizens' digital rights in the AI-driven and post-GDPR algorithmic and city-regional European realm. *Regions eZine*, *4*. https://doi.org/10.1080/13673882.2018.00001038.

Calzada, I. (2019b). Catalonia rescaling Spain: Is it feasible to accommodate its "stateless citizenship"? *Regional Science Policy and Practice*, *11*(5), 805–820. https://doi.org/10.1111/rsp3.12240.

Calzada, I. (2020a). Review of the book Smart City Barcelona: The Catalan Quest to Improve Future Urban Living, by A. Vives. *International Journal of Iberian Studies*, *33*(1), 103–104. https://doi.org/10.1386/ijis_00018_5.

Calzada, I. (2020b). Platform and Data Co-operatives Amidst the European Post COVID-19 Citizenship. In M. Craglia (Ed.), *DigiTranScope: A project on the governance of/with the digital transformation*. Luxembourg: Publications Office of the European Union [Forthcoming]. https://doi.org/10.13140/RG.2.2.12722.22729/1.

Calzada, I., & Almirall, E. (2020). Data ecosystems for protecting European citizens' digital rights. *Transforming Government: People Process and Policy (TGPPP)*, *14*(2). https://doi.org/10.1108/TG-03-2020-0047.

Calzada, I., & Cobo, C. (2015). Unplugging: Deconstructing the smart city. *Journal of Urban Technology*, *22*(1), 23–43. https://doi.org/10.1080/10630732.2014.971535.

Calzada, I., & Cowie, P. (2017). Beyond data-driven smart city-regions? Rethinking stakeholder-helixes strategies. *Regions*, *308*(4), 25–28. https://doi.org/10.1080/13673882.2017.11958675.

Cámara, C. (2017). *Urban Commons: Lessons from Barcelona at the beginning of 21st century*. Barcelona, Spain: UOC.

Campbell, T. (2012). *Beyond smart cities: How cities network, learn and innovate*. Oxon, UK: Earthscan.

Capdevilla, I., & Zarlenga, M. (2015). *Smart city or smart citizens? The Barcelona case*. Retrieved from https://doi.org/10.2139/ssrn.2585682.

Caprotti, F., & Cowley, R. (2016). Interrogating urban experiments. *Urban Geography*, *38*, 1441–1450. https://doi.org/10.1080/02723638.2016.1265870.

Caragliu, A., & Del Bo, C. (2018). The economics of smart city policies. *Scienze Regionali*, *17*(1), 81–104.

Cardullo, P., Di Feliciantonio, C., & Kitchin, R. (2019). *The right to the Smart City*. Bingley: Emerald Publishing.

Cardullo, P., & Kitchin, R. (2018). Being a 'citizen' in the smart city: Up and down the scaffold of smart citizen participation in Dublin, Ireland. *GeoJournal*, *78*, 1–13. https://doi.org/10.1007/S10708-018-9845-8.

Cherry, M. (2016). Beyond misclassification: The digital transformation of work. *Comparative Labour Law & Policy Journal*, *37*(577), 1–27.

Christl, W. (2017). *Corporate surveillance in everyday life. How companies collect, combine, analyze, trade, and use personal data on billions. A report by cracked Labs. 2017*. Retrieved from: http://crackedlabs.org/en/corporate-surveillance/info.

Christl, W., & Spiekermann, S. (2016). *Networks of control: Corporate surveillance, digital tracking, big data and privacy*. Retrieved from: http://crackedlabs.org/dl/Christl_Spiekermann_Networks_Of_Control.pdf.

Chu, B. (2018). Retrieved from: https://www.independent.co.uk/news/business/analysis-and-features/angela-merkel-davos-2018-speech-trump-what-did-she-say-germany-a8176021.html.

Cities Coalition for Digital Rights. (2019). *Declaration of cities coalition for digital rights*. Retrieved from: https://citiesfordigitalrights.org/#declaration.

Coletta, C., Heaphy, L., Perng, S.-Y., & Waller, L. (2017). Data-driven cities? Digital urbanism and its proxies: Introduction. *Tecnoscienza: Italian Journal Science & Technology Studies*, *8*(2), 5–18.

Coletta, C., & Kitchin, R. (2017). Algorithmic governance: Regulating the 'heartbeat' of a city using the internet of things. *Big Data & Society*, *4*(2), 1–16. https://doi.org/10.1177/2053951717742418.

Danaher, J., Hogan, M. J., Noone, C., Kennedy, R., Behan, A., De Paor, A., et al. (2017). Algorithmic governance: Developing a research agenda through the power of collective intelligence. *Big Data & Society*, *4*(2), 1–21. https://doi.org/10.1177/2053951717726554.

Datacity Numa. (2018). Retrieved from: http://datacity.numa.co/.

De Hoop, E., Smith, A., Boon, W., Macrorie, R., Marvin, S., & Raven, R. (2018). Smart urbanism in Barcelona: A knowledge politics perspective. In J. Jens Stissing, P. Späth, & M. Cashmore (Eds.), *The politics of urban sustainability transitions: Knowledge, power and governance*. London: Routledge.

De Jong, M., Joss, S., Schraven, D., Zhan, C., & Weijnen, M. (2015). Sustainable-smart-resilient-low carbon-eco-knowledge cities: Making sense of a multitude of concepts promoting sustainable urbanization. *Journal of Cleaner Production*, *109*, 25–38. https://doi.org/10.1016/j.jclepro.2015.02.004.

De Waal, M., & Dignum, M. (2017). The citizen in the smart city. How the smart city could transform citizenship. *Information Technology*, *59*(6), 263–273. https://doi.org/10.1515/itit-2017-0012.

Decidim Barcelona. (2018). Retrieved from: www.decidim.barcelona.

Decode (DEcentralised Citizens Owned Data Ecosystem). (2018). *D.5.3. Data analysis methods and first results from pilots*. Barcelona, Spain: Decode. Retrieved from: www.decodeproject.eu.

Degen, M., & García, M. (2012). The transformation of the 'Barcelona model': An analysis of culture, urban regeneration and governance. *International Journal of Urban and Regional Research*, *36*(5), 1022–1038. https://doi.org/10.1111/j.1468-2427.2012.01152.x.

Digital Social Innovation. (2018). Retrieved from: http://ateneusdefabricacio.barcelona.cat/.

Edwards, L. (2016). Privacy, security, and data protection in smart cities: A critical EU law perspective. *European Data Protection Law Review*, *2*, 28–58. Retrieved from: https://papers.ssrn.com/sol3/papers.cfm?abstract_id=2711290.

Eizaguirre, S. (2016). Comparing social innovation initiatives in Barcelona and Bilbao. Looking at associative participation in the governance of Citizens' rights. *Revista Catalana de Sociología*, *31*(1), 19–33. https://doi.org/10.2436/20.3005.01.69.

Eizaguirre, S., & Parés, M. (2018). Communities making social change from below. Social innovation and democratic leadership in two disenfranchised neighbourhoods in Barcelona. *Urban Research & Practice*, 1–19. https://doi.org/10.1080/17535069.2018.1426782.

Ethics Advisory Group—European Commission. (2018). *Ethics advisory group, report 2018*. Brussels: European Commission.

Eubanks, V. (2017). *Automating inequality: How high-tech tools profile, police, and punish the poor*. New York, NY, USA: St. Martin's Press.

European Commission. (2017a). *The making of a smart city: Policy recommendations*. Brussels, Belgium: European Commission.

European Commission. (2017b). *The making of a smart city: Best practices across Europe*. Brussels: Belgium European Commission.

European Commission. (2017c). *The making of a smart city: Replication and scale-up of Innovation in Europe*. Brussels, Belgium: European Commission.

European Commission. (2020). *A European strategy for data*. Brussels, Belgium: European Commission.

Evans, J. (2016). Trials and tribulations: Problematizing the city through/as urban experimentation. *Geography Compass*, *10*(10), 429–443. https://doi.org/10.1111/gec3.12280.

Evans, J., Karvonen, A., & Raven, R. (2016). *The experimental city*. London, UK: Routledge.

Evenstad, L. (2018). *Cities key to making data a new form of infrastructure*. Retrieved from: https://www.computerweekly.com/news/252445624/Cities-key-to-making-data-a-new-form-of-infrastructure-says-Nesta.

Fielding, N. G. (2012). Triangulation and mixed methods designs: Data integration with new research technologies. *Journal of Mixed Methods Research*, *6*(2), 124–126. https://doi.org/10.1177/1558689812437101.

Finn, E. (2017). *What algorithms want: Imagination in the age of computing*. Cambridge, MA, USA: The MIT Press.

Foster, S., & Iaione, C. (2016). The city as a commons. *Yale Law & Policy Review*, *34*(2).

Fuster, M., & Espelt, R. (2018). A framework for assessing democratic qualities in collaborative economy platforms: Analysis of 10 cases in Barcelona. *Urban Science*, *2*(3), 61. https://doi.org/10.3390/urbansci2030061.

Gago-Fernandez, A. (2020). *Towards a European strategy on business-to-government data sharing for the public interest*. Brussels: European Commission.

Gascó-Hernandez, M. (2018). Building a smart city: Lessons from Barcelona. *Communications of the ACM*, *61*(4), 50–57. https://doi.org/10.1145/3117800.

General Data Protection Regulation (GDPR). (2018). Retrieved from: https://www.eugdpr.org/.

Gerlitz, C., & Helmond, A. (2013). The like economy: Social buttons and the data-intensive web. *New Media & Society*, *15*(8), 1348–1365. https://doi.org/10.1177/1461444812472322.

Gramano, E. (2019). Digitalisation and work: Challenges from the platform-economy. *Contemporary Social Science*, 1–13. https://doi.org/10.1080/21582041.2019.1572919.

Gray, J., & Lämmerhirt, D. (2017). *Data and the City: How can public data infrastructures change lives in urban regions*. Cambridge, UK: Open Knowledge.

Greenfield, A. (2017). *Radical technologies: The design of everyday life*. London, UK: Verso.

Gruber, H. (2019). Proposals for a digital industrial policy for Europe. *Telecomunications Policy*, *43*(2), 116–127. https://doi.org/10.1016/j.telpol.2018.06.003.

Gutiérrez-Rubí, A. (2017). *Smart Citizens: Ciudades a Escala Humana*. Catalonia, Spain: Ideograma, Barcelona.

Habermas, J. (2015). *The lure of technocracy*. New York, NY, USA: Polity Press.

Hajer, M. A., & Dassen, T. (2014). *Smart about cities: Visualising the challenge for 21st century urbanism*. Amsterdam, The Netherlands: Nai010 Publishers.

Harari, Y. N. (2016). *Yuval Noah Harari on big data, Google and the end of free will*. Retrieved from: https://www.ft.com/content/50bb4830-6a4c-11e6-ae5b-a7cc5dd5a28c.

Hardin, G. (1968). The tragedy of the commons. *Science*, *162*, 1243–1248.

Hatuka, T. (2020). *The digital city: Critical dimensions in implementing the smart city, planning, technology, privacy, and equality*. Tel Aviv: Blavatnik Interdisciplinary Cyber Research Center, Tel Aviv University.

Hemment, D., & Townsend, A. (2013). *Smart citizens*. Manchester, UK: Future Everything Publications.

Hintz, A., Dencik, L., & Wahl-Jorgensen, K. (2017). Digital citizenship and surveillance society. *International Journal of Communication*, *11*, 731–739.

Hollands, R. G. (2014). Critical interventions into the corporate smart city. *Cambridge Journal of Regions, Economy and Society*, *8*(1), 61–77. https://doi.org/10.1093/cjres/rsu011.

Hughes, B. (2016). *The bleeding edge: Why technology turns toxic in an unequal world.* Markham, ON, Canada: New Internationalist Publications Ltd.

Islar, M., & Irgil, E. (2018). Grassroots practices of citizenship and politicization in the urban: The case of right to the city initiatives in Barcelona. *Citizenship Studies, 22*(5), 491–506. https://doi.org/10.1080/13621025.2018.1477919.

Jones, E. (2015). *Smart City Barcelona. A city of the future?*. Retrieved from: http://www.barcelona-metropolitan.com/features/smart-city-Barcelona/.

Joss, S. (2018). Future cities: Asserting public governance. *Palgrave Communications, 4*(1), 1–4. https://doi.org/10.1057/s41599-018-0087-7.

Jun, M. (2018). Blockchain government—A next form of infrastructure for the twenty-first century. *Journal of Open Innovation: Technology, Market, and Complexity, 4*(7), 1–12. https://doi.org/10.1186/s40852-018-0086-3.

Karvonen, A. (2018). The city of permanent experiments? In B. Turnheim, P. Kivimaa, & F. Berkhout (Eds.), *Innovating climate governance: Moving beyond experiments* (pp. 201–215). Cambridge, UK: Cambridge University Press.

Karvonen, A., Cugurullo, F., & Caprotti, F. (2018). *Inside smart cities: Place, politics and urban innovation.* London, UK: Routledge.

Kelleher, J. D., & Tierney, B. (2018). *Data science.* Cambridge, MA, USA: The MIT Press.

Keymolen, E., & Voorwinden, A. (2019). Can we negotiate? Trust and the rule of law in the smart city paradigm. *International Review of Law, Computers & Technology*, 1–21.

Kitchin, R. (2014). *The data revolution: Big data, open data, data infrastructures & their consequences.* London, UK: Sage.

Kitchin, R. (2016). *Reframing, reimagining, and remaking smart cities. The programmable city working paper 20.* Retrieved from: https://osf.io/cyjhg/.

Kitchin, R. (2017a). Thinking critically about and researching algorithms. *Information, Communication & Society, 20*(1), 14–29. https://doi.org/10.1080/1369118X.2016.1154087.

Kitchin, R. (2017b). The realtimeness of smart cities. *Tecnoscienza: Italian Journal of Science & Technology Studies, 8*(2), 19–41.

Knowledge Society Forum. (2019). Retrieved from: https://ec.europa.eu/cefdigital/wiki/display/CEFDIGITAL/2019/11/13/Eurocities+Knowledge+Society+Forum.

Kronsell, A., & Mukhtar-Landgren, D. (2018). Experimental governance: The role of municipalities in urban living labs. *European Planning Studies*, 1–20. https://doi.org/10.1080/09654313.2018.1435631.

Lane, J. (2019). *The digital street.* Oxford: Oxford University Press.

Levy, K., & Barocas, S. (2018). Refractive surveillance: Monitoring customers to manage workers. *International Journal of Communication, 12*, 1166–1188.

Lightfoot, G., & Wisnieski, T. P. (2014). Information asymmetry and power in a surveillance society. *Information and Organization, 24*(4), 214–235. https://doi.org/10.1016/j.infoandorg.2014.09.001.

Lohr, S. (2015). *Data-ism: Inside the big data revolution.* London, UK: Oneworld Publications.

Lupton, D. (2016). You are your data: Self-tracking practices and concepts of data. In S. Seike (Ed.), *Lifelogging: Digital self-tracking and lifelogging—Between disruptive technology and cultural transformation* (pp. 61–79). Wiesbaden, Germany: Springer.

Lupton, D., & Michael, M. (2017). Depends on who's got the data: Public understandings of personal digital dataveillance. *Surveillance and Society, 15*(2), 254–268.

Lytras, M., & Visvizi, A. (2018). Who uses smart city services and what to make of it: Toward interdisciplinary smart cities research. *Sustainability, 10*(6), 1998. https://doi.org/10.3390/su10061998.

Manzerolle, V., & Smeltzer, S. (2011). Consumer databases and the commercial mediation of identity: A medium theory analysis. *Surveillance and Society*, *8*, 323–337. https://doi.org/10.24908/SS.V8I3.4167.

March, H., & Ribera-Fumaz, R. (2016). Smart contradictions: The politics of making Barcelona a self-sufficient city. *European Urban and Regional Studies*, *23*(4), 816–830. https://doi.org/10.1177/0969776414554488.

Martens, B., & Duch Brown, N. (2019). *The economies of B2G data sharing*. Seville: European Commission DG Joint Research Centre JRC.

Marvin, S., Bulkeley, H., Mai, L., McCormick, K., & Palgan, Y. V. (2018). *Urban living labs: Experimenting with city futures*. London, UK: Routledge.

Marvin, S., Luque-Ayala, A., & McFarlane, C. (2015). *Smart urbanism: Utopian vision or false dawn?*. New York, NY, USA: Routledge.

Mazzucato, M. (2015). *The entrepreneurial state: Debunking public vs. private sector myths*. New York, NY, USA: Public Affairs.

Metadecidim Barcelona. (2018). Retrieved from: http://www.metadecidim.barcelona.

Micheli, M., Blakemore, M., Ponti, M., & Craglia, M. (2018). *The governance of data in a digitally transformed European society*. Ispra: European Commission.

Milanovic, B. (2019). *Capitalism, alone: The future of the system that rules the world*. Cambridge and London: Harvard University Press.

Mondragon Corporación Cooperativa. (2018). *Mondragón del Futuro*. Mondragon, Spain: MCC.

Mora, L., & Bolici, R. (2015). The development process of smart city strategies: The case of Barcelona. In *Proceedings of the 1st international city regeneration congress, Tampere, Finland, 3–4 September 2015*.

Mora, L., & Bolici, R. (2017). How to become a smart city: Learning from Amsterdam. In A. Bisello, D. Vettorato, R. Stephens, & P. Elisei (Eds.), *Smart and sustainable planning for cities and regions: Results of SSPCR 2015* (pp. 251–266). Cham, UK: Springer International Publishing.

Mora, L., Bolici, R., & Deakin, M. (2017). The first two decades of smart-city research: A bibliometric analysis. *Journal of Urban Technology*, *24*(1), 3–27. https://doi.org/10.1080/10630732.2017.1285123.

Morozov, E. (2014). *The rise of data and the death of politics*. Retrieved from: https://www.theguardian.com/technology/2014/jul/20/rise-of-data-death-of-politics-evgeny-morozov-algorithmic-regulation.

Morozov, E. (2017). *So you want to switch off digitally? I'm afraid that will cost you*. Retrieved from: https://www.theguardian.com/commentisfree/2017/feb/19/right-to-disconnect-digital-gig-economy-evgeny-morozov.

Morozov, E. (2018). *Capitalismo Big Tech ¿Welfare o Neofeudalismo Digital?*. Madrid, Spain: Enclave de Libros Ediciones.

Morozov, E. (2019). Digital socialism? *New Left Review*, *116-117*, 33–67.

Morozov, E., & Bria, F. (2017). *Roundtable session—A new deal on data: What role for cities? Smart city expo world congress*. Retrieved from: https://www.youtube.com/watch?v=1cakaaip2Vw.

Morozov, E., & Bria, F. (2018). *Rethinking the smart city: Democratizing urban technology*. New York, NY, USA: Rosa Luxemburg Stiftung.

Morozov, E., & Eno, B. (2017). *Debat. Brian Eno i Evgeny Morozov una conversa sobre tecnologia i democràcia*. CCCB. Retrieved from: https://vimeo.com/206060710.

Morozov, E., & Harvey, D. (2016). *Conversation between Evgeny Morozov and David Harvey*. Retrieved from: http://davidharvey.org/2016/11/video-conversation-between-david-harvey-evgeny-morozov-on-post-neoliberalism-trump-infrastructure-sharing-economy-smart-city/.

Nelson, A. (2016). *The school life of DNA: Race, reparations, and reconciliation after the genome*. London: Penguin Random House.

Niederer, S., & Priester, R. (2016). Smart citizens: Exploring the tools of the urban bottom-up movement. *Computer Supported Cooperative Work Cooperative Work (CSCW), 25*, 137–152. https://doi.org/10.1007/s10606-016-9249-6.

Nilssen, M. (2018). To the smart city and beyond? Developing a typology of smart urban innovation. *Technological Forecasting and Social Change, 142*, 98–104. https://doi.org/10.1016/j.techfore.2018.07.060.

Noble, S. U. (2018). *Algorithms of oppression: How search engines reinforce racism*. New York, NY, USA: NYU Press.

Noveck, B. S. (2015). *Smart citizens, smarter state: The technologies of expertise and the future of governing*. Cambridge, MA, USA: Harvard University Press.

O'Neill, C. (2008). *Weapons of math destruction: How big Data increases inequality and threatens democracy*. London, UK: Penguin Random House.

Observatorio Metropolitano de Barcelona. (2018). *Comunes Urbanos de Barcelona*. Retrieved from: http://www.bcncomuns.net.

Ojo, A., Curry, E., & Zeleti, F. A. (2015). A tale of open data innovations in five smart cities. In *Proceedings of the 48th Hawaii international conference on systems sciences, Kauai, HI, USA, 5–8 January 2015* (pp. 2326–2335). https://doi.org/10.1109/HICSS.2015.280.

Ostrom, E. (2010). Beyond markets and states: Polycentric governance of complex economic systems. *Transnational Corporations Review*, *2*(2), 1–12. https://doi.org/10.1080/19186444.2010.11658229.

Parker, G. G., Van Alstyne, M. W., & Choudary, S. P. (2016). *Platform revolution: How networked markets are transforming the economy and how to make them work for you*. NY: Norton.

Pellicer-Sifres, V., Belda-Miquel, S., Cuesta-Fernandez, I., & Boni, A. (2018). Learning, transformative action, and grassroots innovation: Insights from the Spanish energy cooperative Som Energia. *Energy Research & Social Science*, *42*, 100–111.

Platform Cooperativism Consortium. (2020). *Online course to incubate platform co-ops*. Retrieved from: https://platform.coop/blog/a-pcc-mondragon-course-helps-to-incubate-platform-co-ops/.

PWC. (2016). *From concept to applied solutions: Data-driven cities*. London, UK: PWC.

Ranchordás, S. (2019). Nudging citizens through technology in smart cities. *International Review of Law, Computers & Technology*, 1–23. https://doi.org/10.1080/13600869.2019.1590928.

Replicate EU Project. (2018). *City-to-city-learning programme*. Retrieved from: www.replicate-project.eu/city2citylearning.

Reuter, T. K. (2020). *Smart city visions and human rights: Do they go together?*. Harvard Kennedy School—Carr Center for Human Rights Policy, issue 2020-006 Cambridge: Harvard Kennedy School.

Roio, D. (2018). *Algorithmic sovereignty*. Plymouth, UK: University of Plymouth.

Rossi, U. (2016). The variegated economics and the potential politics of the smart city. *Territory, Politics, Governance*, *4*(3), 337–353. https://doi.org/10.1080/21622671.2015.1036913.

Rossi, U. (2019). The common-seekers: Capturing and reclaiming value in the platform metropolis. *Environment and Planning C: Politics and Space*, 1–16.

Sadowski, J., & Pasquale, F. (2015). The spectrum of control: A social theory of the smart city. *First Monday*, *20*. https://doi.org/10.5210/fm.v20i7.5903.

Sassen, S. (2017). Predatory formations dressed in wall street suits and algorithmic math. *Science, Technology & Society*, *22*(1), 6–20. https://doi.org/10.1177/0971721816682783.

Saunders, T., & Baeck, P. (2015). *Rethinking smart cities from the ground up*. London, UK: NESTA.

Schiek, D., & Gideon, A. (2018). Outsmarting the gig-economy through collective bargaining: EU competition law as a barrier to smart cities? *International Review of Law, Computers & Technology*, *32*(2–3), 275–294. https://doi.org/10.1080/13600869.2018.1457001.

Scholl, C., & Kemp, R. (2016). City labs as vehicles for innovation in urban planning processes. *Urban Planning*, *1*(4), 89–102. https://doi.org/10.17645/up.v1i4.749.

Scholz, T. (2016). *Platform cooperativism: Challenging the corporate sharing economy*. New York, NY, USA: Rosa Luxemburg Stiftung.

Scholz, T., & Schneider, N. (2017). *Ours to hack and to own*. NY: OR Books.

Schuurman, D., De Marez, L., & Ballon, P. (2016). The impact of living lab methodology on open innovation contributions and outcomes. *Technology Innovation Management Review*, *1*(6), 7–16.

Senabre, E., & Espelt, R. (2016). *The user experience in platform co-operativism*. Retrieved from: http://www.lab.cccb.org/en/the-user-experience-in-platform-cooperativism/.

Sennett, R. (2020). *Cities in the pandemic*. Retrieved from: https://www.publicspace.org/multimedia/-/post/cities-in-the-pandemic.

Shelton, T., & Lodato, T. (2019). Actually existing smart citizens. *City*, 1–18. https://doi.org/10.1080/13604813.2019.1575115.

Shilton, K. (2016). When they are your big data: Participatory data practices as a lens on big data. In C. Sugimoto, H. Ekbia, & M. Mattioli (Eds.), *Big data is not a monolith*. Boston, MA, USA: MIT Press.

Shin, D. (2009). Ubiquitous city: Urban technologies, urban infrastructure and urban informatics. *Journal of Information Science*, *35*(5), 515–526. https://doi.org/10.1177/0165551509100832.

Shin, Y., & Shin, D. (2016). Modelling community resources and communications mapping for strategic inter-organizational problem solving and civic engagement. *Journal of Urban Technology*, *23*(4), 47–66. https://doi.org/10.1080/10630732.2016.1175826.

Sidewalk Labs. (2018). *Digital governance proposals for DSAP consultation*. Draft proposal.

Solon, O. (2018). *Georges Soros: Facebook and Google a Menace to Society*. Retrieved from: https://www.theguardian.com/business/2018/jan/25/george-soros-facebook-and-google-are-a-menace-to-society.

Sommobilitat. (2020). Retrieved from https://www.sommobilitat.coop/.

Srnicek, N. (2017). *Platform capitalism*. Cambridge: Polity.

Stokes, M., Baeck, P., & Baker, T. (2017). *What next for digital social innovation*. London, UK: NESTA.

Stone, B. (2016). *The upstarts: How Uber, Airbnb and the killer companies of the new Sillicon Valley are changing the world*. NY: Little, Brown and Company.

Stucke, E. (2018). *Should we be concerned about data-opolies?*. Retrieved from: https://ssrn.com/abstract=3144045.

Stucke, E., & Grunes, A. P. (2017). *Data-Opolies*. Retrieved from https://doi.org/10.2139/ssrn.2927018. https://ssrn.com/abstract=927018.

Subirats, J., & Rendueles, C. (2016). *Los Bienes Comunes ¿Oportunidad o Espejismo?*. Barcelona, Spain: Icaria.

Taplin, J. (2017). *Move fast and break things: How Facebook, Google, and Amazon have cornered culture and what it means for all of us*. New York, NY, USA: Little Brown.

Taylor, M. (2020). Retrieved from: https://www.theguardian.com/environment/2020/may/07/world-cannot-return-to-business-as-usual-after-covid-19-say-mayors.

The Royal Society. (2017). *Data management and use: Governance in the 21st century*. London, UK: The Royal Society.

Thomas, V., Wang, D., Mullagh, L., & Dunn, N. (2016). Where's Wally? In search of citizen perspectives on the smart city. *Sustainability*, *8*(3), 207. https://doi.org/10.3390/su8030207.

Tieman, R. (2017). *Barcelona: Smart city revolution in progress*. Retrieved from: https://amp.ft.com/content/6d2fe2a8-722c-11e7-93ff-99f383b09ff9.

Timeus, K., & Gascó, M. (2018). Increasing innovation capacity in city governments: Do innovation labs make a difference? *Journal of Urban Affairs*, . https://doi.org/10.1080/07352166.2018.1431049.

Tõnurist, P., Kattel, R., & Lember, V. (2017). Innovation labs in the public sector: What they are and what they do? *Public Management Review*, *19*, 1–25. https://doi.org/10.1080/14719037.2017.1287939.

Trencher, G. (2018). Towards the smart city 2.0: Empirical evidence of using smartness as a tool for tackling social challenges. *Technological Forecasting and Social Change*, *142*, 117–128. https://doi.org/10.1016/j.techfore.2018.07.033.

Van Dijck, J. (2014). Datafication, dataism and dataveillance: Big data between scientific paradigm and ideology. *Surveillance and Society*, *12*(2), 197–208. https://doi.org/10.24908/ss.v12I2.4776.

Vanolo, A. (2016). Is there anybody out there? The place and role of citizens in tomorrow's smart cities. *Futures*, *82*, 26–36. https://doi.org/10.1016/j.futures.2016.05.010.

Vesnic-Alujevic, L., Stoermer, E., Rudkin, J., Scapolo, F., & Kimbell, L. (2019). *The Future of Government 2030+: A citizen-centric perspective on new government models*. EUR 29664 EN Luxembourg: Publications Office of the European Union. https://doi.org/10.2760/145751. JRC 115008.

Visnjic, I., Neely, A., Cennamo, C., & Visnjic, N. (2016). Governing the city: Unleashing value from business ecosystem. *California Management Review*, *59*(1), 109–140. https://doi.org/10.1177/0008125616683955.

Visvizi, A., & Lytras, M. (2018). It is not a fad: Smart cities and smart villages research in European and global contexts. *Sustainability*, *10*(2727). https://doi.org/10.3390/su10082727.

Von Wirth, T., Fuenfschilling, L., Frantzeskaki, N., & Coenen, L. (2018). Impacts of urban living labs on sustainability transitions: Mechanisms and strategies for systemic change through experimentation. *European Planning Studies*, 1–29. https://doi.org/10.1080/09654313.2018.1504895.

Waag, A. (2016). *Manifesto for smart citizens*. Retrieved from: http://waag.org/en/blog/manifesto-smart-citizens.

Wallace, N., & Castro, D. (2018). *The impact of the EU's new data protection regulation on AI*. Washington, DC, USA: Centre for Data Innovation.

Warren, K. (2016). Cancer clinical research. Enhancing data liquidity and data altruism. In B. Hesse, D. Ahern, & E. Beckjord (Eds.), *Oncology informatics*. https://doi.org/10.1016/B978-0-12-802115-6.00003-3.

West, G. (2013). Retrieved from: https://www.symmetrymagazine.org/article/december-2013/the-scale-of-things.

Willis, K. S., & Aurigi, A. (2018). *Digital and smart cities*. Oxon, UK: Routledge.

Willis, K. S., & Aurigi, A. (2020). *The Routledge companion to smart cities*. Oxon, UK: Routledge.

Wired. (2019). *Americans are abandoning public transit, but don't blame Uber*. Retrieved from: https://www.wired.com/story/transit-center-census-americans-public-transportation.

Wiseman, J. (2017). *Lessons from leading CDOs: A framework for better civic analytics*. Cambridge, MA, USA: Civic Analytics Network, Ash Centre for Democratic Governance and Innovation.

Wyly, E. (2014). The new quantitative revolution. *Dialogues in Human Geography*, *4*(1), 26–38. https://doi.org/10.1177/2043820614525732.

Xnet. (2017). *Xnet installs a whistleblowing platform against corruption for the city hall of Barcelona—Powered by GlobaLeaks and TOR friendly*. Retrieved from: https://blog.p2pfoundation.net/xnet-installs-whistleblowing-platform-corruption-city-hall-barcelona-powered-globaleaks-tor-friendly/2017/01/19.

Yakowitz, J. (2011). Tragedy of the data commons. *Harvard Journal of Law & Technology*, *25*(1), 1–68.

Yin, R. K. (1984). *Case study research: Design and methods*. Thousand Oaks, CA, USA: SAGE Publications.

Chapter 7

PROTECTING smart city citizenship: Citizens' digital rights and AI-driven algorithmic disruption

Chapter outline

7.1 Introduction: AI-driven algorithmic disruption

The 21st century can be characterised as the century of data (Friis-Christensen & Triaille, 2019; Kitchin, Lauriaut, & McArdle, 2018). While data itself has long existed, the current capacity to transform data into action is new (Bigo, Isin, & Ruppert, 2019). Big Data originated with the increasingly advanced data collection capabilities of the Internet, social networks, the Internet of Things (IoT), and sensors. Artificial intelligence (AI) and information technologies (IT) not only allowed for translating code into routines that could previously only be procured by humans but also injected new, previously unthinkable ones, such as massive searches (Almirall, 2019; Calzada, 2019a, 2019b). Finally, the cloud democratised these transformations, converting capital costs into variable costs, providing practically infinite scalability and the ability to package even the most sophisticated routines, such as face recognition and individual profiling, into easy-to-use pre-trained models (Armbrust et al., 2009).

This AI-driven algorithmic phenomenon has led to new consequences—such as hyper-targeting through data analytics, facial recognition, and individual profiling—received by many with both helplessness and threat, and resulting in not-so-desirable outcomes, such as massive manipulation and control via a surveillance capitalism push in the United States (US) (Zuboff, 2019) and the Social Credit Systems in China (Ahmed, 2018; Creemers, 2018;

Smart City Citizenship. https://doi.org/10.1016/B978-0-12-815300-0.00007-1

Kotska, 2019; Sun & Yan, 2020). In contrast, these societal concerns raised a debate in Europe that crystalised into the General Data Protection Regulation (GDPR) coming into force in May 2018 after 4 years of debate. The emergence of this new phenomenon has spurred a call to action for cities and regions in the European Union (EU), establishing the need to map out the techno-political debate on datafication or *dataism* (Calzada, 2019b). Moreover, the phenomenon has also ultimately highlighted the potential requirements for establishing regulatory frameworks to protect digital rights. Such frameworks cover demands on privacy, ownership (Calzada, 2018a, 2018b), trust (Mendoza-Tello, Mora, Pujol-López, & Lytras, 2019), access, ethics, transparency (Brunswicker, Pujol Priego, & Almirall, 2019), algorithmic automatisation (Chiodo, 2019), and ultimately, democratic accountability (Mair et al., 2019; Mora, Pujol López, Mendoza-Tello, & Morales, 2019; Wong, 2019).

Alongside this phenomena, data and data technologies alter not only the corpus of citizens' rights but also the way in which cities and regions conceive and deliver public policy and services (Vesnic-Alujevic, Stoermer, Rudkin, Scapolo, & Kimbell, 2019). This digital transformation pervasively encompasses all angles of policy: the provision of services, the assignment of resources, the approach to solving social problems, and even the complex decision-making process increasingly shifting to software algorithms and evolving towards considering citizens as merely data-providers rather than decision-makers (Calzada, 2018a).

This transformational process stemming from a *black-boxed* algorithmic momentum often gets perceived as a mechanism that increases the efficiency of existing approaches or as simply a process of policy adjustment. Nevertheless, this chapter argues that the data requires and creates data infrastructures and institutions (Ducuing, 2019; Gray, Gerlitz, & Bournegru, 2018; Kotsev, Minghini, Tomas, Vlado, & Lutz, 2020) that empower data, and both should be endowed with an ethical and democratic governance (Cardullo, Di Feliciantonio, & Kitchin, 2019; Ruppert, Isin, & Bigo, 2017). This chapter presents and develops both data infrastructures and institutions, collectively defining them as data ecosystems (Calzada, 2019a; European Commission, 2018a, 2018b; Janssen & Kuk, 2016; Lnenicka & Komarkova, 2019; Oliveira, Barros Lima, & Farias Lóscio, 2019). Data ecosystems are thereby not only data infrastructures and institutions but also related analytics and data capture systems used to take data and relay it to the system owners, who can then alter their provision of goods, services, and marketing accordingly. Currently, some data infrastructures and institutions configuring data ecosystems are either already established or in an embryonic state, namely the following data ecosystems: (i) Data Commons with Open Data; (ii) Code Commons with institutions such as Code for America (2019) and the failed Code for Europe (2019); and (iii) projects such as Ckan (CKAN, 2019) or Decode (DECODE, 2018).

This chapter—stemming eminently from the fieldwork action research carried out for previous publications (Calzada, 2018a) and recent updates and findings (Calzada, 2020) about the Barcelona case study—argues that the

Data Commons model (Calzada & Almirall, 2019a), as initiated and preliminarily implemented during the institutional period 2015–2019 by Barcelona City Council (2019a), has exemplified and contributed to opening up a new policy-data interaction through grassroots-led urban experimentation in Europe (Calzada & Almirall, 2019b). A direct outcome of this period is the Declaration of Cities Coalition for Digital Rights (CCDR, 2019) manifesto, which is ready to be translated into data policy by building networked data infrastructures and institutions. Despite its embryonic and still ideological status, this broad movement has gradually expanded under the leadership of Barcelona, Amsterdam, and New York City (NYC). The movement is now extending into additional cities—including Athens, Berlin, Bordeaux, Bratislava, Cluj-Napoca, Dublin, Glasgow, Grenoble, Helsinki, La Coruña, Liverpool, London, Lyon, Milan, Moscow, München, Porto, Rennes, Roma, Tirana, Turin, Vienna, and Zaragoza in Europe; Amman in the Middle East; and Atlanta, Austin, Cary, Chicago, Guadalajara, Kansas, Long Beach, Los Angeles, Philadelphia, Portland, San Antonio, San José, and Toronto in the Americas; and Sydney in Australia. This network of cities is a worldwide network to advocate digital rights and to start connecting data ecosystems. UN-Habitat is part of this network, which may reinforce its international role.

Hence, this chapter addresses three main aims: (i) to present the urgent need to align and develop these data ecosystems in Europe with the social and public good and democratic choice, unlike the global digital governance paradigms in China and the US; (ii) to elaborate around the case study of Barcelona as the flagship city alongside NYC and Amsterdam, trailblazing the post-GDPR data ecosystem called the CCDR; and (iii) consequently, to explore a strategic roadmap for developing effective European data ecosystems. Accordingly, this chapter is structured in three main sections based on these aims.

7.2 Context: Data ecosystems through data infrastructures and institutions in Europe

In the global context, three main clearly distinguished paradigms on data governance, algorithmic, and AI disruption currently coexist (Just, 2018):

(i) First, China is super-rich in data and is determined to maximise that advantage with systems such as Social Credit Systems (Kotska, 2019) or what is known as technological nationalism (Jiang & Fu, 2018), whereby large technology companies and the state embrace a mutually beneficial symbiotic relationship, in many cases orchestrated by the state in a regime of limited internal competition.

(ii) Second, in the US, the so-called GAFA (Google, Amazon, Facebook, and Apple) is driven by large technological private multinationals who collect massive amounts of data from global citizens without any informed consent. Both models are engaged in a sort of competition with the support of large national technological infrastructures and nationally aligned research agendas.

(iii) Third, in contrast, Europe is focusing on the attempt to start from the bottom-up to build a truly European model—one that is sustainable, locally driven, regionally rooted, and inclusive—while trying to maintain its lead. The European post-GDPR context is attempting to solve this conundrum of addressing citizens' rights in a way generative to societal good while maintaining a competitive lead with comparatively larger, more focused, and possibly more determined players (Warnke et al., 2019). Indeed, the European Commission (2019) is developing an expanded network of digital innovation hubs, which could be central to developing local and regional data ecosystems; these hubs will bring AI training, data, computing, and local partnerships together to develop AI solutions adapted to local and regional issues. Digital Innovation Hubs, in particular those with a specialisation in AI, could serve as the distribution channel for testing and experimentation facilities for smart cities.

Particularly, as the profound implications of algorithmic disruption in European cities and regions begin to surface, considerable fears regarding the hidden power of Big Data evil geniuses—GAFA—operating in porous regulatory systems have also emerged (Crémer, de Montjoye, & Schweitzer, 2019). The perspective of an increase in the already remarkable amount of data being controlled by AI tools and devices owned by multinational corporations has raised concerns in some European cities, such as Barcelona, which is presented as the core case study in this chapter, particularly due to apprehension that the corporations may further exacerbate already-pervasive social inequalities and further marginalise the most vulnerable people (Calzada & Cobo, 2015; Eubanks, 2017). These concerns have aggravated the criticism about the already-controversial technocratic European smart city model initially advocated by the European Commission through its H2020-Smart Cities and Communities policy scheme, raising questions about data privacy and ownership (Borsboom-van Beurden, Kallaos, Gindroz, Costa, & Riegler, 2019; Cardullo et al., 2019; Kempin Reuter, 2019).

Hence, the global digital governance context and the considerably different values of AI among the three global paradigms (China, US, and Europe), in light of the newly released European Data Strategy, in the post-GDPR context, Europe seems determined to lead the debate on the digital rights of citizens by experimenting with data ecosystems (European Commission, 2020). According to Kotsev et al. (2020), this strategy not only establishes an ambitious agenda that aims to leverage the favourable technological and political context but also empowers European citizens, businesses, and public authorities through a data-agile approach which (i) aligns with European values and (ii) reflects the needs of a multitude of stakeholders. Thus, the rationale behind data ecosystems in Europe is to deconstruct data complexity and visualise a multi-stakeholder techno-political process, producing truly inclusive urban spaces that fulfil the right to smart cities (Bigo et al., 2019; Cardullo et al., 2019; Dziembala, 2019; Visvizi & Lytras, 2018, 2019). How do digital technologies and data ecosystems transform the relationships between governments, business, and civil society? What are the defining factors for city and regional differences? How can policies at the EU level steer changing power relationships? As such, the lack of opaque politics concerning the most sophisticated technology, such as deep learning, and its increasing use in cities, particularly in very visible tasks such as facial recognition, has resulted in a push for more regulation and algorithmic transparency.

Against this European backdrop, *data ecosystems* are operationally defined in this chapter as the overarching data policy framework that comprises (i) four types of data infrastructures (political artefact, asset, process, and network) that need to be enabled through (ii) four functions (guidance, advocacy, operationalisation, and exploitation) accomplished by data institutions that create dynamics which mobilise these infrastructures in order to become a real and transformative driver of change.

Regarding data infrastructures (Table 7.1), data can be considered:

- **(i)** a political artefact that infuses societal values into public opinion;
- **(ii)** an asset that has value on its own;
- **(iii)** a process where data is collected, cleaned, and analysed; and
- **(iv)** a network where organisations around data trigger public good by overcoming political imbalances.

Specifically, data as a political artefact, as an instrument that enables the emergence of individual and collective rights, has attracted significant attention

TABLE 7.1 Data Infrastructures.

Four types	Data infrastructures	Specific examples
Political artefact	Digital rights	GDPR Manifesto in favour of technological sovereignty and digital rights for cities Barcelona ethical digital policy toolkit
Asset	Data commons Code commons Model commons	Open data Public-sector open source (e.g. Ckan)
Process	Public cloud Public analytics Public AI	AWS GovCloud in the US Anonymisation procedures Privacy-preserving procedures
Network	Moonshot projects Civic tech accelerators Grassroots networks Open data networks	Barcelona civic tech house Open data Hackathons Civic tech London Meetup

in Europe in the form of legislation on digital rights (Calzada, 2018b, 2019b). GDPR is a good example of this incarnation. Similarly, data as an asset is at stake and is arguably the most widely developed area where Data Commons is well represented by Open Data, but where Code Commons and Model Commons are also urgently needed (Calzada & Almirall, 2019a). The public sharing of code and AI models will not only spur innovation but also focus development into fewer and better solutions to the benefit of multi-stakeholder policy schemes in European cities and regions. Accordingly, a pressing necessity in Europe exists for a Public Cloud, Public Analytics, and Public AI workflow processes with ethical and social considerations and standards. Regarding Public Cloud, in June 2020, GAIA-X, as a federated data infrastructure for Europe, was presented by the Economy minister of France and Germany (GAIA-X, 2020). Thus, France and Germany work together to pioneer a new cloud computing process in order to reduce the EU's current dependence on American Silicon Valley tech giants such as Amazon, Microsoft, and Google. This joint initiative was announced in October 2019, but its current push by the end of year 2020 comes on the heels of a cooperation between both countries to boost the European *technological sovereignty* in the wake of the COVID-19 pandemic. Finally, a network comprising Moonshot projects, Civic Tech accelerators, Grassroots networks, and Open Data networks with many similarities to the entrepreneurial/innovation network is also essential for achieving a strong digital European policy in the public sector (Mazzucato, 2017).

Consequently, this chapter differentiates four functions of data institutions (Table 7.2) in operationalising the related data infrastructures (previously presented through Table 7.1):

- **(i)** those devoted to providing guidance in the governance and policy, such as Open Data Institute (2019) and GovTechLab (2019);
- **(ii)** those focused on advocacy, such as the CCDR (2019);
- **(iii)** those that operationalise the infrastructure, such as the Data Commons policy scheme through the Open Data Ecosystem, City Data Analytics Office, the Open Software Ecosystem through CityOS, and the DECODE-DECIDIM-METADECIDIM experimental and strategic triad of initiatives (Aragón et al., 2017; Barandiaran et al., 2017; Barcelona City Council, 2018, 2019b; Bass, Sutherland, & Symons, 2018; Calzada, 2018a; Calzada & Almirall, 2019b; Marras, Manca, Boratto, & Laniado, 2018);
- **(iv)** and finally, those devoted to exploiting the commons, such as organisations that use open source data together with those who have the political intent to reserve post-capitalistic logics through new grassroots-led urban experimentation, such as platform co-operatives (Borkin, 2019; Calzada & Almirall, 2019a; Scholz, 2016) and data co-operatives (Hardjono & Pentland, 2019). A platform co-operative is a co-operatively owned democratically governed business model that establishes a computing platform and uses a website and/or mobile application to facilitate the sale

TABLE 7.2 Data institutions.

Four functions	Cases	Analysis
Guidance	Open Data Institute (ODI)	The ODI, based in the UK and founded by Sir Tim Berners-Lee, is a non-profit private company that aims to connect, equip, and inspire people around the world to innovate with data
	GovTechLab	The purpose of GovTechLab is to facilitate the discussion, adoption, and exploration of new digital technologies (AI, IoT, Big Data, and Blockchain) with the view to support the adoption of these technologies in the public sector (Mora, Pérez del Hoyo, Sirvent, & Gilart-Iglesias, 2019)
Advocacy	CCDR	The CCDR cities—already encompassing 41 cities worldwide (Europe, America, Australia, and the Middle East), with the support of the United Nations Human Settlements Program (UN-Habitat)—share best practices, learn from each other's challenges and successes, and coordinate common initiatives and actions
Operationalise	Data Commons policy scheme: Open Data Ecosystem City Data Analytics Office Open Software Ecosystem Through CityOS DECODE-DECIDIM-METADECIDIM experimental and strategic triad of initiatives	According to previous research by the authors (Calzada, 2018a; Calzada & Almirall, 2019a), the Data Commons policy scheme could be defined as a way to negotiate the techno-politics of the smart cities as a contentious and dynamic process among several stakeholders, reconfiguring sociopolitical and power interrelations through conflicting trade-offs, of the ownership of the data, and ultimately, of the technology itself
Exploitation	Companies and organisations using the data Infrastructures (e.g. Open Data): Platform and data co-operatives	According to Scholz (2016, p. 16), 'platform co-operatives is a term that describes technological, cultural, political, and social changes' Complementarily, according to Borkin (2019, p. 5), 'platform co-operatives are digital platforms that are designed to provide a service or sell a product—and are collectively owned and governed by the people who depend on and participate in them' And according to Hardjono and Pentland (2019, p. 2), 'data co-operatives refer to the voluntary collaborative pooling by individuals of their personal data for the benefit of the collective group or community membership'

> of goods and delivery of services. Examples of platform co-operatives include Fairbnb, Denver's Green Taxi Co-operative, and Resonate. Data co-operatives may help rebalance the relationship between those who create data (citizens as data providers) and those who seek to exploit that data while also creating an environment for fair and democratic exchange. Data co-operatives with fiduciary obligations to members provide a promising direction for the democratic empowerment of citizens through their personal data. Examples of data co-operatives are flourishing around credit unions. As not-for-profit institutions owned by their members, credit unions are already chartered to securely manage their members' digital data and to represent them in a wide variety of financial transactions.

In the next section, this chapter briefly presents several elements to illustrate the relevance of data ecosystems through the case study of Barcelona, researched in-depth since 2017 by the author (Calzada, 2018a, 2019a, 2019b; Calzada & Almirall, 2019a, 2019b). Barcelona ultimately illustrates that Europe may be speaking with its own voice. In the final section, this chapter proposes a preliminary roadmap to make data policy effective for European local and regional authorities.

7.3 Barcelona protecting its citizens' digital rights

In the contours of this chapter, the case study of Barcelona illustrates the leading role that this city has played since 2015 by shifting the smart city policy agenda and starting to construct data ecosystems from scratch in not only Barcelona but also in Europe by leading the CCDR. In fact, during the policy period starting in May 2015, Barcelona attempted to cover the four techno-political perspectives of data infrastructures (Table 7.1) and the four functions of data institutions (Table 7.2). Accordingly, this chapter reveals that the intensity of the outcomes for the four types and four functions differs considerably, requiring further nuanced fieldwork research to produce conclusive results. Obviously, regarding data infrastructures, the political artefact defined through the Manifesto for Digital Sovereignty and Digital Rights and the Barcelona Ethical Digital Policy Toolkit was the main driver of the data ecosystems in Barcelona. Regarding data institutions, the advocacy function facilitated through the CCDR was remarkable but so, too, was the way in which the Data Analytics Office was operationalised to be strategically supported through the efforts to create a pan-European data infrastructural asset such as Code Commons. In this endeavour, contributions made by participants of the Decode-Decidim-Metadecidim experimental and strategic initiative triad clearly operationalised a solid digital policy ground for establishing pan-European data institutions (as seen in Chapter 6). In addition, there were several attempts to nurture platform co-operatives (Scholz, 2016) and data co-operatives (Hardjono & Pentland, 2019) such as Som Energia (Calzada & Almirall, 2019a) as a social and ethical alternative to existing commercial platforms (Just, 2018).

Methodologically speaking, the author's previous research spanned from September 2017 to March 2019 by putting into practice a fieldwork action research methodological approach (Forester, Martien, & David, 2019) in two gradual and complementary steps. Preliminarily, the author actively participated in the CCDR and the subsequent actions aimed at establishing Data Commons and Code Commons. In parallel, he actively carried out direct participation in three core events and conducted 20 in-depth interviews with a diverse set of strategic stakeholders—following the Penta helix multi-stakeholder framework—including the private sector, the public sector, academia, civic society, and (social) entrepreneurs/activists (Calzada & Cowie, 2017). Thus, the previous fieldwork showed several key findings as shown in Chapter 6, which could be considered the point of departure for this specific analysis in this chapter.

From a strategic standpoint, the governmental period in Barcelona starting in May 2015 could be examined as follows: the team led by the former Chief Technology and Digital Innovation Officer of Barcelona City Council, Francesca Bria, largely supplanted the role of several data institutions by accomplishing core strategic functions. Clearly, this approach may present abundant hindrances (Bria, 2019), despite the fact that the significant impact is worth considering and highlights the main benefit of this chapter: to suggest a roadmap for governance and institutional empowerment to allow for creating effective and democratic data ecosystems in Europe. Barcelona (alongside the leading cities of the CCDR, such as Amsterdam and NYC) presented what can be described as an embrionic version of a set of data ecosystems for the European city-regional realm, particularly on its institutional side. Hence, in this section, this chapter briefly examines Barcelona's data institutions as structured in Table 7.2.

In guidance, all 20 interviewed stakeholders (stemming from previous fieldwork research; Calzada, 2018a) agreed upon the large impact of the accomplishments, exemplified through two main data infrastructures under the GDPR umbrella (Table 7.1): the Manifesto and the Toolkit. There was, however, also a consensus on the lack of diversity in the guidance, based on the unilateral ideological vision of the given data infrastructures—the political artefact.

Advocacy was probably the more fertile data institution in this policy analysis during the period 2015–2019. Despite the fact that directly promoting this approach on digital rights (also known as technological sovereignty; Calzada, 2019a, 2019b) from local authorities is rather unconventional, it is equally true that CCDR proved to be very effective, particularly in terms of already mobilising 41 cities worldwide and creating techno-political awareness.

Operationalisation took four different directions under the policy programme Data Commons:

(i) The first operationalisation involved updating the Open Data Ecosystem with an Open Source Portal (CKan) while fostering its adoption.
(ii) The second involved creating the City Data Analytics Office.

(iii) The third involved the code-sharing effort via the Open Software Ecosystem Through CityOS through the CCDR to identify and encorage software to share.

(iv) And finally, the fourth involved three experimental and strategically intertwined initiatives:
  - **(a)** cutting-edge, innovative EU-funded projects, such as DECODE led by Barcelona and Amsterdam,
  - **(b)** the DECIDIM grassroots-led co-operative platform, and
  - **(c)** the METADECIDIM process for reflecting upon DECIDIM's operation and future development through a meta-lab of open debate.

However, exploitation of data institutions has materialised bolder and more innovative projects around two new organisational forms for data: platform co-operatives and data co-operatives. Alongside the launch of the CCDR in 2018—jointly led by Barcelona, Amsterdam, and NYC—updated and ongoing fieldwork research revealed (Calzada & Almirall, 2019a, 2019b) a tension between two different business models on data governance: platform capitalism exemplified with the conflict between Cabify and Uber and the local taxi association, Elite Taxi BCN, and platform co-operativism exemplified by the successful case of Som Energia, a co-operative in the energy field that is actively supported by city hall. While it is much too soon to accurately appraise the initiative, it certainly extends beyond what has been attempted by city halls so far, raising the bar for local politics in general and digital policy in particular, and opening up new and promising data policy pathways.

Updated and ongoing fieldwork research also surfaced the underlying tension between a government that tries to push the limits of what a local administration can achieve and what it should achieve given its inherent internal restrictions (Purwanto, Zuiderwijk, & Janssen, 2020). The will to push the boundaries of digital competences in local authorities is highly visible in advocacy, particularly in the construction of the coalitions in 41 cities worldwide pushing to establish digital rights (and technological sovereignty) and primarily gaining momentum from the European post-GDPR realm. Furthermore, this push not only explicitly expresses the techno-political will, but also introduces the novel ambition in local governments aiming to redefine modes of production by creating platform and data co-operatives.

However, the tension, which often turns into frustration due to limitations, has mostly surfaced in uncommon and unexpected data policy areas. One of them is Code Commons. Certainly, sharing code developed with public money among cities, on the surface, seems unproblematic. There are, however, many details in the implementation that create insurmountable barriers. Among them is the lack of incentives for cities to start a collective process that hypothetically will ultimately benefit all despite the complexities involved in prioritising this process as a pressing matter for local authorities. Likewise, the same occurs with analytics: data scientists are expensive to hire and not eager to work for bureaucracies like city councils, particularly if the scientists have not already established leadership in the field that ensures the progression through a career path.

Hence, looking past these tensions and returning to the assessment of guidance, this chapter discovered the main issue: the lack of external validation and guidance for governance—while the need to continuously invent its model—without the endorsement and advice that external organisations, such as GovTechLab (2019), could have provided.

7.4 Conclusion: Towards pan-European agencies?

The conclusion of this chapter revolves around the evidence that local digital policies are no longer local, in neither their objectives nor their instruments for implementing data infrastructures and institutions. The interpellation of global actors that interdependently shapes the digital governance realm cannot be understood from an extremely local perspective of each city council. This chapter, therefore, suggests data ecosystems as a need for a pan-European post-GDPR digital policy (Kotsev et al., 2020). Thus, currently, the embryo of data ecosystems consists of several forms of cooperation with universities serving the CCDR in a broader Penta helix multi-stakeholder policy scheme (Calzada & Cowie, 2017; Olsen & Welke, 2019).

In the contours of the previously published and further ongoing and updated fieldwork action research carried out in Barcelona and briefly presented in this chapter, the author concludes by proposing a preliminary roadmap for data ecosystems among European cities and regions. Fieldwork research overall clearly shows that code sharing cannot be established from a local perspective with pressing only local interest. Rather, it needs neutral agencies driven by incentives to create a common ground. Code development also needs the guidance and common motivation that non-profit foundations such as Apache or Numfocus brought to Open Source. Previous attempts witnessed a tentative translation of these efforts done by Code for America or the failed Code for Europe, but they lacked the breadth and necessary influence to trigger the movement effectively, among other things, because of the lack of perspective of future growth, finance capabilities, and a feasible vision that European cities and regions will firmly adopt their contributions (Ulo, Hidayanto, Sandhyaduhita, Fitriani, & Abiding, 2019).

After previous and ongoing fieldwork research, a clear final remark emerged: it is highly unlikely that these new European data ecosystems appear with the present digital policy scheme. Cities acting independently will have neither the opportunity or the sense of urgency to establish a set of commons in terms of data infrastructures and institutions, nor the resources and the power of influence to develop pan-European collaborations among cities and regions. There is certainly a need to pursue a different approach through a European roadmap for digital policy and the emergence of data ecosystems.

The following three main priorities stand out from the previous and ongoing fieldwork action research and could constitute a preliminary roadmap for local and regional governments that aim to establish post-GDPR data ecosystems for protecting citizens' digital rights in Europe.

Advocacy: There are already organisations where cities and regions can collate their points of view, such as Eurocities, or intensive knowledge exchange activities such as the City-to-City Learning programme in the Replicate EU project (Replicate, 2019). However, the rise of other networks with a substantial critical approach to the techno-politics of data science, such as CCDR, shows the need for further critical policy approaches for data. Cities and regions in Europe need arenas where they can speak louder among a set of diverse voices, arenas that should be better connected to European policymakers.

Governance: There is a lack, particularly in continental Europe, of guidance and applied research in policy, especially in modern areas such as AI, data spaces, behavioural analytics, and digital transformations. Much of the problem lies not in the existing capacities but in the financing of these activities with a neutral non-partisan view.

Pan-European agencies: Probably the most stringent problem is the one of mobilising capacities in AI, analytics, and modern software development by putting them at the service of European cities and regions. Without such mobilisation, data infrastructures and institutions will not happen, and the benefits of AI will not be reaped. Among all potential solutions, pan-European agencies—either public, private or in the form of a partnership through the Penta helix framework (Calzada & Cowie, 2017)—that promote Open Source code, model sharing, and standardisation look like the best possible solution.

Cities and regions have, so far, followed a bottom-up approach with limitations, as uncovered by the current research. In parallel with that, the rise of new needs surfaced the increasing limitations of this approach. European local and regional governments are still endowed with old governance structures that clearly cannot overcome 21st-century challenges. These challenges ultimately boil down to protecting citizens' digital rights while relying on the capacity of European cities and regions to deal with self-governing and interdependent data policies as the only possible way to ensure fairer European democracies.

References

Ahmed, S. (2018). Personal risk and algorithmic opacity: An investigation of user-identified concerns in the construction of the social credit system. In *Freie Universität Berlin, Workshop on digital transformation in China—Recent trends and impacts, Berlin.*

Almirall, E. (2019). *From competing on analytics to companies as code*. Retrieved from: https://www.forbes.com/sites/esade/2019/01/10/from-competing-on-analytics-to-companies-as-code/#15e5700c7af1.

Aragón, P., Kaltenbrunner, A., Calleja-López, A., Pereira, A., Monterde, A., Barandiaran, X. E., et al. (2017). *Deliberative platform design: The case study of the online discussions in Decidim Barcelona*. Cham: Springer.

Armbrust, M., Fox, A., Griffith, R., Joseph, A., Katz, R., Konwinski, A., et al. (2009). *Above the clouds: A Berkeley view of cloud computing*. Mimeo, UC Berkeley RAD Laboratory. Retrieved from https://www2.eecs.berkeley.edu/Pubs/TechRpts/2009/EECS-2009-28.pdf.

Barandiaran, X., Calleja-López, A., Monterde, A., Aragón, P., Linares, J., Romero, C., et al. (2017). Decidim: Redes políticas y tecnopolíticas para la democracia participativa. *RECERCA, Revista de Pensament i Análisi, 21*, 137–150. https://doi.org/10.6035/Recerca.2017.21.8.

Barcelona City Council. (2018). Retrieved from: https://www.decidim.barcelona/.

Barcelona City Council. (2019a). *Barcelona digital city: Putting technology at the service of people*. Barcelona: Adjuntament de Barcelona.

Barcelona City Council. (2019b). Retrieved from: www.metadecidim.barcelona.

Bass, T., Sutherland, E., & Symons, T. (2018). *DECODE D.1.10 policy requirements and models of implementation*. London: NESTA.

Bigo, D., Isin, E., & Ruppert, E. (2019). *Data politics*. London: Routledge.

Borkin, S. (2019). *Platform co-operatives: Solving the capital conumdrum*. London: NESTA.

Borsboom-van Beurden, J., Kallaos, J., Gindroz, B., Costa, S., & Riegler, J. (2019). *Smart city guidance package: A roadmap for integrated planning and implementation of smart city projects*. Brussels: EIP-SCC.

Bria, F. (2019). Retrieved from: https://www.wired.co.uk/article/reboot-britain-francesca-bria.

Brunswicker, S., Pujol Priego, L., & Almirall, E. (2019). Transparency in policy making: A complexity view. *Government Information Quarterly*. https://doi.org/10.1016/j.giq.2019.05.005.

Calzada, I. (2018a). (Smart) citizens from data providers to decision-makers? The case study of Barcelona. *Sustainability, 10*(9), 3252. https://doi.org/10.3390/su10093252.

Calzada, I. (2018b). Deciphering smart city citizenship: The techno-politics of data and urban cooperative platforms. *Revista International de Estudios Vascos, RIEV, 63*(1-2), 42–81. https://doi.org/10.13140/RG.2.2.24498.35524/3.

Calzada, I. (2019a). Data spaces and democracy. *RSA Journal, 3*. https://doi.org/10.13140/RG.2.2.26821.60641/1.

Calzada, I. (2019b). Technological sovereignty: Protecting citizens' digital rights in the AI-driven and post-GDPR algorithmic and city-regional European realm. *Regions eZine, 4*. https://doi.org/10.1080/13673882.2018.00001038.

Calzada, I. (2020). Review of the book Smart City Barcelona: The Catalan Quest to Improve Future Urban Living, by a. Vives. *International Journal of Iberian Studies, 33*(1), 103–104. https://doi.org/10.1386/ijis_00018_5.

Calzada, I., & Almirall, E. (2019a). *Barcelona's grassroots-led urban experimentation: Deciphering the 'data commons' policy scheme, in Data for Policy 2019*. London: Zenodo. https://doi.org/10.5281/zenodo.2604618.

Calzada, I., & Almirall, E. (2019b). Is Barcelona establishing a sustainable paradigm in Europe by grassroots-led smart urban experimentation through the 'data commons' policy? In *American Association of Geographers Annual Meeting 2019, Washington DC*.

Calzada, I., & Cobo, C. (2015). Unplugging: Deconstructing the smart city. *Journal of Urban Technology, 22*(1), 23–43. https://doi.org/10.1080/10630732.2014.971535.

Calzada, I., & Cowie, P. (2017). Beyond smart and data-driven city-regions? Rethinking stakeholder-helixes strategies. *Regions Magazine, 308*(4), 25–28. https://doi.org/10.1080/13673882.2017.11958675.

Cardullo, P., Di Feliciantonio, C., & Kitchin, R. (2019). *The right to the smart city*. Bingley: Emerald.

CCDR (Cities Coalition for Digital Rights). (2019). Retrieved from: https://citiesfordigitalrights.org/.

Chiodo, S. (2019). The greatest epistemological externalisation: Reflecting on the puzzling direction we are heading to through algorithmic automatisation. *AI & SOCIETY*, 1–10. https://doi.org/10.1007/s00146-019-00905-y.

CKAN. (2019). Retrieved from: https://ckan.org/.

Code for America. (2019). Retrieved from: https://www.codeforamerica.org.

Code for Europe. (2019). Retrieved from: http://codeforeurope.net/.

Creemers, R. (2018). *China's social credit system: An evolving practice of control*. Retrieved from: https://ssrn.com/abstract=3175792.

Crémer, J., de Montjoye, Y.-A., & Schweitzer, H. (2019). *Competition policy for the digital era*. Luxembourg: Publications Office of the European Union.

DECODE. (2018). Retrieved from: https://www.decodeproject.eu/.

Ducuing, C. (2019). Data as infrastructure? A study of data sharing legal regimes. In *Competition and regulation in network industries*. https://doi.org/10.1177/1783591719895390.

Dziembala, M. (2019). Smart city as a steering centre of the region's sustainable development and competitiveness. In A. Visvizi, & M. D. Lytras (Eds.), *Smart cities: Issues and challenges. Mapping political, social and economic risks and threats* Elsevier, ISBN:9780128166390.

Eubanks, V. (2017). *Automating inequality: How high-tech tools profile, police, and punish the poor*. NYC: St. Martin's Press.

European Commission. (2018a). *Communication from the Commission to the European Parliament, the Council, the European Economic and Social Committee and the Committee of the Regions "Artificial Intelligence for Europe" COM/2018/237 final*. Luxembourg: Publications Office of the European Union.

European Commission. (2018b). *Communication from the Commission to the European Parliament, the Council, the European Economic and Social Committee and the Committee of the Regions "Artificial Intelligence for Europe" COM/2018/795 final*. Luxembourg: Publications Office of the European Union.

European Commission. (2019). *Call for digital innovation hubs on artificial intelligence*. Retrieved from https://ec.europa.eu/digital-single-market/en/news/call-digital-innovation-hubs-artificial-intelligence.

European Commission. (2020). *European data strategy, 2020*. Retrieved from: https://ec.europa.eu/info/strategy/priorities-2019-2024/europe-fit-digital-age/european-data-strategy_en.

Forester, J., Martien, K., & David, L. (2019). Enacting reflective and deliberative practices in action research. *Policy Studies*, 1–20. https://doi.org/10.1080/01442872.2019.1618445.

Friis-Christensen, A., & Triaille, J. P. (2019). *JRC data policy*. Luxembourg: Publications Office of the European Union.

GAIA-X. (2020). Retrieved from: https://www.data-infrastructure.eu.

GovTechLab. (2019). Retrieved from: www.govtechlab.org.

Gray, J., Gerlitz, C., & Bournegru, L. (2018). Data infrastructures literacy. *Big Data & Society*, *5*(2), 1–13. https://doi.org/10.1177/2053951718786316.

Hardjono, T., & Pentland, A. (2019). Data cooperatives: Towards a foundation for decentralized personal data management. *arXiv*. 1905.08819v1.

Janssen, M., & Kuk, G. (2016). The challenges and limits of big data algorithms in technocratic governance. *Government Information Quarterly*, *33*(3), 371–377. https://doi.org/10.1016/j.giq.2016.08.011.

Jiang, M., & Fu, K.-W. (2018). Chinese social media and big data: Big data, big brother, big profit? *Policy & Internet*, *10*(4), 372–392. https://doi.org/10.1002/poi3.187.

Just, N. (2018). Governing online platforms: Competition policy in times of platformization. *Telecommunications Policy*, *42*(5), 386–394. https://doi.org/10.1016/j.telpol.2018.02.006.

Kempin Reuter, T. (2019). Human rights and the city: Including marginalized communities in urban development and smart cities. *Journal of Human Rights*, 1–21. https://doi.org/10.1080/14754835.2019.1629887.

Kitchin, R., Lauriaut, T. P., & McArdle, G. (2018). *Data and the city*. London: Routledge.

Kotsev, A., Minghini, M., Tomas, R., Vlado, C., & Lutz, M. (2020). From spatial data infrastructures to data spaces—A technological perspective on the evolution of European SDIs. *ISPRS International Journal of Geo-Information*, *9*(3), 1–19. https://doi.org/10.3390/ijgixx010005.

Kotska, G. (2019). China's social credit systems and public opinion: Explaining high levels of approval. *New Media & Society*, *21*(7), 1565–1593. https://doi.org/10.1177/1461444819826-402.

Lnenicka, M., & Komarkova, J. (2019). Big and open linked data analysis ecosystem: Theoretical background and essential elements. *Government Information Quarterly*, *36*(1), 129–144. https://doi.org/10.1016/j.giq.2018.11.004.

Mair, D., Smillie, L., La Placa, G., Schwendinger, F., Raykovska, M., Pasztor, Z., et al. (2019). *Understanding our political nature: How to put knowledge and reason at the heart of political decision-making*. Luxembourg: Publications Office of the European Union.

Marras, M., Manca, M., Boratto, L., & Laniado, D. (2018). *DECODE D.5.3. Data analysis methods and first results from pilots*. London: DECODE.

Mazzucato, M. (2017). *The value of everything: Making and taking in the global economy*. London: Penguin.

Mendoza-Tello, J. C., Mora, H., Pujol-López, F. A., & Lytras, M. D. (2019). Disruptive innovation to cryptocurrencies in consumer acceptance and trust. *Information Systems and e-Business Management*, *17*(2), 195–222. https://doi.org/10.1007/s10257-019-00415-w.

Mora, H., Pérez del Hoyo, R., Sirvent, R. M., & Gilart-Iglesias, V. (2019). Management city model based on blockchain and smart contracts technology. In *Springer Proceedingss in Complexity. Research & Innovation Forum 2019, RIIFORUM 2019*. Cham: Springer. https://doi.org/10.1007/978-3-030-30809-4_28.

Mora, H., Pujol López, F. A., Mendoza-Tello, J. C., & Morales, M. R. (2019). Virtual currencies in modern societies: Challenges and opportunities. In A. Visvizi, & M. D. Lytras (Eds.), *Politics and technology in the post-truth era* (pp. 171–185). Emerald. https://doi.org/10.1108/978-1-78756-983-620191012.

Oliveira, M. I. S., Barros Lima, G. F., & Farias Lóscio, B. (2019). Investigations into data ecosystems: A systematic mapping study. *Knowledge and Information Systems*, *61*(2), 589–630. https://doi.org/10.1007/s10115-018-1323-6.

Olsen, T., & Welke, R. (2019). Managerial challenges to realizing IT shared services in a public university. *Transforming Government: People, Process and Policy*, *13*(1), 76–92. https://doi.org/10.1108/TG-04-2018-0030.

Open Data Institute. (2019). Retrieved from: https://theodi.org.

Purwanto, A., Zuiderwijk, A., & Janssen, M. (2020). Citizen engagement with open government data: Lessons learned from Indonesia's presidential election. In *Transforming Government: People, Process and Policy*. https://doi.org/10.1108/TG-06-2019-0051.

Replicate EU. (2019). *City-to-city-learning programme*. Retrieved from: www.replicate-project.eu/city2citylearning.

Ruppert, E., Isin, E., & Bigo, D. (2017). Data politics. *Big Data & Society*, 1–7. https://doi.org/10.1177/2053951717717749.

Scholz, T. (2016). *Platform cooperativism: Challenging the corporate sharing economy*. New York: Rosa Luxemburg Stiftung.

Sun, Y., & Yan, W. (2020). The power of data from the global south: Environmental civic tech and data activism in China. *International Journal of Communication*, *14*, 2144–2162. 1932-8036/20200005.

Ulo, K. L. M., Hidayanto, A. N., Sandhyaduhita, P. I., Fitriani, W. R., & Abiding, Z. (2019). Factors influencing internet users' intention to sign e-petitions. *Transforming Government: People, Process and Policy*, *13*(3/4), 257–275. https://doi.org/10.1108/TG-01-2019-0006.

Vesnic-Alujevic, L., Stoermer, E., Rudkin, J., Scapolo, F., & Kimbell, L. (2019). *The future of government 2030+: A citizen-centric perspective on new government models*. Luxembourg: Publications Office of the European Union.

Visvizi, A., & Lytras, M. (2018). It's not a fad: Smart cities and smart villages research in European and global contexts. *Sustainability*, *10*(8), 2727. https://doi.org/10.3390/su10082727.

Visvizi, A., & Lytras, M. (2019). Reflecting on oikos and agora in smart cities context: Concluding remarks. In A. Visvizi, & M. D. Lytras (Eds.), *Smart cities: Issues and challenges. Mapping political, social and economic risks and threats* Elsevier, ISBN:9780128166390.

Warnke, P., Cuhls, K., Schmoch, U., Daniel, L., Andreescu, L., Dragomir, B., et al. (2019). *100 Radical innovation: Breakthroughs for the future*. Luxembourg: European Commission.

Wong, P.-H. (2019). Democratizing algorithmic fairness. *Philosophy & Technology*. https://doi.org/10.1007/s13347-019-00355-w.

Zuboff, S. (2019). *The age of surveillance capitalism: The fight for a human future at the new frontier of power*. London: Profile.

Epilogue. RESETTING smart city citizenship: Amidst the post-COVID-19 hyperconnected-virialised societies

1 The new normal: Pandemic citizenship

Over the last decades, global smart cities have led to a new hegemonic class of global citizenship. While the access to this global citizenship is still not spread evenly, many citizens have enjoyed the freedom to move, work, and travel with no limits (Arendt, 1949; Birnie & Bauböck, 2020; Bridle, 2018; Carey, 2018; Kallio, Wood, & Häkli, 2020; Lepoutre, 2020; Nordling, Sager, & Söderman, 2017; Schou & Hjelholt, 2018). In the meantime, as it has been addressed in Chapter 1 through the idea of *unplugging* smart city citizenship, the urban phenomenon and its sociotechnical controversies (Duarte & Firmino, 2018) have been explicitly surfacing until we have reached this unknown and highly unexpected status of a hyperconnected-virialised society called 'the new normal'. Against the odd, cities and communities are beginning to develop new ways of responding to the COVID-19 pandemic that seek to make the most of the Social Innovation (SI) of urban areas. Richard Sennett optimistically argued that the pandemic could provide the final shift in how technology is used in smart cities to one that is primarily about building communities. According to him, 'pandemic may, finally, humanise the use of high tech in cities: what's emerging in this pandemic are good programmes and protocols which create community' (Sennett, 2020, p. 1). But, amidst the COVID-19, how the rise of algorithmic need could not be bad for humans and democracy (Allam & Jones, 2020; Amat, Falcó-Gimeno, Arenas, & Muñoz, 2020; Bastani, 2019; Broussard, 2018; Floridi, 2017; Floridi, Cowls, King, & Taddeo, 2020; Frey, 2019; Hatuka, Toch, Birnhack, & Zur, 2020; Kuziemski & Misuraca, 2020; Zuboff, 2019)?

The so-called 'the new normal' may be approached through four pillars to developing smart cities:

(i) People first: Combining a citizen-centric approach to urban governance. This pillar may imply actions for the smart city as a service being extended through multiuse, sharing, and cohabitation to almost all urban functions.

Smart City Citizenship. https://doi.org/10.1016/B978-0-12-815300-0.09987-1

(ii) Transmobility: A service view to transportation. This pillar may imply actions for the smart city that bring together the mobility chain of citizens with goods and services.
(iii) Retrofitting: Sees built environment as a generative asset. This pillar may imply actions for the smart city that retrofit underused urban infrastructures to contemporary life.
(iv) Data commons: Knowledge is an infrastructure. This pillar may imply actions for the smart city that regain public commons in the new landscape of digital services (see Chapter 6).

However, 'the new normal' should be seen beyond the smart city through a broader lens called *pandemic citizenship.* All of a sudden, the cosmopolitan globalisation rhetoric of a borderless world has been drastically slowed down by COVID-19. This pandemic has introduced a new level of uncertainty in global affairs and led many to question whether citizens will be able to continue enjoy the freedom of movement once the crisis is 'over'. Ironically, this resonates with the former UK Prime Minister Theresa May's popular quote in reference to the *de facto* Brexit, 'If you believe you are a citizen of the world, you are a citizen of nowhere'. Actually, we are now *pandemic citizens*, increasingly stuck inside closed nation-states surrounded by contradictory new walls and old borders. Against this backdrop, it can be argued that borders still matter—at least as much as nations do. But the significance of nations and citizenship might be rapidly shifting through a sort of *pandemic adjustment*, with different consequences for citizens depending on which country they call home and their living conditions. In other words, and bluntly speaking, it seems borders are making a temporary comeback affecting everyone directly but not all equally. We are in the transition heading towards a new world order where smart city citizenship should be adjusted and adapted. How should smart city stakeholders face this novel scenario?

What we might call a shared pandemic citizenship—where citizens worldwide share exactly the same fear, uncertainty, and risks—is here to stay. This has different levels of techno-political implications, as it intersects with another global trend—how algorithms are increasingly shaping our lives. In other words, the Epilogue of this book argues that the current pandemic crisis is pervasively related to data governance issues, which exposes citizens' vulnerability in a potential surveillance state and capitalistic and extractive forms of digitisation.

The responses to this pandemic emergency have been extremely different from case to case: from the drastic lockdowns first seen in China, which were eventually followed by several European countries including Italy and Spain, to more targeted measures like those implemented by South Korea, Singapore, and Israel. Several governments have, in an attempt to tackle the spread of the virus, begun operating, whether consciously or unwittingly, as *algorithmic nations* (Calzada, 2018). Algorithmic nations are driven by a new mode of governance where algorithms such as contact tracing apps, blockchain, facial recognition, or data mining, and other technological tools are a cornerstone. The downside is that these algorithms may negatively affect the ethical and the democratic life of citizens (Rose, 2020). We must therefore ask what are the democratic trade-offs of such algorithmic strategies? What are the consequences for citizens? There is clearly a merge between the pandemic and a data crisis.

Apps can help fight COVID-19 in many ways: through telemedicine, help with isolation, and online education among many others. Regarding contact tracing apps, a high number of citizens using them is required (60%). The data interoperability between apps is a real issue. Currently, Google and Apple are preparing a version that will easily become the mainstream approach to the issue. There is an intense period of developing and testing expected. Probably several contact tracing apps will be soon published in stores. But most importantly from the smart city citizenship perspective, two distinct approaches have emerged and created controversies mainly represented by the (i) centralised (Pan-European Privacy-Preserving Proximity Tracing, PEPP-PT) and (ii) decentralised (Privacy-Preserving Proximity Tracing DP-3T). The question here would be regarding the citizens' attitudes towards apps and data sharing. It is clear that European strategy for data (European Commission, 2020) (GaiaX, 2020), including business to government data sharing, data altruism, data donation, innovation of public services, and implications on digital governance, will be at stake.

It appears that this pandemic crisis is forcing us towards an algorithmic crisis, in which the data of citizens could be used for unfair or unethical purposes by governments or other organisations. Do we have a good understanding of how China has implemented its social credit systems, or how South Korea has used the app to track and treat citizens? Why Singapore and Germany, in very different geopolitical contexts, have very few deaths and been able to control so quickly the spread of infection? How will Israel use the data that people are providing to the government to control the pandemic spread? Are all means justified to fight the pandemic? Should governments protect citizens from being infected even if this might mean establishing a new digital non-privacy norm? Will this pandemic crisis become an algorithmic crisis, with serious side effects for governments worldwide?

There may be evidences of governments misusing data collected to fight the coronavirus for nefarious aims. Thus, it is a systemic risk that we must not be blind to, as these new data tools are incredibly potent. Surprisingly positive though, scientists worldwide are working continuously to experiment and design unprecedented AI systems to (hopefully) detect the virus without violating democratic norms while protecting our fellow citizens. It is a massive mobilisation of knowledge that we cannot easily dismiss.

Global thinkers, such as the philosophers Harari (2018) and Innerarity (2016), constantly advocate for transnational cooperation among algorithmic nations. According to them, the real antidote to an epidemic is not segregation, but political leadership and cooperation. In the near future, governments may take different techno-political approaches to how data could be used and exploited to tackle such an unprecedented situation. Algorithmic nations of various political ideologies are already carving out different futures for their citizens. Among the resilience strategies adopted by various governments, collective intelligence should be considered to further avoid dystopian measures that could exacerbate existing social inequalities and techno-political vulnerabilities among pandemic citizens. Collective intelligence is created when people work together, often with the help of technology, to mobilise a wider range of information, ideas, and insights to address a SI challenge.

Among the various resilience strategies stemming from SI that are worth considering are predicting and modelling AI systems, citizens science projects with real-time data, social media mining, open-source do-it-yourself (DIY) coronavirus detection tests, and most importantly, sharing policies and strategies among algorithmic nations.

Ultimately, algorithmic nations should strive to manage this extraordinary situation by taking advantage of the unprecedented masses of data now available, but without using it as a shortcut to undermine democracy and the rights of our fellow pandemic citizens, wherever they are located on the planet (Calzada, 2019a, 2019b). This has brought to the fore a new old dilemma, whether key tenets of European democracies, including the protection of the fundamental right to privacy, should be set aside during the pandemic to enable a more effective response (Kuziemski & Misuraca, 2020). Here once again the current COVID-19 outbreak comes in our help, as it is often remarked that crisis like wars is always dramatic accelerators of change. So as discussed by Geoff Mulgan (2020), 'Coronavirus could be used to accelerate changes that were long overdue' as it served as an extreme stress test for governments of all kinds and with specific impacts on digital resilience, institutional governance capacity, and welfare systems.

2 Digital, algorithmic, and liquid citizenship

Hence, the world may face a gradual return to another citizenship stage over the coming months or even years as a 'new normal' emerges before a vaccine becomes available on a mass scale, large enough to inoculate billions of citizens worldwide. With much of the world closed for business, and no widely available vaccine in sight, it may be months, if not years, before citizens travel and freely move (if sometimes) as they did before the crisis.

In parallel, from a closer look at the old continent, regarding European smart city citizenship landscape (Calzada, 2020), as Bauman (2000) suggested, solid bodies of European nation-states are abruptly liquefying through *data-opolies* (Stucke, 2018) and algorithmic disruption. The giant technological flagship firms of surveillance capitalism, such as Google and Facebook, have already assumed many functions previously associated with the nation-state, from cartography to the surveillance of citizens, which deterritorialised liquid and algorithmic citizenship. Now they may extract pandemic citizens' daily routine by sucking all their data. While liquid citizens remain highly distributed in a global grid of networks and data ecosystems, the data they produce are concentrated in the hands of a few companies by implementing *dataism:* the emerging ideology or new form of religion in which citizens are dispossessed of their data and digital rights (Harari, 2015). In the aftermath of the General Data Protection Regulation (GDPR), Amsterdam, Barcelona, and New York launched the Cities Coalition for Digital Rights, a joint initiative to promote and track progress in protecting citizens' digital rights. The digital philosopher Evgeny Morozov (2019) has argued that the economics of these giant firms' data extraction enables the emergence of a new global geopolitical order called *AI nationalism* (Hogarth, 2018), which contrasts with the needs and claims of citizens' digital rights. According to the billionaire investor and social philanthropist George Soros, these giant platforms have become obstacles to innovation and are a menace to citizenship (Hindman, 2018; Sadowski, 2020).

In recent years, European city and regional authorities have claimed that (smart) citizens are as important to a successful smart city program as the underlying data and technology, and these citizens must be convinced of the benefits and security the initiatives offer. Cities like Barcelona and Amsterdam are leading a new digital transformation agenda that complements the EU's GDPR, which mandates the ethical use of data to protect (smart) citizens from risks inherent in new, data-intensive technologies. In the contours of the digital, algorithmic, and liquid citizenship debate, this book has explored the problem of how city and regional authorities can proactively establish policies, strategies, and initiatives to locally enhance digital rights and give citizens more control over personal data by protecting them from discrimination, exclusion, and the erosion of their data privacy and ownership (Arrighi & Stjepanović, 2019; Birnie & Bauböck, 2020; Cardullo & Kitchin, 2018; Datta, 2018; Davies, 2020; De Koning, Jaffe, & Koster, 2015; De Waal & Dignum, 2017; Eizaguirre, Pradel-Miquel, & García, 2017; Ferronato & Stan, 2018; Hintz, Dencik, & Wahl-Jorgensen, 2017; Jašina-Schäfer & Cheskin, 2019; Joss, Cook, & Dayot, 2017; Kallio et al., 2020; Keith & Calzada, 2018; Kitchin, Cardullo, & Di Feliciantonio, 2018; Mark, 2014; Nguyen, 2017; Piccoli, 2019; Purcell, 2003; Sassen, 2002; Smith, 2019; Stahl, 2020; Stuurman, 2019; Swyngedouw, 2005; Tammpuu & Masso, 2019; Zandbergen & Uitermark, 2019).

In the European data-driven economy, AI, big data, machine learning, and blockchain technologies are reshaping the notion of citizenship in Europe, on the one hand, by pervasively challenging the rescaling of nation-states' fixed dynamics and, on the other hand, by demanding a counter-reaction from city-regions to bring the control of data to citizens (Craglia, 2018). Claims of technological sovereignty through data commons policy programmes and the Decode EU experimental project taking place now in Barcelona and Amsterdam (Calzada, 2019a, 2019b; Couture & Toupin, 2017; DECODE, 2019) are presented as the flagship of this movement, which has already been replicated throughout other European city-regions. In the post-GDPR scenario (smart) citizens' data privacy, security, and ownership ultimately need to be protected by localising personal data via grassroots innovation and co-operative platforms. This type of citizenship that will be influenced and shaped by the geopolitical dynamics between city-regions and big firms is still unfolding. Thus, how could liquid and algorithmic citizens' data and digital rights be protected through further democratic empowerment to avoid digital dissent and dystopia (Pilkington, 2019)?

3 Algorithmic nations: Technological sovereignty through platform and data co-operatives

But how can we foresee algorithmic nations operating through technological sovereignty? Technological sovereignty is a political outlook that information and communications infrastructure and technology is aligned to the laws, needs, and interests of the city, region, or country in which users are located. In the post-COVID-19 societies the major challenge for Europe is to establish its cyber-sovereignty policy aligned with data ecosystems stemming from the city-regional scale (Calzada & Almirall, 2020). In this endeavour, the emerging generation of digital co-operatives, the so-called data and platform cooperatives, can clearly contribute to this challenge. Europe is at the moment a living lab for creating data and platform co-operatives stemming from data altruism and donation. How will new versions of co-operatives evolve over the years? How can data and platform co-operatives contribute to further democratic smart cities? How can citizens be self-governed and organise themselves to establish new social capital that could overcome the post-COVID-19's social distancing measures and consequently the loss of social capital (see Chapter 1)?

Europe is focusing on the attempt to start from the bottom-up to build a truly European model—one that is sustainable, locally driven, regionally rooted, and inclusive—while trying to maintain its lead. The European post-GDPR context is attempting to solve this conundrum of addressing citizens' rights in a way generative to societal good while maintaining a competitive lead with comparatively larger, more focused, and possibly more determined players. Indeed, the European Commission (European Commission, 2019) is developing an expanded network of Digital Innovation Hubs (DIHs), which could be central to developing local and regional data ecosystems; these hubs will bring AI training, data, computing, and local partnerships together to develop AI solutions adapted to local and regional issues. However, how to leverage this aim reactivating digital economic and SI from the bottom-up for protecting citizens' digital rights? Co-operatives have been many times in history the answer for this (Calzada, 2013).

However, cities and regions have, so far, followed a bottom-up approach with limitations, as uncovered by the current research (Keith, 2020; Kempin Reuter,

2020). In parallel with that, new needs surfaced increasing the limitations of this approach. European local and regional governments are still endowed with old governance structures that clearly cannot overcome 21st-century challenges (Susskind, 2018). These challenges ultimately boil down to protecting citizens' digital rights while relying on the capacity of European cities and regions to deal with self-governing and interdependent data policies as the only possible way to ensure fairer European democracies.

4 Reset

Probably, post-COVID-19 societies may establish a new world order and will transform the way we understand the concept of smart cities. The question here is: Where will this general reset leave citizens? How will algorithmic disruption and surveillance capitalism affect citizens and their rights? Ultimately, how could (should?) we start building *the city* (again) from this reset? How citizens can define the city through democracy in a world that will not be back *normal* as we have known so far. And maybe unlike the suggestion made by the Irish writer Samuel Beckett with his famous quote 'try again, fail again, fail better', we all, representing citizenship, may not have a second chance (to try and to fail). We must sharply hit the nail on the head, in this, final occasion. RESET.

References

Allam, Z., & Jones, S. D. (2020). On the coronavirus (COVID-19) outbreak and the smart city network: Universal data sharing standards coupled with artificial intelligence (AI) to benefit urban health monitoring and management. *Health*, *8*(1), 46. https://doi.org/10.3390/healthcare8010046.

Amat, F., Falcó-Gimeno, A., Arenas, A., & Muñoz, J. (2020). *Pandemics meet democracy: Experimental evidence from the COVID-19 crisis in Spain*. Preprint. Retrieved from: https://osf.io/preprints/socarxiv/dkusw/

Arendt, H. (1949). The rights of man: What are they? *Modern Review*, *3*, 4–37.

Arrighi, J.-T., & Stjepanović, D. (2019). Introduction: The rescaling of territory and citizenship in Europe. *Ethnopolitics*, 1–8. https://doi.org/10.1080/17449057.2019.1585087.

Bastani, A. (2019). *Fully automated luxury communism*. London: Verso.

Bauman, Z. (2000). *Liquid modernity*. Cambridge: Polity.

Birnie, R., & Bauböck, R. (2020). Introduction: Expulsion and citizenship in the 21st century. *Citizenship Studies*, *24*(3), 265–276. https://doi.org/10.1080/13621025.2020.1733260.

Bridle, J. (2018). *New dark age*. London: Verso.

Broussard, M. (2018). *Artificial unintelligence: How computers misunderstand the world*. Cambridge: MIT Press.

Calzada, I. (2013). Knowledge building & organizational behaviour: mondragon case. In F. Moulaert, D. MacCallum, A. Mehmood, & A. Hamdouch (Eds.), *International handbook of social innovation. Social innovation: Collective action, social learning and transdisciplinary research* (pp. 219–229). Cheltenham, UK: Edward Elgar Publishing.

Calzada, I. (2018). 'Algorithmic nations': Seeing like a city-regional and techno-political conceptual assemblage. *Regional Studies, Regional Science*, *5*(1), 267–289. https://doi.org/10.1080/21681376.2018.1507754.

Calzada, I. (2019a). Data spaces and democracy. *RSA Journal*, (2), 40–43. https://doi.org/10.13140/RG.2.2.35392/89601/1.

Calzada, I. (2019b). Technological sovereignty: Protecting citizens' digital rights in the AI-driven and post-GDPR algorithmic and city-regional European realm. *Regions eZine*, (4). https://doi.org/10.1080/13673882.2018.00001038.

Calzada, I. (2020). Emerging citizenship regimes and rescaling (European) nation-states: Algorithmic, liquid, metropolitan and stateless citizenship ideal types. In S. Moisio, N. Koch, A. E. Jonas, C. Lizotte, & J. Luukkonen (Eds.), *Handbook on the changing geographies of the state: New spaces of geopolitics*. Cheltenham, UK and Northampton, MA, USA: Edward Elgar Publishing.

Calzada, I., & Almirall, E. (2020). Data ecosystems for protecting European citizens' digital rights. *Transforming Government: People, Process and Policy*, *14*(2). https://doi.org/10.1108/TG-03-2020-0047.

Cardullo, P., & Kitchin, R. (2018). Smart urbanism and smart citizenship: The neoliberal logic of 'citizen-focused' smart cities in Europe. *Environment and Planning C: Politics and Space*. https://doi.org/10.1177/0263774x18806508.

Carey, B. (2018). Against the right to revoke citizenship. *Citizenship Studies*, *22*(8), 897–911. https://doi.org/10.1080/13621025.2018.1538319.

Couture, S., & Toupin, S. (2017). What does the concept of 'sovereignty' mean in digital, network and technological sovereignty? In *Paper presented at the Giganet 2017 conference*.

Craglia, M. E. (2018). *Artificial intelligence: A European perspective*. Luxembourg: EC.

Datta, A. (2018). 'Cityzens become netizens': Hashtag citizenships in the making of India's 100 smart cities. In C. Coletta, L. Evans, L. Heaphy, & R. Kitchin (Eds.), *Creating smart cities*. Oxon: Routledge.

Davies, G. (2020). European Union citizenship and the sorting of Europe. *Journal of European Integration*, 1–16. https://doi.org/10.1080/07036337.2020.1723577.

De Koning, A., Jaffe, R., & Koster, M. (2015). Citizenship agendas in and beyond the nation-state: (En)countering framings of the good citizen. *Citizenship Studies*, *19*(2), 121–127. https://doi.org/10.1080/13621025.2015.1005940.

De Waal, M., & Dignum, M. (2017). The citizen in the smart city. How the smart city could transform citizenship. *Information Technology*, *59*(6), 263–273.

DECODE. (2019). *The people, not governments, should exercise digital sovereignty*. Retrieved from: https://decodeproject.eu/people-not-governments-should-exercise-digital-sovereignty-financial-times.

Duarte, F., & Firmino, J. F. (2018). *Unplugging the city: The urban phenomenon and its sociotechnical controversies*. Oxon: Routledge.

Eizaguirre, S., Pradel-Miquel, M., & García, M. (2017). Citizenship practices and democratic governance: 'Barcelona en Comú' as an urban citizenship confluence promoting a new policy agenda. *Citizenship Studies*, *21*(4), 425–439. https://doi.org/10.1080/13621025.2017.1307609.

European Commission. (2019). *Digital innovation hubs (DIHs)*. Brussels: EC.

European Commission. (2020). *A European strategy for data*. Brussels: EC.

Ferronato, P., & Stan, R. (2018). Smart citizenship: Designing the interaction between citizens and smart cities. In *Limerick: DRS 2018 design research society 2018 catalyst*.

Floridi, L. (2017). *The rise of the algorithm need not be bad news for humans*. Retrieved from: https://www.ft.com/content/ac9e10ce-30b2-11e7-9555-23ef563ecf9a?mhq5j=e2.

Floridi, L., Cowls, J., King, T. C., & Taddeo, M. (2020). How to design AI for social good: Seven essential factors. *Science and Engineering Ethics*. https://doi.org/10.1007/s11948-020-00213-5.

Frey, C. B. (2019). *The technology trap: Capital, labor, and power in the age of automation*. Princeton: Princeton University Press.

GaiaX (2020). Retrieved from: www.data-infrastructure.eu/GAIAX/.

Harari, Y. N. (2015). *Homo deus: A brief history of tomorrow*. London: Harvill-Secker.

Harari, Y. N. (2018). *21 Lessons for the century*. London: Vintage.

Hatuka, T., Toch, E., Birnhack, M., & Zur, H. (2020). *The digital city*. Tel Aviv: Blavatnik Interdisciplinary Cyber Research Center.

Hindman, M. (2018). *The internet trap: How the digital economy builds monopolies and undermines democracy*. New Jersey: Princeton University Press.

Hintz, A., Dencik, L., & Wahl-Jorgensen, K. (2017). Digital citizenship and surveillance society. *International Journal of Communication*, *11*, 731–739. Retrieved from: http://ijoc.org/index.php/ijoc/article/view/5521.

Hogarth, I. (2018). *AI nationalism*. Retrieved from: https://www.ianhogarth.com/blog/2018/6/13/ai-nationalism.

Innerarity, D. (2016). *Governance in the new global disorder: Politics for a post-sovereign society*. NYC: Columbia University Press.

Jašina-Schäfer, A., & Cheskin, A. (2019). Horizontal citizenship in Estonia: Russian speakers in the borderland city of Narva. *Citizenship Studies*, 1–18. https://doi.org/10.1080/13621025.2019.1691150.

Joss, S., Cook, M., & Dayot, Y. (2017). Smart cities: Towards a new citizenship regime? A discourse analysis of the British smart city standard. *Journal of Urban Technology*, 1–21. https://doi.org/10.1080/10630732.2017.1336027.

Kallio, K. P., Wood, B. E., & Häkli, J. (2020). Lived citizenship: Conceptualising an emerging field. *Citizenship Studies*, 1–17. https://doi.org/10.1080/13621025.2020.1739227.

Keith, M. (2020). *Future cities: New economy and shared city prosperity driven by technological innovation*. Nairobi: UN-Habitat.

Keith, M., & Calzada, I. (2018). Citizenship in a changing multi-scalar post-brexit European context. In *Urban transformations ESRC report on 11th September 2017 workshop entitled 'Scaling migration through the European city-regions'*. Retrieved from: http://www.urbantransformations.ox.ac.uk/blog/2018/citizenship-in-a-changing-multi-scalar-post-brexit-european-context/.

Kempin Reuter, T. (2020). *Smart city visions and human rights: Do they go together?*. Harvard: Harvard Kennedy School.

Kitchin, R., Cardullo, P., & Di Feliciantonio, C. (2018). *Citizenship, justice and the right to the smart city*. The programmable city working paper 41.

Kuziemski, M., & Misuraca, G. (2020). AI governance in the public sector: Three tales from the frontiers of automated decision-making in democratic settings. *Telecommunications Policy*, 101976. https://doi.org/10.1016/j.telpol.2020.101976.

Lepoutre, J. (2020). When losing citizenship is fine: Denationalisation and permanent expatriation. *Citizenship Studies*, 1–16. https://doi.org/10.1080/13621025.2020.1733259.

Mark, D. (2014). From the city of bits to e-topia: Space, citizenship and community as global strategy. *International Journal of E-Adoption (IJEA)*, *6*(1), 16–33. https://doi.org/10.4018/ijea.2014010102.

Morozov, E. (2019). Digital socialism? *New Left Review*, *116/117*.

Mulgan, G. (2020). *How not to waste a crisis: Possibilities for government after COVID-19*. Retrieved from: https://www.geoffmulgan.com/post/how-not-to-waste-a-crisis-possibilities-for-government-after-covid-19.

Nguyen, J. (2017). Identity, rights and surveillance in an era of transforming citizenship. *Citizenship Studies*, 1–8. https://doi.org/10.1080/13621025.2017.1406456.

Nordling, V., Sager, M., & Söderman, E. (2017). From citizenship to mobile commons: Reflections on the local struggles of undocumented migrants in the city of Malmö, Sweden. *Citizenship Studies*, 1–17. https://doi.org/10.1080/13621025.2017.1341660.

Piccoli, L. (2019). The regional battleground: Partisanship as a key driver of the subnational contestation of citizenship. *Ethnopolitics*, 1–22. https://doi.org/10.1080/17449057.2019.1584494.

Pilkington, E. (2019). *Digital Dystopia: How algorithms punish the poor*. Retrieved from: https://www.theguardian.com/technology/2019/oct/14/automating-poverty-algorithms-punish-poor.

Purcell, M. (2003). Citizenship and the right to the global city: Reimagining the capitalist world order. *International Journal of Urban and Regional Research*, *27*(3), 564–590. https://doi.org/10.1111/1468-2427.00467.

Rose, G. (2020). Actually-existing sociality in a smart city. City, 1–18. https://doi.org/10.1080/13604813.2020.1781412.

Sadowski, J. (2020). Cyberspace and cityscapes: On the emergence of platform urbanism. *Urban Geography*, 1–5. https://doi.org/10.1080/02723638.2020.1721055.

Sassen, S. (2002). Towards post-national and denationalized citizenship. In E. F. Isin, & B. S. Turner (Eds.), *Handbook of citizenship studies* (pp. 277–291). London: SAGE Publications Ltd.

Schou, J., & Hjelholt, M. (2018). Digital citizenship and neoliberalization: Governing digital citizens in Denmark. *Citizenship Studies*, 1–16. https://doi.org/10.1080/13621025.2018.1477920.

Sennett, R. (2020). *The state of exception becomes the norm*. Retrieved from: https://newcities.org/the-big-picture-the-state-of-exception-becomes-the-norm/.

Smith, W. (2019). Deliberative citizenship: A critical reappraisal. *Citizenship Studies*, *23*(8), 815–830. https://doi.org/10.1080/13621025.2019.1664404.

Stahl, K. A. (2020). *Local citizenship in a global age: How cities are changing what it means to be a citizen (part III)*. Cambridge: Cambridge University Press.

Stucke, M. E. (2018). Should we be concerned about data-opolies? In *Georgetown law technology review*. Retrieved from: https://ssrn.com/abstract=3144045.

Stuurman, S. (2019). Concluding observations: Citizenship in cities, states and empires. *Citizenship Studies*, 1–18. https://doi.org/10.1080/13621025.2019.1603273.

Susskind, J. (2018). *Future politics: Living together in a world transformed by tech*. Oxford: Oxford University Press.

Swyngedouw, E. (2005). Governance innovation and the citizen: The janus face of governance-beyond-the-state. *Urban Studies*, *42*(11), 1991–2006. https://doi.org/10.1080/00420980500279869.

Tammpuu, P., & Masso, A. (2019). Transnational digital identity as an instrument for global digital citizenship: The case of Estonia's E-residency. *Information Systems Frontiers*. https://doi.org/10.1007/s10796-019-09908-y.

Zandbergen, D., & Uitermark, J. (2019). In search of the smart citizen: Republican and cybernetic citizenship in the smart city. *Urban Studies*. https://doi.org/10.1177/0042098019847410.

Zuboff, S. (2019). *The age of surveillance capitalism: The fight for a human future at the new frontier of power*. London: Profile.

Glossary

Prologue

Data ecosystems Data ecosystems are not only the data infrastructures and institutions but also the related analytics and data capture systems used to take data and relay it to the system owners, who can then alter their provision of goods, services, and marketing accordingly.

GDPR The General Data Protection Regulation (EU) 2016/679 (GDPR) is a regulation in EU law on data protection and privacy in the European Union (EU) and the European Economic Area (EEA).

AI According to English Oxford Living Dictionary AI is the theory and development of computer systems able to perform tasks normally requiring human intelligence, such as visual perception, speech recognition, decision-making, and translation between languages.

Digital rights According to the Cities Coalition for Digital Rights, there are five digital rights. (i) Universal and equal access to the internet, and digital literacy. (ii) Privacy, data protection, and security. (iii) Transparency, accountability, and non-discrimination of data, content, and algorithms. (iv) Participatory democracy, diversity, and inclusion. (v) Open and ethical digital service standards. According to the author, even 15 digital rights could be identified: (i) the right to be forgotten on the Internet; (ii) the right to be unplugged; (iii) the right to a person's own digital legacy; (iv) the right of a person's personal integrity to be protected from technology; (v) the right to freedom of speech on the Internet; (vi) the right to a person's own digital identity; (vii) the right to the transparent and responsible usage of algorithms; (viii) the right to have a last human instance in the expert-based decision-making processes; (ix) the right to equal opportunities in the digital economy; (x) the consumer rights in e-commerce; (xi) the right to hold intellectual property on the Internet; (xii) the right to universal access to the Internet; (xiii) the right to digital literacy; (xiv) the right to impartiality on the Internet; and (xv) the right to a secure Internet.

Chapter 1: Unplugging

Unplugging Unplugging is a novel trend that offers a corrective from the corporate, top-down direction of the smart city mainstream in favour of a transition towards the critical use of digital technologies enabling the construction of a more democratic citizenship.

Social Innovation Social Innovation is the capacity to elaborate alternative discourses and actions that are counter-hegemonic in terms of resistance and/or innovative transformations.

Context collapse It refers to the infinite audience possible online as opposed to the limited groups a person normally interacts with face to face.

Networked individualism A theory first put forward by Barry Wellman, which describes the increasing importance of personal networks. This reflects a decreasing emphasis on communal and family bonds, and is supported by technologies such as the Internet, social networking, and personal communication devices.

Social capital According to Putnam we can define social capital as the connections among individuals—social networks and the norms of reciprocity and trustworthiness that arise from them.

Chapter 2: Deciphering

Living labs The notion of urban living labs is normally attributed to Professor William Mitchell of the Massachusetts Institute of Technology (MIT). Living labs are intervention mechanisms to bring together interdisciplinary experts and stakeholders represented through the Penta-helix policy framework to develop, deploy, and test—in actual living environments—new technologies and strategies for design that respond to societal translocal challenges.

Platform co-operatives Platform co-operatives are digital platforms that are designed to provide a service or sell a product—and are collectively owned and governed by the people who depend on and participate in them.

Data co-operatives Data co-operatives are voluntary collaborative pooling by individuals of their personal data for the benefit of the collective group or community membership.

Data commons Data commons is a policy scheme that co-locates data with cloud computing infrastructure and commonly used software services, tools, and apps for managing, analysing, and sharing data to create an interoperable resource for research community and extensively considering data a communal asset. Inspired by the management of common pool resources, help organisations or people collaborate to create and maintain shared data assets.

Techno-politics According to Edwards and Hecht (2010), techno-politics are hybrids of technical systems and political practices that produce new forms of power and agency.

Chapter 3: Democratising

Penta helix Penta helix is defined as a joint interaction of the four established helixes of the so-called Quadruple helix (the public sector, the private sector, academia, and civil society) being intermediated and activated by the fifth-helix (social entrepreneurs/activists).

Quadruple helix Quadruple-helix framework is defined as a partnership convened by universities as key civic institutions to shape the future development of their cities bringing together academia, the public sector, the private sector, and the civil society.

Triple helix Triple-helix framework was developed to conceptualise public innovation and the flow of knowledge in open innovation systems. Initially the focus was on technological innovation that benefits economic development. This framework was useful for the interconnectedness among universities, industry, and government.

Multi-stakeholders Multi-stakeholder policy framework seeks to bring stakeholders together to participate in the dialogue, decision-making, and implementation of responses to jointly perceived problems.

Public-Private Partnerships (PPP) According to Forrer et al. (2010), PPP could be defined as an ongoing agreement between the government and private sector organisations in which the private organisation participates in the decision-making and production of a public good or service that has traditionally been provided by the public sector and in which the private sector may or may not share the risk and the profit of that production.

By contrast, Mazzucatto (2015) argued that the public sector should not only be perceived as a passive corrector of market failure in the PPP but also as an entrepreneurial partner with a broader range of roles in stimulating innovation.

Chapter 4: Replicating

City-to-city learning City-to-city learning is a replication strategy among smart cities that reformulates the unidirectional, hierarchical, mechanistic, solutionist, and technocratic approach by attempting to overcome it through a multidirectional, radial, dynamic, iterative, and democratic learning process.

Scalability The scalability could be defined through the composition of the multi-stakeholder's policy scheme, such as their interdependence and power relations (examined through the Penta-helix policy framework).

Replication Replication is desired solutionist mechanism by which one city copy-pastes and reproduces exactly the same urban intervention implemented in another city, resulting in a panacea deadlock.

Chapter 5: Devolving

Dataism Dataism is a term that has been used to describe the mindset or philosophy created by the emerging significance of big data. The term was coined by David Brooks in the New York Times in 2013 and thereafter have been popularised by Yuval Noah Harari.

Datafication Datafication is a technological trend turning and thus coding many aspects of our life into data which is subsequently transferred into information realised as a new form of value.

Data devolution The devolution is the process by which the ownership of data could be scaled down from the control of big tech towards lower levels of the multilevel governance by reaching ultimately citizens.

City-regions City-regions are widely recognised as pivotal socictal and techno-politic-economic formations that (i) are key to national and international competitiveness and (ii) rebalance political restructuring processes into nation-states, even changing their geoeconomic, geopolitic, geodemocratic, and geotechnologic dynamics beyond and between them.

Smart citizens Smart citizens are the citizens guided by the following set of behaviours and values: (i) take responsibility in caring for the environment they live and work in, and the places they like; (ii) value access over ownership and involvement over power; (iii) ask for tolerance, not authorisation; (iv) ethical algorithms rather than extractive algorithms; and (iv) offer assistance to less technologically savvy individuals.

Technological sovereignty Technological sovereignty is a political outlook that information and communications infrastructure and technology is aligned to the laws, needs, and interests of the city, region, or country in which users are located.

Chapter 6: Commoning

Experimental cities Experimental cities could be defined as a current transition towards more socially constructed (smart) cities and particularly suggesting a new role for citizens who are considered decision-makers co-operatively setting up platforms to avoid the monopolistic control of extractivist multinationals' algorithmic governance.

Big data Extremely large data sets that may be analysed computationally to reveal patterns, trends, and associations, especially relating to human behaviour, interactions, and predictions.

Chapter 7: Protecting

Data infrastructures Data infrastructure is a collection of data assets, digital infrastructure, and the bodies that maintain them for promoting data sharing and distribution.

Data institutions Data institutions are an organisation, establishment, foundation, society, or the like, operating independently of data providers and beneficiaries and therefore able to balance existing power relations and conflicting interests among stakeholders. They frequently seek a collective, social, or public good purpose, which might include redressing power imbalances, promoting competition, or supporting economic activity as well as more traditionally social good purposes such as improving health outcomes.

Pan-European agencies Pan-European agencies might mobilise capacities in AI, analytics, and modern software development by putting them at the service of European cities and regions through a vast network of Digital Innovation Hubs (DIHs) being at present distributed across the European geography. They can foster open source code, model sharing, and standardisation.

Digital government Digital government is about new ways of delivering public value and making services and government procedures digital by design.

Epilogue

The new normal The new normal is understood as a non-normality as we have met so far as a result of the post COVID-19 aftermath globally in the society and economy.

Pandemic citizenship Pandemic citizenship represents a global category of citizens worldwide who share exactly the same fear, uncertainty, and risks.

Liquid citizenship Liquid citizens could be defined as citizens who remain highly distributed in a global grid of networks and data ecosystems, by which the data they produce are concentrated in the hands of a few companies by implementing *dataism*.

Data altruism Data altruism refers to the option made by citizens to allow to use of the data they generate for the public good, if they wish to so, in compliance with the GDPR.

Data donation Data donation could be understood as a specific type of transaction encompassing three distinctive characteristics: relationality, indirect reciprocity, and multiplicity.

Algorithmic nations Algorithmic nations could be defined as (i) a non-deterministic city-regional and techno-political conceptual assemblage, (ii) for a transitional strategic pathway, (iii) towards the nation-state rescaling, and (iv) through a contextual set of drivers.

Index

Note: Page numbers followed by *f* indicate figures and *t* indicate tables.

T

U

W

Z

FSC
www.fsc.org
MIX
Papier | Fördert gute Waldnutzung
FSC® C083411

Kolibri 360 GmbH
Ferdinand-Jühlke-Straße 7
99095 Erfurt, Deutschland
produktsicherheit@kolibri360.de